Building Rainmakers

The Definitive Guide to Business Development for Lawyers

Building Rainmakers

The Definitive Guide to Business Development for Lawyers

David King Keller, PhD

AMERICAN BAR ASSOCIATION
Defending Liberty
Pursuing Justice

Cover design by Kelly Book.

Printed in the United States of America.

27 26 25 24   5 4 3

ISBN: 978-1-63425-083-2
e-ISBN: 978-1-63425-084-9

Library of Congress Cataloging-in-Publication Data
Names: Keller, David King, author.
Title: Building rainmakers : the definitive guide to business development for lawyers / David King Keller.
Description: Chicago : American Bar Association, 2016. | Includes index.
Identifiers: LCCN 2015047009 | ISBN 9781634250832 (alk. paper)
Subjects: LCSH: Lawyers—United States—Marketing. | Law firms—United States—Marketing. | Practice of law—Economic aspects—United States. | Legal services—United States—Marketing.
Classification: LCC KF316.5 .K455 2016 | DDC 340.068/8—dc23 LC record available at http://lccn.loc.gov/2015047009

Discounts are available for books ordered in bulk. Special consideration is given to state bars, CLE programs, and other barrelated organizations. Inquire at Book Publishing, ABA Publishing, American Bar Association, 321 N. Clark Street, Chicago, Illinois 60654-7598.

www.ShopABA.org

Contributors

Adam Severson/Baker Donelson
Adam Stock/Allen Matkins
Allen Chichester/Barnes & Thornburg
Barbara Lauterbach/Daniel Coker Horton & Bell
Bill Flannery/The WJF Institute
Bill Mooz/University of Colorado Law School
Casey Flaherty/KIA Motors America, Inc.
Clare Ota/Murphy Pearson Bradley & Feeney
Daniel Kloke/Sheppard Mullin
Dave Bruns/Farella Braun + Martel
David Ackert/The Ackert Advisory
David Boies/Boies, Schiller & Flexner
David Freeman/David Freeman Consulting Group
Despina Kartson/Morgan Lewis
Don Goewey/ProAttitude, *The End of Stress*
Erin Corbin Meszaros/Sutherland Asbill & Brennan
Gerry Goldsholle/FreeAdvice.com
Gil Purcell/Brayton Purcell
Hans Haglund/Blank Rome
Jan Kang/AOptix Technologies, Inc
Jeanne Hammerstrom/Benesch
Jeff Berardi/K&L Gates
Jeffrey F. Silber/Silber, Vasquez & Associates
Jill Weber/Stinson Leonard
Jonathan Fitzgarrald/Equinox Strategy Partners
Jonathan Waldrop/Kasowitz, Benson, Torres & Friedman
Karen Bell/McCarthy Tétrault
Karen Febeo/Goodwin Procter
Karie Trujillo/Markowitz Herbold
Larry Bodine/Lawyers.com
Lisa Konie/Adobe Systems
Lisa Salazar/Norton Rose Fulbright
Louise J. Muldoon/Baker & McKenzie
Marian Lee/Brownstein Hyatt Farber Schreck
Marilyn Klinger/Sedgwick
Mark Karkazis/Ungaretti & Harris
Mark Usellis/Davis Wright Tremaine
Matthew Taylor/Duane Morris
Melanie Green/Faegre Baker Daniels
Michele Silva/Association of Business Trial Lawyers
Mike Haven/NetApp, Inc.
Mike O'Horo/RainmakerVT
Nancy Kostakos/Goodwin Procter
Peter Johnson/Law Practice Consultants

Peter Symons/*Brain Fuel* Author
Roger Epstein/Cades Schutte
Sally J. Schmidt/Schmidt Marketing, Inc.
Scott Kessler/Business and Personal Coach
Shanda Zavalsky/Brownstein Hyatt Farber Schreck
Silvia Coulter/LawVision Group
Stephen Fairley/The Rainmaker Institute
Steve Bell/Womble Carlyle Sandridge & Rice
Tasneem Goodman/Akina Corp
Tom Helm/Bryan Cave
Wayne Hogan/Terrell Hogan Yegelwel

Contents

Chapter 1

Learn from the Experts

The American Bar Association Book Division believes this is the most comprehensive and most collaborative "How-To" book on business development techniques for lawyers ever published.

This book was designed for the busy lawyer and law firm business development professional looking for fast and proven answers to their questions. This manual can help you guide and coach very talented attorneys into becoming very successful rainmakers.

If you don't have time to read a whole book, but just want to read the subject you're interested in, this is the guide for you.

You need to improve **cross-selling**. No problem. Pick up this book. Go to the C's in Chapter 2's A to Z Guide. Look up "Cross-Selling" and find a few cross-selling solutions that have already proven successful in a major way. Presented by people you can trust. People you already know personally or know by reputation.

You're considering a **mentoring** program. Pick up this book. Go to the M's. Look up "mentoring" and find out what others have learned so you don't have to re-invent the wheel.

How do you identify your **ideal client target list**? Pick up this book. Go to the Exhibits section and find six different Exhibits describing techniques to create your perfect target list.

Do you need an effective **business development plan template**? Pick up this book. Go to the Exhibits section and select one of the five plans that have already been time tested.

Go to **Chapter 3's *Disasters To Avoid*** to learn from the mistakes of others in order to prevent the loss of a valued client or potential client relationship.

The topics covered in this guide are a **must-read for anyone charged with increasing firm revenue**, whether you are a member of the firm's management committee, chief marketing officer, business development director, director of sales, practice group chair, professional development director, client services manager, solo practitioner, consultant, coach, partner, associate on a partner track, or, in any manner responsible for maintaining and growing your law firm's clients and receipts.

This book will help **make sure you are not leaving any stones unturned** in the effort to support your firm's financial stability and growth, and to find out what your colleagues are doing in order to improve your own performance.

Our new market reality requires a new level of business development skills. According to **Jeff Berardi, CMO for K&L Gates**, "Lawyers now are increasingly in situations where a client or potential client is choosing among multiple law firms, each of which is considered extremely competent. This means that the potential client will be making decisions based on trust in the relationship and just how comfortable the client is with you and your law firm. At that point, **business development skills will be the differentiator** that sets you and your firm apart from the other lawyers and law firms.

Now, more than ever, **the onus is on lawyers and on the firms to really deliver that value proposition and the way you do that is through effective business development**, strengthening client relationships, and making sure that the client really understands what the differences are between a particular lawyer or law firm and what you bring to the table beyond just the legal knowledge. If our lawyers are better trained, and feel more comfortable with business development, then they have a better opportunity to actually deliver that win for the client engagement."

What follows is the **combined wisdom of more than 50 professionals** charged with growing firm revenue and building strong sustainable law practices. These contributors represent some of the best and brightest business development professionals in the legal field with more than 700 years of collective experience. Included here are their best practices when it comes to successful rainmaker strategies.

Most of the comments presented are fast, easy to read, **short excerpts** from my conversations with these highly regarded thought leaders. I asked our contributors/interviewees to allow me to preserve their largely unedited words as they were first spoken in order to maintain the fresh feeling as if they are speaking directly to us over a cup of coffee. I requested that they set aside their natural desire for written perfection so that we could share their wisdom in more of a one-to-one personal conversation. Granting us this permission was vital and is a testament to their courage and trust. Flexibility like that is the hallmark of a true leader.

Louise Muldoon, North American Director of Business Development, Marketing and Communications at Baker & McKenzie, shares how she helps maintain and increase the revenue at one of the largest law firms in the world.

Matt Taylor, Chairman of the Trial Practice Group at Duane Morris, has consistently maintained an eight-digit book of business for many years. In the coming pages, Matt explains how he does it and how you can use those same rainmaker strategies to dramatically increase your firm's revenue.

Jill Weber, Chief Marketing Officer and Business Development Officer for Stinson Leonard Street, explains how she helped 20 attorneys collectively grow their practices by $7.5 million over a two-year period with just a $150,000 investment. That's an approximate 5000% return on investment (ROI). A decade later, nine of those 20 initial participants have sustainable seven-figure books of business. In the past decade, the 70 partners who participated in the *Fast Forward* programs at her firm have experienced an average revenue growth rate ten times that of their peer group.

Karen Bell, National Senior Director, Professional & Client Education at McCarthy Tétrault LLP, shares her "client magnets" that keep clients stuck to her firm.

These experts and **more than 50** other successful law firm business development thought leaders answer the question—

"How do you help a skilled lawyer become a skilled rainmaker?"

Chapter 2

A to Z Business Development Guide For Lawyers

How to Make Best Use of the Guide

There are over 400 topic-centered discussions in this Chapter. To make searching for a specific topic easier, the topic title headlines are listed in alphabetical order, **A to Z**. In many cases, though, the expert's comment covers more than one subject related to the title headline. So the topic title is only indicative of the content, but cannot always convey in one keyword what is being discussed within a quarter page to many pages.

For example, one title starts with a "T", *The Solution: Here's How You Turn Skilled Lawyers into Skilled Rainmakers*. So, it is critical that you scan all the titles because, as in that example, not all titles fit neatly into one A to Z keyword.

I highly recommend that you take one minute right now and go to the **Chapter 2 Index of Topic Titles** at the end of this chapter on page 352 to review a complete listing of all 400+ topic titles. Check off those titles that you would like to review as soon as possible.

Each headline title is followed in parenthesis by the name of the professional who made the specific comment. Their bios can be found in *Appendix A*.

When reading these short subject-based discussions by a specific business development professional, take note of those techniques and approaches that are commented upon by more than one speaker. Repetition of a particular strategy is a good sign that it represents a successful revenue generating idea that you, too, should consider. Or, someone may have developed an entirely unique approach you should examine. Some topics, such as the "Elevator Pitch" are so essential to creating a positive first impression and generating a "next step" that more than a dozen experts are asked how they address this topic with their attorneys.

Every business development technique in this book is designed to help you thrive in today's highly competitive legal marketplace.

Refer to the *List of Contributors* and read their biographies in *Appendix A* and you'll know why you'll want to dive right in and start benefiting from their wisdom. The consultative value of their 700 plus years of combined experience in growing law firm revenue is inestimable.

Build more rainmaker skills within your firm and watch your revenue numbers grow.

Rainmaker Topics Listed in Alphabetical Order

Accountability

(Hans Haglund)

No matter what law firm you are with, there is someone at the top that is managing a team to execute on objectives. As a business development (BD) support team, you need to manage in the same way. For example, tell attorneys they need to make five business development calls a day, to a mix of new and existing clients. Then follow-up to make sure they are making those calls. You should swing by their office and make sure that if they don't have something to send to clients or have an engaging inquiry about their business issues, you help them figure out ways to re-connect with those clients and potential clients. Some really appreciate the follow-up, some are not as grateful, but most people seem to respond more effectively if someone holds them accountable. It's the old saying, inspect what you expect.

When you get down to the individual level, all lawyers are not all alike, but there are certain ways that you can present business development concepts that makes it more appealing or at the least more concrete. [See also *Business Development: A Tactical Approach: Do The Math*, and *Client Development: Getting Into Their World Using 70/30.*]

Advice to an Associate: Going from Skilled Lawyer to Skilled Rainmaker: Part 1

(Gerry Goldsholle)

Let's face it, the typical recent law graduate is clueless about the economics of law practice, how a law firm operates, what's involved in running a law practice, and what's truly important to becoming a financially secure lawyer. No matter how capable a lawyer you may be, no matter how prestigious your coveted position as an associate at a top law firm may be, and no matter how hard you work, if you fail to learn what's really important – not what the firm claims is important – the odds are that at some point you'll have to begin looking for a new job.

Your perceived ability to bring in new clients and generate more business from existing clients – in other words your rainmaking ability – is often far more important to upward mobility and financial success at a law firm than legal brilliance, the ability to write outstanding memos and briefs, dazzling oratory, or the capacity to work 24/7. Although each of those elements may contribute to success, something you've been graded on since kindergarten is also at play – your ability to "work well and play well with others." That one is at least as important as any other factor in being seen as a rainmaker.

Law firms generally don't expect new associates to be bringing in new clients – especially the type of clients and matters the firm would be willing to handle. So unless you were hired because you're the scion of an extremely wealthy or politically influential family, or because one of your parents is a senior executive of a major corporation, the good news is that actual rainmaking is neither anticipated nor required for the first few years. Criteria the firm will be using to evaluate you – how pleased the partners are with you, whether or not you are someone who consistently does great work, meets deadlines, avoids surprises, and can be relied upon, form the basis on which you will be judged in your early years.

It's an absolute certainty that the partners will be eliciting informal feedback on your performance from more senior associates, and from each of the partners you work with, as well as from the firm's clients you interact with. During an associate's initial years the ability to keep the partners and the firm's clients happy serves as a far better proxy for your eventual business generating ability than any stray client, with a one time, relatively modest matter you might otherwise attract.

Another great proxy for your potential as a rainmaker is the ability to spot legal problems and areas of vulnerability your firm's existing clients are not, but should be aware of, and would want your firm to address. If, working with the partners, you can parlay those legal problems into an additional or expanded assignment that generates meaningful revenue for the firm, you'd likely be recognized as a future rainmaker. Make sure that you receive at least some of the recognition for generating that new business.

Advice to an Associate: Going from Skilled Lawyer to Skilled Rainmaker: Part 2

(Gerry Goldsholle)

Rainmaking is the primary route to financial success from the practice of law. Given the ever-changing nature of legal practice, being a rainmaker, and having a book of portable business – clients who rely on you and will likely follow you to a new law firm should you change firms – makes you valuable to your existing firm, and many new firms. It gives you power so that if your current law firm fails to treat you properly, folds, merges, or changes direction – you're in control of your destiny, and that's more than just a "good thing." Having a block of portable business is becoming increasingly critical. Without portable business, or an essential expertise in a lucrative area of practice, you are just one of many very skilled but relatively fungible lawyers.

Regardless of your status in a law firm, without a meaningful client base you're just the "hired help." While you may be well paid, particularly if you have some unique knowledge or skill, are highly productive, and are willing to work extraordinarily long and hard, you're unlikely to land in the corner office, have your name on the door, or receive the large partnership share. In contrast, the law firm's rainmakers – even if they are not the best lawyers in the firm – make the big bucks, just as the big rewards in pro sports tend to go to those who score the most points in football, basketball and baseball.

One of the factors that goes into rainmaking is being recognized as having an in-demand skill. During my tenure at MetLife we would try to hire outside counsel on the basis of need and skill, as needed. Unlike many other large companies we did not have any one firm to which we'd look when we needed outside counsel. We'd go to the law firm that we regarded as the best specialists to address for the particular problem. Today, more and more of corporate America's legal work is being done in-house – going out only when needed, such as for rapid coverage, specialized experience, geographic location or the like. And clients can and do change outside counsel at the drop of a hat.

Every lawyer has to realize that the key to success is not how good the work is objectively – that's the ultimate client decision, which often is very subjective – but how satisfied the client is with the work given the costs and hassle incurred. Let me emphasize that I am talking not only the actual financial cost – the bill – but also the client's internal costs. If you are viewed as someone who bothers the client's executives with what they regard as needless requests for information, or someone with a propensity for taking up a lot of their time, such as making them hang around while you polish that affidavit they have to execute – particularly when the need for doing so is not fully appreciated by the company's executives – the executives' perceived difficulty in working with you will be communicated to your law firm and remembered long after the bill and the matter's outcome are forgotten.

Unlike a law firm, the priority of almost every American business is to do even more business, and get any legal matters over and done with as rapidly as possible and with the least possible disruption, cost, or distraction. On many matters a business would be far happier "losing" quickly than winning after a lengthy, time absorbing battle that, in the scheme of things, takes far more time than it's worth. For example, most companies would prefer their VP for Product Development to be out developing new and improved products or evaluating acquisitions rather than spending time and effort dealing with lawyers on an old and often otherwise forgotten matter. In such circumstances insisting on spending the time and client money to win may be good for one's ego, but it's not going to get you anywhere if the client is dissatisfied, not with the outcome but with the process. And it's not only the client's executives' time that is important. I've seen otherwise wonderful lawyers totally failing to appreciate how valuable the client's inside counsel's time is, at least in the mind of inside counsel. All it sometimes takes to derail a career is a client saying to a partner "I'd prefer working with someone else next time. . . ."

Advice to an Associate: Going from Skilled Lawyer to Skilled Rainmaker: Part 3

(Gerry Goldsholle)

To be a rainmaker you have to understand what's important to the client, and what each client's real needs and objectives are. If you find somebody who has a problem and you can provide a feasible solution, you have a client. So, what is the pain-point for the prospective client? What are they worried about? What would they like to get done more easily, or more quickly, that ideally has something to do with the law? How can you help them?

What is the biggest problem that most lawyers have? Generating new clients. That's rainmaking. How can a lawyer go from an unknown associate to a rainmaker? Probably the best, most efficient strategy a lawyer can take to become regarded as an authority in a particular field of law is to publish. If you write a book or a law review article, once it is published you often will be regarded as an authority. If a book is out of the question, and law review articles aren't feasible, a series of shorter articles or even blogs – ideally aimed at a broad audience – could help. The short articles or blogs can live on your website or a third party website, such as my firm's FreeAdvice.com which attracts 20 million visitors each year.

As associates, we used to write client advisories. A new law would be enacted and we'd write an article and send it to the firm's clients. I recall doing one about a law that required all businesses with glass doors to put some visible markings on the glass so people would not try to walk through the glass.

Perhaps there's been a case recently where someone was injured by walking through an unmarked glass door. Well, you could write an article on the subject and have the firm send it to your current and prospective clients. Should a new law impact clients you can write a short article, get the firm to send it to the firm's clients, and/or get it published elsewhere. A short, readable article that would discuss what the new law says, and how your client can comply and protect itself. Be neutral. Explain the reason for the law, and how they can avoid what otherwise might be a problem. You need not be a literary genius. It need not have lots of citations. It's just a simple letter to clients – one that would make people say, "Gee, I remember seeing that." Nowadays, you can also get every one of those little client letters published to a broader circulation.

Every morning I spend some time scanning a compilation of law firm advisories that are summarized in an email newsletter called Lexology[1]. There usually are 30 to 40 summaries of articles in my fields of law that were already written by law firms around the country. I've learned many new things that are useful to my practice and my business, and find Lexology to be a good starting point to generate ideas for articles that also would be of interest to our readers and clients.

If I were a new lawyer, I would mine resources like Lexology every day, see what would be of interest to my firm's clients and what can I then write or blog about. Getting your name out there, with many articles, and ideally articles that are picked up and cited by others is one of the best ways to build a reputation among people who don't know you and otherwise wouldn't know you. It also keeps your name in front of clients if you have clients; and if nothing else, it might help you bring in clients by periodically becoming a top-of-mind legal resource. Of course, if you expect immediate gratification, then writing articles is not for you as that's not the way it works.

Another important thing on the path to becoming a rainmaker is billing fairly. While not all clients are price sensitive, none wants to feel ripped off. Consider writing off billable hours that you don't think were as productive as they should have been. All associates used to "get lost in those stacks" before everything was online. Today even with the best technology we all still go down dead ends from time to time. Those are hours that firms used to write off as a learning experience for the associate, rather than something that should be billed to the client. So even though you may have logged 20 hours for the client this week, if 6 of the hours were truly wasted, only billing the 14 that were productive usually makes long term sense. Clients look at their legal bill and will run it through a does-this-look-reasonable filter in their mind. You always want their answer to be, "Yes."[2]

[1]Lexology is a web-based service that provides law firms with a depth of free practical know-how by collaborating with the world's leading commercial law firms. Lexology is able to deliver fully tailored intelligence to the desktops of business lawyers.URL: http://www.lexology.com/. Compare to JDSupra.com, Law360.com, and Google Alerts.

[2]*Author's note:* In my Excel-based time sheets that can double as invoices, I have columns titled time invested, cumulative time invested, time billed, and cumulative time billed. This "time invested" vs "time billed" approach allows the client to see all the hours you put in along with any "discount" for time not billed. This is not interpreted as you being any less competent, but as you being extremely judicious with the client's limited resources, which will garnish you goodwill and more business.

AFA: See *Fees: Alternative Fee Agreements*

Asking for the Business

(Matt Taylor)

I spent several years at my father's law firm. My dad was the greatest trial lawyer I have ever seen, and he's heard me say it, but he was not the best at running a business. So I learned a lot from that experience. One, how to try cases. Two, I watched him rely on one client, and when that client was gone, I was forced to learn how to bring in business because, quite frankly, we were dying on the vine.

I'm certainly not a psychiatrist, but in my experience people are flattered when you ask them for business because they either think, "Well, I don't know, maybe this guy's too fancy, or she's too fancy for my business," or, "They're too busy to have my business." One, I think people like to be asked. Two, the answer "no," to me, is an okay answer. Even if someone says, "You know, Matt, I can't right now," or, "We're using someone else," there is still no doubt in my mind that that person was impressed that you asked them for business. No one is ever going to disparage you—no one is ever going to hold it against you for asking for business. If the answer is "no," that's okay because, guess what? They have you in mind. Whether it's at the top of their mind or it's more subliminal, they feel bad. In my view, they feel bad. They're going to want to get you business in the future. Don't wait to ask, is my point. It will usually bear fruit at some point.

Associate Billing Credit: go to: Billing Credit to Associates

Associate to Partner Transition

(Steve Bell)

In the case of an associate who becomes a partner and now has billable hour requirements on top of his or her new partner responsibilities, the partner billable hour requirement should be lower than the associate billable requirement. The delta between the two is intended to be spent on enterprise activity, much of which is supposed to be development of clients. The new partner is relieved of some of their billable hour pressure and they're expected to devote it to the enterprise.

Associate to Partner Transition: Not for the Faint of Heart

(Peter Johnson)

In the case of the transition of an associate to partner, I draw on my extensive background as a managing partner to help the associate through the process. It can be challenging for an associate who is simply taking instruction and knocking out maybe up to 1800 to 2100 hours. The associate then becomes a partner, he or she is still supposed to hit the billables, say, 1800 hours, but then the new partner has got all the non-billables: the meet and greets, partner meetings, the hiring of associates, and training associate laterals.

We tell people that their billables affect their current income, but their non-billable time is their future. To answer directly, regrettably, there are no silver bullets. If the firm is doing their job, hopefully, it's not a deer in the headlights type of situation. If the firm is doing a good job of mentorship, et cetera, then this is not going to be a shock to the system. By the time they get to seventh or eighth year, they're being mentored in some of these initiatives. The reality is the bar rises every year and the minimal level of accountability increases every year.

When we ask the question, "What's the biggest or most significant challenge you have to business development," not surprisingly, the number one answer is time. When I started practicing, I used to call it juggling. Now, they call it multitasking.

Somehow they seem to do it. When you divide the number of billable hours and non-billable hours into an actual year, it's nuts. You hear complaints about sleep deprivation and work/life imbalance. It's a challenge. It's a profession that's transitioned into a business years ago. It's not for the faint of heart.

Associate to Partner Transition: Our Criteria

(Matt Taylor)

A young lawyer who's been at a firm for probably 8 to 10 years and makes partner is making partner because they're probably already doing most of the things partners do. They're probably already a leader. They're probably already doing many valuable activities that are just not billable. To make partner at our firm you have to be an excellent lawyer. There's five criteria. One, you are an excellent lawyer, a master of your trade. Two, you must be a productive lawyer, so that means you've added to the bottom line. Three, you have significant first chair type of experience, including leadership roles in cases. Four, you've been involved in the firm – you're a volunteer and great Firm citizen. And five, you need to demonstrate the actual or potential ability to excel at client development.

These partners do a lot. They're mentoring. They're out marketing. Of course, that's what you are supposed to do. Some do it better than others, but you have to be out there. I always talk to our young partners and then let them know, just as I would talk to them when they were a fifth-year associate, "How can I help you? What are you doing about your contacts? Remember I met your friend four years ago? What are you doing with that guy?"

Most of those people that just made partner, in this environment, are already doing all that and they've never even asked a question about the transition.

Associate to Partner Transition: Preparation Needed

(Marian Lee)

On the subject of associate to partner transition, I believe there have been many instances where that transition hasn't been very smooth. When you become a partner, there are a number of responsibilities beyond just meeting your billables. What we are trying to do at our law firm is to educate the associates from day one that their billable hour requirement is not the only measure of being a good associate and a good future partner. When you join the firm, you're going to bill 1800 or 1900 hours. That's just part of what's expected. You are also expected to develop yourself, to attend training, to network, and to engage in other activities. We're not expecting you as a junior associate to bring in any clients, but you absolutely have to start planting the seeds and making the relationships that will later help you develop business. From day one, we set a range of expectations on what it means to be a successful associate at our firm.

It's really important to educate associates throughout their career that the billable requirement is only a piece of the total career commitment that they have to make if they want to be successful. This is the life they've chosen and depending on the size of the firm and their practice area, of course, the actual total hours can vary. The message we convey is that you have a billable component to your career commitment and a non-billable component. And if the associate has been doing a range of activities, such as joining firm committees, attending trainings and getting out in to the community, then when they become a partner, the transition is not so abrupt. Yes, their billable hours are probably going to drop and they're going to spend a little more time on those other non-billable activities, but it's not going to be as much of a culture shock if they have been properly prepared from the beginning.

It's very late to get started on business development when you're a partner, especially these days when you have so many two-tiered partnerships. You don't have 8 or 10 years after making partner to start developing business; you have three to five years, depending on the firm, to really show that you can gear up. If you didn't lay the groundwork years earlier, it's just too late.

We're trying to educate our associates that it's a matter of their own career protection and their best interests to make themselves valuable and marketable. To set themselves up to do whatever they want later, they must orient their thinking to include business development from the beginning.

Associate to Partner Transition: Pure Effort

(*Hans Haglund)*

This question comes up regularly, "How do you assist associates who have become partner and are finding it difficult to maintain billable hours along with new partner responsibilities?" I believe, in that transition, you have to add a few more hours to your day. If you have been working 9 hours to achieve your billable hours, then, as a new partner, you're going to work 11 to 12 hours. If their current billable is 2,000 or 1,800, or whatever their target is, there is no getting away from those billable hours, while now adding partner responsibilities along with maintaining and building your business. That takes pure effort.

The question that has come up in every place that I have worked is, "How do I have a life and do this?" You already know the answer. For the rainmakers—you don't. If you want to make equity partner money, you make it balance later in your career. But in your first ten years . . . accept it, embrace it, and change your mindset.

> When you go from associate to partner, the next phase is building your business. That takes pure effort. Associates who become partners have raised this question in every firm I have ever worked, "How do I have a life and do this?" You already know the answer. For the rainmakers—you don't. If you want to make equity partner money, you make it balance later in your career.
>
> —*Hans T. Haglund*

You are going to have to put in "x" number of additional hours and it's going to take much more work. You have to balance that with the benefits to family and other longer term benefits. It's a personal decision that you have to make. After the transition to partner, we can get into various tactical options and discuss ways to expand current clients. For example, you have these two small clients that are small in revenue, but they are good-sized companies and you are only doing a little bit of their work. One strategy is to look at them, dive in, and make yourself their key person whom they cannot do without. There are many other tactical actions we can help you with in making the transition from associate to partner.

Associate to Partner Transition: See also Flannery Rainmaker Training: Part 10

Associate to Partner Transition: The Sweet Spot

(Jill Weber)

The associate-to-partner transition is the sweet spot. That's where an attorney is really interested in fine tuning their understanding of business development, because they now have to bring in new business. They are no longer an associate with someone assigning them billable hours. They now have to bring in new client files that have billable hours.

Associate Training: go to: Business Development Training: Associates

Associates: Educating the Reluctant Marketer

(Silvia Coulter)

Associates should definitely start learning some good business development habits early on. A lot of associates are really good at staying in touch with their colleagues in the way that yesterday's people weren't because of LinkedIn and Facebook. That's good. The key is that they need to understand that regardless of the fact that they're young and their colleagues are not yet in a decision-making role, that their friends and contacts can still be influential within their organizations. I had a young associate say, "Yeah, but my friends will think I'm marketing to them." I said, "Take them to lunch with one of your partners. Your partner will show an interest in what they're doing. Start getting used to having business discussions. It's always about the connections. It's will always be about that."

Associates: Remember Business Development Is Relational, Not Transactional

(Jonathan Waldrop)

A partner gave me and the other associates opportunities to run cases. That partner provided us with experience which in turn gave us confidence in how to grow and build a practice. Now, it may take a long time.

His big thing, too, that changed my life, was that most lawyers are transactional, but this business is relational. You have got to move from being transactional to relational because all lawyers are skilled in transactions. I do this, you do that. But business development is relational. Sometimes in a client relationship, you may give, give, give, but it's going to all equal out. At the end of the day, no one's going to be behind. That partner gave me that, and it changed my career. Best thing that ever happened to me.

[Read more: *Mentoring: The Lesson That Saved My Career*]

Attitude: Mine

(Barbara Lauterbach)

There is no point in doing this job if I don't enjoy the company of my lawyers and their clients.

I am sure there are some attorneys who would just as soon never hear my voice on the other end of the phone because they know I'm going to ask them to do something that they're either uncomfortable doing or don't think that they have the time to do. The biggest challenge in a trial law firm is trying to show the attorneys that they really do have the time to develop business and help them make that process instinctive and natural. I can never waste their time, and I have to make their tasks as easy as possible to accomplish.

You should know, that helping attorneys develop their practices is personal to me. One of my children is an associate attorney developing a complex practice in DC. I try to assist my attorneys the way I hope someone is assisting her. Helping good lawyers develop their businesses is important to me, and each attorney's practice is unique and requires a unique approach.

Attorneys as Clients: Nota Bene: CMO and BDD

(Allen Chichester)

First, giving marketing and business development staff the perspective that the attorneys they work with are their clients, and then helping staff understand how to deliver great client service to them makes a big difference. Treating our firm's attorneys as clients is precisely my perspective. Coming from the ad business, I saw immediately that if we treated our firm partners as employers or bosses then from a business development and marketing perspective, we wouldn't get much done. Only by viewing them as clients and encouraging them to do the thing that is in their own best interest, which they might not be asking for, would we pave the way to success. Leo Burnett used to say, "First, you give the client what they ask for and then you give them what they need."

The reasoning behind that was you have to show clients respect, and until you build a trust-based relationship with them, you darn well better give them what they ask for. But you need to go above and beyond that and give them the best solution as well, regardless of what they ask for.

Best Client Strategy: Bring Them Business, A Key Introduction

(Karen Bell)

"Don't overlook the possibility that you can bring business to your client."

Connections. In business it's all about connections. We have clients who other clients want to meet. So, we set up ways for them to meet through our Client Continuing Professional Development (CPD) program.

And, by having different clients come to our seminars and panel discussions, we are gathering folks in the same room who have a common interest. Everyone has a nametag and, they see who's there, and they can meet on a more social basis and have a practical discussion around a given topic. And then partners have an informal environment to introduce their clients to partners from other practice disciplines. Clients win. The firm wins. [See *Client Professional Development: A Value Add That Sets Us Apart.*]

Billing Credit to Associates: On Originating a New Client

(Matt Taylor)

We also give our associates billing credit on originating a new client or new client matter. We bonus our associates out on collections for those clients.

Billing: A Simple Trick to Make It Easier, More Accurate and More Effective

(David King Keller)

The bottom line is getting the bills out so that you can get paid. That's also business development. Many attorneys put off the billing activity till the last second because they hate to do it. When they finally get around to it, it's a real chore to recall the details. As a result, a bland summary can result that can upset a client who sees it. How are you helping your lawyers become more efficient in the billing process? One way, of course, is to ask all of your current rainmakers how they do it. Another simple trick I always recommend to my attorney coaching clients is to set their smart phone to vibrate every 2 hours, e.g., 9am, 11am, 1pm, 3pm, 5pm, and 7pm. Pause for one minute, ask the question, "What am I doing," and dictate a voice-to-text email exactly what you're doing for a client in detail in the active voice and send it to accounting and/or to yourself for review later when structuring your client invoice. If your work is very detailed and varied, you may consider going to 60 to 90-minute intervals.

Billing: The Good, the Bad, and the Ugly

(Sally Schmidt)

Based on extensive interviews with clients, I developed a number of tips for lawyers in terms of how to describe their billable time in such a manner that the bill is something that the client finds appealing and informative. It should reinforce the client's decision to pay for the legal services provided because tremendous value is being received.

When it comes to describing time and making the bill more appealing to clients, I give the following advice: Don't use passive language, and describe what you're doing in detail. If there are two people in a meeting, explain what they're doing; it's not just "reviewing a file," because that sounds to the client like they're paying for some new person to come into the matter and it sounds duplicative. Instead say, "Discussing various options and strategies to improve ABC's outcome given the surrounding circumstances and set of facts" or something like that. It's not really about what you're doing, but, again, what's the value in what you're doing? How are you adding value to the client by what you are doing for the client? For example, "Meeting with so and so to discuss such and such a thing." Not just "Meeting, 2.5 hours." I think the proper description of the time is key to getting paid. If you think of billing as an extension of your marketing and business development and as a way to improve client rapport, you'll do a much better job of it.

[Author's note: Sally Schmidt's point about billing was recently validated at an "In-House Counsel Summit" held in Silicon Valley, which was sponsored by the Legal Marketing Association (LMA). The LMA seminar hosted a panel of general counsel discussing what they like and don't like about outside counsel. One general counsel from a well-known high-tech firm said, "I'll tell you one thing that irks me. Bills that don't tell me what

I'm paying for. I got a bill from one of our law firms and one line item said, '7.5 hours strategy meeting.' That tells me nothing. So, I simply crossed it out, and sent it back with payment less the 7.5 hour charge. I simply didn't pay it. I just marked it off. And if the firm was smart enough to look at their bill when it was returned, they could ask me about it, and we could have a discussion around it. I just found that charge to be virtually insulting because it was so non-descriptive." Also, please note that Sally Schmidt provides a more detailed discussion on billing strategies when consulting law firms.]

Bio: An Attorney's Website Bio

(Shanda Zavalsky)

I help our lawyers develop a business development friendly bio. I use a "word cloud" tool to create a visual to assist in presenting a clear picture to the attorney of which topics are being given the most emphasis. I use the site: http://worditout.com/word-cloud/make-a-new-one.

Bio: It's Step One

(Lisa Salazar)

Every attorney needs to make sure that they have a good online bio.

If it's not established as a separate web page on the website, it definitely should be. Each attorney should have their own space on the web and take ownership of it.

One of the things that I have heard is, "I don't want to be involved with digital or social media. I am too busy and it takes up too much time." Lawyers have all these different reasons for not being in the digital arena. What I always respond with is "Are you a member of your state bar association?" Inevitably, they say yes. Then I say, "Well, it's more than likely that you have a profile page on the State Bar site. If you're not taking control of that page, you're running the risk of being overlooked and other people speaking for you. So it's important to take ownership of that page and what is said about yourself." The same is true for online directories. There are so many these days. If a lawyer is listed in a directory that is not a good forum for them, ask to be removed from the directory. Lawyers are public figures—officers of the court and so when sworn into office, it entails managing your digital space.

To answer your question, "Are there some things that should be in your website bio that can help make an existing client feel more assured and a potential client feel more attracted to you as their new prospective attorney?",

I would just reflect on the adage "to thine own self be true." A lawyer needs to know who he or she is—know their skills and know their goals. Once these are identified, this will set the framework for how to develop and write a bio to attract and target clients.

This is also true for their LinkedIn profile or Twitter profile, even though it may be a shorter representation of the lawyer.

Bio: The Attorney's Website Bio: First Impressions Count

(Despina Kartson)

One tip I have, which sounds somewhat simplistic, make sure that you have a very strong, current, and compelling biography.

How many lawyers do you run across who have phenomenal backgrounds, phenomenal client experience, and when you look at their bio it's a two-paragraph statement, so-and-so works in the corporate practice group and specializes in mergers and acquisitions, and you know this lawyer is fantastic but he has just done himself such a disservice, or it's not current.

I was talking to a newly elected partner once and I said, "Now that you're a partner, make sure that you update your biography" and they said, "Oh, yeah, I guess I should. I haven't updated it in about six years." I said "That means that you were a junior associate when you last updated your bio and now you're a partner. That's not good." I think that the bios are important because, number one, it's the most commonly visited portion of a law firm's website. Number two, it's the most publicly visible representation a lawyer has to describe what they do and what they're good at. Will a client necessarily retain a lawyer solely based on their biography? I'm not suggesting that, but having a strong bio certainly validates reasons to hire and showcases a lawyer's great experience and expertise. [See Chapter 3, *Disasters to Avoid, Quickest Way to Lose a Business Opportunity: Outdated Bio.*]

Blogging: Every Survey Shows It's Growing

(Lisa Salazar)

Blogging. It's becoming common knowledge that some lawyers can get new business from blogs. Is it something that you recommend that people actively consider from the business development standpoint? What do you say to the lawyers when they ask about blogging?

American Lawyer magazine has gone into its fourth year of surveys on blogs in the legal community with statistics showing that it continues to be a very popular medium for lawyers. It is something to be considered for marketing purposes; if nothing else, it allows lawyers to follow clients and competitors.

There are a number of blogs that have gotten to be quite well-known: the IP blog by Dennis Crouch called PatentlyO, the Scotus blog, or the Wall Street Journal law blog.

You asked me to comment on the "Three Geeks and a Law" blog. I am a founder of the blog, and spent a few years actively involved with the blog, but I have not posted in a very long time. But I'm happy to say that I created a forum that has given other people an opportunity to shine. It is an award-winning blog, and listed as one of the top 100 blogs in the legal community for a number of years. I can't speak highly enough of the people involved. I think we've got a good host of writers that are highly regarded in the industry and I'm just really proud to be associated with them.

What's interesting to me is nobody's really wanted to change the style of the blog since it was first built. It's rather homely, a little crude-looking, but that kind of says it all. It typifies how we think of ourselves, and it's definitely a labor of love. We don't get paid for this. It's simply done for the pleasure of it.

Blogging: One Way to Differentiate Yourself from the Crowd

(Casey Flaherty)

Do something that differentiates you in a way so that everybody knows you're good.

And, so maybe . . . you write *the* "go to" blog on a very narrow issue. Or, you are forever speaking on a very technical topic so that people recognize you as *the* expert in that area; because if you don't get that separation, if you're just a commercial litigator—albeit a fairly good one—why choose you as opposed to the 1,000 others?

Blogging: The More You Blog, the More Business You Get

(Larry Bodine)

The more you blog, the more business you'll get. There's a direct correlation. Two or three times a week is good, but every day is better. I was asked, "Should the website or blog be refreshed Monday through Friday?" I do it Monday through Friday because the sites I work with are both business sites. It depends on what you're writing about. If it's an amusement park, you should refresh on weekends and holidays. [See Content Marketing: Blogging Examples.]

Blogging: Versus Face-to-Face

(Silvia Coulter)

We encourage people not to hide behind marketing activities as an excuse to avoid sales activities. Don't write 30 blogs to the exclusion of direct one-to-one connections. Yes, you want to brand yourself. You want to demonstrate expertise and experience. Marketing with written material is important, but it doesn't replace voice-to-voice or face-to-face. At some point, make a connection that's not at arm's length. Marketing tools like blogs, articles, and speaking are all very important in emphasizing that you have expertise and experience, because those are two vital legs of the three-legged stool of business development. But the third leg, which is just as vital, is relationships. Leverage those experience and expertise marketing tools you've created to complete the foundation of the three-legged stool. Say, "Here's an article that I wrote that you or someone in your network might be interested in reading or might find useful." Take the marketing opportunity that you spent all this good time on and leverage it to a direct connect relationship-building opportunity.

Bonuses

See also *Origination Bonus.* See also *Billing Credit to Associates.* See also *Cross-Selling: Incentivizing the Attorney to Cross-Sell.*

Bonusing Origination

(Tasneem Goodman)

Creating compensation systems that create the right incentives around business development, client service and good substantive work product is a tough nut to crack, and I sympathize with managing partners, executive committees, and others who lead firms and have to create those systems. I think it's a tough one.

My perspective is that those systems are extremely important, as you are, in fact, incentivizing behavior. At the end of the day, a big part of our motivation in our professional lives is the compensation that we get for our work. And the way that compensation is structured is undoubtedly going to create incentives. I went to the University of Chicago for law school. It's a law and economics shop. It's all about incentives and how do we incentivize behavior. How do we create legal systems that incentivize the right behavior? So lawyers know all about that. They're creating incentive systems through their work constantly. And yet it's a tough nut to crack because there are so many different kinds of behaviors that you want to incentivize and a relative order of priority of those behaviors, and how they get compensated presents a challenge on how to design the perfect system.

As it relates specifically to compensating origination versus compensating doing the work or growing the relationship or serving the client, my personal perspective is that origination credit is important, and you have to reward that. And my perspective is also that origination credit only matters for a certain amount of time. My perspective is that there should be a time horizon over which origination matters. So, when a client is new to a firm or when a matter is new to a firm, origination matters because who made that happen, who brought that in is important. But it's only important at the beginning of the relationship. Then what matters is how well are we serving that client and what's the quality of the work product that we're creating and delivering. And that's when I think the other kinds of credit, whether it's proliferation, or client service credit, or working attorney credit, or another type of credit are all really important, as well.

I think where too many firms go wrong is when they do incentivize origination, there's no time horizon on which that origination credit ultimately expires. Because what you don't want is 10 years from now that client's been with us forever, and that originating attorney has barely touched it but there's a really hardworking number two that's serving that client really well, and keeping them happy, and that person is getting nothing for it other than the hours they bill. That doesn't seem to be the right solution.

Fair and precise compensation strategies are a tough nut to crack. Compensation is very dependent on culture, history, and how the firm has evolved. There's so much at play. But if there are a couple of truths about compensation, the first one is that it is important to reward origination if, in fact, you want to incentivize that activity; and you have to if you want to have a going concern as a law firm. The second truth is that it only makes sense for that origination credit to exist for a finite period of time in the client relationship, and the client relationship may last much longer than the origination credit lasts. It's that initial contribution. Yes, you made a great contribution. You brought that client in, or you brought that case into the firm. That's awesome, and we're going to reward that. But that can't last forever.

And I can't put a percentage on the origination bonus. I don't have a good answer for that. It is all over the place because there's so much that goes into it. It's very hard for me to say 1 percent, 10 percent, or 20 percent because I bet you you've got everything from zero to 25 percent out there.

It's very hard to say in a vacuum what the number should be because it is so contextual. [See also *Origination Bonus.*]

Bonusing: Firm Bonus of Specific Business Development Activities

(Stephen Fairley)

There was a study cited in an ABA publication reporting that fewer than 25 percent of law firm partners will participate in marketing and business development unless there's financial compensation. The compensation can take any number of forms including origination credit, a flat fee paid towards bringing in new work, or credit towards billable hours, but the principle remains—very few attorneys will participate unless they are somehow credited.

Other firms require the creation of individual marketing plans that you must review with the managing partner or with the partner in charge of your department. Completion of that plan is directly tied to your annual bonus.

Owners, partners, and chief marketing officers must specifically identify what they want the attorneys to do (an approved list of marketing activities) and they must compensate or reward them for doing so.

Building Rainmaker Skills: Part 1: Three Steps

(Tasneem Goodman)

"How do you turn skilled lawyers into skilled rainmakers," is the multimillion dollar question, and I think there are a few layers to it.

First, somebody has to want to be a rainmaker. I think it's worth pausing to think about that. And I don't make any assumptions about what percentage of the lawyer population wants to be a rainmaker. What's more interesting to me is answering the question, what are the underlying motivations that make someone want to be a rainmaker? For some people it's the money, but there are all kinds of other reasons why people want to create their own book of business.

For some people it means greater security and predictability in their future. They're not beholden to anyone or their success at a firm is not dependent on anyone else's ability to keep them busy, for example. I think for some people, having a book of business of their own means greater satisfaction in their work because they are the person who is on that frontline with the client in the relationship seat, and for many that's very satisfying. So I think it can be different things for different people. Pausing for a moment to think about that is important. Otherwise you could have a lot of training, and mentoring, and even business development activity that doesn't stick because somebody's heart isn't in it; or they're not really making it the kind of a priority it needs to be if you want to be successful at it because it's not easy. It takes time, and energy, and resources.

All of us make decisions about how we spend our time, and energy, and resources based on our priorities, and whether business development is going to get the time, energy, and resources it deserves. It has to be a priority to someone. You have to tap into what would make it a priority. What makes being a rainmaker fit up there with your other priorities of being a spouse, or a parent, or a part of a community, or a religious person, or someone who does service for others? There are all these other activities that take up our time and energy, and if you're going to be good at rainmaking, it has to fit among all of your priorities. So tapping into what makes it fit, whether it is more money, or greater satisfaction, or greater control over your future, or a louder voice inside of your firm, or whatever the motivation may be, is what you've got to tap into first. Otherwise you can do lots of other things, train people, coach them, mentor them, give them resources, give them skills, make them go to a lunch-and-learn, etc. But it's hard to stick with it if you don't have that underlying motivation.

Once you've established that foundational motivation, where do you go from there?

I think there are three things. First, people need the basic skills of business development, the basic skills of rainmaking. And some of them are skills that are similar to the skills that lawyers use in law practice and some of them are different, but they are specific skills. What do you need to actually be successful at rainmaking? You need to understand that in order to develop business, you have to first develop a very good understanding of the audience that you're trying to attract. Once you've done that you have to figure out what is it about you and your practice and your firm that you need to communicate that will, in fact, attract that audience. You have to develop good relationship-building skills. And relationship-building skills take work. You've got to do preparation and planning. You have to execute well. You have to follow through. So there are many different kinds of tools that you have to have in your toolkit. Those are the *what* of business development, which are the actual skills that are needed to be successful in business development. That's number one.

Number two is the *how* of how those things I've just described get implemented. Specifically, *how* do you implement *what* needs to be done? I've often seen where we'll do training programs in which we'll give people those *what* skills, but they will still need help with the *how* those specific activities get done. For example, here's what you do that allows you to define a target market. You have to figure out what you're good at, and what you care about, and what the opportunity is in the marketplace. When those three things align you can figure out what's a good target market for you to pursue, which you can define by industry, or company type, or buyer type, or a situation that that buyer of legal services needs to be in to make them a good fit for your practice. You can give people those kinds of *what*, but if you don't actually help them put that into action, give them the *how* in addition to the *what*, I often find that some will make the translation, and others won't.

Most people can't make it to the full extent of their potential. That's often where we'll do things like coaching or mentoring. Whether us or a senior rainmaker or other professional inside the firm who can sit beside the lawyer and say, "All right. You're going to have lunch with this person. Talk to me about what you're trying to accomplish with him. What kind of conversation points are you going to build into your conversation? And what do you need to learn from him to figure out whether there might be some opportunity for you there? And what do you need to get him talking about in order for you to pursue that opportunity? And when you leave lunch what are you going to do to make sure that you don't say, 'Great, let's do this again sometime,' only to have six or twelve months go by and that 'sometime' never seems to roll around?"

So I think there is, in addition to the *what* of the skills, it helps to give people the *how*, of how do you actually put those skills to work. That added support can happen through mentoring through a more experienced attorney who's been successful at rainmaking already, or a professional inside of the firm, or a professional outside of the firm. I think it's important to be able to sit down with that lawyer and say, "Okay, tell me what your game plan is for this lunch. What do you want the conversation to look like? What are you trying to accomplish? What do you want to communicate? What do you want to learn?" Similarly, if it's somebody who's come back from the conference, and they say, "Oh, I made this really great connection, but I don't know quite how to follow through on it. What do I do next?" I sit next to them and help them draft an email that says, "Hey, it was great meeting you at the conference. Would love to have a phone call or meet for coffee to learn more about you and your business or your career trajectory," or whatever it might be. I think it's really helpful to give attorneys a little bit of that mentoring/coaching/advice on the actual implementation of those business development skills. Some will do it naturally, and they can take those skills, and apply them, and be great and successful. For others it won't be as natural. It won't come as intuitively or easily, and so giving folks some support in how they actually take those skills and implement them, the *how* in addition to the *what* is helpful. And I think even for people for whom it comes naturally or intuitively, some additional help on that *how*, somebody who can serve as a sounding board, just helps you sharpen it.

I think that's just helpful, whether it happens in a formal or informal way. Just like when you're a lawyer you need the substantive knowledge of the law, and you need the skills of how to try a case or draft a compelling brief or negotiate an agreement between your client and their counter party. Most of us, as practicing lawyers, watch other lawyers doing that, and we cobble together a style that works for us. I think that works very well for lawyers in business development as well, and yet, there's not as much transparency to it. So often more junior lawyers don't have the opportunity to see more senior lawyers executing on business development because the opportunity doesn't present itself, or it's not as well entrenched into the way that we do business. And so some help is needed there—"This is how you actually make this happen. This how you go to a lunch and have the kind of conversation that's going to get you somewhere in this relationship that might create opportunity for business over time." I think that's an important part of it.

The third part, after you have the *what* and the *how* is what I like to call the *fuel*. I think it's really helpful to celebrate successes in business development no matter how small they are and that's the *fuel*.

So I spend a lot of time with my clients, individual lawyers who are developing business, celebrating when they send an email or come back after a lunch, and they know exactly what they're going to do to follow up on that lunch, or come back from a conference and actually send the email to the person that they met while they were there asking them if they can get back together for coffee or a phone call or something like that. I give people lots of high fives. Pop lots of champagne. Because I think that's so very important to keeping people on the track to be successful.

As lawyers when we practice we get pretty immediate feedback. It's very easy to see the results of our efforts because most of them are tangible. We do a deposition, and we've actually done it. Or we write a brief, and now we've got a brief. With business development you go to lunch or you speak at a conference or you write an article and you don't immediately have clients or new dollars rolling in the door. Measuring and celebrating the success of doing things right, I have found in my experience working with lawyers, keeps people motivated and on track to continue to do those things, do them well, and do the right things so that over time new clients and dollars will roll in the door. There's a lot that has to happen before that, and so if we can measure and celebrate some of those successes along the way, it's easier to stay on track using that approach because there's a long haul, in many cases, before the dollars start coming in the door.

Building Rainmaker Skills: Part 2: Three More Elements

(Tasneem Goodman)

Here are three other thoughts on turning a skilled lawyer into a skilled rainmaker.

Number one, I think one of the things that happens when you break it down simply like this is that it demystifies business development for people. I think in the profession of law, certainly my experience as a practicing lawyer and what I've seen in the lawyers that I've worked with is that business development often seems like a black box, where people have a friend who comes in one side of the black box and money rolls out the other side. We don't know what happens in between that makes that happen. And oftentimes what I find is that people see a successful rainmaker, and they think that it's very personal to them. So, you'll see that guy, Peter, who builds that multi-million dollar practice that keeps 10 lawyers busy, and you think it's about Peter. You think it's about where he went to school, and the friends he has, and who he socializes with, and how long he's been at this, and the fact that he's really well-known in the profession and all those kinds of things. And we think of it as very personal to them. Oh, he's a great backslapper and glad-hander. He's really great at earning people's trust, and people just want to hire him. And many think it's completely unique to them. But when you break down their activities into smaller steps, you can identify specific concrete skills that anyone can use to develop business, and here's how you implement them. Business development is a process and a knowable process. And while it's organic and its relationships and its people, it is also predictable. Business development is a process, and there are some universal truths about it that we know.

I think knowing that aspect of business development really helps because for many lawyers, we didn't have that training in law school or even in our firms. Just opening the black box and saying, "Here is the six-step process or the five-step process or three-step process." I've seen multiple processes for business development. They all share many of the same concepts and truths, but it almost doesn't matter as long as it is a process because as lawyers we're pretty good at process. We're good at understanding process and understanding that if there is a process I can master the parts of the process, and I can be good at it. Knowing that really helps, one, because it demystifies it. Two, because it divorces it from the person and makes it accessible no matter who you are, or where you went to school, or what your personality type is.

Oftentimes when you see a successful rainmaker or a couple of successful rainmakers in your firm, and if you believe you don't fit into their mold of personality, or background, or education or whatever, you may not think that you can be good at it. But if somebody breaks it down into a process and concrete skills that go along with that process, now all I have to do is hone those specific skills and translate that *how* into a *how* that works for me.

So, number one, the demystification of the business development process helps tremendously. The other thing I think along those lines is that business development is about three simple things: making friends, solving problems, and doing it in a disciplined and strategic way.

And if you really unpack those three elements, you can grasp everything that is business development. Making friends, i.e., building authentic relationships. It's a relationship business. And the ability to build authentic relationships with clients, potential clients, referral sources, people with whom you want to partner to develop business. That's a key part of it.

Number two, it's about problem solving and in particular, other-centered problem solving. So solving problems for people in a way that's generous and that helps them even if it puts your self-interests at bay for a moment. You need to understand that if you are building relationships with the right people and you're making investments in those relationships by solving problems that should be solved, not just the ones you get paid to solve, business will come.

Number three, you've got to do it with strategy and discipline. You've got to figure out who the right people are, and you've got to make sure that you prepare, and you've got a plan, and you've got a strategy, and you're doing your business development activities with purpose and discipline and consistency. If you do those things, if you make friends, solve problems in ways that truly help people, and do it consistently and with discipline and purpose, you'll be good at it. And all of those things are very human. It's in our human nature to connect with people. It's in our human nature to help people, to be generous. It's in our human nature to be disciplined about the things that we care about and are a priority to us. [See also *Business Development Training*.]

Building Relationships: The Process Is Generic, Implementation Is Unique

(Silvia Coulter)

The generic "sales process" is the same for everybody. How you implement the process is really based on your style and personality and what fits for you. A big piece of acquiring new clients is about building relationships because very few of us want to buy anything from someone we don't like. Decide on what style works best for you to deepen a connection. One person is going to be really effective at speaking at a conference. Maybe they didn't go to the dinners and all the cocktail receptions at the conference. They may have gone back to their room to do work, but they can still be very effective at building relationships as long as they keep in touch. How you remain in touch with those individuals is really based on your individual personality and style. For some people blogging works. That's not the most direct route, certainly. For some people, going out every night for dinners, and to receptions works. Do whatever works best with your style. Remember though, at some point face-to-face or voice-to-voice is a critical element to building a long-term binding relationship.

A high volume of activity across a broad group of individuals within your targeted audience is always going to get you feedback that can be converted to leads, then prospects, then clients. It's a proven formula for success. Your only decision is to decide how specifically you are going to conduct a high volume of awareness-creating activity across a broad group of individuals within your targeted audience. A good measure is to be in touch with at least 50 individuals at least four times a year. Share resources the firm is putting out there or articles from the daily news journals. Keep in touch.

Business Development Coaching versus Business Development Training/Consulting

(Peter Johnson)

There is coaching on a group or firm level which could be practice-based, firm-wide, or customized cohorts. The setting can be onsite at the firm's offices, offsite, online, and/or via conference calls. This is usually called training or consulting. Then there is one-on-one attorney coaching. Coaching can be as individualistic as the coach and customized to each individual attorney's personality and needs.

Business Development Coaching: Setting Priorities: Rainmakers First

(Silvia Coulter)

When asked how to set up a firm-wide business development coaching program, and how much of that would be focused on the associates, my response is, there's certainly good associate programing we can do, but I wouldn't say start with the associates. I would start with the rainmakers. Now, not every firm is willing to do that, but let's think about this. If you've got a person who can bring in half-a-million dollars consistently or a million dollars or $7 million consistently, they can double that. They've already demonstrated they can do it. Why not put your money with the fast horses in the race? You can certainly help develop the associates. But, you're not going to be getting an associate going to U.S. Steel to get a big piece of litigation, or an ITC case, or any of those bigger dollar decisions. It's unlikely. There is room for associate business development training. Group coaching can be very effective and consistently teaching about business development is important since it is an important part of their career track at a firm. Training at all levels helps keep the focus on client retention, client growth, and new business development; and it's a good way to build camaraderie across the firm as well.

When prioritizing coaching dollars, I say start with the rainmakers. If you've got a person who can bring in half a million dollars consistently or a million dollars or $7 million consistently, they can double that. Why not put your money with the fast horses in the race?

—*Silvia Coulter*

Now, that doesn't mean your associate is not capable of leveraging some of their contacts at their level in the law department of in-house counsel and secure an introduction to senior people who would meet senior people at the firm. That's what we'd advise associates to do—be the eyes and ears of the firm. Look for opportunities and sell the team—and stay in touch with everybody. These are the basic things that associates need to learn and do to help them lay the groundwork for the future. But in terms of making an investment go with your equity partners, and those income partners, or younger partners not yet equity who are on the partner track, because they're the future of the firm. I've never worked with an equity partner I couldn't teach something to, and I think that's often overlooked in firms.

Some say, "Oh, well, this guy has a big book, he's got a great practice. So, he doesn't need any help." It's not that he or she doesn't need help, but super talented people hire coaches all the time. Serena Williams, Olympic champions, or any great athlete, they all have coaches. They're at the top of their game, but they still have coaches. So, give us your best players, and we'll help them refine their skills. I haven't had any rainmakers who haven't found it valuable. We don't need to work with them for 12 months, but six months is a good period to help them sharpen the focus of their energy and their efforts. We know they can do it. It's a matter of just having a sounding board, and brainstorming, and tightening the game up a little bit. I say go with your talent, your top talent.

And you've got to have senior sales coaches. The coaches have to be people who have sold. If you're going to coach a rainmaker, you better have stood in highly competitive shoes, carrying a commission-based practice, and have had success because you've been there, you know how to compete and win. With the income partners or, the seniors, the next level down—people who are on the partnership track—I think that's a significant investment, recognizing that not everybody is going to become an equity partner, but we don't know who necessarily will and who won't. Let's give these people the skills that they are going to need because we're going to expect it from them.

Business Development Committee

(Jill Weber)

The business development committee is separate from our board of directors. We have eight members from different offices of the combined firm. They are key business generators from a variety of disciplines. We meet once a quarter to talk about business development initiatives.

Business Development Motivation: See "*Motivation*"

Business Development Plan: Less Is More

(Despina Kartson)

The second tip is to develop a simple one-page actionable plan and stick to it. I'm very much the "less is more" type and I'm in favor of easy to follow templates. I know that lawyers are reluctant to hear, "So, have you prepared your business development plan?" and they assume it's a six-month project of sitting down and writing a treatise on how they're going to tackle developing business. I like to have a one-page strategic plan that's also very practical, very tactical, and very actionable. This approach will make you stick with it because it's simple, it's direct, and to the point.

I think in working with lawyers across the firm, for example, there should be a template and a format for this. Lawyers should be given a template that they can then craft into their own words.

Business Development Resource Library

(Jeanne Hammerstrom)

In addition to pushing out information, we also provide access to a resource library where we put various articles on elevator speeches for example, or a podcast by Alycia Sutor of Akina Corporation who did a program for us on leadership skills and how to work with people. And I'll tell you one of the things I use over and over again for associates is Ross Fishman's Associate's Marketing Checklist by year of practice. I use that all the time. [Ross Fishman's Associate's Marketing Checklist can be found in the ABA book titled, *The Associate As Rainmaker.* See *CRM: Data That Makes Me Look Brilliant*, and *Information Aggregators: Using Third Parties for Critical Research* by Jeanne Hammerstrom.]

Business Development Resource Library

(David King Keller)

If you don't have a Business Development Resource Library that is well known and easily accessible to all of your staff and attorneys, you're losing revenue.

Business Development Strategy: Not Always about the Revenue . . . Initially

(Sally Schmidt)

In the last five years, it's been all about growing law firm revenue. But, it should sometimes be about growing visibility. For example, a law firm will say, "We want to target the nanotechnology industry," or some other new industry for the firm. They think it's a growth area, but it's one in which they don't have any clients or any experience; it's just a new area they want to develop as a revenue source. To me, our first goal isn't to get business. The first goal is to get people in that industry aware of the firm, and get the firm on the shortlist of firms to be considered when new legal matters come up. So that's more about getting involved in the proper associations and writing and speaking and blogging and a whole variety of industry-related activities. Because, it is a two-step process to being hired. First, you have to make the shortlist and then, second, hopefully, get the business. But how do you make the shortlist if you're not even perceived to be a player ? So, the first step isn't necessarily about bringing the revenue in. It's about growing the firm's visibility.

Business Development Support Staff

(Erin Meszaros)

We have my level, Chief Marketing and Business Development Officer; then we have directors. Then we have senior BD managers, managers, and coordinators. The coordinators are the ones who are doing the lion share of the hard administrative work (i.e., research, pulling the RFP material together, providing analytics, tracking return on investment (ROI), etc.). I do worry . . . the coordinator's job is such a demanding job with a lot of repetitive routine activities they deal with and for the most part it is not the most exciting. I try to make sure that they're interested in what they're doing and getting enough variety that they will stick around. As to the total team size, today we have six coordinators and 24 on the team total. It's 12 and 12. So I have 12 on the business side who focus strictly on business development, and I have 12 on the Mar-Com side who focus on PR, marketing, website, graphics, etc.

Business Development Support Staff: Structure

(Nancy Kostakos and Karen Febeo)

We have a marketing and business development department comprising 40-plus people that is responsible for strategic brand and integrated marketing for the firm and its practice areas, internal and external communication, event planning, and business development strategy, coaching and support.

The firm is organized around business units with a business development strategist and at least one support person within each one of those units. There is obvious value in having these strategic, higher level business development individuals in each department. Some firms have gone beyond the coaching and support role into true non-lawyer sales roles. We're not there yet, but we are seeing more and more partnering between non-lawyer professionals and lawyers in our business development efforts.

The marketing, communications, and professional development and training teams provide centralized support to the business development teams embedded in each unit. Our business development team is the front-line service team that works directly with the lawyers and with the business unit leaders on setting strategy to develop additional business. Our professional development and training team works closely with our marketing and business development teams to bring business development training and coaching into the mix.

When the firm reorganized into business units at the end of 2013, we made a substantial increase in business development resources to support the business units. Our management committee expects to see a favorable return on investment on the additional resources that have been allocated to business development. We are rigorous about requiring ROI information on all of our investments. If we find that investments are not providing tangible results, we will recommend that the dollars get redistributed to something that will be more impactful.

Business Development Support: A Success Story

(Barbara Lauterbach)

This happened several years ago—this is one of my favorite stories. I was at a firm in Florida that had never had a marketing professional . . . sitting down with a named partner and going through my usual initial interview questions - tell me who you are, tell me what you want to do, tell me who your biggest disappointments have been, tell me who you want. This partner said, "I want a particular manufacturing group's business. It's driving me crazy." By the way, when I tell this story I don't mention any names and I change the industry group type to preserve confidentiality.

So, here we have this partner who is president of a well-known firm, one of the best transactional people in the State, and he lives a mere six blocks away from the chairman of the board of that particular manufacturing group. He could not get an appointment with the General Counsel. He could not get these people to give him the time of day. So, I said let me do some research, let's figure this thing out; and it took me a little while, but I figured out that the chairman of the board, who really did make the decisions about choice of legal counsel in spite of the fact that they had a general counsel, was very involved in a major non-profit organization. It had been his personal passion for several years. He had been responsible for closing the organization down and rebuilding it and reopening it and starting to fund it.

So, you know what happens now. I become friends with the people at the non-profit so that I can get some inside information. Specifically, I became friends with a guy who was in charge of Public Relations and News for the non-profit and he told me how the members of the board were chosen. I put my partner in a position to become a member of the board. He was elected to the board and within six months of him joining the board, once the chairman of the board realized what a wonderful man he was, what a committed attorney, what a consummate professional he was, of course they started talking about the transactional work for his manufacturing group. And about a year later, we were doing all of their new transactional work.

All of the new files were going to us. That's probably the proudest moment of my life - because it took such cunning and it really wasn't that difficult, but it was an unorthodox approach.

> All of the new files were going to us. That's probably the proudest moment of my life - because it took such cunning and it really wasn't that difficult, but it was an unorthodox approach.
>
> —*Barbara Lauterbach*

Sometimes an unorthodox approach is the best approach. You just have to figure it out and keep at it, and you also have to understand that most of these accomplishments require process skills.

And what I mean by that is you're not out at a skeet shoot where you say, "pull," and the target goes up in the air and you shoot it. You have to identify the target and find out where it is. So, even in this situation where I clearly knew relatively early on who the person was who was going to make the decision, it was not a matter of getting my attorney in front of him and making a pitch. It was a matter of putting someone in the chairman's way who he would bond with and who could do the work. So, it wasn't going to happen overnight. We were 18 months into my tenure with that firm before we pulled in the first file.

And now, seven years later – my attorney is still doing all of their transactional work.

He landed his dream client. I'm sure he has more lucrative clients than this restaurant group, but that was a burr under his saddle. He just couldn't get over the fact that he couldn't get in there. When you give someone the tools and opportunity to land a dream client, there's a true relationship developed.

All business development folks talk about the importance of relationships, but until you develop a true trusted advisor relationship with a client, it's all academic.

We did all sorts of things for this non-profit before we got any of their business. We had an attorney working on the board. He raised money for them, he donated money to them. We took the firm holiday card and turned it into a tribute to the non-profit. We made a donation for every card sent, and encouraged our clients to also contribute. We partnered with that non-profit in ways that other members of the board weren't and certainly their lawyers weren't. And, yes – we took him to dinner, and golfing, and sailing.

And some of that cost us money. Also, it certainly took much of the partner's time. I know he gave a fair amount of free legal advice to them as well, but my attorney got the business that he wanted and the satisfaction of landing a dream client.

Business Development Team: Structure

(Allen Chichester)

We have three groups within our marketing department: Business Development, Marketing Communications, and Marketing Services. Each has a director, with managers who report to the director. The directors of each group report to me, the CMO.

I love working with organizational structure. For me, the optimal structure is always based on the talent and passions of your staff, the marketing and business development tools and systems you have, and the needs and priorities of the organization. I prefer a relatively simplistic structure versus complicated roles and responsibilities. One of the challenges of working within a distributed network, like most law firms are, is managing the matrix nature of staff responsibilities.

In my view, it's not simply the physical structure and the job responsibilities, it very much has to do with the culture that you want to build within the staff and the organization, to make sure that whatever structure you've got in place actually works. Of course, there are the basics as well, like people have to understand what's expected of them and the people that they engage need to understand what their roles are.

Business Development Tip #1: Find Attorney's Comfort Zone

(Despina Kartson)

Define what business development means to you and what you're comfortable with and play to your strengths. This addresses an individual's concerns such as, "I don't really like to network. I don't like to go to cocktail parties. I don't have time for cocktail parties." If you are a social person and you have the ability to do a lot of client entertainment, that's great. On the other hand, if you're more the type who thinks "I just want to write some articles and get them published and then follow up with people," then do that, but play to your strengths because your approach will be genuine; it will be authentic and it will work for you.

Business Development Tip: Leverage Firm Resources

(Despina Kartson)

Leverage resources within your firm. For example, most firms have Client Relationship Management (CRM) systems, with contact information shared with personnel across the firm. If you're interested in targeting a particular company that may not be a client, then check in your CRM system and see who in the firm has a relationship with that company and ask if they'll make an introduction for you. Does your firm put on different events for clients at the firm level or at the practice group level? Make sure you have access to the firm calendar and figure out which of those firm events you should attend. Decide that you're going to attend, reach out to the BD Team, ask for a list of clients and prospects who have RSVP'd to the event and prepare yourself.

If the firm doesn't have a calendar that's available on their Intranet, someone in the Business Development and Marketing department is going to have a master list.

Also, understand who else in your firm has a particular area of expertise that would be useful for you in your outreach to clients and prospective clients. If you know that a client has a particular need and you don't necessarily have that area of expertise, find out who within your firm has that area of expertise and work with them. Take them to a client meeting.

When it comes to internal resources, leverage your PR, BD, and marketing team. Let your PR team know that "Part of my business development plan for this year is that I want to publish two bylined articles. How can you help me?"

Work with your internal business intelligence and competitive intelligence teams. Many firms have competitive intelligence groups either within the BD teams or in the library groups that can do great research. Leverage all resources within your firm to which you have access.

Business Development Tools: Templates, Guides, Videos, E-Learning , and More

(Karen Bell)

We have a wide variety of business development tools accessible to our attorneys on the firm's intranet. We are constantly reviewing these tools for effectiveness, while researching and developing new ones that can be added. Our BD team works very hard to make sure that there are a number of templates and guides our lawyers can use for client development. For example, we have an amazing guide to successful pitches. We also have a large e-learning initiative underway and we put that pitch guide into an e-learning module that includes a feedback feature that allows our attorneys to provide their insights.

And our plan is to have many more e-learning primers. In our BD Ideas discussions, we're looking at transferring the key points in our BD instruction modules into little video vignettes—so that they are available for quick access before our attorneys meet with clients or a potential client.

A big focus in terms of business development skills is the notion of being oriented around an objective and being well-prepared, even if you're "just" going out for lunch with someone. The point is not to waste anyone's time. Be very clear on the objective. Do some research or have someone help you, so that you go there with some specific questions and takeaways and follow-ups. It's that rigor we encourage.

To support that rigor continuing, we make sure that we have tools that are easily accessible to our attorneys. By working hard upfront to create these tools and the system that makes them easily accessible, the attorneys benefit and there's some element of self-serve to the BD team, as well. We have a very lean BD team. There's only so much they can be doing. So, we spend a lot of our focus on empowering our attorneys with systems and tools that they can use on their own for the majority of their business development needs. This allows our BD team to put more of their attention on situations that require more unique and customized solutions along with the potential for a significant ROI.

To achieve this level of multi-tiered business development activities by our lawyers and our team means our lawyers have to develop BD habits. Making BD a habit sounds really easy. It's a simple statement. It's hard to do.

We experience moments of great gratification from our efforts when we hear one of our attorneys saying, "Oh, yes! I did it! I followed the instructions in your video on how to use the pitch guide and it worked. We won the client's business! " And so now what we're doing is saying, "How do you make that happen, again?" Well likely, just three or four simple little things. When they start seeing that once they give it a try, it works, that makes the next time a little easier, a little more routine, and those business development habits a little more ingrained.

We incorporate a range of programs, workshops, and experiential learning exercises, as well. We have a variety of business development coaching programs in place that include one-on-one and group sessions. By incorporating more planning and a more strategic and disciplined approach in all our efforts, it results in a more integrated program that connects the education, the tools, the programs and our *Dialogue Project Management*® processes. Once attorneys see how things connect, they feel far more supported and enabled.

Business Development Training: Associate/ Baker Donelson

(Adam Severson)

I have hosted a variety of associate round tables across a variety of offices and I think one of the things that I really emphasize in that context is our lawyers need to own their career and have an intentional plan to shape its future and borrowing from the book [of the same name] basically saying that hope is not a strategy. So, I tried to break it down into some tangible things that they can do and I've put it into **four categories**. The **first** is to delight your clients and ensure that you do good work and that you meet and exceed the service expectations of both your ultimate clients as well as your internal clients. **Second**, would be to differentiate yourself to be known for something; and to try to understand what your experience is and what you'd like your experience to be; and then look at ways to capitalize and build on that and coupling with the firms strengths. **Third** would be to get involved; and there is a variety of ways in our firm and other firms that folks can position themselves both as thought leaders and team members, whether it is on a practice group or serving as a substantive resource to another group to write a white paper or to participate in industry groups or on board participation or committees, or alumni groups and all those things; and make sure that in some way you are getting involved, I always recommend that people get involved with something that they or their clients are passionate about, because if you, join the Humane Society Board but you cannot stand dogs, you're not going to really do a terrific job and put your all in to that particular organization. And the **fourth category** would be to build and mine your network; telling our folks at an early age that their colleagues from law school and college can very well become future colleagues or referral sources down the road and so one of the things that I really recommend as part of building and mining their network is what I call a **DIRP** analysis. This analysis is designed to take a concerted look at your network and figure out who is a **D** for decision maker, **I** for influencer, **R** for referral source, and **P** for personal contact. In many instances those positions like personal contact and decision maker may very well overlap. The goal is to ensure that people are working with what I call high potential professionals. Those might be bankers or accountants or other lawyers. By doing this analysis they are trying to align the frequency of their touch points with these influencers or decision makers in a weighted fashion as compared to some of the other contacts that they may have.

The other piece relative to fostering and growing our lawyers' business development skills is that we've got a couple of coaching programs. The one that has the greatest visibility within the firm is the program that we call **Baker Rain,** which is intended to support our junior shareholders in the development and training of their skill set in business development. Also we partner with a third-party resource to provide both training as well as individual and group training; first, in a group session to build a peer group within the firm and then individual one-on-one sessions that are tailored to that particular individual's practice. [Read more at: *Business Development: Cultural Expectation/Two Day*

Training at Baker Donelson; and *Business Development: Client Teams, SWOT and DIRP.]*

Business Development Training: Associate/Partner: See also *Communication Skills*

Business Development Training: Associate: Learning Firm's Resources

(Matt Taylor)

An associate checklist item: If I'm a first-year associate, I am looking at our firm website. I am learning everything about every practice group leader, and their practice area skills. You have to invest some time. Too many lawyers go about their work with blinders on and don't pay attention to who is around them. You have to know who is around you so that you can sell the full range of legal services offered by the firm.

Business Development Training: Associates

(Mark Usellis)

Associates: mid- to senior-level associates: elements of BD program:

- Day-long training program followed by six months of limited coaching.
- The concepts of business development.
- The sales pipeline.
- Building and developing a network.
- How to develop a business plan.
- Understand the capabilities of the firm outside of their office and their practice group.
- Learn how to do a referral interview.
- How to meet with a referral source.
- Fundamentals of how to understand the legal needs of a business.
- Multiple ways you can be helpful to a business prospect or client.
- How to build rapport.
- Other basic fundamentals of business development.

Benefit of this program: when they became partners and came into the partner business development training program, we didn't have to spend so much time on remedial topics, rather we could focus on the needs assessment and pitching.

Business Development Training: Associates

(Jeff Berardi)

I can only personally do so much. I can only get to so many offices. Although I travel frequently, I am not out on the road constantly. So, although I offer training programs within a local office, when I travel to that office, it is just one element of our entire training program.

Part of our business development training occurred during our associate symposium, a global associate symposium. We brought together approximately 80 associates from all over the world – representing all of our offices. The attendees included one or two associates from each of the offices, who were selected to serve as liaisons to the rest of their office, and who reported back on activities for those that were not able to attend. This past year, we basically had the entire program focused on business development and client development skills. The reason was the content was entirely based on what the associates said they wanted to hear in the surveys conducted prior to the event. The associates really wanted to learn more about client development activities and what to do and how to do it.

So, we built the program over three days, basically, two and a half days' worth of programs, on all different topics. Some programs were more plenary session discussions where we talked to the entire group, but many were breakout sessions, where we had concurrent sessions going on. We talked about setting the stage for success; determining what the client needs to hear; how do you build an effective client pitch; how to maximize relationships within the firm and outside the firm; world-class client service; and how to understand the difference between standard client service and world-class service and many other important related issues that gave the associates in attendance a much better perspective.

The symposium was very focused on building these business development skills for them in a variety of different ways. The program really seemed to be appreciated by the associates in attendance, and it helped us as well, because it meant that then we had a platform and a template to use for other training programs as well, not just for associates. For example, we actually took some of these programs and built them into a separate learning program that was intended for all lawyers across the firm. The symposium experience was the catalyst to really build out a more robust program that we could share with all lawyers.

We had a number of members of my senior director team and the marketing department who were heavily involved in the symposium's development. Everything was done in conjunction with our professional development department. At a high level, we are working closely together on what the lawyers' needs are. It was members of the professional development department that contacted me and said that the associates are interested in client development. So we worked collaboratively to add business development to the agenda.

My team is involved with the professional development directors and their managers, and my managers work together. So it's definitely a joint approach and I certainly can't take credit just in the marketing and business development department. It's very much a concerted effort between the two administrative departments.

> We had a global associate symposium. We brought together approximately 80 associates from all over the world – representing all of our offices. We worked collaboratively with our professional development department to include a robust business development program to the agenda.
>
> —*Jeff Berardi*

Business Development Training: Associates/Benesch

(Jeanne Hammerstrom)

One rainmaker training exercise that we have done is a mock pitch. We will involve three of our partners. One will be the CEO, another will be the GC, and the other will be the HR person. They will present a case to our associates, who we have formed into little teams. We conducted this exercise at an associate retreat a couple years ago. Our partners had a few weeks to prepare the mock client presentations which were conducted at a retreat for the associates. We found this to be a very successful training.

Ross Fishman's Associate's Marketing Checklist by year of practice is one of the support tools I use over and over again in my business development program for associates. I use that checklist all the time. [Two checklists for a year-to-year approach to associate marketing, including a copy of Ross Fishman's checklist for associate marketing, can be found in *The Associate As Rainmaker, Building Your Business Brain*, an ABA book by David King Keller located at http://bit.ly/1dAxob6.]

Business Development Training: Associates and Partners Together?

(Jeff Berardi)

We typically try to have the associates participate in separate discussion sessions from the partners. In some situations, it's perfectly fine to mix them, but I think that you don't always get partners being as honest as they would be talking about things if they are in front of the associates, and vice versa. I just feel like sometimes it makes sense to break them up because you're going to have a little bit of a different discussion angle and people are going to talk more open and honestly, and feel more comfortable doing so when they're in their own group. It's not intended to segregate too much, but I've found that if you have it for all lawyers (inclusive of both partners and associates) you often don't get as many partners in attendance.

I will say, however, that when I am talking about digital communication activities, such as how to use LinkedIn and other social media, that has been—more so than probably any topic I have discussed in recent years—more universally interesting to both associates and partners, and, as a result, we don't seem to experience any of the same issues with attendance. I think it may be that whereas our younger lawyers are probably savvier about this social media, they also haven't been really focused on it from a business perspective, having viewed it more on a personal basis. On the other hand, some of our older lawyers haven't been doing so much with social media even though they might be very established in their careers; therefore they don't have as much of a digital presence, which doesn't really fit with their market recognition more generally in the marketplace. So, I think it's interesting that for whatever reason, that topic has no challenges in blending the two groups together.

Business Development Training: Associates Trained by Firm Rainmakers

(Louise Muldoon)

In Australia, we had our top rainmakers talk to our associates about how they had become successful. We would run panels with two or three successful business developers, so that, they could deliver the information in person. They'd share war stories and talk about what it was that set them apart. In one presentation we had one of our anti-trust lawyers speak about how he'd spent a couple of years with a regulatory authority that cleared mergers, in addition to other things, and how useful that had been later on when growing his practice. The associates were given many great strategies that these rainmakers had used to their advantage, both from a business development and career development perspective.

We do these panels on a regular basis, and I would be surprised if any of the partners or lawyers that you talk to aren't prepared to take some time off the timesheet to help educate associates. I believe many partners look at their business holistically and see helping associates improve their skills as something that goes beyond the timesheet, because it creates a very positive culture within their institution. Sharing information and knowledge is seen as important and mentoring goes hand-in-hand with other non-billable activities our lawyers perform, such as pro bono legal work. I have never had a problem getting any of our lawyers to spend whatever time was needed in preparation and delivery for one of these sessions. We usually did this over a lunch. Occasionally, we did this in the evening over a drink.

Business Development Training: Associates: A Formal Program

(Allen Chichester)

Over the past few years, we have begun to formalize our business development training for associates.

They are very smart and they can pick up whatever theory you want to give them. So, there is no "dumbing-down" here. In fact, they probably have more ability to pay attention and absorb new things when they're associates, so if anything, we crank up the theory. However, if you're telling them things that they're not going to be using, then they may or may not retain it. We try to focus on those business development challenges that are relevant to them. We also try to get a lot of discussion going so that we understand the barriers that they see in terms of working on their own business development.

Another activity we encourage is to create opportunities for associates to sit down with their office managing partners on a regular basis to talk about business development. We love to hear associates talk about their own business development experience. What have you done lately? Have you gone to networking events? Tell us about it. Often, an expectation gets created that they should be active in business development simply because they're going to be asked what they've done lately. It is amazing to me how quickly associates become sophisticated in their business development activity when expectations are made clear.

We have fourth year associates doing the sales pipeline management that would rival any partner I've seen. It's very rewarding for us as trainers, and just a reminder that these are very people. If you give them the right tools and the right expectations, they'll deliver.

A huge challenge is to create appropriate expectations across a distributed network of offices, where the associates come into contact with different local business development cultures. So, I'm not saying we do it perfectly, but we have seen a lot of positive responses from the associates when they're given the opportunity and clear expectations.

> We have a couple of good things going for the associates. One is, we have formal business development training, and all associates are encouraged to participate. The second thing we do, and this is an office-by-office activity, is that we try to create opportunities for the associates to sit down with the office managing partners on a regular basis and talk about their business development experience.
>
> —*Allen Chichester*

Business Development Training: Associates: Activities

(Karen Bell)

Our business development training for associates is geared to the attorney's level of experience. For example, we work with our associates on the basics of profile building and networking and we do that during two stages in their career. Specifically, our mid-level associates, four years and up, are supported in creating their personal plans. We provide them with a lot of good guidance in an interactive workshop format, with a focus on the need for planning for these activities. For our more junior associates, we start with the very basics of networking and what client service means. That program is more general and emphasizes how client service needs to be woven into one's approach to networking and communicating. In order to "cement" their understanding of service, we ask them to observe others doing/speaking client service acts and then report back on their observations about the effectiveness of the approach. Another part of our foundational training for our first-year attorneys is to examine how social media can be a valuable tool to build their online profile. We encourage all of them to develop a LinkedIn profile and to understand the various ways LinkedIn can be used as an effective way to network. I consider LinkedIn as another form of elevator speech where you're encouraged to create a brand and, in the space of a few sentences, to really nail down what your value proposition is and what you offer in terms of a business opportunity.

[For more on business development programs for this firm's attorneys, please go to the following topics by Karen Bell: *Business Development Tools: Templates, Guides, Videos, E-Learning & More; Business Development Training: Role Playing: Mock Pitch Presentations; Client Communication: The Platinum Rule Leads To More Business Development; Client Development That Leads To Business Development: The Umbrella Approach; Dialogue Project Management®: A Client-Centric Approach; Elevator Pitch: Tell Them Your Value; Project Management: Six Sigma and Six Sigma Lean; and Solutions-Based Marketing.*]

Business Development Training: Associates: Core Competencies

(Marian Lee)

I am the Director of Professional Development and we have a Director of Business Development. We work together in a number of areas starting with the junior associates, or even summers. Very early on we give them a presentation on some basic skills around networking followed by a cocktail reception where they can practice some of those new networking techniques.

Our associates go through four levels of development before making partner. Each level is approximately two years, except Level 4, which may be 1 or 2 years. Our Level 1 associates participate in an apprentice program where they are expected to bill a certain number of hours, do a certain number of pro bono, get in some shadowing hours, and attend in-house training. As part of that in-house training, this year we had a senior associate talk to them about what he's learned about time management. That seemed to resonate fairly well. It wasn't from an expert. But what the senior associate did was conduct some research, gathered some information on best practices from a variety of sources, applied it to what he's experienced and turned those into some tips and pointers. We also present effective ways on how to use the marketing department and what you should be doing right now in the area of marketing. We also encourage them to do something in the area of leadership.

We are essentially starting with raw recruits. By the time they get to partnership, we've spent a great deal of time helping them polish a whole array of skills. A really important piece that we've added in the last four years was the development and implementation of our core competencies. We have 16 competencies. They're grouped. We have legal excellence which includes research, oral communication, writing communications, etc. We have self-management, organization and development, and professional development. We have teamwork, leadership, client development, and service. The competency groups also include professional values and commitment. There are 16 of them in total, and each competency has a description of the performance expected at each level. For example, the Level 1 performance expectations for legal research are different from those of Level 4 associates.

For example, at Level 1, a competent associate is able to write a decent memo with one or two changes, good grammar, and other criteria. A Level 2 associate can write a slightly more complex piece with a little bit of partner oversight. A Level 4 can write something that goes right out the door with very little editing. So, each level's performance criteria will be different.

Our idea was to describe for associates what's expected in each area of competency at each level. We do have a business development competency, and it's broken into levels. At Level 1, it may include, go attend an event, learn to meet people, and learn to follow up. It's very basic, yet an essential activity and skill. Keep in touch with your law school classmates, for example. At Level 2, more activities are added. Level 3, join a board. Level 4, get a board leadership position, etc.

We tell them what they're supposed to be doing at each of these levels. This provides them with greater awareness and understanding of what's expected in order for them to be successful. It goes in all 16 categories, but especially for business development and for community involvement. We spell it out pretty directly for them.

> When you break those business development skills down into small activities, and you look at what's really expected as a series of smaller steps, it's not that hard at all. The goal of the checklist is to spell out those little incremental steps.
>
> —*Marian Lee*

Shanda Zavalsky, our Business Development Director, has done a great job of creating an associate marketing checklist. This list tells the associates what they should do at each level. Sometimes a Level 1 hears about business development and may respond, "Oh, my God. I can't do that. I don't even want to think about that." But when you break those business development skills down into small activities, and you look at what's really expected as a series of smaller steps, it's not that hard at all. The goal of the checklist is to spell out those little incremental steps. And Shanda did a great job of putting that together.

Business Development Training: Associates: Designed Using Personality Research

(Melanie Green)

Our associate career model was developed based on feedback from focus groups and interviews with a number of different successful partners within the firm. The model includes behavioral and technical competencies. In designing the model, we also looked at the innate behavioral traits of lawyers. Since personality drives behavior, we considered personality trait research as well. You have to have that level of knowledge at the forefront of developing any kind of program. Our associate business development curriculum program was developed with the associate model, competencies, and personality trait characteristics in mind.

We worked with Dr. Larry Richard, of *LawyerBrain LLC*. He's done personality profiling of thousands of lawyers using a test called the Caliper Profile, and then measured those against the million plus profiles of other professionals also in the Caliper Profile database. He has identified six or seven personality characteristics where lawyers are categorized as either very high or low compared with the general population.

Dr. Richard's research reveals that on average, compared to general population, lawyers have *low sociability* and *low resilience*. If you're dealing with people who are low in resilience, what does that mean? For us that means, the people, trainers, and coaches who we have working with the lawyers must have über resilience, combined with patient persistence. We have to be patient working through the process and understand where the lawyers are coming from. At the same time, be really persistent in trying to make sure that we're coaching them to fully understand how to get through the sales process.

> Since personality drives behavior, we considered personality trait research as well. Our associate business development curriculum program was developed with the associate model, competencies and personality trait characteristics in mind. We worked with Dr. Larry Richard, [who] has come up with six or seven personality characteristics where lawyers are categorized as either very high or low compared with the general population.
>
> — *Melanie S. Green*

On the other hand, his research reveals that on average, compared to the general population, lawyers are very *high in autonomy*. So, you can't go in and just say, "Here's how you're going to do it." They're also very *high in skepticism*. All of those personality traits can make you a really good lawyer, but it will make them question the training programs that we put together, the sales cycle, the prospect to client timeline, and how to make that happen. I give this as a framework to say when we think about these programs internally, that's the context that we have to have behind whatever we build.

Business Development Training: Associates: 3 Levels, 12 Programs

(Melanie Green)

At the associate level, we have a training and development program that is client and business development focused. It's part of a broader training and development curriculum that includes professional development skills. We have three associate levels in the model. We have offered four programs a year to each of those levels. And they're all client relationship/business development focused.

For **Level 1**, we provide insight into what goes on behind-the-scenes in client intake and billing. Programs are not just about selling. They include what a client relationship manager or a client billing manager needs to do, what the client expectation is, and refer to outside counsel guidelines. How all of these issues, actions, and relationships fit together is a teaser into the bigger picture. We provide "Ten Ways to Become an Expert on a Client." That includes reading their 10Ks, setting up Google Alerts, internal information resources, and other research that you can do to be more informed about the clients you're working with.

These educational forums progress throughout their career. **Level 2** has "Can a Bill Be a Business Development Tool?" We expand the associates' awareness about the multi-dimensionality of the impact of a bill, rather than just the ins and outs of entering billable time. How can you use a bill's financial information as a way to enhance a client relationship through clarity or simplicity?

In **Level 3,** we have a billing conversation called, "Well, That Was Awkward." This addresses a situation where somebody's upset about a bill, and how to handle those situations?

Business Development Training: Associates: Duane Morris

(Matt Taylor)

We have a Marketing 101 for first-year associates. We have a Marketing 201, 301, and 401. These are big video presentations where every associate in the firm participates, along with key partners and key business development managers trained on marketing. I give a big piece every year to all of our associates on marketing, along with tips on business development. They ask incredible questions. This is something in our firm's DNA where we are training our associates about marketing and business development. We ask all of our associates, and this is crucial, to do a detailed business plan every year. I review every single one of them in the trial group and comment on them. I think some of our associate business plans are better than some of our partners' business plans.

"Okay. This is my plan of attack. I'm president of my alumni association. I'm going to do this." Or, "I'm on this committee at my synagogue," or whatever your networking is, become a leader in whatever group that is the big thing. Some of these business plans are awesome and they redo them every year. Then, the next year, they report on what they did to execute on that business plan. Some of these folks' business plans are incredible and they execute on it, so it's something that we are really aggressive about from day one with our associates. And, it's great for the firm. We're training them how to be rainmakers. Again, not everyone is going to be a rainmaker, but some are. So, from day one, we have our associates trained in thinking that way. That's something we're proud of. We talk about it with them—to be rainmakers. We also give our associates billing credit. We bonus our associates out on collections.

For our 101, 201, 301 training, we set aside at least an hour, but in connection with our annual meeting it's a full-day program. The day before our annual meeting, the associates come in and they do a much more in-depth seminar internally. We've got an excellent marketing department and the business developers run it with the practice group heads.

> We ask all of our associates, and this is crucial, to do a detailed business plan every year.
>
> —*Matt Taylor*

By the way, there's no magic to the business development plan. There's no right or wrong answer of what to put in there, but it makes you think about, "Where could I possibly get business?" I think that's what freaks people out the most. I really do. I think people are so intimidated by the thought of, "How the hell do you get a client? Why is anyone going to hire me as their lawyer? At this firm? At these rates?" I just think that some people get freaked out by it. Instead of just saying, "Okay. There's a great deal of business out there. This other joker got business? I can get business."

If you're not talking to your associates about this, then I don't even understand why you're in business. Of course, you should be talking to your associates. Educate them. Calm those down a little bit. Let them know, "Hey, your next door neighbor? The guy with the Ferrari? Guess what? He's doing something." You don't knock on the door and ask him for business right away. But, that person is a potential client. Another thing that drives me crazy is when associates say, "Matt, I can't ask him for business. He's a good friend." Or, "That's my cousin." Literally, I want to come off the floor, saying, "Okay, think about it. If you don't ask people that you know and like for business, who are you going to ask?" I always tell the associates, "It's a thrilling feeling when you land your first client and you open your first file. It's very exciting."

Business Development Training: Associates: Time Management

(Marian Lee)

When we do an orientation for new associates, we give them a new associate's guidebook. The guidebook has some tips for time management, managing your email, and other suggestions. But we have yet to find one great source of time management training that seems to resonate with every person.

Business Development Training: Baker & McKenzie, Part 1: Key Skill Factor

(Louise Muldoon)

We take a step back from the question, "How do you help a skilled attorney become a skilled rainmaker?" and say, "What are the sorts of things we need to think about when we're training lawyers to be rainmakers?" I was in practice myself and I found that experience helps in recognizing and understanding the pressures of practice, management of the timesheet, as well as managing client expectations and meeting deadlines. We are dealing with skilled, highly trained professionals, so we need to make sure that we are delivering training and observations that add value.

Empathy is one skill value that I think is vitally important, but which may not be the first thing that comes to mind. When I talk to lawyers, I often say, "You need to have a good level of empathy with your client, so that you will be able to identify what pressures they are experiencing." Everyone talks about client "needs," but I dislike the word "needs" which I think is a very simplistic word in this case. As a lawyer, you need to be aware of your client's business pressures, the politics of the environment in which they operate, and think holistically about the client's situation. So, we spend—I spend—a great deal of time talking with clients and asking them about these things in addition to the core question of "how are we doing?" from a client service perspective. We do that to identify key concerns that are on clients' minds. We know how important it is for our lawyers to be knowledgeable about the client's business, so, we spend a lot of time gathering information about the different factors impacting our clients in various industry sectors, and share it, so our lawyers can be sensitive to the organizational and other influences on their client. This enhances empathy because often our clients are working in pretty stressful situations. We know that if we also understand how things are structured at the client's organization, what their culture is like, what the people are like that the client interacts with, and what the politics of the situation are, that we are going to do a much better job. We take all of those various data points, distill them, and take that information to the lawyers during training and say, "Here are some of the component parts of how to be a successful rainmaker. It's not enough anymore to simply give excellent legal advice." However, we don't take the focus off excellent legal advice at all. We're very focused on legal training and that's a key element of making a lawyer a skilled rainmaker. Lawyers need to be very, very proficient at what they do, but empathy, really understanding every aspect of what the individual client is experiencing, is extremely critical, as well.

Business Development Training: Baker & McKenzie, Part 2: Firm-wide Expectations

(Louise Muldoon)

We obviously don't exclusively focus on client empathy; we're doing many other things. I'm very lucky to work for a larger organization which has many resources at its disposal, and is focused on all facets of a lawyer's development. I know this from experience having been a practicing lawyer in this firm. I joined in Sydney as a junior litigator, and I spent 12 years in litigation and have experienced first-hand the firm's focus on legal skills development and the effective delivery of legal services as being the all-essential foundation of a successful legal career. In addition, I received a great deal of training on business development. We have a tool called the "development framework," which sets out expectations in a number of areas core to legal practice and is based on extensive research into what it takes to be a successful high-performing lawyer at Baker & McKenzie. From a junior lawyer to principal partner of the firm and every level in between—expectations are defined based on key performance areas and personal qualities that the Firm has identified as key contributors to high performance. While I won't go through them exhaustively, some of the core areas are legal knowledge and expertise, client service, matter management, and people management. For each of the key performance areas, we've set out, in quite some detail, what the expectations are at every level, and business development is a key component. We have training modules for each skill set. We also have training modules that deal with all the other skills that impact business development, like listening skills and presentation skills. As a senior associate, I was sent to a course designed to specifically teach rainmaker skills.

This course was focused on how to have conversations with clients. The course also covered many of the core competencies around effective business planning and measurement. The rainmaker course was a three-day course in Ho Chi Minh City, so, you can see it was something that the firm took very seriously. They flew their top senior associates (I was lucky enough to be thus considered) in from all around Asia Pacific, and so we were able to talk about business development in Japan, in Vietnam, and what the situation was like in Indonesia. It was fascinating. The training took a global perspective because culturally there are some different things in different jurisdictions that you need to address. We do a considerable amount of training at all levels and we do this within a multi-jurisdictional context, and that definitely and specifically includes our business development activities.

Business Development Training: Baker & McKenzie, Part 3: Grads, Associates, Partners

(Louise Muldoon)

We offer a good deal of training at all levels. I saw your question about BD training for associates and BD training for partners. I facilitate business development training for associates, beginning at the first year level. In fact, I talk to law school summer associates about this area, as well. We tell them that the lawyers of today need to be good at business development. We also tell them the lawyers of tomorrow are going to think about the delivery of legal services in a completely different and evolving way. We want to create a mindset that will enable their thinking to evolve. As an example, we give training on writing effective proposals with the intelligence we get from our clients' feedback. Client service is an area that the firm is particularly focused on at the moment. We're running training on that topic at all levels of our organization right across all of our 77 offices in 47 countries. We run a Business Development Academy for our Senior Associates. We also run courses for our partners that cover a number of topics and also includes business development. So, as you can see, we are very focused on business development training and will continue to do so.

Business Development Training: Baker & McKenzie, Part 4: Managing Expectations

(Louise Muldoon)

We have an extremely skilled talent management department. They are really, really fantastic. They carefully set out very detailed expectations at each level and use that structured development framework to assess quality. Quality is incredibly important to this firm. We spend a lot of time talking about quality; what it means; and how to deliver it effectively. Through this development framework we can ascertain whether an individual has the skills required to be promoted to the next level. So, for example, if you are a midlevel associate and want to be a senior associate, not only do you need the core competencies as outlined in that framework at associate level, but you also need to demonstrate that you are capable of meeting core competencies required of a senior associate in order to be promoted. Having business development skills is one of the key performance areas.

The expectations for a junior associate for business development are obviously very different from those of a partner. At a junior level, lawyers will be assisting with things such as the preparation of presentations and publications for internal and external audiences. At the more junior associate level, we look at things such as whether you're building relationships with your peers at the client organization. At a senior associate level, one is expected to have—often, with the right client—primary responsibility for managing the client relationship, and, as a senior associate, I had that responsibility. While there was always a partner in the wings, there still was an expectation that a senior associate would be capable of managing a client relationship to the client's satisfaction. This is something that we measure.

We have spent significant amounts of time detailing those expectations for skills in the area of business development at the various levels of experience and tenure. Our talent management team has done this in consultation with the business development team. It's very much a team effort. But we've also worked with consultants—with external people to say, "Well, do these sound right? Are these fair? Are we looking at the individual's development and measuring it in an appropriate way?" Because for a junior associate, for example—and that goes back to my initial point—the rigors of developing your skills from a legal perspective are pretty high and that needs to be the focus. Junior associates are on a pretty steep learning curve and how much can you expect them to do from a client management perspective while doing everything else we expect of them? So, it's balancing out improving legal knowledge and expertise, client service skills, and all the other core areas that are quite important. We see business development as one of those core skills that must be attained and demonstrated.

I feel that area is going to continue to evolve and business development as we know it now is going to change quite dramatically. It's a fast evolving area and we recognize that we have very, very sophisticated clients in a highly competitive market, and that leads to dynamism and change.

Business Development Training: Best Time?

(Despina Kartson)

We have found, overall, the best time to train lawyers with a short program is over lunch.

Business Development Training: Best Time?

(Jeff Berardi)

Well, I will say that offering a meal during one of my programs is almost always a much better draw than simply offering me as a speaker! So, I think it's a rare situation that these are not over breakfast or lunch and, in some cases, cocktails in the evening. First of all, it just makes more sense. The lawyers have to eat and I think they will come out for free lunch and maybe learn something new. We have a number of these things that happen and most of the time, they are either during a breakfast or, and most often, during lunchtime. So, I'm a big advocate of that. I think it is well worth the money you put out for some sandwiches and some drinks. It's hopefully getting the lawyers there and having them engaged and interested.

Business Development Training: BT Law Academy

(Allen Chichester)

Several years ago we created an internal institution for business development training called the BT Law Academy.

To create the Academy, we really bootstrapped our training programs by harnessing the talent of the firm, and by licensing some core curriculum and focusing on a train-the-trainer approach. It has all worked as a kind of virtuous circle. Since our business development staff often serve as trainers, we have had to up our game to be able to provide high-quality courses. At the same time, serving as trainers helps boost the credibility of the business development staff. We also tap talented attorneys with proven business development acumen to provide specific workshops and seminars.

One thing that has really made a difference for us is the follow-up, the coaching and mentoring that happens, as a way of keeping the training going to change the actual behavior of the attorneys as they implement what they have learned. We try to have some type of follow-up in place for each of our programs. While we have had some success working with groups of lawyers, we have found that successful training often involves working with individual attorneys on their business development acumen. That takes coaching and it's more of a long-term process.

We have evolved over time to the point where every business development manager here is a coach, and that is their highest and best training purpose. In many ways it has become our highest calling. It is also very granular in nature, and is always focused on the next best step for any business development opportunity.

From where I sit in this organization, nothing we have done has been more effective than this type of business development support for our lawyers. Success breeds success. When it starts to get done, when they start seeing results, attorneys will keep doing it, they truly change their behavior and that's a beautiful thing.

> Our highest calling is when we get into an office of a partner and we help them take the next step in business development, whatever that it is; and then we come back in a couple of weeks and we talk to them again about what happened as a result and where they go next. From where I sit in this organization, nothing we have done has been more effective than that.
>
> —*Allen Chichester*

We try to take advantage of any and every opportunity to create branded BT Law Academy training events. We will do lunch-and-video conferences, we'll do webinars, we'll do virtually anything, but probably our most effective approach is to host a live, in-person-type conference. On any complicated subject, we have found that between 8 and 15 attorneys is optimal; it's good to have a similar experience base when possible, and we try to pepper in a lot of exercises with the theory so that we give them as much opportunity as possible to engage in discussion and compare notes about what's going on. We do some theory, we give them some "expert" points of view, and we give them statistics, but in the end what they really benefit from is working with each other.

Business Development Training: Business Development Off-The-Shelf Catalog

(Jeff Berardi)

Our global associate symposium was the impetus behind a new business development asset, which we have developed recently. It's called the "Business Development Off-The-Shelf Catalog." It is a resource we are launching for all lawyers. It provides a collection of the business development training we have done over the years.

The catalog contains a variety of business development materials that include PowerPoint presentations, or in some cases, a video, with me or someone else presenting the business development topic. The Catalog is also meant to give a sense of the various programs we offer. This allows everyone to review what we've done in the past and then we can perhaps customize a specific program that might use the materials or the PowerPoint from previous sessions, but it would be done in a live setting or via video conference to that particular audience.

There are a number of different sections to the Catalog. There's a section on business pitches, business intelligence, cross-marketing, and so on. There is a section on knowing your firm, which talks about global integration and how you take what we have done with the brand and use it in a personal way. There's something on understanding your client's business, which talks about client challenges, AFAs, legal project management, and so on.

The Catalog highlights the business development instruction that we have done in the past while providing a starting point to create entirely new programs going forward. What we haven't always done a great job of is pulling it all together, because a lot of this happens at the office level, as opposed to doing it at a firm-wide level. But when you do put it all together, it's pretty incredible, all the things we've done for the lawyers.

Now we can say, "You know what? Let's take advantage of that particular approach as a reference and build something specifically designed for a particular office or a particular group." The Catalog allows us to say, "Here is just an example of the kind of things we presented on in the past and if something piques your interest then we can do it pretty quickly because we have the framework for it now." So it is like a catalog of off-the-shelf materials that we're providing for lawyers. It's almost like a coursework catalog.

In some cases an individual will just watch a video or look at a PowerPoint from the Catalog. There is value in that, but it's not as powerful as stimulating an office-wide initiative saying, "Oh, this session looks really interesting. Maybe we can do something in my office that would fit that." Then, we can do it at the local level with my managers or professional development, or the library in some cases, where it is not just from the top down. It's much more of a bottom-up approach.

On a global level we do the associate symposium pretty well because we can pick out the best administrative professionals and key associates and pull them in and do it in a very clear way for them. But it's more challenging when you have 2,100 lawyers and a video conference with me talking. That is to say, we've done it and it has some limited benefit and it is certainly better than not doing something, but it's hard to engage people using that format. It's hard to ask questions and have that back and forth. So, what we would really rather do is give them the materials. Here's some information in this new Business Development Off-The-Shelf-Catalog you may want to watch or read which we have determined to be of value. Here are some links to other resources that might be helpful, articles and so on. So, the lawyers can do a lot of this research on their own.

One benefit of the Catalog is now our local managers can view the material and we hear from them directly, "Oh, I really like the sound of this. Maybe we should build something locally"; and maybe it's my business development manager in that office that can run it, because we have the materials and they are very familiar with it, but no one ever thought to ask them to develop a local office-centered program.

It's really trying to maximize the impact of our resources in as broad a manner as possible and that's something we have always struggled with because we are so big and vast, and that it's just not easy to do. Because there is some value in doing it through e-learning and video and video conferences and so on and we don't want to just take that off the table completely, but I think that the real power is at the local level and I think we are able to offer that, but we just need to know where the interest is in a given topic or subject.

> We have recently developed the Business Development Off-the-Shelf Catalog, which includes PowerPoints, videos and other materials. There's a section on business pitches, business intelligence, cross-marketing, knowing your firm, which talks about global integration and how you take what we have done with the brand and use it in a personal way, understanding your client's business, which talks about client challenges, AFAs, legal project management, and so on.
>
> —*Jeff Berardi*

That said, I think that when it comes to the bigger picture for all the lawyers, there is more work to be done for sure. In some places, in some offices, and in some practices it has been done very well. In other places, it's an area of need and so that's where we are going with this Business Development Off-the-Shelf Catalog. I think it will allow us to spot some of those areas of need a little bit better, because we just don't always hear about it now the way that we probably should. So, it's meant to serve as a bit of a catalyst for that.

Business Development Training: Client Needs Assessment Interview and Pitching

(Mark Usellis)

We've approached business development training in a few ways. From a programmatic standpoint, we started several years ago with a business development training and coaching program for select groups of young partners.

The firm had never done anything like that before, so we had a pretty big pool of people. I looked from 8 to 16 years of practice and worked through those people. There are some we didn't include because they either weren't interested or didn't seem like they were really going to be adept at this. We had a year-long program that was a combination of training sessions and then individual coaching where we would teach them the fundamentals of what the business development process is, how you create a business plan, how you target a client, what the sales pipeline looks like, and how you move a prospect through the pipeline.

The two main skills that we focused on were the client needs interview, or the needs assessment interview, and the second was pitching. Number one, the needs assessment interview was very important to me because if you wanted to single out some of the most common weaknesses in how lawyers do business development, identification of a client's or prospect's needs is number one. Lawyers tend to be responsive or reactive and not sufficiently proactive, which means they almost always end up in a competitive situation. Number two, they tend to sell and pitch what *they* do as opposed to what the *client* needs. They don't understand the full spectrum of the client's situation. They don't really know what their firm can do for the client, because they don't, yet, fully grasp everything that needs to be known about the client. Mostly they go into a pitch with a mindset of "what can the client do for me" as opposed to "what can our firm do for the client?"

So, we focused on those two skillsets, needs assessment and pitching. We did that for a few years. During that time, though, I had this growing feeling that we were spending too much time on what I consider to be very remedial business development subject matter, I didn't blame the lawyers for that because nobody had ever taught them this. So, I thought it would be worthwhile to create an additional program for mid- to senior-level associates where we could, first of all, expose them to the concepts of business development, a sales pipeline, building a network, and other business development fundamentals. With this new program we didn't wait until they became a partner before we started working on those new business generating skillsets.

Second, we wanted the associates to realize there are certain activities that you can do at a younger age to start laying a business development foundation. The reason that I had focused on young partners initially was I wanted to be working with the people who were in a position to get hired by clients. I believe in giving people the information that's relevant for them at that point in their career and at a time when they're actually going to use it. I didn't want to teach a group of third year associates a number of skills that they weren't ever going to use until they become partners. Having said that, because nobody had ever helped these folks when they were associates, we had to do quite a bit of remedial awareness training and skill building. I worked with our professional development department and created a somewhat truncated program for mid- to senior-level associates, which was a daylong training program followed by six months of limited coaching. The main purpose, the metrics, were: we wanted them to develop a business plan, we wanted them to learn about the firm and understand the capabilities of the firm outside of their office and their practice group, we wanted them to learn how to do a referral interview, how to meet with a referral source, and we wanted them to start developing a network. Even if they weren't going to be pitching people for work, they need to start developing, and learning how to develop relationships, to start getting the fundamentals of how do you understand needs, how can you be helpful, and how do you build rapport, along with a number of other functional skills and mindsets.

We went upstream and started teaching foundational skills to younger lawyers, so that when they became partners and came into the partner program, we didn't have to spend so much time on remedial matters and we could emphasize and focus on the needs assessment and pitching. Those were the two areas where people were weakest as a general rule.

Business Development Training: Coaches; See *Coaches*

Business Development Training: Fast Forward®

(Jill Weber)

Fast Forward® is an innovative program designed to accelerate business and boost legal revenues. The Fast Forward program offers several unique program elements that differentiate it from any other training and coaching service, including: an integrated program, a system for establishing measurable benchmarks to evaluate participant progress, established investment parameters, ideas for sales incentives and awards, and a brand identity to create a "buzz" within the law firm. See expanded description and ROI details of Fast Forward program in *Fast Forward: A Formal Business Development Program: Parts 1–7.*

Business Development Training: For a Firm of 50 to 60 Lawyers: Part 1

(Barbara Lauterbach)

Our law firm has about 55 lawyers, largely trial attorneys, and I am a one-person CMO, MarCom, and BDD department all rolled into one. So, my approach has to be tailored to my circumstances. Also, at my firm I was the first to hold this position, so, much of what I have done was new to the firm culture. Given that formal business development is new to the firm and the fact that attorneys in general, and trial lawyers in particular, don't like to be caught in a misstep, or shown that there may be a better way to approach their practice development versus the way they've always done it in the past, I need to be particularly sensitive to their feelings and sentiments. The occasional misstep by them is "OK" but only if it's invisible—which is why I find that in this environment and frankly in other law firm environments where I've been, I know some people like to do groups and get attorneys to compete with each other, but I find it easier to work with people confidentially, invisibly, so that no one else is watching.

Well, it's not something that I caught on to 15 years ago. It took a while to figure this out. Once they've started to succeed, it's wonderful to be able to publicize their success within the firm.

Then, other people get interested. In the last three years, I've coached a few young partners and worked with them very closely and we've had some significant success.

I got an email this morning from someone who was attending the Mississippi Association of Builders and Contractors Annual Event. We started going to those events three years ago. We've been members for a longer time, but nobody had ever actively taken a role in that trade association and I now have four attorneys who've been working with that organization regularly. They've been going to local and regional meetings and speaking and having lunch-and-learns. I had one senior associate who applied and was accepted into their leadership program so that she was in a leadership program, not with other lawyers, but with people who were in the construction industry who were taking these leadership classes. In the email I got this morning was the news that she picked up a new client last night from her efforts.

And that's wonderful. That's the sixth new client we've gotten from this relationship and we've been working it for three years. That's not a whole lot of litigation. These six clients are not really big clients, but the more we work with those six people, the more visible we'll become in the industry, the better it will be, and the more referrals we will get. So, I let everybody in the firm who is important to know that we picked up another client last night and why we picked them up and also that it was directly related to this one attorney's involvement in the leadership program of a trade association. Publicizing the wins is good, but you can never, ever let the stories about losing propositions out there because it discourages and sometimes embarrasses people.

Business Development Training: For a Firm of 50 to 60 Lawyers: Part 2

(Barbara Lauterbach)

I've had one senior associate who had tried twice and failed to make partner, but who made partner this year through the additional business that he picked up following my coaching him for a while. Guess how many people want to be on my coaching list for next year? Visible success is a real game changer.

I think it's really important to make initial assignments during coaching relatively simple opportunities and I like to make sure that I give my attorneys enough information, so that they don't have to create the strategy. Either I have or we've done it together because once they've had a little success, they can take the next one and take a little bit more ownership of it and by the time they've had three successful projects or assignments they don't need a whole lot of coaching anymore.

Then, I become the person they call and say, hey, this is what I'm thinking about doing. What do you think about it as opposed to me calling them and saying, this is what I think you ought to do, what do you think?

I have built a relationship with them, protected their ego, supported them in getting some wins and now they're being more proactive. Now, my function is cheerleader—cheerleader and the person who celebrates and reinforces.

Business Development Training: For a Firm of 50 to 60 Lawyers: Part 3

(Barbara Lauterbach)

My role as Director of Business Development is starting to be a great role. It was very frustrating in the beginning because business development simply was not part of the culture, but Mississippi, which is where I am, hit the recession late and we were noticing diminished revenue, two years later than the firms out East were, most definitely.

So, when I came, we were just starting to experience the recession even though everybody else was starting to come out of it. So, to come into an environment where that was happening and they had no culture for business development or coaching or even no thoughts contemplating the acquisition of new business and during this period of time was very challenging. Through this coaching and other activities of our marketing committee, we've changed the culture of the firm to one that is open to business development opportunities and able to envision the possibilities.

Although we continue to do insurance defense work, we have acquired a number of direct hire matters through hard work, strategic thinking, and lots of research. And that's made a huge difference in our revenue. This represents a nice change in the business culture and is easier with the younger attorneys than those who've been doing this for 40 years. I think that it's not impossible to teach an old dog a new trick, but it's a lot easier to teach a middle-aged dog a new trick. They don't have as many preconceived ideas. They don't have enough experience to say that this is a stupid idea or to say, "I'm a great lawyer, as long as I continue to try good cases and I do a great job, I don't need to do any business development." Of course, there will be people who will come back to you time and time again, but we're trial attorneys. We can try a case for people that we won't need to do anything for, for three or four years, or ever. They're not necessarily repeat clients, so building a reputation is important, but building a sales force, so to speak, that's comfortable speaking to people and engaging with people and eventually making an ask, if not for a file, an ask for information— getting that whole process started is— well, you know how complex it is. I don't understand how people turn this into a science because perhaps I have too much of an artistic background, but I think of this as an art. I think that you have to understand when and how to move to the next level and that's a nuanced mechanism that is not easily categorized. It can be very nuanced. Obviously, listening is very important and trial attorneys have these skills. They're simply not used to using them outside of the courtroom.

Business Development Training: For a Firm of 50 to 60 Lawyers: Part 4

(Barbara Lauterbach)

Attorneys have to be very good listeners to think on their feet in the middle of a trial or a deposition. They have to be active listeners and they have to be able to react to what they're hearing. Unfortunately, they're just not used to taking that skill into a lunch or a conversation in the hallway that's not related to a case. So, they have to be taught that it's okay to bring those skill sets out of their normal legal environment into a business situation. They also have to learn that there's nothing demeaning about asking for work. People ask me, "How do you convey that? How do you get that across?"

Well, again, that can be difficult. It depends upon the person, but it's not dissimilar to any situation they would run into in the beginnings of preparation of a case. It's all exploratory. It's gathering your facts.

Recognizing the fact that this prospect is a potential case and you have to start gathering your information in order to even find out if you're interested in having the case and trial lawyers all love to do closing arguments, but they know that they can't give closing arguments until they've presented their case . . . you have to take that same slow methodology that they use in trial work and put up at the front end of developing a relationship with somebody. It's really not very different from what they do regularly in the practice of law.

I draw a parallel to what they're doing and business development. I think this works with transactional attorneys too. It's a matter of getting them to see that the whole process is information gathering, gathering your evidence, organizing it, presenting it, and asking for action and asking for the right action. There's a timing to it and it varies from situation to situation just like it does in front of a jury or a judge.

If you can put your attorneys at ease by drawing comparisons to what they do regularly to what you're asking them to do, it's just a lot easier. I learned this a long time ago when I was first writing brochures and pitch materials for a large law firm in Chicago and I was trying to get someone within the firm to understand something that I was saying and the director of the marketing department pulled me aside and said you have to think of every conversation you have with an attorney like a legal process and if you want them to decide in your favor, you have to give them all the facts and figures, all the evidence, all the arguments for, all the arguments against, and make sure that they get where the emphasis is and can draw the same conclusion that you have. He was very smart. How can you argue with a lawyer if you don't have your facts and figures together? You can't, you better not try. Or, if you're like I am, you're going to end up in the ladies' room in tears if you try very often.

Business Development Training: For a Firm of 50 to 60 Lawyers: Part 5

(Barbara Lauterbach)

In a firm of our size, I wear a lot of hats and we're members of all the local bar associations. We have three offices and there are a lot of moving parts on a daily basis. I have a second-year associate who is supposed to be playing golf with a foursome at the Capital Area Bar Association Golf Tournament at the end of July and I asked him yesterday if he found anybody to play and it has to be lawyers, it has to be people from our firm. He's known about it for a month and he hasn't done anything and he's a good lawyer, but he's a little shy and very interested in being proper.

So, I sent him a short list of people that I knew in this office who play golf regularly, who would probably welcome the opportunity to play golf with the firm if they had time, if they weren't at trial. He still hadn't done anything about it.

So, today I had a little conversation with the president of our firm, who mentioned to me that one of our senior people has recently decided to get re-involved with golf and he's been making an effort to play on a pretty regular basis. So, I just ran into this associate attorney's office today and said, hey, Partner "X" has really been trying to play golf more lately, so why don't you ask him? So, he did. Now he's got one person committed to play with him and now it's going to be easier for him to ask a third and fourth person.

It's just a matter of supporting the attorney in experiencing a new behavior with a "win," so that he or she will be able to do it on their own more easily in the future.

Another example: I helped a senior associate who has been trying to make partner the last two years with no success. I helped him get an AV rating with Martindale Hubbell. I got him in Super Lawyers, I got him in 40 over 40. I didn't do these things, but I got him to do it. He's been doing some government liability work and I got him some speaking engagements and then he put together a summary of claims under the Mississippi Tort Claims Act, which is relatively new, but really important here and he did a whole list of all the cases that were pertinent in 2013 and then we marketed that paper. One thing led to another and he just developed a fair amount of confidence and his numbers went up and people noticed and it was impossible for them not to make him a partner. It wasn't one thing. It was a number of small wins. How could they say no? He's done so many things and gotten us some positive press, and some positive clients and some expanded revenue. His hours were up. He lifted everything. I even looked at his collections with him and pointed out where his collections were hurting him. I helped him make a couple of tactful phone calls to people who could take care of those collection issues for him. You just have to put that person in a position where nobody really can say no to them being a partner because there is no reason to. Now he's a partner.

Business Development Training: For a Firm of 50 to 60 Lawyers: Part 6

(Barbara Lauterbach)

And when I first start closely coaching somebody, I'm likely to have a couple of one-hour meetings with them or sometimes a meeting will go even longer than that, but once that kind of rapport is established, we should be able to have a 15-minute phone call every Thursday that says, okay, these are the four things we talked about doing last week, have you gotten anywhere on any of them? Where have you gotten, what do we need to do, what prevented you from getting further, how can I help, what can I do, do you need more names, do you need more contacts, do you need somebody to get in touch with this person's secretary, what do you need?

It also means that you can't do this effectively for 15 people at the same time, though.

People ask me, "How many can you give that degree of support and attention to at a time?"

My response is that I could probably do a lot more if I weren't still doing all the marketing collateral here. We're a small firm and the demand has been relatively low because we've never done it before and I've taken 6 people through a full year of coaching at this point. So, I've got those 6 people that I'm still touching base with once a month or so, or at specific times. Meanwhile, we're trying to give the associates some basic skills so that they can ask people to play golf and can go to lunch with a prospect and can hold their own in a conversation at a convention.

Initially, I didn't think with my workload that, I could coach more than three people actively in a year. It takes a lot of time and I have to be involved in what they're doing. I can't just let them go. They don't have those kinds of skills. It might be different if a firm has a culture of that with people who have had several years of basic training. Every situation is different, but I don't think anybody can be coached well in less than a year and I think it requires a fair amount of involvement on the part of the coach to do it.

Sometimes I am asked, "What is my coaching plan of action?" Well, first of all, in my environment, I've written this person's attorney profile. I know what their publications are. I know what their presentations have been. I know this person before I start working with them. I have studied their numbers. I know their working hours versus their managing hours. I know their clients and their caseload. I know all of that going in. So, I'm not wasting their time when we first start talking. Initial conversations generally go along the lines of, tell me what you're doing, tell me what you want to do, tell me where you want to be five years from now, tell me who your favorite mythological client is, and tell me who you're going to feel really good about getting as a client.

I always ask, "Who is it that you really want as a client?" And then, I try to help them get it.

At the same time, we were doing things like going through old client lists and trying to identify clients that we hadn't had any business from in a while and talked about that too and that's one of the things that you always do with somebody you're coaching. You look at who their clients have been and whether they've been repeating or not and how long it's been since you've seen them. You want to know about their client service and their existing relationships so that you can enhance them, deepen them.

I follow a checklist. It's a checklist that I developed once upon a time when I was interviewing for a job and they wanted me to tell them what my approach was going to be. So, at that point, I had to actually sit down and talk about how I would do this and I think up until that point, there was a mental list, but it wasn't written down.

I look at everybody else's list. I look at Mark Mariah's materials and I look at David Freeman's articles and I look at Ross Fishman's checklist and I still use his Associate's Marketing Checklist. I give it to all my new lawyers when they come in. There's no sense in reinventing the wheel when the wheel is perfectly fine. [A copy of this checklist is contained in the ABA book, *The Associate As Rainmaker.*]

I have had the good fortune to hear Mark Mariah and David Maister address business development issues and I have had access to some of their forms, and those of other big names in the industry. I have had access to some excellent forms such as when I worked at Schiff Hardin, I was at the "let's learn how to do this stage," but I was an excellent listener and a great note-taker. So I now have some of the best checklists and forms. I've cherry picked some really good information and then kept it within easy reach.

Business Development Training: Four-Tiered Program to Grow Rainmakers

(Jonathan Fitzgarrald)

In response to your question as to how do I help skilled lawyers become skilled rainmakers, I do this through implementation of a four-tiered rainmaker training program. This is a very thorough business development training program. In any given year, a third of the attorneys in the firm are in some way involved in one of our business development training programs. Here are some of the highlights from our program.

<u>Tier One</u>: Top Rainmakers

Tier One is for the top rainmakers, one each from each of our 10 practice areas. Therefore, we have 10 attendees per training session meeting. Lunch is served at every meeting.

Our tiered approach to business development allows each attorney to receive targeted customized business development coaching. This is a very focused business development coaching program. The metrics show that regardless of their experience level, they improve productivity by 20 percent.

First benefit: increasing booked revenue. A 20-percent increase in a top rainmaker's book is a big increase! We meet monthly and everyone attends. At each monthly meeting, we spotlight one member and during the meeting we give an overview from his or her practice to the other nine. We find that the preparation alone for anyone who is presenting really focusses the lawyer on their own business development efforts.

Second benefit: cross-selling improved significantly. The presentation and communication to the other lawyers at the meeting is very impressive to the senior management of the firm because they see how much it helps cross-selling. Don't let anyone tell you, "I already know what he/she does." That's BS. They don't really know what the other attorney is doing. These meetings really help to enlighten all the others, which significantly improves cross-selling.

Third benefit: this tiered approach builds camaraderie. The interpersonal relationship building is awesome.

<u>Tier Two</u>: All partners that are not in the Top Rainmaker group.

These are second-tier revenue generating partners of all ages. They each have a capacity for a big book. Don't let anyone tell you differently. They all have the capacity. It is just a matter of training.

Again we have a meeting once a month for the entire group. Half the time is focused on skill building, the other half on the individual attorneys' business development wins and challenges. We also go over an element that is challenging to one or more of the attorneys, and the group offers their ideas on how to address the challenge. Then we challenge the specific attorney to do something with that element prior to the next monthly meeting. Discussing these challenges increases the esprit de corps and the camaraderie. Someone is solving problems for one of the others. It gets to the point where they all want to report something for the group to address.

<u>Tier Three</u>: Senior Associates

We follow the exact format as in Tier Two. Half the monthly meeting is on skill building. Half is spent addressing individual wins and challenges and includes the same element of accountability where we ask the associate to have done something with their challenge prior to the next meeting and report on what happened.

<u>Tier Four</u>: Alumni

The "alumni" are the lawyers who have gone through a full one-year program in Tier One, Two, or Three. After one year of participation in one of the three Tier groups, the attorney can elect to go into the alumni group, which meets monthly, so they can be rainmaker partners and rainmaker associates. This group focuses exclusively on prospecting and developing new client matters and new clients. They must come up with a list of potential prospects.

In between each meeting, every single member of each tier group gets visited by a member of the Marketing Department for anywhere from one or two minutes up to an hour. This is the accountability follow-up that we discuss with each member. This allows us to determine if that specific attorney is tracking on the previous discussion. This is a very important meeting because it allows for privacy. Many attorneys do not want to bring up certain issues in a public forum. So, this allows for a private discussion. We are extremely time conscientious and in some cases it's just a head pop-in for a quick check-in.

This program was started four years ago. The first year had some rough edges because we were just developing the program. But by year two we were off and running and it's been extremely successful.

Today, our program is far different from four years ago. Every year it grows in sophistication. We track the hell out of everything we do by using metrics. We provide a scorecard to each attorney that includes about half a dozen different metrics, so that they can score themselves. This measures their individual progress in each of the different categories from month one to month 12.

The best part about the program is the accountability. Accountability is key. Having to report back to their peers every month on how they are doing is a tremendous motivator.

We do find participation is different between the boomers and the Gen X'ers. The boomers find the accountability is okay, but the Gen X'ers don't seem to be particularly fond of the peer pressure element of accountability.

The collaboration within each group is very significant. The specific set of metrics is designed to work within each group. We have a very simple formula for who should be in the room and who should be in the group. This way we are able to avoid any political issues.

For someone to be eligible, it has to be known that they are staying with the firm for at least another six months and that these are people with marketable skills. So that we don't play favorites, we let management decide who should participate in the group specifically. We have the chair of each practice section make the decision of who will participate from that practice group. We have about 10 practice sections at our firm. Each practice director decides which partner goes into Tier Two, and which senior associate goes into Tier Three. The attorneys that are going to the rainmaker group is fairly simple. We just look at the book of each attorney and go down the list.

This takes all the pressure off of the marketing department and places that decision making squarely on to the practice leader. Anyone with a beef regarding who is in the group can simply take their issue directly to the department chair.

The first year of this program was like pulling teeth. We did not have much traction. But by year two and going in the future, we created cachet around participation as to who gets to be selected; and so, now we have people coming up to us and saying, can you please consider me?

Business Development Training: Four-Tiered Program: What We Measure

(Jonathan Fitzgarrald)

Here are the categories we are measuring:

(1) Number of new business pitches.
(2) Number of prospecting interactions, for example, meeting over a meal, at office, etc.
(3) Number of networking events attended.
(4) Number of emails sent out and follow-ups conducted.
(5) Number of referrals received.
(6) Number of referrals given.
(7) Number of client visits.
(8) New revenue received.

It is very activity-based. Of course the bottom line, the final bottom line, is did they get a new client?

This is a very, very ambitious program and because it is very, very, very time-consuming, it's very challenging for most firms to implement.

As to your question about LinkedIn. Yes, we do LinkedIn training. We found LinkedIn to be a resource for new clients. This is one of the skills we discuss and one of the topics that we review in our tier group meetings.

At a recent Legal Marketing Association seminar where I addressed the topic "R.O.I: The Only Technology Acronym That Matters," I informed the audience that we hired MK Partners (http://www.mkpartners.com/) to customize our *SalesForce* (www.salesforce.com) program. Now, instead of having to go to six or seven different databases, we have one depository for everything related to business development, and it works seamlessly with our CRM program, *Interaction* (www.interaction.com). These are just some of the tools that we use to support our four-tier rainmaker training program.

[Author's comment: Jonathan Fitzgarrald served as an in-house CMO—most recently for Greenberg Glusker—for almost two decades. He now manages a business developing coaching and training consultancy, Equinox Strategy Partners. Expanded bio in Appendix A.]

Business Development Training: From the Ground Up

(Lisa Salazar)

Please see my comment titled, *Bio: It's Step One.*

Business Development Training: Groups: Length of Meeting

(Peter Johnson)

Generally, our business development group training is a half day. We find that if you put lawyers in a room for more than four hours, they get carpel tunnel syndrome looking at their watch. We usually have it from 8:30 to noon, and then we have a lunch where everybody stays and we answer questions. At lunch, we frequently have graduates from the previous program come in and have an informal discussion about what they learned and their experiences. Then the attorneys can go back to work that same day following a 90 minute, one-on-one meeting to identify specific business development actions and set up a calendar of one-on-one follow-up coaching calls.

The evening before a group training, we have an informal reception to connect the attendees with each other and the business development program leaders. This reception acts as a nice bridge into thinking about business development. It allows for a warm, friendly, and fast start the next morning. Without the reception the evening before, many of the attorney attendees will show up at 8:30 am saying to themselves, or out loud, "I should be at work. Why am I here?"

[For more details on group coaching see: *Coaching: The Johnson Technique: "Getting Started"* by Peter Johnson.]

Business Development Training: Individualized Coaching

(Nancy Kostakos and Karen Febeo)

No one learns to drive a car by watching someone speak to a PowerPoint presentation. So, too, with business development—you actually have to try things out, and practice those skills. Therefore, we offer individualized coaching for our partners and counsel. We start with external coaches, then transition to our embedded business development leaders. The one-on-one coaching we offer to our partners and counsel gives them an opportunity to meet on a regular basis with a coach who can focus on our attorneys' individual needs, take a look at their pipeline and their contact list, and discuss how they are engaging their contacts. The coaches encourage individual attorneys to develop a systematic way to approach their prospects and make it a part of their day-to-day activities. Our goal is to give our attorneys the tools and resources to develop successful habits.

> I always say that no one learns to drive a car by watching someone speak to a PowerPoint. So, too, with business development—you actually have to try things out and practice these skills.
>
> —*Karen Febeo*

The external coaching then transitions to internal coaching with our business development team continuing to check in and make sure that business development efforts stay on track. We have also experimented with an additional element where a senior equity partner is paired with a coaching participant as a mentor. This is a great way to validate what the newer partner is learning, and share business development strategies and ideas. It also encourages collaboration with other partners across different practices or different geographies.

Coaching will not work unless the participant is motivated and engaged to do the work that's required. Some of the partnering with external coaches worked very well, and some never really blossomed, and that was an interesting experience. We found that even in instances where partners were not particularly motivated to say: "Okay. What am I going to do next? How am I going to implement this in my day to day?" Just getting them talking about these issues was valuable. In other instances, talking about why business development efforts did not work was also helpful. We learned a great deal by playing Monday morning quarterback and figuring out what we could do differently next time.

Our managing partner is a real proponent of collaboration and team tackling. Now that we've done a number of one-on-one coaching programs, we are considering some small-group coaching, leveraging cross-selling and enhancing relationships beyond an individual and his/her particular practice area. We are starting to shape our business development coaching to help teams understand how to go out and effectively pitch together. How do you make an impactful institutional pitch as opposed to just doing it individually?

> The liaison concept between business units is about increasing awareness of what's happening elsewhere in the firm and ultimately institutionalizing client relationships more effectively.
>
> —*Nancy Kostakos*

The other result that we've seen from increased focus on revenue generation, collaboration, and team tackling is the realization that there is still much to do internally in terms of educating everyone on the firm's collective strengths. To deal with this, we've begun to see business units designating liaisons to other business units. The liaisons are ultimately tasked with finding opportunities to introduce members of their business unit to clients of another business unit. Often this starts with simply asking to be on the agenda for partner meetings in the other groups and introducing their practice – truly marketing their practices internally.

Business Development Training: It's Not a One Size Fits All. Here's My Approach

(Jeff Berardi)

I certainly do a lot of training and presentations. Whenever I am traveling to different offices, which is fairly frequently, I try to set up some type of workshop or presentation with either associates or partners, in some cases both. The program content is based on the interests of the local office, usually it is built after discussions I have with the office administrative partner, and I listen to what they feel like is going to be most relevant to their particular office and the lawyers within it. Usually, it's a business development workshop on how to build some of those skills. It might be talking about building a personal brand and thinking about it from a digital perspective. We are doing more and more of that now. It might be client development tips and networking. So, there are a whole host of different topics and, really, it's not a one-size-fits-all model. It's more of "what's this office like, what are their needs, what are they most interested in hearing." Then, I structure my presentation and discussion, and really it is more of a discussion usually than a presentation, because I learn a lot when I talk to our lawyers about what's going on in that market, where the challenges are and where the opportunities are, and what works and what doesn't. So, I tend to view it as if I'm going to facilitate a conversation. I can give them some examples of what I think has worked in other places and in my own experiences, but at the end of the day, I have got to listen, too, because that helps to inform me as to what's going to apply. For instance, in some markets, talking about us being global is not an advantage—companies may think we don't know the local market. So it's just a matter of trying to make sure that we communicate the right message in the right situation.

Business Development Training: Law School

(Louise Muldoon)

In the UK, people can embark on a law degree straight out of high school. So, if they pursued a law degree in the university, it's the equivalent of having gone to law school in the US. If you've received a law degree, you do an additional year at the University of Law (formerly the College of Law) which is designed to give you the practical skills needed in order to practice law when you go into a law firm. After that, you do two years supervised. My point is that the curriculum of the University of Law now includes options for business development training. That curriculum is looking to equip lawyers with practical skills that they can use when they're training to be lawyers and actually working within a law firm. The changes demonstrate how proactive the University of Law is in anticipating and addressing the needs of today's law students as they enter a very demanding legal marketplace.

Business Development Training: Our Approach: Part 1: Start Day One

(Erin Meszaros)

Turning really skilled attorneys into skilled rainmakers is not an easy feat. I believe you have to start when they set foot in the door as a young associate; and I think to truly maximize and build upon what they learned in law school you continue to help them develop business development skills into their 40s so that they are not saying when they become partner, "Oh, my gosh. How do I go get business," when it is too late. Now, I will truthfully tell you, though, that I personally don't spend a lot of time with the associates, but I try to assign someone on each BD team to focus on the associates and encourage the coordinators that are also learning and coming up through the ranks to learn together and to help guide the associates. I may do the opening meeting with the first-year associates through a lunch-and-learn session and let them ask me any questions they may have from how the firm is run, to how they develop business, to how they target their friends. I try to build rapport with the associates as we are there to support them with the understanding that after the initial lunch-and-learn they will be supported, probably, at a lower level. And it's not because I don't want to support them, it is just with everything that's on my plate my time is limited.

We are starting the business development education efforts with associates when they walk through the door, so it is there from the beginning and hopefully will become second nature. Then they can start to pull it into the foreground as they go forward with developing their career and business. To me it's also beneficial for their career internally because I teach them they need to be focused on their first client, and their first client is the partner they are working for.

If they can master pleasing a partner, which is not always easy, then they can please any client. I tell them your first order of business is to learn how to be an excellent lawyer, and that's the first step in business development.

The legal filed is extremely competitive and now a few tough clients trying to get a negotiating edge will tell you rather unkindly that, "Lawyers are a dime a dozen, and being a good lawyer is a given." So, I tell my young lawyers you have to get over the hurdle of just "being a good lawyer," or you won't get to the next level where you are able to meet the decision makers who will hire you. The clients don't want to be questioning your skillset.

They expect you to *have* the skillset they need. They expect you to know the law. That doesn't differentiate you anymore, if it ever did. I tell folks, take the first one, three, five years to really focus on learning how to practice law. Learn how to be effective, efficient, and sophisticated in the level that you practice. Tie that to exceptional client relationship skills with those they service internally and you have created a knock-it-out-of-the-park rainmaker when they hit their stride at 40 or 45.

If the young lawyer develops client relationship skills, early on with internal clients, the firm's partners they work with, as well as mastering legal skills, then they are going to be rainmaking with external clients before they know it.

I tell folks, take the first one, three, five years to really focus on learning how to practice law. Learn how to be effective, efficient, and sophisticated in the level that you practice. Tie that to exceptional client relationship skills with those they service internally and you have created a knock-it-out-of-the-park rainmaker when they hit their stride at 40 or 45.

—Erin Meszaros

A great way to bring law practice development to the attention of the young associates just starting out is to give them the proper frame of mind early on to set themselves up for business development success down the road. But be careful as it may be a different path you need to take when looking at someone, possibly a lateral, who didn't grow up under that guise. That's why when working with the younger associates it is important to teach the business development team to treat the associates as individuals as much as possible.

Business Development Training: Our Approach: Part 2: Six Buckets

(Erin Meszaros)

I recently held a meeting with our coordinators to check and see how things were going. "Ask me any question you want to ask." One of them responded, "Well, I've been working with two different groups. I have to say that we don't have a standard business development template. Wouldn't we be more effective if we had one template that everyone used?" And I said, "Not necessarily. While that would be nice to make our jobs easier, in essence, our job is to figure out the individual who is sitting in front of us, what makes them tick, what helps them be most effective, how they go to [the legal] market and that information will drive revenue." And the way we think as marketers, with our standardized forms, may not be what's best for them. So my whole career I have not really "standardized" things. I have centralized things, I have provided *best practices*, commonalities, things that I know are tried and true, but I tend not to limit people to a particular X, Y, Z form. I want you to talk to me about some basic elements of which clients we need to grow across the firm. Who are the prospective targets you have?

There are six buckets I will talk to them about and then I will build the right approach from the discussion around those six buckets. We are always trying to customize things and listen to our external clients, so it is not one size fits one, but what works best for each client.

When I refer to the "six buckets," there are six discussion areas that I bring up when talking to my attorneys about business development. First, I generally tell them, "Talk to me about your current client base and the firm's client base; are there opportunities within those two areas to grow your practice? Second, talk to me about the prospective clients which happen to be other partners' clients within the firm in other areas that you think we should grow. Third, talk to me about prospective clients that are not clients of the firm that you think are either a good target for you or someone else in the firm."

I don't want to digress too far, and I'll come back to my six buckets, but I want to make sure that the attorneys think about not only themselves but about the firm, and so we try to have conversations around, yes, you are our first priority as far as how do we help you, but don't discount the contact if we don't find an avenue for you, we will find one for someone else in the firm that gets credited back to you. So if you've got the relationships but we can't find the opportunity for you, don't write that off. Go back and look and say, "Oh, but you know what? They could do this kind of work, and let me tell my buddy down the street." I think a lot of lawyers get so myopic that they forget it's a bigger puzzle than just one piece. If they are truly part of an institution they'll want to sell whatever they can in the firm.

So back to my six buckets. Fourth, I then say to them things like, "Talk to me about whether you like to write, speak, or teach. What are some of the ancillary things that you like to do that you may think don't lead to business development, but in my mind I think they add credibility and can potentially capture the attention of a potential client or a referral source." Once in a while you luck out, and you'll be teaching something—be it a CLE or be it a seminar where you speak and somebody comes up afterward and you land a client. That's awesome. But that is far-fetched and rarely happens. I do think, however, that it is very possible that somebody sitting in the audience listening to you speak will two, three months down the road have a buddy who says, "I need someone with X, Y, Z expertise, and none of my law firms have it. Have you heard of someone that you would recommend?" and that person who was in the audience says, "I heard this guy speak who was phenomenal. Let's at least check him out." I think it adds credibility, which you then want to back up by adding that CLE to your web bio, LinkedIn or other resource you've put out in the market place. You want all of it together to say "Yes, I am the skilled, talented person you thought I was."

I also believe good leadership skills help with rainmaking, and so, in my fifth bucket, I will ask them do they have an interest in leadership in the firm? Do they have an interest in mentoring? And I try to build upon those things.

It would be interesting to interview successful rainmakers to see what they attribute to their success. I think high-level rainmakers are probably very well-rounded individuals. And it's not about the dollar. They are recognized and rewarded because of that well-roundedness, but I don't think they chase the dollar. I believe they truly care about the clients they are servicing, have top notch legal skills, and have exceptional people skills.

In the sixth bucket, I will ask them, do we need to do something with your bio? Do you need to have more than one bio? When you go to market and you're trying to talk to clients, you want to be able to send them exactly what they're looking for, not a bunch of stuff they don't care about. I'm not a big collateral person. I don't like sending a bunch of collateral, but I do think the website is critically important. Recently I revamped a website, and I walked into the partnership, and in front of all the partners I said, "While I know I constantly tell you it's not about you, I'm now going to eat my words. The website is totally about you." We conducted client research to determine the best approach to this redesign. We sent a survey to many of our clients, and every one of them, when asked, "Why do you come to our website," said it was to read attorney bios, to grab attorney information, to look at their latest experience data, client alert, publications, or speaking engagements. Everything drove back to the attorney. I think that's a very important piece of information. For the website I really focus substantive content on what can we tell our clients about the attorney they are using or looking for. It's the reason they are coming to our website anyway. So, the website bio may be the last bucket I discuss, but it may also be the most important in some cases.

As a brief summary, six buckets to discuss with your lawyer before preparing their individual business development plan includes: your current client base; other partners' clients of the firm that may provide an opportunity for you or someone else in the firm; non-firm potential client targets that may provide an opportunity for you or someone else in the firm; do you like to write, speak, or teach; do you have an interest in leadership in the firm or mentoring; and do we need to do something with your website bio and/or add a second bio to your legal resume?

Business Development Training: Partners

(Hans Haglund)

If the partner is not a "natural rainmaker," someone that does not develop relationships naturally, that's OK. But he or she must be willing to learn new business development strategies, and you start with changing their daily habits.

In the process you need to respect what these attorneys are going through. There's a great deal involved. Successful partners are amazing. Those partners have to go get the business, then they have to do it, and then they have to collect on it. There are a number of ways the administrative staff and the business development team can help with many aspects of those activities, but partners really are a business in themselves. [See also *Business Development: A Tactical Approach: Do The Math*, and *Client Development: Getting Into Their World Using 70/30*.]

Business Development Training: Partners Training Other Lawyers

(Jeff Berardi)

When it comes to business development training, we just try to keep the needle moving in the right direction. You can never do enough training. We really want to make sure we provide the lawyers with the tools and perspective, but at some level too, some of this business development awareness you can't totally train. Some partners have some of these extensive business development abilities already and are simply putting them into action. So, taking advantage of their perspectives is part of what we do.

Periodically, we get together a panel of partners that are really good at business development and we say, "Okay. Let's do a session." We tee up some questions and I moderate it or some member of my team moderates it or the office administrator partner moderates the session. We might not be all that directly involved during the session itself from a business development or professional development perspective. All we do, in some cases, is choose the people, get their buy-in, and give them the focus. Then, it is hearing from the partners whom we've selected. I think that our lawyers really value that. So, in a lot of cases, it's just making sure we're giving them the opportunity to hear from influential partners, and then setting it in motion, rather than saying it's a particular systematic approach or some exact science. I think it's a blend of art and science.

Business Development Training: Partners: Year-Long Training

(Mark Usellis)

Partners who are graduates of the associate business development training program receive group training that focuses on refining the client needs interview, or the needs assessment interview, and fine tuning pitching strategies. They also receive more advanced individual coaching.

Partners who are not graduates of the associate business development training program receive a combination of group training sessions that includes how do you create a business plan, how do you target, what the sales pipeline looks like, how do you move a prospect through the pipeline, and other fundamentals of new business generation. This is followed by individual coaching where the fundamentals of the business development process are reinforced and tracked.

The two main skills that we continually focus on are the client needs interview, or the needs assessment interview, and pitching.

Business Development Training: Role Playing: Mock Pitch Presentations

(Karen Bell)

We run mock client presentations. Senior partners take on various client roles and then the junior partners make their pitch to the clients. Afterwards, people come out of their roles and have a very rich discussion about what it was like to be the client, what were the strong points, and what could have been better. These are senior partners in the firm who are sharing their knowledge and skills with more junior partners and that, essentially, is a type of a mentoring experience.

We provide different types of role-playing sales training over the course of three-and-a-half years.

Within our mock presentations, our coaching, and our client team structure, we're trying to ensure that our lawyers understand that everyone has a role to play and can be effective in business development. We place particular emphasis on the classic rule around focus: 80 percent of your time on current clients and 20 percent of your time on prospects. And when working with your current clients, building those strong relationships, expanding them, understanding their needs, and being proactive about bringing solutions in language which is their language, not our language—those are some of the core messages that we impart in our discussions.

Business Development Training: See also *Training a Future Rainmaker*

Business Development Training: See Building a Business Development Culture

Business Development Training: Selecting Trainees

(Barbara Lauterbach)

I am very careful about which attorney I select to work with when it comes to business development training and support. I review all potential candidates and then select the ones that I believe have the most promise.

When I first came here to this firm, I was trying to show value and find ways to motivate people and also trying very hard to understand who did what and how, so that I wouldn't waste anybody's time. I think that's the single most important thing that a person in my position can do is be strategic, but also be very strategic in the use of the attorney's time because that time is very valuable.

So, I think that the single most difficult thing is to identify a few people who are going to be motivated and pliable and willing to make some missteps. Those things don't necessarily come easily to trial attorneys.

Business Development Training: Some Resources I Use

(Steve Bell)

I use the same approach for associates and partners: Focus on sales training and sales awareness.

Two of my many resources include "Just in Time" sales training or sales coaching program that's available to people using "Rainmaker VT," V as in video, T as in technology from Mike O'Horo. We have used Mike O'Horo as a sales coach. I also use relationship development coach Mark Maraia, and LawVision sales trainer Silvia Coulter. All excellent.

Business Development Training: Start at the Beginning

(Nancy Kostakos and Karen Febeo)

Helping talented attorneys become talented rainmakers happens incrementally over the course of each individual's career. Our goal is to provide associates with building blocks from the moment they walk in the door. We help them to understand, for example, the importance of having a network, maintaining a network, and working that network in an authentic way. We emphasize that it is much easier to keep in touch consistently over time than it is to cold-call people out of the blue later in one's career. We view attorneys' development much like a triangle with the three vertices being: legal skills, professional skills, and business development skills. When attorneys start out, their main focus must be on developing their legal skills and learning how to become a great technical lawyer. But they also need to start developing their professional skills (communication, leadership, project management, etc.), and establishing the habit of maintaining their networks for potential future business. We talk to them about how their focus in each of those areas will shift and flex over time reflecting where they are in their career.

As attorneys advance, we present leadership programs where we cover these concepts in a comprehensive manner. For example, for our third-year associates, we conduct a session on networks and have them create a network map where they identify who is in their networks from different areas of their lives, and who they reach out to when they need help. By just getting them to think about their connections a bit more intentionally, it reminds them that this needs to be a part of their day-to-day focus. At the senior associate level, we talk about the importance of cultivating those networks. We show them that as they're working on client matters, it is important to make personal connections with people at their level on the other side of the table because one never knows where people may end up, and where those relationships may lead as everyone develops in their careers. We talk about laying a foundation now, so that they have broader networks later on when they will be looking to tap into their networks to develop new business. Over time, we remind people to refresh and expand their network mapping tool. We also teach our younger attorneys to focus on their career narrative. We teach them to answer simple questions like, "What's new?" or "What are you doing these days?" in an engaging way so the inquirer can quickly know them better, and have a better sense of the issues and problems they can help solve, or that other lawyers at the firm can help solve.

Of course, we do a lot more robust training at the partner level. That's where we take a much deeper dive. We've done full-day and half-day workshops on business development and how to sell legal services. Selling is not something lawyers are terribly comfortable with. They were trained to deliver legal services – not to sell their services. The economic downturn, combined with continued consolidation in our industry, has helped people realize the importance of focusing on and learning these skills.

Our firm is focused on remaining profitable by growing top line revenue, and not by carving back on expenses. While the economy certainly has a huge impact on profitability, the way we've chosen to manage our law firm can also have a significant impact. By creating revenue and profitability targets at the business unit level, there is now greater accountability across the firm. Collaboration and teamwork are essential to success, and we are seeing more and more of that now that the consciousness around revenue generation has been raised.

Starting our associates with the right kind of education and continuing it throughout their careers is also essential to our success as a firm. The business development conversation continually grows as our associates develop. We tell them, "Now that you're more advanced, here's a couple more things you should be adding to your to-do list around business development and marketing." We don't want them to be in the dark on business development and then be completely overwhelmed when they get close to partnership.

Business Development Training: Summers

(Jeanne Hammerstrom, Wayne Hogan, Marian Lee, Matt Taylor)

The Florida State University (FSU) College of Law offers a unique program to undergraduates who want to continue on to law school. The Summer for Undergraduates Program is the largest of its kind and has become a national model for other law schools. Sixty undergraduate college students are chosen to participate in this month-long program. During the program, undergraduates attend daily classes taught by law school professors and writing instructors. In addition to classes, the program provides guest lecturers from the legal community, observation of courtroom proceedings and visits to local law firms where the subjects of growing a practice and business development are introduced. Recognizing that the legal field should reflect the diverse population that it serves, Wayne Hogan, who provides economic underpinning of the summer program states, "This is why our FSU College of Law Summer for Undergraduates Program seeks a range of students from an ethnically and socially diverse background." (See Diversity by Wayne Hogan.)

"And so from the beginning, we start training associates as they come in the door. We even do some training with our summer associates. We engage them in the Legal Mocktail that Roberta Montafia and Catherine MacDonagh, JD do for our summers." (See more on Legal Mocktail at *Business Development Training: Associates/Benesch,* and *Business Development: How Do You Turn Skilled Lawyers into Skilled Rainmakers?* by Jeanne Hammerstrom.)

"We include business development strategy awareness as soon as a lawyer or law student begins a relationship with our firm. So, starting with the junior associates, or even summers, we've done a presentation on *networking with some basic skills and then we provide a cocktail reception* afterward where they can practice some of those new networking techniques. [See *Business Development Training: Associates: PD, DBB and Core Competencies* by Marian Lee.]

Matt Taylor explains, "We just had our firm introduction for 15 summer associates. Every year, each practice group head meets with them over a brown bag luncheon and teaches them about their practice group. I'm the head of trial and before I go into anything about trial, I always say the same thing to these young summer associates. They all went to incredible schools, so, they're surrounded by brilliant people, accomplished people, and I always say, "Start day one to be a networker. Do not wait." (See *Network and Networking* by Matt Taylor.)

Business Development Training: The Mock Pitch

(Jeanne Hammerstrom)

One rainmaker training exercise that we have done is a mock pitch. We have three of our partners participate and role play. One will be the CEO. One will be the GC, and one will be the HR person. The partners then present a case to our associates who have now been formed into little teams. We did this at an associate retreat. And the associates had a few weeks to prepare for it. So, they had to use my department, use available research and say, "Jeanne, we're doing this pitch. We need business development support." They would then make their presentation to the mock client decision makers followed by a critique. The partners would say, "Here's what I would have said, or here's what I would have done differently."

Business Development: A Basic Guideline

(Sally Schmidt)

Some things may be more effective than others, but they're all going to be more effective if you're targeting the right people and doing something you enjoy.

Business Development: A Firm-wide Strategy: Senior Management Role Critical

(Sally Schmidt)

For a firm-wide business development culture, it would be best if law firms would approach their organizations on a very strategic basis and say, "Here's the role that we expect everybody to play." And then, "What do we need to give them in terms of support, resources, training, information, etc. to get that done?" But, that does not always happen.

Business Development: A Tactical Approach: Do the Math

(Hans Haglund)

Compared to classroom-style training I believe working one-on-one tactically to grow a practice provides a better result. Lectures generally don't get down to that personal level, and business development is absolutely different for every person. You need to understand the attorney's strengths and weaknesses, general approach to developing relationships, and other differentiators. We can speak theoretically about how to build relationships, how to enter new markets, and how to develop a new client base. But it really is a tactical discussion. You need to better understand your clients at a business and personal level.

> Get down to a tactical level. Ask how many people they're connecting with on a daily basis.
>
> *Hans T. Haglund*

We can talk theoretically about how to market, how to go into new markets, and how to develop a new client base and so forth. But it is really more of a tactical exercise in that you need to create the habit of talking to people every day and following up. This is how successful sales people achieve their goals.

Using a basic math approach, if you have a million dollar annual quota and your average sale is, let's say, $50,000, you need to close two new clients a month. From a statistical and tactical approach, how do you back into your revenue goal? What's your close rate? If half of the people you contact wind up doing business with you, that means you need to contact at least four people per month in order to acquire two new clients per month—basically one per week. You need to have a disciplined approach. If your close rate is 10% that would mean you need 20 viable people per month that you're talking to about buying your product or your service in order to close 2 per month, or basically one per workday.

If your call and email outreach "warm response" rate is 20%. Then, in order to have 20 people to connect with every month you need to have a general outreach to 100 connections every month. 100 x 20% = 20, 20 x 10% = 2 new clients per month. Your percentage may vary. If it is 100 per month, that means you need to make 25 "warm response" connections a week. That's a lot. I'm not saying that these are the numbers. What I am saying is that if you have to be reaching out to 25 a week then that means 5 a day.

The first component of a tactical approach is to understand the math. The second component of developing into a rainmaker is that you need to have a disciplined approach. You must have the attitude that, "this is what I do every day." Within your outreach approach, of course, you are demonstrating your legal skills, business acumen, and genuineness. If you make high-quality connections that creates a higher percentage of potential clients to bubble to the surface, then your required outreach numbers go down dramatically. You may only have to make half the connections if you are getting the results of two new clients a month. As long as you know that's what number you need to get to as your objective, then your business development daily activities, tactically speaking, become clearer and better defined.

Business Development: Building In BD Time

(Shanda Zavalsky)

It's all about efficiency. The more efficient you can make your marketing, then the more you're going to be willing to do it because you're not out there going to an event that didn't produce results. Our roadmaps are very results driven.

The first page of our Visibility Roadmap specifically lists the initiative, what the purpose is, who the targets are, and what that action is. And then on the second page, we call it the Visibility Scorecard, we track everything you do to accomplish page one of the Visibility Roadmap.

If you hold lunch and learns for clients and really nothing came out of those, then at the end of the year we're going to go, "Hmm, what did we do wrong? What could we change about these activities? Or maybe we try to reach these targets in a different way because these didn't work. Or maybe something did work really well, so how can we leverage that approach even more?" I don't really have a time management system that meets all of our needs, but I do have a tracking system that tells us what's working, what's not working, and what needs to be changed.

The scorecard informs us of what worked and what didn't work. We can easily view our efforts and determine those efforts that did and did not produce results. We are then able to repeat what did work and leverage the success and change the efforts that didn't. The added benefit is that no effort is for nothing, we learn something from each one. There is no failure, which helps to get attorneys past the fear of failure.

Business Development: Client Teams, SWOT and DIRP

(Adam Severson)

We have put a great deal of focus on our key client teams. When working with lawyers on these client teams, a significant part of our program is dedicated to the development of their client plans. There are a couple of fundamental questions that rainmakers need to ask as they develop their plans and documents for recruiting new business.

The first questions are: "What are the significant developments in their client's business? How do those developments affect their needs for legal services? And how are you positioned to capitalize on those opportunities?" The legal business is episodic and derivative, and you need to ensure that when an episode or something happens in the client's business you are aligned to be engaged for that matter. To support that preparation for new opportunities we go through a SWOT (Strengths, Weakness, Opportunities, and Threats) analysis of how they are situated with that client, and we conduct a DIRP (Decision maker, Influencer, Referral source, Personal contact) analysis. These need to be specific to each company, as many large institutions have a variety of decision makers that are part of their process.

Within our SWOT review we analyze the competitive dynamic that exists within an individual client. We want to identify how close we are to the C Suites, how do we stack up to our competitors, and how ingrained is our client with various members of our firm. Hopefully, the client works extensively with several firm members, not just one or two individuals.

The second question is, "What is your action plan?" We set out an action plan and identify a particular next step for each client. We identify who on the team is going to lead the charge and when it's going to happen.

In the very first implementation of our enhanced client plan approach, the client team leader agreed to personally act within 10 days on two of the identified four most important next steps. This led to a reenergized group of lawyers for a very significant client of the firm. The client visit was a key component of the plan and one of the client visits occurred within those next 10 days. By the time his plane landed, returning from that client visit, we had gotten five new matters.

> We introduced the notion of an enhanced key client team approach which included a detailed client plan, SWOT and DIRP. Within 10 days of implementing this program for a key client, we received five new matters.
>
> —*Adam Severson*

Recognizing we are in an increasingly competitive environment and the more our lawyers can be intentional about their efforts with their clients, the greater the likelihood of success we will have in fending off some of the competition and hopefully increasing our market share with any given client. Part of our enhanced client plan includes a competitive analysis in the form of a "gap analysis" which identifies the total legal services purchased by a client and our firm's share of their current legal budget. [Read more: look up *Severson, Adam* in Index]

Business Development: Cultural Expectation/ TwoDay Training/Baker Donelson

(Adam Severson)

We have a one-size-fits-one approach to servicing our clients. Culturally, we set that as an expectation. We've structured our business development team strategy to enhance client relationships. Customizing client service is an essential part of the agenda of a two-day internal training program. This program emphasizes the need to both increase the frequency of client visits as well as improve the quality of those client visits. With support from management and the budget, we have emphasized the importance of seeing clients in person. We inform the attorneys of the many benefits of a client visit. For example, it is rare for somebody to go and visit a client and not have a terrific result, whether that's cementing an existing client relationship or obtaining new work. In some instances, we learn of a client problem that we're able to resolve simply because we were able to hear about it in real time. The training helps our people sell in teams and to examine the importance of questions in the business development process to ensure that we understand and clarify the needs of our clients in allowing us to explore potential solutions for that client. Our lawyer leaders speak to large and small firm groups to ensure that everybody knows that marketing and business development are no longer options. It is only a matter of what are you going to do, specifically. Client visits and a very intentional exploration of the client's business and needs are an integral part of the firm's cultural expectations of its lawyers' activities. [Read more at: *Business Development: Client Teams, SWOT and DIRP* by Adam Severson.]

Business Development: Exception Proves Rule

(Hans Haglund)

The exception to consistent business development is that rare specialist who provides a service or an expertise that is so unique and specialized, like a brain doctor with a high-demand expertise, they don't need to go out and develop new relationships. In that case, you don't care about his bedside manner. It's a different matter when you're talking about a relationship with your attorney. The best rainmakers are trusted advisors, and they are regularly and consistently communicating with their clients, and potential clients at a very high level. You want to be able to say to your clients, "I know your business. I know you and how your executive team operates. I know your strategy, and I know how to help ensure your success with the best available legal advice." This message needs to be a mantra proactively generated in a variety of different ways with every existing and potential client. Rainmak ers know you cannot sit by idly thinking the phone will ring.

Business Development: Finding the Time

(Sally Schmidt)

Attorneys often say, "I don't have time for business development," or "I'm so busy, how do I find time for business development?" This subject is a corollary to our discussion on prioritizing your time. Time well invested will correlate with business in the door. And by investing their time well, they can usually find an activity that includes effective business development opportunities. I find sometimes that what the attorneys are doing for marketing is being so poorly done that they shouldn't even do it at all. They think they are marketing, for example, by going to a chamber of commerce lunch or something like that, but they get there late, they sit right down at the table, they miss the networking time, they listen to the speaker and, as soon as he is done, they get up and run back to the office. They haven't used any of the opportunities in that situation to network or build relationships. So, the concept here is they can stop going to those meetings—figure out something else. In other words, if you are going to do it, do it right. Many lawyers are doing the wrong things; they are doing ineffective things. There are so many different options. It's a matter of reviewing them, and finding something they are going to want to commit to, as well as being efficient at achieving the business development objective. [See *Business Development: Prioritizing Time.*]

Business Development: Finding Time

(Barbara Lauterbach)

To answer your question, "How do you show them that they have time even though they're busy trial lawyers?" Sometimes it's a matter of finding time for them, finding ways that they can push some of their work on to associates or paralegals, so that they've got a little bit more time. Sometimes it's the matter of showing them that this doesn't really take a whole lot of time. What's been taking time is their mental attitude that says, "Oh, I don't have the time to do that. I've got to go ahead and do this."

Trial lawyers have blinders on, particularly when they're getting ready to do something, when they're dealing with a bunch of discovery, or when they're getting ready for a summary judgment hearing, for example. They're just focused on that one thing and they don't generally understand that they can take a break from that and make two phone calls and go back to it. So, sometimes that means coming in early, catching them in the elevator, staying in for lunch, and sometimes that means going into their office and helping them do it. "I know you're having a tough time getting started on this, let's sit down and make these two phone calls now."

It's been on their list for a while and they just haven't got to it and part of that is apprehension, why am I going to call somebody that I don't have an open file for, what are they going to think, are they going to think I'm desperate for work? It's a mental thing. They're thinking too much about it.

So, there is a little time there where you try to get past that and when it gets right down to it, when you laid that groundwork and they still haven't done it, checking the time, realizing that it's not lunch time wherever they're calling, running in and saying, hey, let's do this now, here's the number.

I'm not beyond calling to see if somebody is in before I do that, either.

Once they get comfortable doing it, I'm not going to have to do that again, at least not very often. There will be times if somebody's having problems getting to a certain point, but it's the fear of the unknown that stops them every time, which is why again, you've got to make it as parallel to what they do regularly if you possibly can.

Lawyers don't want to fail. Nobody does.

In some cases my role is laying the groundwork. In other cases the training wheels are off and that's part of developing that business development muscle.

And sometimes they are going to fall over. That's part of cheerleading.

And although it's important to get out of the room and let them go at it on their own, it's also important to go back in and check and make sure that if they fell off the horse they get right back on it before they think about it too much.

At the associate level, it's more of a habit-forming activity. You want them to understand business development and networking and building relationships is something you do every day. It's not something that you turn off and on. It's not something that you get to think about only once in a while. [See also topics beginning with *Time*.]

Business Development: Forms: We Don't Use a One-Size-Fits-All Template

(Erin Meszaros)

When one of my business development coordinators asked me, "Should I have one template that applies to everyone?" My answer was, "Not necessarily. You could, but in my experience it needs to be specific to the individual and his/her needs." I told him you may go in with your template as a starting point, but make sure you are listening to what the lawyer needs to have done, as you may end up filling out your standard template, but you may have to change it, as well. Yes, it takes a lot longer, I know, and it makes our job harder, but I am big on "customizing" for each attorney so they will be effective. I want to make sure I'm doing what that person across the table needs help with. [See also: *Business Development Training: Our Approach: Part 1: Start Day One*; and *Business Development Training: Our Approach: Part 2: Six Buckets*.]

Business Development: Foundational Question

[See *Revenue: Growing Firm Revenue: Job One*]

Business Development: Guides, Forms, Templates

(Matt Taylor)

Our business development team has put together a very good guide on how to do a successful pitch and we turned it into an e-learning module that includes their insights. I have video of the team presenting the pitch material and we've found that to be useful. The team has built a number of tools, templates and checklists. The pitch program we've been running is well beyond pilot stage. It's now into its fourth year. We've run a couple of other programs that have been piloted and now they're ready to share across the country.

Business Development: Have a Disciplined Process

(Sally Schmidt)

How does a skilled attorney become a skilled rainmaker? Well, for the people who are not natural rainmakers, which is, to be honest, probably the vast majority of the legal profession, I think there are still many things that they can do to become good rainmakers. Some can become great. Some might be good. Some might be fair, but they can all certainly be better. One thing that I think is important, and it sounds kind of process oriented, but it's true, is discipline– develop a discipline of routine business development practices.

Fundamental activities like organizing your contacts and figuring out a system for how you track how long it's been since you've seen somebody . . . maybe spending two hours every Thursday afternoon to schedule next week's lunches, or send thank you notes, or follow-up with clients that you finished projects with, or other relationship-building activities. I frequently work with people to either set up Outlook appointments or calendar business development activities, or put reminder notes in Outlook, or to code their clients[*], things like that. It becomes a little bit easier to manage business development activities when you have a good process.

We help attorneys develop a type of activity muscle, a habit. Creating behaviors that make it easier for them. For example, I am coaching an attorney later today over the phone—he's pretty senior and we're organizing his target list. We're talking about people he knows and how he's going to stay in touch with them and how he's going to organize them. In his case, he's going to keep them in a handwritten notebook with sections devoted to these different people; and when he contacts them; then he'll keep notes so he can look back at the dates and what they discussed. I don't care how the lawyers do it. It doesn't matter to me if it's through technology or if it's on a notepad. The point is to have a disciplined system that is consistently followed and is shown to be effective over time. [*See also *Code Your Clients*.]

Business Development: How Do You Turn Skilled Lawyers into Skilled Rainmakers?

(Jeanne Hammerstrom)

We have a variety of programs that we incorporate to help turn skilled lawyers into skilled rainmakers. First of all, we have Benesch Business Development Institute, which is part of our Benesch University. In all of these activities we work very closely with professional development.

We start training associates as soon as they come in the door. We even do some training with our summer associates. We incorporate the Legal Mocktail that Roberta Montafia and Catherine MacDonagh do for our summers.

The Legal Mocktail is an experiential program to teach networking skills to lawyers. Roberta Montafia reviews the key concepts of relationship building and the do's and don'ts of networking in her video "Essential Networking Tips for Legal Marketers." She discusses common networking habits and how to exhibit proper etiquette at networking events. In the video, the attorneys learn about the top three networking tips, how to gracefully enter and exit conversations, and how to follow-up once an event has concluded. As Roberta says, "What location is to real estate, follow-up is to networking." [Author note: here's a link for more info on Legal Mocktail: http://legalmarketing.bizyeti.com/view/content/YpCVT2.] The associates are going to be included in that Legal Mocktail training as well as presentations on dressing for success, etiquette, how to mine your contacts, and a number of the essential softer skills.

> "What location is to real estate, follow-up is to networking."
>
> —*Roberta Montafia*

In our Benesch Business Development Institute—we have topics broken down by years in practice, 1 to 3, 3 to 5, all the way up to the partner level, the 8-plus, who receive a different type of training.

We also have a two-and-half-day program that we use for business development training, finding client's needs, pitching, client development, client service, and related topics that all the partners and almost all associates have been through. It's a very expensive program. It's sizable. So, we use that program, and actually, I should tell you it's Bill Flannery's program out of Austin. [Author's note: Act fast if you wish to experience this program as Bill Flannery is threatening to retire. You can find various contributions to this book by William Flannery by going to the *Index*.]

Another part of the Benesch Business Development Institute is coaching from a coach outside the firm who works with our attorneys. We do a program every 16 to 18 months with this gentleman, Peter Johnson, out of Boston, who works with about a dozen of our attorneys. And it used to be more for those we think we can get to the million-dollar club, but he really has done everything—he's worked with some of our highest rainmakers . . . on their plans, to up-and-coming associates who are really showing good promise in the whole business development area. So Peter is another key resource in our business development program—he's like a partner of this firm.

And I'd like to point out that whenever I talk about developing and supporting rainmaker skills, we also provide really awesome resources. For example, we have a suite of six or seven competitive intelligence tools. We have a business intelligence resource called Data Fusion that we layer on top of our competitive intelligence tools. We also use article aggregators, and other information aggregation resources.

We're constantly pushing these resources out to the attorneys and making ourselves valuable to them. They have these resources, so before they go out on the pitch, they know everything they need to know about the person or company. And once they figure out what the content of pitch should be, we have put in place some really great templates that are easy for them to use to help finish their pitch presentation.

There's a couple other things. We also started, a couple years ago, pipeline meetings. We have them every other week on Friday. And all partners are invited from every office, every practice group. And sometimes we'll get 20 on a call and sometimes we'll get five, and everyone's helping each other. I know that person at ABC Hospital. I can reach out . . . that kind of support is generated. So they're helping each other. Although it can be competitive sometimes, it's really very collegial and very team-oriented.

In addition to those pipeline meetings, we are also starting a more casual program in our Cleveland office just to talk about business development and then we'll expand from there. We're calling it "What's On Tap?" We're going to have business development, beverages, and brilliance. We begin around 4:00 or 4:30pm, have some cocktails, sit around and talk. Discussions can be about anything from trends to let's talk about JD Supra and what they do. Let's talk about the pitch that I just had and how we could use the comments that resulted. Let's talk about the latest client assessments and maybe what we've learned from those, topics like that. We do have a formal client assessment program so, that can be an ongoing rich source for our discussions.

That covers a number of different business development-oriented activities that we're doing. I have six staff members and we support 180 attorneys. Which, for us, is a good ratio. The firm has been really good to me in letting me invest in outside resources as well as my own professional development and a couple of my other people. So I take advantage of that, which includes my membership in LMA national and the LMA state-wide networks. LMA and so many of its members are so important to me because they've been a valuable resource of people who have been there to help me.

Business Development: Incentivizing

(Shanda Zavalsky)

I incentivize people to want to do more business development by trying to make it easy. Years ago, we tried to make these generic cookie cutter templates outlining Step 1, Step 2, etc. And while we still do that, I try to sit down and discuss with the attorneys where their passion is, and what they enjoy doing. If you despise speaking, I'm definitely not going to try to sign you up for some speaking gigs. But maybe you love writing, so let's look at how we can leverage some of your knowledge through writing.

That's why these Visibility Road Maps that we create play such an important role. Every single one is different because every single attorney has a different preference. Although some preferences do overlap and have commonalities across different attorneys, they're unique to them, so is the roadmaps are very individualized.

The persuasive part is probably the most difficult. How do I persuade you that this is really something that's worthwhile to spend your time on? Attorney time is incredibly precious. So, we work hard to say if you do this, this outcome will be achieved and this is what we will do next – hopefully, you'll connect with these potential clients, a relationship will develop, and then we determine our next step. We try to give them a clear picture.

If you're pitching a client, you need to give them a very clear picture of what it's like to work with you. How we are going to benefit them. We try to do that with our attorneys, too.

For example, when you're pitching, you want to say, "This is what it's like to work with our firm." For associates whose minds might be considering 16 different tracks of conversation, ultimately, one message must be, "This is going to be your experience if you work with our firm and work with me." And, in some way, allow them to experience your passion for your work.

> You must remember that they became attorneys for some reason. There had to be a little passion in there somewhere. And it's easy to lose if you let a big firm suck you into a whirlwind of action that is disconnected from your original purpose for going into law. So I try really hard to keep them focused on that passion.
>
> —*Shanda Zavalsky*

You must remember that they became attorneys for some reason. There had to be a little passion in there somewhere. And it's easy to lose if you let a big firm suck you into a whirlwind of action that is disconnected from your original purpose for going into law. So, I try really hard to keep them focused on that passion.

Business Development: Locating Outside Consultants, Trainers, and Coaches

(David King Keller)

How do you find great business development consultants, trainers, and coaches outside of the firm? Many talented people were mentioned by name during the course of the many interviews in writing this book. Most would belong to the Legal Marketing Association (LMA). A call or email to the executive director of LMA, the LMA national President, or the President of your local LMA Chapter will help you find an excellent marketing and business development resource. Some would have written books on the subject.

Business Development: Motivation Using Jedi Mind Games

(Shanda Zavalsky)

I find that Jedi Mind Games Work.

Part of increasing motivation is that when working with lawyers you have to make the idea theirs. So, when I go into meetings, I don't ever go in and say here's what you need to do. I ask a lot of questions and say a lot of what do you think about this? What if we did this? And they will soon come up with their own idea. When they do that, they are much more engaged than if it's someone else telling them what they should do. By coming up with the idea themselves, then they get a little more motivated, and they'll actually act upon it.

Business Development: Multiple Approaches

(Despina Kartson)

Consider multiple approaches to business development which can take many different shapes. It can be client entertainment, it can be providing CLE programs, it may be cross-marketing with and to other partners and practices in your firm, and it could be writing articles, publishing, speaking engagements, attending industry associations and conferences. Focus on the industry or industries that a lawyer works in, whether it's the energy sector or the pharmaceutical sector.

Business Development: Our Form and What We Measure

(Stephen Fairley)

When it comes to business development and marketing, I have found templates and checklists can be very helpful. Several years ago I created an individual Attorney Marketing Action Plan (AMAP). It's about seven pages long and goes through each major area of a marketing plan. It starts with identifying the individual attorney's annual goals: number of new clients per quarter, number of new consultations you will do each month, how many networking events you will attend, how much new revenues will you bring in, the number of new referral sources you will meet with, number of articles you will write, number of blog posts you will write, number of new connections you will make on LinkedIn®, and so on. As much as possible you want to use metrics to hold the attorney accountable.

For business development, we focus on activities like client retention and satisfaction: who are your top 10 existing clients? How will you connect with them each quarter (other than sending them an invoice)? What is your plan for developing the account and asking them for additional business? Who are your top 10 prospects you want to target? What is your plan for connecting with them and asking them for business? Who are your existing referral partners? How are you going to connect with them: face-to-face, email, phone, weekly, monthly meetings, quarterly business review sessions, dinners, or some other manner?

Cross-selling is always a major opportunity, especially in mid to large law firms. It's far too easy to keep the right hand separate from the left hand. Many times a client doesn't even know your law firm X, Y, and Z because they hired you for A, B, and C. What's your plan for cross referring those clients? Who are you going to refer them to? Have you identified other needs that your law firm could help them with?

There is also a section on external marketing activities such as seminars and presentations you commit to giving, topics you will speak on, networking groups you will join and attend, leadership in bar associations and other professional trade associations, article topics you will write on, blog posts you will write, and personal development courses you will take. It asks the attorney to carefully and completely fill this out and then review it with the managing partner. The managing partner invests an hour or two reviewing it with the attorney, providing suggested changes and improvements. Both retain a copy and review it quarterly to establish progress. Successful completion of their AMAP is figured into their bonus.

Business Development: Overview

(Allen Chichester)

In my view, if business development isn't driving the boat, then your marketing department's rudder is probably not well managed. The business development function is all about creating incremental revenue, which is the highest and best calling of marketing.

In the professional service world, the only reason to build a public profile, to manage your brand, to be consistent about your branded communications, to engage in content marketing, to do any of these marketing communication things and more, is to help soften the ground for people who are building business. Law firms, like other professional organizations, need to grow. It's difficult to manage in an environment where you're declining or where resources are continually scarce. Growth is fundamental and I view my job is to contribute to the growth of the firm through incremental revenue, full stop.

For these reasons I first focus on business development. Business Development Managers (BDMs) and business development staff need to have their own unimpeded access and clear roles related to supporting attorneys in business development activity. By this I mean don't lumber them with a bunch of other responsibilities because they happen to be in the right place at the right time. Also, because they tend to be focused on industries or practices and not geographies, I work as hard as possible to make all the business development functions national in scope. We are a national firm and if we cut up responsibilities based on geography, it will make coordination across jurisdictions that much harder. There is some specialization within the business development group as well. We have one manager that is focused on industry groups, for example. And even though we have business development staff assigned to departments and practice groups, we have specializations within that.

Of course, there are other business development functions that we have centralized. We have a small centralized group that work on pitches and proposals, mainly the large complicated RFPs. This is the same group that leads our competitive intelligence efforts, although all the BDMs are responsible for competitive intelligence and for pitch support.

One of the critical things in our culture that we try to foster is a teamwork approach to the job. The main reason for that is-any manager would understand-you can't staff to the peak levels of your demand, otherwise you would go broke, so you staff somewhere in the middle and sometimes people may be not very busy, while other times they may be overworked. In order to balance all that out, you have to be able to share and support each other when it comes to projects. Like a pendulum, demand tends to be focused on one group or another in terms of workload and if you don't have a mechanism to spread that work out, then people go from being panicked to being bored and it's just not very effective. We have a high value placed on the ability to step in and feel comfortable asking for help or volunteering help on projects that you have nothing to do with.

Business Development: Prioritizing Client Search Time

(Steve Bell)

Your best prospective client is a company that closely resembles an existing client with whom you have just a fabulous relationship.

Business Development: Prioritizing Time

(Sally Schmidt)

I am frequently asked, "How does Schmidt Marketing help attorneys prioritize their business development time?" Many attorneys might be thinking they're doing a lot of marketing because they're going to a lot of lunches, but it's because they're getting invitations from brokers or insurance agents and different people that want to see them, but not necessarily the people the lawyers need to see in order to grow their practices. So, there are two things I do to help people prioritize how they spend their business development time.

One, is doing a better job of figuring out who exactly is your target. For instance, giving speeches or writing articles. A fellow recently I was working with was interested in wage and hour work, and yet he was writing articles about the Family and Medical Leave Act. It was just because a publication came to him or his firm came to him and asked, "Would you write an alert on this?" Well, sure, he can do it; he's capable. But my point is: if you're going to spend the time marketing, market the things you want to attract. So, part of it is: who are the targets; who are we really trying to reach; and, what do you want them to know about your practice?

Two, in terms of prioritizing, is helping the lawyers figure out what they like to do, because they're going to be more inclined toward things they enjoy. So, when people tell me, as one young woman did, "I'd rather teach 100 hours than take someone to lunch", my reaction is that she's not real big on networking so let's find other ways for her to get out there. Find what people like to do. If someone loves to write, for instance, and some people say, "I *love* to write," I'll say, "Well, let's think about a blog, or let's think about a quarterly update, or writing a series of articles." Some things may be more effective than others, but they're all going to be more effective if you're targeting the right people and doing something you enjoy.

Business Development: Setting Expectations

(Dave Bruns)

The expectations of success of a business plan vary, depending on the level you have attained as a lawyer. At the associate level, it's expected they maintain communications with their law school friends, maintain an updated LinkedIn bio, join some LinkedIn groups, and get involved in a bar group or other organization that can be supportive of their legal career. They're starting to build their networks. At the associate level, it's more of a habit-forming activity. You want them to understand that business development, networking, and building relationships must be done every day. It's not something that you turn off and on.

> At the associate level, it's more of a habit-forming activity. You want them to understand that business development, networking and building relationships must be done every day. It's not something that you turn off and on.
>
> —*Dave Bruns*

As an associate grows in her/his career, from first year to second, etc., the specificity and the amount of activity in their plan grows. At the earlier stages, join your alumni group and engage in a few other networking activities, but junior associate activities should be more focused on achieving excellent lawyer skills and understanding how to be a lawyer.

At the same time, the associate must understand the importance of building brand and maintaining communications with their contacts, realizing that at most firms junior associates don't have any client contact as a junior associate.

If you wait until you're a partner to start reaching back to your old classmates and contacts they're going to think, "Who are you? I don't know you."

You've got to maintain those contacts from the beginning. As you move up in the associate ranks, you should go to conferences, start to specialize a little bit in your practice area, start to do content development, or something along those lines. You want to brand yourself, and, as you roll into your partnership, you've built the habits of being a strong business developer and it becomes something you do naturally.

As you get into the partner ranks, your plan becomes a little more specific. As a senior partner, it becomes a great deal more specific. It's, "I'm going to go after these 8 clients." The expectations are based on where you are in your career.

Although we have a Farella process, it's not a one-size-fits-all process and there's some flexibility in it. Is it Gumby and you get to do backflips? Probably not that flexible, but it's certainly flexible. There's enough flexibility that you can individualize it to your specific goals, objectives, commitments, and where you are in your life. It takes into account familial needs. Do you have young kids, old kids, or no kids? How much can you commit?

Business Development: Strategies and Priorities

[See also Industry Marketing.]

Business Development Support Staff: Structure and Titles

(Jonathan Fitzgarrald)

Chief Marketing Officer: oversees the entire department. As to business development activities: individual and group attorney coaching.

Business Development Manager: spends most time on visiting with attorneys one-on-one throughout the month to follow-up on business plans and initiatives. Also handles research for new business pitches/opportunities.

Marketing Coordinator: spends time planning/coordinating events, updating the website and blogs, and managing the firm's CRM.

Marketing Assistant: spends time handling all the administrative duties of the department, e.g., logging attorney expense reimbursements, record keeping, recording metrics, etc.

Business Development: Support: Internal

(Melanie Green)

We do have a group that I rely upon or go to for feedback on things worth thinking about. And they're not necessarily like a marketing committee. There are a group of people who have been successful, and we draw upon them for various firm business development programs.

Business Development: Support: Internal: Size of Firm BD Support Staff

(Despina Kartson)

We have BD Staff supporting every one of our offices around the globe. We support every office and all of the practice areas of the firm, as well as all of the industry sectors. We have internal resources like PR graphic design, CRM, a full complement of internal resources.

Business Development: The Moment of Truth

(Mark Usellis)

Procter and Gamble talks about the customer moment of truth. It's when customers are standing in the grocery aisle and they're deciding which mustard to buy? To me the first meeting—the first encounter you have with someone—the needs assessment and the pitch are really the moments of truth.

Business Development: Zavalsky Technique: Part 1: Three Unique Concepts

(Shanda Zavalsky)

We have *three unique concepts* that we've created over the past year that seem to be working really well. They work well because they effectively address the new market environment where you have to be very targeted and generally have to do more than one thing to effectively engage your target.

Years ago, you could put your name out there with a certain amount of advertising and people might call you and give you some work. Today, people are keeping more of that work in-house. Clients are more particular about who they're giving work to, which requires you to meet them in person. The client has to build some trust in you before they're going to hand you any work.

To address today's client within the highly competitive current market environment, we've created three unique business development concepts: one is based on the individual; one is practice group based; and the third is a mentorship, pay-it-forward program that we've begun.

In the past, I would send out a generic business development plan questionnaire to the attorneys who would fill in the blanks to certain activity questions, and hopefully they would stick with that plan over the year. But we weren't good about checking in on them and making sure they were making progress. So we came up with a new approach using three programs

The *first* program is called "Ready, Aim, Fire: Your Personal Brand." We call it "Ready, Aim, Fire" because what we found by watching attorney's behavior was that many attorneys, once they made partner, would suddenly come to the full realization, possibly for the first time, that they need to bring in some new work. So, they start thinking, "I have to do some business development." So, they just go straight to "fire." I'm going to join an organization. I'm going to write a client alert. I'm going to go speak at some event.

But what they're not doing is starting with pre-planning. Who's my audience? What's relevant? How am I going to reach my target audience? Answers to these questions and others must be known before truly effective action can take place. We've made them step back by incorporating that "ready." And the "ready" is identifying what you want to be known for. Does it match with what you're currently known for? How do people think of you and describe you? How do you get where you want to be with that description? And that description should match your website bio.

We start "ready" by taking their bio and putting it into a word cloud. Within the word cloud, the words in your bio become larger or smaller based on relevancy, placement, and emphasis. The word cloud gives us a quick snapshot of what you're telling the world about yourself. For example, a word cloud might highlight a State in large letters, or the word "corporate." If these are not relevant within their practice, they are emphasizing the incorrect areas of their bio. If they are a gaming attorney and "gaming" appears small. They are not highlighting their gaming expertise enough.

> We start "ready" by taking their bio and putting it into a word cloud. Within the word cloud, the words in your bio become larger or smaller based on relevancy, placement and emphasis. The word cloud gives us a quick snapshot of what you're telling the world about yourself.
>
> —*Shanda Zavalsky*

The word cloud gives us an opportunity to say here's what we need to focus on. What do you want to be known for? We update their bio. We make sure that they have the right speaking engagements and they highlight the fact that they are a player in the market. Now that we've talked about what you want to be known for, we then ask, "Who needs you?" Who needs you, and why are they going to hire you over every other attorney out there who is great and offers the same legal services? So, we go through why you're different. This is why they would, hopefully, be impelled to get to know you or work with you. What are some key successes? Maybe there's a certain niche area in which you are an expert.

Once we know who the target is, and why they want you, we can determine where they are. From that point we ascertain the best venues to reach the target audience. You're not just running around out there speaking at random events trying to get visibility or trying to get your name in the paper, but you're connected to something that's going to connect you in the end to that right audience. So, that's what we do in lieu of a generic fill-in-the-blanks business development plan.

Next, we create a Visibility Road Map to connect the attorney with the target audience. This map has a combination of business development tactics and communications tactics. There are some direct things we do, like lunch and learns or speeches at a client industry meeting, or those more in-person meetings. We include networking at specifically identified associations conferences and sponsorships of targeted industry events. We also include profile building and expert positioning by using bylined articles, media sources, public relations, and client alerts.

The *second* program is called The One-Pager Process, which we use for each practice group. We take the individual attorney's "Ready, Aim, Fire" approach and apply it to practice groups. For example, within a particular practice area, I might have three very dynamic people in that group, but if all of them are going to market and describe us in a different way or are going after different people and we're not unified in our message, then our message is scattered and diluted instead of being collaborative and powerful. So, we get them together as a practice group and ask what is it we do, who we do it for, why we do it best, and what are some examples of success? We then put this information together into what we call the One-Pager. The result is a nice looking and cogent one-page hand out. But what's great about it is now we're a team. And we've identified where we're strong, why we are different than others, and we can all communicate this message increasing its effectiveness.

Marketing can use that one-pager to help you target. It can help you with your Visibility Roadmap, and it can help you with your communications.

Advertising can use language developed for the One-Pager. And we tie the One-Pager language with our goals. Maybe we're known for the small deals, but we can do the big deals. Then we're going to start trying to highlight our big deal work.

I'm very passionate and excited about this approach to business development. I think that we do things really well here, and so I love talking about it.

Our *third* program is an individual mentorship Pay-It-Forward program. We're just kicking it off. What we've done is we've identified a really good rainmaker within the firm. And, then, he has taken a few people under his wing that he is going to talk to about how he develops business. If there's any one thing you need to be successful at business development, it's to be prepared. And this rainmaker is a master at preparation.

This rainmaker-mentor has certain things that he does if he's going to a networking event. He will research who the audience is and what kind of needs they might have that relate to his expertise. So he shows up knowing the message he wants to send to the potential clients. In addition to attending the conference, he'll get together a targeted dinner. Then he'll follow-up with some materials from the office after the event so that he's connecting. Or he'll invite them to lunch. But he has a definite process for networking. He has a definite process for holding an event, or speaking engagement. We're creating informational packets on what we're learning from this rainmaker. For example, if you're going to speak, here's Step 1, Step 2, and Step 3. If you're going to attend a conference, here's what you do. If you're going to a pitch meeting, here's what you do.

We're putting together these informational packets as the rainmaker mentors people. The idea is the Pay-It-Forward concept. After our current attorneys go through this mentoring program, then they're going to identify a few people that they can mentor on how to conduct successful business development.

It's an internal coaching process that we're organizing, and what I like about it is every firm has its unique set of challenges, just like every attorney does. So internally, hopefully, we're going to have each individual work with people that they've built a relationship with, so there's a good deal of pre-existing trust. You can share openly, but you feel like this is another lawyer who works at the same firm and understands the challenges that you might have.

We just recently implemented the Pay-It-Forward program. It's a test case. We've chosen our first four participants. We're are putting together the materials and trying to see how it works. It's going really well and people are excited about it. They seem pretty engaged, more so than when I've hired expensive external coaches. After our external coaching program ended we noticed that slowly people just quit answering the phone or they quit doing their actions that they're supposed to do. That one-time insertion of external coaching ends up being a waste of money.

There are a number of factors that are supporting our Pay-It-Forward program. One, it's totally customized to their particular situation. Another is that they don't want to fail their peer. In many cases whereas an attorney won't mind failing a program that has them working with a paid outside coach, they feel I can live with that, but I don't want to fail a peer who may speak to others, and before you know it, I've disappointed a lot of people I work with. So there's more accountability related to this internally-sourced mentoring-coaching program.

Business Development: Zavalsky Technique: Part 2: Associate Training

(Shanda Zavalsky)

Our associate business development training, utilizes the associate marketing checklist.

When I started at this firm, there was a difference in thinking with leadership and myself that when you become an associate and you become an attorney, really, you need to focus on becoming a good lawyer first. Don't worry about business development. Don't think about it. Well, I disagree.

I do agree with the fact that you need to become a good lawyer first and foremost. But I do think you should start creating business development habits from the beginning. And they're simplified, nothing that takes a lot of time. I don't expect you're going to be bringing in a client the first two years.

> I do think you should start creating business development habits in associates from the beginning.
>
> —*Shanda Zavalsky*

But you can start building a mailing list of your contacts from day one. Make sure that when you meet people you put them in your contacts you also create a tickler to follow up and maintain that relationship. Make sure you're sending out holiday cards. Make sure that you're reading the right legal and targeted industry publications. And make sure that you're thinking about where you want to go with your career.

The biggest mistake you can make as a new attorney is not thinking about where you want to go, because if I know right now I want to specialize in a certain area or, where my passion is, then I'm going to connect with the right people. I'm going to build a relationship with the firm's shareholders who have that expertise so I can be assigned that type of work. I'm going to join organizations and attend conferences that will allow me to learn about my field of interest and meet decision makers who hire attorneys within my desired practice area. If I don't choose my path, the firm will choose it for me. And five years down the road I may be a very unhappy attorney because I'm not doing what I love. So make sure you're thinking about what is it that I want to do? Who do I want to be? And set yourself up for success down that path.

For associates our professional development director, Marian Lee, changed our process awhile back to not approach marketing training on a first year, second year basis. Instead, we have levels based on levels of experience with business development. So, we have Level 1, Level 2, and Level 3. So I created my marketing checklist to match up with those levels. It's truly just a simple checklist. If you're sitting there and think, "Oh, I should do some business development and I don't know what to do." I can pull out my checklist and look. And I've created a whole book for our new associates and it just has the seven areas that I think that you need to be thinking about when you're an associate. And it's being a good lawyer (1). It's client service development (2). It's internal marketing (3). It is knowledge building and industry research (4). It's selecting a niche (5), building external relationships (6), and then building your reputation (7).

I have found articles within each of these areas that I thought were good, or I wrote some of them myself. So, if an associate thinks, "Oh, one thing I need to do is figure out client service, they can go to that tab and read a little about it." Same with building a niche. I don't know how to build a niche. What do I need to think about? They can go to that section.

These support tools work most of the time, however there are still issues. One open question is, "How many people do we need in marketing?" It's hard to keep up with 250 attorneys. It's also difficult because not all of them want to develop business. So trying to get people to do things they don't really want to do is sometimes hard, so it's definitely not perfect, but it's organized.

Business Intelligence: See *Information Aggregators*

Business Plan Templates: Firm-wide Standard Can Be a Lifesaver

(Dave Bruns)

We have a standardized business plan template and we let the lawyers work within the structure of that template. Some lawyers stick with the basic template format. Some convert it to a spreadsheet. Others write a 52-page memo. We need them to be in a comfort zone with their plan and if they're comfortable with a 52-page memo, go for it. In all cases, I'm going to end up saying, "Okay, what are the action items and let's create a small list of high priority action items. "What are you doing? For whom? When? What are the next steps?" I want action items to be fairly specific and direct.

There's tremendous value in having a standardized template. When multiple attorneys from different offices are all going after the same client, why not put them all together and have them act as a team? Because how embarrassing is it when you're competing against yourself? That's when a firm-wide standard business plan template can be a lifesaver.

Checklists: The Power of Checklists

(David King Keller)

How powerful are checklists?

Dr. Atul Gawande determined that a checklist of just 19 items that could be completed in two minutes lowered surgical complications and deaths by more than one-third. Another study in the Netherlands determined that a pre-surgery checklist reduced complications and deaths by 47 percent. [Source: The Power of Checklists, interview of Atul Gawande, MD, available on a 2011 YouTube at https://www.youtube.com/watch?v=CGwOMM896Po.]

The pilot's checklist is now commonplace, but it started in WWII with Model 299, which was so complex the army feared no one could master its pre-flight complexities. One of the army's most veteran pilots died during a test take-off that was later determined to be pilot error because he forgot one simple pre-flight step prior to taking off. As a result of that error, this vital plane's production was side-lined. A team put together the first pilot pre-flight checklist that allowed this plane to go back into production; and now the B-17 bomber is legendary in how it helped turned the tide of the war. More than 1.8 million miles were flown in the Model 299/ B-17 without one preventable accident. [Source: *The New Yorker*, December 10, 2007, "The Checklist" by Atul Gawande.]

Two variations of "The Associate Marketing Checklist by Year" is in an ABA best-seller I wrote, *The Associate As Rainmaker, Building Your Business Brain*, available at http://bit.ly/1dAxob6.

Chief Client Officer: Consider Having a CCO to Manage Client Teams

(Karen Bell)

We have a Client Team and Industry Group framework, which is led by our Chief Client Officer. [See *Client Teams* by Karen Bell.]

Civility Matters: Have Warrior Skills While Being Collaborative and Vulnerable

(Michele Silva)

The most successful business people I have worked with, including attorneys who wish to be rainmakers, are those who demonstrate a desire to be "collaborative" instead of "competitive." When someone thinks their success is based upon being covert and closed to collaboration with other attorneys, they are ultimately operating from a position of fear, which can only produce weak and disappointing results. If, however, they can exhibit a spirit of collaboration while remaining wise and confident, their openness and willingness to be vulnerable will attract new clients, cooperative juries, and referral business from other firms that is either outside the other firm's practice areas or that they can't take on due to conflicts of interest. Firms who refer business outside the firm have to trust the attorneys they're recommending, and how can someone know whether they trust you if they have only seen the "warrior" side of you? Collaboration dictates the allowance of opportunities to flow to you and requires an attitude of inclusiveness which fosters generative energy that will elude a person who is furtive and combative.

Civility Matters: Rainmakers Don't Burn Bridges to Opposing Counsel

(Wayne Hogan)

I'm on the National Board of The American Board of Trial Advocates, the ABOTA organization, and I'm one of the trustees of their ABOTA Foundation. A very substantial focus that they have in addition to the importance of the Seventh Amendment Right to Trial by Jury is professionalism and civility. "Civility Matters" is the program they are instilling in law schools across the country and the point of the organization, which is basically half plaintiff and half defense lawyers in the civil side, in insurance or commercial defense, is the idea that lawyers can not only handle cases, but also handle them professionally and civilly, and, at the end of the case, still be friends. Hopefully, if it's within a town, you'll begin the case as friends and you'll end the case shaking hands and going on to the next work for the next client.

We call it an adversary system, on the theory that at least that gets the most important communication about the different sides of the topic in front of a neutral arbiter, whether it's a judge or a jury, depending upon the setting, but also, it means each side putting forward their best case. Sometimes, and maybe oftentimes—most of the time because of mediation and the like—it helps to resolve the dispute in a civil way. So, we call it "adversary," but in reality that's just because it's the mechanism for getting down to the key points of difference so that it can be resolved.

It's not all just shaking hands and saying, "Hello." It has to do with understanding your work and presenting it. But, that said, doing it in a professional way and realizing that in part, it's because you're going to see that lawyer and you're going to see a number of those lawyers time and time again and you need to develop a reputation for reliability and truthfulness.

Those are the kinds of basic qualities that help you have a sustained practice over time and then, the hope is, and I think it's been the case, that other opportunities come your way. For us and for me personally, after Governor Lawton Chiles and I, as President of the Academy of Florida Trial Lawyers had been on opposite sides of a legislative battle about workers compensation, there was the opportunity at a later time, when the call came out from Governor Chiles that he was looking for lawyers who had the kind of background that would be required to represent the taxpayers of the State of Florida against the cigarette industry. I happened to be included in the ones that were asked to be part of the governor's legal team and said, "Yes." [Author note: which led to a multibillion dollar settlement.] In the end, at base, you probably know better than I what it takes to be "a rainmaker" these days; there's advertising, there's all ranges of things and everybody does that in some way or another, but my opinion is that, in the end, there's got to be substance and the ability to work with people. And, the other thing is engagement in professional organizations. [See the Ted Olson comment that supports this at *Civility Matters: Ted Olson Discusses Working with Former Opponent David Boies*, which led to a national partnership that won a U.S. Supreme Court Decision.]

Civility Matters: Ted Olson Discusses Working with Former Opponent David Boies

(David King Keller)

The San Francisco Fairmont Hotel Ballroom was packed on the one-year anniversary of *Hollingsworth v. Perry* as we listened to a riveting presentation by David Boies and Ted Olson to the Commonwealth Club of the inside story on how these former opponents in *Gore v. Bush* came together to win a landmark ruling on The Defense of Marriage Act before the U.S. Supreme Court. On June 26, 2013, the U.S. Supreme Court issued a pair of landmark decisions, reinstating the freedom to marry for same-sex couples in California. Boies and Olson joined forces to forge the unique legal argument that would carry the day. This decision reverberated around the world, causing many jurisdictions to change their policies. In presenting their story of the five-year struggle to win the right for gay couples to marry, Ted Olson took a few minutes to explain the importance and significance of maintaining civility with opposing counsel when he said that working together with David Boies "has ennobled us, it has enriched us, and it's inspired us . . . I think we lead a little by example, by saying that you can be friends and have great admiration for your opponent in the courtroom and that you can work together." Olson added that they both found common ground working together on an American Bar Association task force to support more funding for the courts all across the country. Later, David Boies added, "I predict that one of the civil rights we'll be focused on down the road is education." Today your opponent. Tomorrow your partner in making the world a better place. Civility matters.

Client Communication: The Platinum Rule Leads to More Business Development

(Karen Bell)

We strive to help our lawyers develop a mindset that business development is an everyday activity and not a case of just blocking Saturday off to do all your BD planning or follow-up. The fact is that you are doing business development every day when engaging in client conversations. It's about adjusting your approach just a couple of degrees.

And, it's not about what you want to say. It's about what the client wants or needs to hear. Attorneys are slowly becoming more comfortable with that. For example, I might be very excited to talk to you about the five recent appeals from our highest court, and yet, what the client will value is hearing the impact on their business of some of those decisions. They couldn't care less, typically, about the appeal, or the fact that I spent hours on it and was successful in my own right. They say, "Well, so what?"

Some of the consultants will say, "Well, it's not the Golden Rule we need to follow, it's the Platinum Rule which means thinking of what the client wants or needs." And that is the key to success; and then do it in an economic, timely manner. That is how to build the client relationship. So, that's underlying our messages in the various activities. We believe that's what will make attorneys effective as they come up the ranks, not just in BD, but in terms of their career; and they'll have a lot more fun.

Client Development That Leads to Business Development: The Umbrella Approach

(Karen Bell)

When asked to speak about the integration of client development and business development, I tell people about my umbrella metaphor.

How do I stay client focused and client centric in order to best facilitate client development? It's my umbrella. One spoke on my umbrella is classic business development: relationship building, profile building, relationship management, pitching, sales, sales pipeline, client loyalty, all that. Then, there's business acumen: business intelligence that makes you savvy to the world of your clients, their business or businesses, the world that they live in.

Communication is another spoke. Your analysis and insights need to come out in an articulate, compelling fashion. We all talk about, "Let's become trusted advisors," and absolutely, that's the end goal. I just say, "It's something we earn. It's not something that we can buy." You can have training around, or discussion around how to earn trust, but it's the client's to give—to place trust in you. It's not something you can take for granted. It's your behavior that then delivers or fosters in the client a sense of trust.

Client Development: Getting Into Their World Using 70/30

(Hans Haglund)

You must understand your buyer. Here's what used to be typical at law firms when meeting with prospective clients. If there was three people from the client, the law firm will bring 8 to 12 partners who will try to cover everything that the law firm does within that hour conversation. Today it's different, and it goes back to those big themes, the importance of getting into the client's world. Ask about what the general counsel cares about and uncover their most important issues. The initial phase of your meeting is a consultative approach where you start to understand their world. On a tactical level, we tell our lawyers the client should talk 70% of the time, we talk 30%. It should never be flipped. The firm's lawyers need to be the ones that are getting the information, finding out how the client works, how they operate, and their goals and objectives. We can only help after we know all the issues, objectives, and goals. Rainmakers understand that.

Client Development: Learning from Australia and the United Kingdom

(Louise Muldoon)

Australia is a very competitive market in which there is a limited client base. Accordingly, leading edge practices for client development and client management have evolved because of that environment. I continue to be impressed by what comes out of Australia. I feel very fortunate to have spent the amount of time there that I did. It's not that they've got all the answers, but I believe the more competitive the legal market becomes, the more pressure there's going to be to develop new and different ways of engaging with your client base. It's a trend in the world of business development and when you review what we do today compared to five years from now, the landscape will look quite different.

We believe that, as a firm, we are ahead of the curve. Currently I'm focusing on a couple of initiatives that I believe will keep us slightly ahead of that curve. We were the first firm to see the potential of a globalized economy, and a globalized law firm. This way of thinking very much feeds into our culture in the area of business development. We're always looking at business development and saying, "How can we be better? How can we be more innovative? How can we see around the corner? What is it that our clients are really looking for?" We note that what our clients are really looking for is continually evolving and, so, we're trying to stay on top of their desires. For example, look at the area of client feedback, which is incredibly well-developed in Australia, and in London, and which is just starting to really get a head of steam in the U.S. While there are firms doing it, it's not something that's just part and parcel of what law firms do. That exercise of engaging clients, talking to them, asking them, "How are we doing?" Systematically doing that on an institutional level and taking those findings, feeding them back into how you're delivering legal services, how you're responding to what your clients need, is very important. And we're very focused on that as a business. I know there are very good lawyers and law firms right across the spectrum in the U.S. that are doing that, but I believe it will become a more universal approach.

Client Education: A Relationship and Business Development Program

(Karen Bell)

One of the other things I'm responsible for is education for our clients and we see that as a very important business development opportunity. We want to do more in this regard than simply deliver a one off CLE. We work to position ourselves as the experts—as the firm with the connections and with the practical or innovative solutions. Our lawyers have therefore become quite good at saying, "Okay. In terms of expanding the business, we want to put a spotlight on this particular area." It might be something in M&A. It might be something in products. It might be something in privacy, or, it might be on a new piece of legislation being enacted. We use video-streamed webinars to deliver the information, with the idea that it should be strategically aligned with the plan for that product or that industry – and demonstrate some kind of expertise on our part. Or, we might have regulators or other key players in the industry involved in a panel discussion so that our audience is getting access to very credible, hard-to-reach resources. We might focus on some new solution and innovation in a particular area. The whole point is, you're sharing insight, so to that end, it's a very important business development tool—not necessarily used in every case with every initiative, but when it can really deliver the results we are looking for. It's part of that value add and everyone's being asked now, by clients, to articulate the value for what we're charging. Because we develop those seminars very strategically, it works for both sides, our attorneys and our clients.

Client Feedback Surveys Can Increase Revenue

(Sally Schmidt)

Once a firm identifies its top 10 clients, I recommend implementing a client feedback process where somebody goes out and talks to them and says, "What do you think of the firm? Are there other opportunities? Is there anything the firm could be doing for you that it's not?" My guess is, over time, 50 percent of those interviews result in new business, so that, to me, would be job one.

Client Feedback: Best Practices

(Louise Muldoon)

When speaking of the frequency of client feedback, most of our attorneys would say, "I get feedback from my clients all the time." And, they do. We have some very, very talented lawyers that are incredibly close to their clients, understand what their client's strategies are, understand the machinations of the client's board, how the board approaches the company's business, and understand where the organization is headed. We have some classic rainmakers here that are very, very good at what they do. They live and breathe their clients' businesses. They're incredibly responsive. They give great legal advice. They're fantastic. In an organization that's promoting quality,

I think most of our lawyers would say, "Yeah, I talk pretty regularly with my clients." However, what I'm talking about is an institutional approach to client relationships that says, "We're not going to otherwise impact your client relationship, but what we'd like to do is talk to your clients on an institutional level and ensure that from an independent point of view, we're doing everything your client needs us to do. We don't want to do anything to interrupt your relationship, Lawyer X, but we know from both the work that we've done in the area and, generally, from research, that a client will likely talk in a more frank and open way if they're not talking directly to the person who delivers the work on a day-to-day basis." It's human nature, really, and I always say, "It's a very human business" and the decision to buy legal services is, fundamentally, a very human one.

We like to make sure that we're checking client satisfaction at an institutional level. You asked me how often we get involved in that. "As often as we can," is the answer. With our most significant clients—we talk to them very regularly. With all our other clients, we talk to them as often as we can. We also talk to them if we're doing a piece of work for them. So, if there's a particular matter that we have worked on, at the end of that matter, or deal, or transaction, or dispute, or whatever it might be, we have a mechanism whereby somebody independently calls the client up and asks, "How did we do?" Another thing we are doing is that rather than wait until the end of the work, we now call clients midway through and ask on an independent basis, "Are you getting everything you need?"

I have certainly spent a lot of time talking to lawyers about that exercise, and the way I describe it is as, "an exercise in business intelligence." It's an exercise in what are our clients thinking about. What were they trying to achieve when they engaged us, and did we help them to achieve that? What organizational influences have come into play with this particular project, and can we respond to that? And can we deliver in a more effective way moving forward? It's really getting business intelligence from the client and then responding to that information on a case-by-case basis in a way that improves our client service. You then take that business intelligence and ask, "What is that information actually delivering to us in terms of themes and trends and issues in the aggregate?" How do we use that intelligence and distill it into key areas that we can then take to our lawyers and help them respond more effectively to their clients' requirements? We can then be much more responsive, and comprehend what's around the corner. So, bringing it back to the topic of business development, I say to everyone in the business development team, "This is a business and we're here to build a business and we need as much business intelligence as we can get about our client's wishes to make sure that as a business, we're responding to them."

You are correct when you say that we select our wording and phraseology very deliberately to optimally engage our lawyers. We refer to our client feedback process as gathering business intelligence, not selling or marketing. As business development professionals—and I say this having sometimes been skeptical when I was in practice—we've got to add value to the business and provide the business with professional advice. I feel that in order to provide professional advice, we have to speak in a language that lawyers will understand and will respond to. As a lawyer, if someone talks to me about business intelligence, I'm going to be instantly interested in that. It takes the exercise of getting clients' feedback from beyond a "let's check the box" exercise, to "this is going to have an impact on your business and it's going to actually affect the way in which you conduct your business moving forward." And, when you put it in those terms, lawyers respond. I think any individual would respond to it, frankly. I don't know that lawyers are the breed apart that everybody likes to say they are.

You're talking about—and this is something I always feel strongly about—people who are under enormous pressure, who every minute of the day have client demands. These individuals have the pressure of giving accurate legal advice, and the pressure of having looked at every aspect that might affect the way in which they respond to the client's issue. They need to keep on top of some fast-developing areas of law, and while trying to do all of that, need to work on business development skills and being business people. I think if you're going to be an effective business development professional, you've got to give the lawyers things they can take and use in the most effective and efficient manner possible. Or, putting this in another way, I see every single lawyer in this whole organization as my client and I want to give them the same value I tell them they've got to give to their clients.

> I see every single lawyer in this whole organization as my client and I want to give them the same value I tell them they've got to give to their clients.
>
> —*Louise Muldoon*

In response to your question about who actually conducts these client interviews, whether an outside service or members of the firm, the answer is the latter. That's not to say our clients aren't approached by third-party agencies that look at similar issues. Acritas is one of them. They measure law firm brands based on a variety of metrics, including name recognition. But they also look at areas like client service, delivery of services, and brand quality. And they use all of those metrics collectively to work out which are the best law firm brands. I'm happy to say that globally, they rank us number one. When it comes to research compilation, they have people that do nothing but interview clients, gauge client satisfaction, and monitor client perception for the brand.

Again, we're very structured about conducting client interviews. We've thought about questions in advance, but our people are all trained to go in there in what I call a "spirit of open inquiry" and try to find out, genuinely, how we're doing, but in a very structured way. We run training programs, and we have trained some of our most senior partners who then interview clients, with whom they've had no previous contact. This is all done under the umbrella of business development and it's just one part of a full spectrum of business development activities. So, as an example, for some of our really significant clients our Global Chairman, Eduardo Leite, will visit those clients pretty regularly.

Client Intelligence: Useful Information: Lower Billing Rate Increased Revenue

(Erin Meszaros)

I'll tell you something that I think is interesting that I'm not sure a lot of folks are focused on—and this drives back to where I talked about needing to be a good leader to be able to be a good rainmaker— the financial aspect of the practice. They need to focus on leveraging from the pricing aspect. It's very important that they understand how to be efficient and push the cost of the legal work down.

One of the things the executive director and I have been doing, is going and meeting with folks, and instead of having a business development meeting where all I do is talk about targets, how are we going to go after them, what are we going to look at, what resources do you need, what support do you need, are you tracking your efforts and the like, he and I will go in with a more collaborative approach to say, "Let's look at this holistically. Let's look at all aspects of the client interface from A to Z, from the time you identify the target, to the closing of the sale, to how you will manage the matter you have been hired to handle. It has made a difference to incorporate on the front end the discussion to include the financial metrics of how you will "manage" the matter in addition to how you will bring it in the door.

It's been really interesting to watch these discussions evolve and to determine the appropriate approach. I had an attorney on the East Coast who came to me and said, "I get all the high dollar work on litigation for a particular client, but I want the day-to-day work as well." I then asked, "Have you asked the client whom he or she uses for that day-to-day work?" During his next contact with the client he decided to ask to which the client replied, "Well, I don't use you because I didn't think it was the kind of work you would want to do." This opened the door to a discussion with the client regarding why it might be more efficient for our firm to do the high dollar and the day-to-day work. If you can provide the right platform and leverage without sacrificing value and client service, it seems that would be most beneficial to the client.

Client Interviews: Another Way to Develop Business

(Erin Meszaros)

Client interviews are another great way to develop business. The best resource for more business is a happy, current client. Making sure your clients are secure is the best thing you can do. The client interview process allows you the opportunity to check-in and make sure you are providing superior service. Checking in also keeps you top of mind, so when that next new matter comes in the door you may be lucky enough to have just had your client meeting, and, voilà you are even luckier as you are the call they make to work on that new matter. We don't go in with the attitude that the client interviews are done to obtain new work, but by making sure we are handling the work we currently have to their satisfaction and exceeding their expectations, it may just put us a rung above the other firms they use who don't check in.

Client Magnet: Become a Client Magnet with Your Connections and Information

(Karen Bell)

It's possible to become a client magnet by having connections and information that clients want.

It's great for our business when clients say, "We have to work with you because you've got all the great connections."

Our message to clients is, "We want to understand your business and part of our rationale behind that is not only to be better strategic partners, but to share connections that can bring you business or support in some way."

Our program mantra is, "Your Partner in Your Development," and development is used very broadly. Our job is to make our clients' jobs easier, to provide more innovative solutions, and to help them answer their challenges. If it's a connection they need—the dialogue with the regulator or a financier—or, if it's turning a typical litigation process around to make it work for the client and not just be a process, but a strategic tool . . . we're very focused on presenting our clients with these types of innovative solutions. Our market leaders are out there speaking to our clients, as others are on our team, about what innovation can mean for the client when they're trying to solve a problem—and not necessarily a legal one—or they're searching for an opportunity; and we come along and certainly have the legal expertise, but also bring along some innovation to the whole approach, so that it ends up being both a legal and a business solution.

What I'm saying is that when our firm's attorneys have a conversation with a client, part of the goal is for the attorney to expand the client's thinking process . . . to understand we're coming in not just as legal advisors, but also are able to assist more broadly from a strategic standpoint.

The client has business issues. Some of them are complex; some of them are exciting. And, our attitude is we're there to make things happen – either make the problems go away or help them realize the opportunities. And in order to do it in a cost-effective and timely manner, you have got to do things differently. So, we're spending a lot of time looking at how we can do things differently. It starts with listening to the client a lot – perhaps a lot more than attorneys have been accustomed to, because client expectations have changed.

Client Magnet: Ways We Keep Our Clients Stuck to Us

(Karen Bell)

One way we make ourselves attractive to clients is to offer free education programs to all in-house counsel, their legal team, and the C-Suite. We put a "Seminars" tab on our website home page where we list them. [See also *Website: Home Page as Magnet*.]

Client Meeting: Initial Meeting: Old Versus New Approach

(David King Keller)

The old paradigm for the first client meeting was to have three to twelve firm partners meet with a GC and two assistant GCs and the law firm partners spent between 80 to 95 percent of the hour discussing firm capabilities.

The new paradigm is for the firm to send to that initial meeting only enough partners needed to achieve a 1:1 match of the number of in-house counsel staff attending, listen 70 to 80 percent of the time, and ask probing questions that reveal the company's operations, goals, opportunities, challenges, legal needs, and latent legal needs. The genuineness and quality of the law firm attorney questions reveal the expertise of the attorneys and the firm. Law firm attorneys are familiar with the Stanford University research on a fairly quick trust building technique (see "Trust Building").

The future Paradigm? Two senior partners accompanied by a veteran sales executive listen 70 to 80 percent of the time, and ask open-ended and closed questions sufficient to supplement the extensive research done prior to the meeting for the purpose of taking a holistic approach to the company, its decision makers and its decision influencers. [See "holistic" in Index.]

Client Meetings: Annual Off-the-Clock Meetings

(Despina Kartson)

Schedule annual review meetings with clients—off-the-clock—for the purpose of listening to them. Don't go in and *talk to them*, but go in with the purpose of *listening to them*. What are their key business challenges? What are their priorities for the coming year? What's on their strategic plan? Ask "How has our firm done from a client service perspective? Are there any ways in which we can help you? Is there any added value that we can offer to make your life better?" Schedule an annual discussion with your clients solely for the purpose of listening to them. Find an easy and convenient time for the client . . . whether it's a lunch or a coffee or drinks, whatever works for that particular client personality. Some firms have "client listening programs."

Client Professional Development: A Value Add That Sets Us Apart

(Karen Bell)

We call it our Client CPD program, i.e. Client Continuing Professional Development, and it is delivered under our McCarthy Tétrault *Advance* ™ platform. If you're on our website, just go to the "Seminars" tab on the home page. In brief, what we say to clients on that page is that we are their partner in their continuing professional development and that they are our top priority. We are committed to advancing their professional knowledge, growth, and development, and will ensure that they meet all of their continuing professional development (CPD) needs. Through our platform we deliver a variety of programs in each of our offices in the form of seminars, meetings and talks about timely topics, led by our attorneys, as well as industry experts. We regard our clients as partners in this endeavor, learning together and learning from each other.

Our seminars include content that provide all clients who are attorneys with the credit hours required for CPD requirements under the various regional regimes governing lawyers in Canada.

It's very much about being in partnership with our clients. It's one of a number of value adds that we provide, and our clients tell us it's very important and very valuable to them.

Client Prospecting: How to Select Appropriate Targets: Fishing Hole Concept

(Steve Bell)

Fish where you've already been successful. Rainmakers target their audience and find a way to engineer a meeting with that audience. Your best prospective client is a company that somehow closely resembles an existing client with whom you have a fabulous relationship. Rainmakers know how to select targets that are appropriate, prospective clients that are more likely to end up as clients than not. They get to the right fishing hole. All of this should be terribly simple, but when it plays out it turns out to be more complex for many. What are the characteristics of your current fantastic client relationships? For example, you have a close relationship with the buyer, the technical content is the same, the company has the same capital structure, etc. Find more companies like that, and you may have found your fishing hole.

> Your best prospective client is a company that closely resembles an existing client with whom you have a fabulous relationship.
>
> —*Steve Bell*

Client Service: Assessment First, Pitch Later

(Mark Usellis)

For any relationship, a lawyer needs to have the mindset of—and this is why needs assessment is so important—I want to understand what's going on in my client's business and what the related legal needs are, and then think about, "How can I help them?"

Client Service: Assessment Programs: Internally Sourced and External

(David King Keller)

Michael Rynowecer of BTI Consulting is recognized worldwide as one of the leading client service analysts. He can conduct an external client service audit or help a firm set up their own internal client assessment program.

Client Service: Everything, Everything, Everything Comes Back to This

(Steve Bell)

In my opinion and based on research by BTI Consulting, four client service attributes really distinguish law firms and individual lawyers: they understand the client's business, they demonstrate commitment to the client's success, they deliver value for the dollar, and they exhibit tremendous focus on the client and its needs. Lawyers who put these attributes to work for clients perpetually end up in the top of client-service ranking lists. When lawyers focus these same attributes on prospective clients, they end up with a lot of new clients.

Client Service: Resource: Michael Rynowecer of BTI Consulting

Client Service: Website Home Page Says it All

(Hans Haglund)

This message on our website says it all, "At Blank Rome, we see the world through our clients' eyes."

Client Teams

(Karen Bell)

Our firm has a history of innovation. We were the first in Canada to be a national firm. We also were one of the first with a structured client-team approach across the firm. We link innovation, service delivery, efficiency and excellence. We put ourselves in our client's shoes and work with them as a business partner.

Each client faces different challenges and requires unique solutions. Our client-focused solutions are built using project management, alternative fee and creative staffing arrangements, and process re-engineering.

We have national market leader roles (Leader of Markets and Chief Client Officer) and client-team relationship partners. This framework creates opportunities to expand the client relationships and make sure we have good succession planning. This is our plan that we're working on now. You can see that it's coming together. It's very exciting, but there's still lots to be done and, as I said, one of the fun things I get to do is work with our leaders to identify the skills they need and how best to develop them. So, whether that's leading teams on working together, leading teams on planning, and leading teams on plan execution—those are the things that we're looking at.

And, when I say teams, I am referring to client teams as well as industry groups or industry teams.

We organize ourselves internally as practice groups. We have five main practice groups and multiple subgroups. For example, we have a litigation practice group that subsumes subgroups like environmental and intellectual property. For marketing purposes, we are trying to move, as other law firms are, to a more solution-based model. While we may not sell litigation, we can sell a product around it. It might be a focus on privilege or it might be a focus on e-discovery. Taking a page from the accountant's book 20 years ago, the idea is to sell by industry and then more micro-level by client.

Client Teams: Make Sure the Client Is on the Client Team!

(David King Keller)

If you set up a Client Team, which is recommended for every major client, be sure to include a representative of the client on the team.

Client: A Client Is Really an Individual

(Steve Bell)

A client is an individual. A client is not a corporate entity. It seems the great rainmakers have a passion for understanding what's driving and motivating these individual buyers.

Clients: How to Make a Client a Raving Fan

(Karen Bell)

If you want to turn a client into a raving fan, don't overlook the possibility that you can bring the client business and grow their bottom line while, at the same time, turning the attorney who made the introduction into a real hero in the client's eyes.

We also use our economic acumen, industry knowledge, and contacts, and when we can, we show our clients ways to cut costs or build in more predictability. That is appealing to their CFO and lays the groundwork for the CFO and our contacts there to go from satisfied client to raving fan.

We have clients whom other clients want to meet. Absolutely, we will make those introductions.

People ask me, "How do we go about taking actions that can benefit our client's business strategies other than through our legal services?" One way is through our Client Continuing Professional Development program, Client CPD for short.

Our whole commitment to professional development at our firm is delivered under our platform McCarthy Tétrault *Advance*™. We have a French version of that, as well. The larger part of that is capabilities development of our students, our lawyers, and our paraprofessionals across the country; and part of it is for our clients, which is the Client CPD program I just referenced. And, by having all these different clients come together there's a common interest because they're all in the room wanting to hear about this particular topic or problem or opportunity. We hold meetings where we do a number of other kinds of activities that allow for clients to meet on a more social basis, as well as gatherings focused on personal development and professional development. So that's certainly an opportunity. And then, partners will put clients in touch with each other in certain practices that lend themselves to that.

Clients: Key Client Program

(Despina Kartson)

Develop a strong *key client program*. Identify the criteria that the firm is comfortable using, consider who the key clients are that you want to focus on in the coming year, and then build teams around those clients. It's important from a client relations perspective, but it's also important from a business development perspective. Effort should be spent cultivating and expanding existing client relationships.

Coach: External: Absolutely Essential to Optimizing Success

(David King Keller)

In addition to the firm's internal business development support team, it may not be as obvious to the average managing partner, that you also need a very skilled outside coach who complements the inside business development team which may also include a trained inside coach. For optimal results and more ecologically complete coverage, you must have someone outside the four walls. Let me explain.

Using an outside coach has many benefits. One, the coachee, the attorney being coached, knows that this outside coach is not part of his or her internal political life. It offers the advantage of confidentiality without the fear of being misinterpreted internally with the attorney-coachee suffering potential negative blowback to his or her career. The outside coach – coachee relationship allows the attorney being coached to make mistakes, to stumble, to have incomplete thoughts . . . in other words to be more of a person and less of a public persona, and converse without fear of negative impact on one's public and political stature within the firm's internal culture.

The coaching environment, a good coaching environment, allows the attorney to explore ideas, not to be the one in the room with all the answers, allows the attorney to ask really dumb questions, and allows the attorney to bring up very personal matters that may be seriously impacting his or her work but that he or she could never, would never, mention to anyone at the firm, not even a partner-mentor.

The outside coach does not replace the inside business development team but complements that team. The inside team knows about firm strategies and politics that the outside coach can never fully know about. Yet the outside coach brings an environment of strict confidentiality that the inside coach can never really offer. Yes, a great inside coach can offer confidential conversations but in the back of the mind of the attorney-coachee will know that whatever he or she says to someone in an administrative role at the firm may have conscious or subconscious negative blowback at some point down the road. Experience shows that the best rainmaker training includes both internal and external coaching environments.

It should be noted that there are many different kinds of external coaches. There are those that have purely and strictly business development training and that's fine . . . up to a point. The best external coaches also have life coaching skills, certified, bona fide life coaching skills. These are coaches that have been trained to pick up on nuances of internal belief patterns that are consciously or unconsciously impacting the career of the attorney. A business development coach with excellent life coaching credentials may be in a better position that a firm staff member to discern when a "personal" issue may require professional help, e.g., psychological, psychiatric and/or medical help.

It is not hard to understand that only in a very confidential environment which is external to the law firm environment would an attorney discuss certain aspects of stress, anxiety, and/or depression. All of these could impact and probably are impacting their career and their business development opportunities. Every law firm professional knows how stressful being an attorney is, and that this stress can lead to a high level of anxiety, and that stress and anxiety can lead to depression. Probably the highest return on investment that a law firm can make is one where a skilled external coach is able to reduce the level of stress of a highly skilled attorney.

Yes, every law firm has a good medical program and that a stressed or depressed attorney can easily avail themselves of that medical resource, but there are two symptoms that work against that avenue: one, the attorney is just too damn busy and too distracted by work to set up medical or psychological appointments; and two, it is very important to keep in mind that one symptom of advanced depression is that there can be a cognitive inability to self-prescribe a visit to a medical health care professional. In other words, a depressed attorney may not actually be neurologically in a very good condition to diagnose him or herself and make that call to secure medical attention, but in the confidential environment with a skilled business development coach that has certified life coaching skills may be able to gently yet persuasively explain the hazards and dangers of the attorney's current course of action and could gently yet persuasively steer them toward making that professional medical support contact and also provide the follow-up accountability to make sure that it has been done. Certified life coaches cannot dispense medical advice, but they are in a position to recommend a visit to someone who can.

External coaching occurs outside the very complex political environment within the firm culture. So as part of your interview of an external coach ask yourself what are the range of skills that you really want to bring to your firm's attorneys. Some external coaches have an excellent business development program where all the blanks are filled in on the attorneys activities that need to be accomplished to move their business development forward and to hold those regular accountability discussions to make sure those are taking place, but do they have work-life balance and executive life coaching skills that go beyond just knowing how to structure and follow-up on a good business development plan. Do they have the training that allows them to discern nuances of speech behavior, language patterns, vocabulary usage, and the required empathetic skills that allow them to listen very deeply and to determine when some aspects of the attorney's personal life, mental state, and/or physiological life may need additional professional support and the persuasive skill sets to effectively steer the attorney in the right direction.

Wearing the business development and work-life balance hat is a lot to ask of an external coach and yet the external coach is the one person that the attorney may actually open up to, given that that person has the skill sets to engage in that type of conversation without ever overstepping any ethical boundary and never giving medical advice. And yet, can be that one person that provides insight into what additional support that attorney needs and can point him or her in that direction and can actually track it on a very personal and confidential basis to hold that attorney accountable to that follow-up action.

Coaches: Advice from Google's CEO

(David King Keller)

Google CEO Eric Schmidt shared that some of the best advice he ever got is to have a coach.

Eric Schmidt, CEO of Google, was asked in a Fortune TV interview, "What was the best advice you ever received?" Schmidt said, "Well, I've received lots of advice. One that comes to mind is to have a coach. Every famous athlete, every famous performer has somebody who's a coach. Somebody who can watch what they're doing and say, "Is that what you really meant?' They can give them perspective. But one thing that people are never good at is seeing themselves as others see them. The coaching really, really helps." [See Chapter 3, *Don't Ignore Eric Schmidt's Advice*, for the expanded quote and more details from this recorded interview, along with the YouTube URL link.]

Coaches: Outside Coaches

(Melanie Green)

For the sales training we have to pick a little bit on who we're going to invest additional time in with the expectation that everybody has to play some role. But where we have identified those, who we think fit that criteria, we've done more customized one-on-one—or it's a smaller group. Say we pick 15 to go through a program. And in that program we have sessions that they all go through together, but then it's one-on-one coaching with an outside coach for a 12 to 24-month period depending on the program._

We used three outside coaches from different places, and we aligned—we matched those to the personalities of the lawyers by what we knew and the style of the coach.

Following the merger, we're getting back to some common language. But trying to come up with that Faegre Baker Daniels way of talking about it, and then working with outside coaches to use their coaching styles, techniques, but using the Faegre Baker Daniels language.

And how many sales funnels or cycles have we seen that have the same five steps but all worded differently?

Coaching Objection: It Just Didn't Work

(Silvia Coulter)

A firm will say, "Yeah, we hired those guys, and it was an okay program, but nothing really happened as a result of it." Well, nothing really happened because you've got to go to the gym every day and do all the sit-ups, and do all the leg lifts, and all the other exercises your gym trainer taught you. It's the same thing with sales. You've got to flex your sales muscles or else you're not really conducting sales. At some point you have to ask for business. At some point you've got to close the deal just like you would in a trial. You've got to ask the jury to vote for you.

They've got to use their new business development and sales and marketing strategies for a while before they can become habits. Sometimes we've talked for three months to the same lawyer about connecting with a few people that we've identified as reasonable potential clients. Pick two people, and let's put this into action by calling them. I've sat in rooms where I've said let's pick up the phone right now. Most people don't really want to do that. Once in a while they will. You've got to make something happen here. What's standing in the way? Wait for a clear honest answer, then address it. I had someone say to me the other day . . . I said, "How did it go?" He said, "This was so easy. I am so over being worried about this."

Coaching: A Blend of Approaches

(Erin Meszaros)

At my last firm I did have a very formal coaching program for the lawyers. Currently we have internal coaching from my team on a 1:1 basis as needed or requested. In addition, a number of attorneys are using external individual coaches that they have hired. Coaching is a great resource for the attorneys whether it be from my team or someone else.

Coaching: Business Development Mindset Must Come from the Top

(Despina Kartson)

In order for coaching to be effective, there should be a firm-wide commitment and it needs to come from the top. If the approach is one-off where you are going to coach a few partners, and it doesn't have the rubber stamp and the full endorsement of the leadership of the firm, it will not be given as serious consideration as it should be.

The concept of building a business development culture across the firm and for individual lawyers has to be something that is embraced at the top levels of the firm. If you have commitment from the senior leadership of the firm, then the resources will be made available, whether it's time, personnel or financial resources.

Coaching: External versus Internal

(Despina Kartson)

The best approach is a hybrid one – use of both external and internal coaches. Business development coaching using external consultants is very effective for a number of reasons: they're truly the experts, this is what they do for a living, so they have lots of experience. They've coached numerous individuals. Also, every coach has his or her own particular approach or methodology.

External coaching may not—depending on the size of the firm and the results that the firm wants to achieve—be sustainable if you have 500 or 1,000 or more lawyers that you want to coach.

The next approach is internal coaching. This has a lot of viability because it is sustainable. If you develop a core group of senior professionals within the firm's BD team who can work with lawyers on an internal consultative and coaching approach, it's sustainable. You maintain both the institutional knowledge, as well as the technique within the firm.

I've developed a train-the-trainer program, working with external coaches who train your internal professionals on coaching, and this is the best of both worlds. You are trained by the experts and can develop an internal, sustainable program.

Coaching: Internal

(Allen Chichester)

Every business development manager here is a coach and that is their highest and best purpose. *Yes,* we chase competitive intelligence information, yes, we chase events formation and conceptualization, yes we chase RFPs and pitch support, but our highest calling is when we get into an office of a partner and we help them take the next step in business development, whatever that it is, and then we come back in a couple of weeks and we talk to them again about what happened as a result and where they go next.

From where I sit in this organization, nothing we have done has been more effective than that, because success breeds success and once you can help show a partner how a diligent application-a disciplined approach where they spend some time every day or every week on the process of networking and qualifying referral sources and clients-a permanent change takes place. When it starts to get done and they start seeing results, they keep doing it; they truly change their behavior and it's a beautiful thing.

Calendaring business development time as part of the coaching process, we think, is one of those things that has direct positive results. Bringing the actual practice of business development into the lawyer's experience, making it a part of their calendar, that's the key.

Coaching: Summary Research on Five Firms, 26 to 1,000 Attorneys in Size

(Karie Trujillo)

As the marketing director at Markowitz Herbold PC in Portland, Oregon, I wanted to better understand how others were coaching attorneys into being rainmakers. So, I reached out to five of my colleagues at four other law firms. Here is a brief summary of my research, which was published by the ABA in their online publication called *The Practice Today* on November 17, 2014 under the title, *With Attorney Coaching Programs, One Size Does Not Fit All.*

In 2006, my firm was a 13-attorney boutique commercial litigation firm in Portland, Oregon. More than 80 percent of our revenue was generated by David Markowitz, the firm's cofounder. It became clear that this model was unsustainable. Dave would eventually retire and without his rainmaking abilities, the future of the firm was in question. Leadership realized it was crucial for other attorneys in the firm to cultivate rainmaking skills. The goal was to eventually get to a point where Dave originated 20 percent or less of the firm's revenue, without reducing the amount he generated.

Dave, one of the most prolific rainmakers in Oregon, created an attorney coaching program that has since changed the trajectory of the firm. Now, eight years later, the firm has reached its goal, with Dave generating 20 percent of revenues, while the dollar amount of revenue he generates has increased, not declined. Our firm has grown to 26 attorneys, and the firm now has a rainmaking culture that encourages all of our attorneys, from junior associates to senior partners, to participate in business development activities.

The program, outlined below, works well for our firm. However, many other types of law firm coaching programs are available. I have spoken with several of my fellow marketing colleagues at firms of various sizes who have robust coaching programs. The scope and approach of their programs vary, but all agree that they have made a significant difference in their firms' bottom line.

<u>Markowitz Herbold PC has about 26 Attorneys.</u>

The Markowitz program is simple. All attorneys in the firm are invited to participate; however, participation is not mandatory. Currently, all associates and most shareholders are in the program. Every three months, individual attorneys meet with Dave and me. Each attorney in the program is required to have a marketing plan. During the meetings, we discuss how the attorney's marketing activities are going and what we can do to help. Dave offers advice, gives guidance, and encouragement. Attorneys commit to action items based on their plan. My role is to take away barriers and excuses for not following through with their action items. For example, if they agree to write an article, I help pitch the article to the publication and run interference with the editor.

It's simple, but it works. We have found that origination for an attorney in the program typically doubles after two to three years in the program.

<u>Ungaretti & Harris has about 110 Attorneys.</u>

Mark Karkazis, Director of Marketing at Ungaretti & Harris, said his firm started to offer coaching eight years ago because leadership recognized the benefit of giving attorneys direct guidance from an experienced sales professional. Mark, who has a sales background, serves as the program's coach. Any attorney who wants coaching can participate. Attorneys of all levels work with Mark regularly, or as needed, to get advice on specific situations such as how to get their first matter from a prospect, how to network, or how to prioritize opportunities. This type of situational coaching has enhanced the sales culture within the firm and has been helpful to attorneys in generating business. The back story to this program is that we started with a more structured model, with limited participants, regular reporting, metrics, etc. But that was out of alignment with the culture of the firm, which gives individual attorneys a lot of autonomy. Maintaining the structure of the program started absorbing time that should have been used for actual coaching. So I ended the formal program and just started coaching on whatever basis individual lawyers wanted. That has ended up working very well here.

<u>Greenberg Glusker has about 87 Attorneys.</u>

Jonathan Fitzgarrald, Chief Marketing Officer at Greenberg Glusker, told me that his firm started its program three-and-half years ago when firm revenues were declining due to the recession. Firm leadership felt that developing rainmakers was vital to their ongoing success.

Among the firm's business development initiatives is an annual program called the Rainmakers Roundtable. Composed of 10 of the firm's top revenue generators, the group meets once a month for 10 months. At each meeting, one of the 10 attorneys presents on their practice (practice overview, how they have historically attracted clients, typical referral sources, etc.), as well as on plans for future growth. The other attorney participants then provide feedback and ideas for generating additional revenue, like introductions to their contacts and ways for cross-selling the firm's services. When time permits, the group also will engage in a spirited discussion surrounding a business development topic, like overcoming obstacles or closing. Jonathan reports that attorneys in the program have increased their productivity by 20 percent or more.

Bryan Cave LLP has about 1,000 Attorneys.

When Steve Sunshine, a senior partner in the Irvine office, was in his late 30s, he realized that all rainmakers had certain characteristics and behaviors that made them good at what they do. He talked with rainmakers inside and outside the firm to learn what made them successful. Implementing what he learned, Steve saw his origination increase. Over the years, others recognized his success, and attorneys started coming to him for advice. Seven years ago he decided to share what he'd learned, and created the firm's Coaching the Coaches program.

According to senior marketing and business development manager Tom Helm, Coaching the Coaches teaches people to ask the right questions, truly listen, build relationships, and genuinely care about others.

The program is based upon three pillars: Authenticity, Seeds, and Scanning for the Gap. Authenticity is being oneself all day, every day, a consistent characteristic of rainmakers. Seeds are "deep meaningful relationships" that rainmakers develop with others, not for the purpose of bringing in business, but for their own fulfillment. Scanning for the Gap involves rainmakers thoughtfully engaging with potential clients who may need the rainmakers' services.

More than 800 attorneys have participated in Coaching the Coaches. Participants advance through the 12-month program via monthly one-hour calls with Steve and other partners who are graduates of the program and demonstrated rainmakers. A different "lesson" is presented each month, and homework is assigned for the next meeting. Participants are required to actively participate on the calls by sharing success stories and what they learned from the previous lesson. These participants or "coaches" are required to take what they have learned and share it with another attorney in a one-on-one session throughout the 12-month program.

Murphy Pearson Bradley & Feeney has about 46 Attorneys.

Clare Ota, marketing director at Murphy Pearson, said her firm needed to build its attorneys' business development skills and opted to hire Practice Boomers, an attorney coaching and training company, to implement its program. Clare says that Murphy Pearson started the Practice Boomers program about six months ago. Participants in the nine-month program include

10 junior partners and three senior associates. Practice Boomers has developed a series of business and practice development-focused video modules designed specifically for attorneys.

Before the coaching meetings, attorneys watch a series of videos, most of them only five minutes in length. During the bi-monthly meetings, participants discuss the lessons from that particular module. Topics include how to build business development routines into your day, how to set achievable goals for your practice, how to differentiate yourself from your competitors, and how to develop productive referral sources, to name a few.

Clare said that the firm has seen immediate results in the six months since starting the program. Participants are actively engaged in business development and are enthusiastic about rainmaking.

Jonathan put it quite succinctly. "If a firm is serious about moving the needle forward, they should consider implementing an attorney coaching program."

Successful coaching programs require buy-in from firm leadership, committed participants, an investment in resources (both money and time), and a focus on execution. The bottom line is this: If you want to increase rainmaking efforts in your firm and create a sales culture that will develop the next generation of rainmakers, you should consider implementing a coaching program that is tailored to meet the needs of your firm. [Article reprint by permission.]

Coaching: The Johnson Technique: "Getting Started," Part 1

(Peter Johnson)

We don't provide coaching in a vacuum. We provide coaching in the context of the law firm. Every law firm has a personality. Every law firm has a culture.

Our responsibility is to assist the attorney in the context of the law firm's business development culture. The way we work, not surprisingly, is the same way the firm's successful lawyers work when they spend considerable time doing research on projects. We all know that he or she who's the most prepared and has done the most research, generally, is the most successful.

The way we approach our coaching assignments is the same. We get as much information as we can about the firm, about goals and objectives, about measurements and rewards, about any obstacles that may get in the way of business development. We do that before we even meet or speak with the individuals with whom we may be working.

We've been doing coaching for about 14 years, and the process has been iterative. Experience tells us that we have a system and a program that works. We also think that there are other coaches and coaching consultants that have systems that are different from ours and they also work. The good news is that there are so many firms that are now providing attorneys with coaching that there is a large number of programs available. They'll find a coach or a coaching program that's compatible with their needs, their philosophies, etc. That's what we've found that has worked. Let me tell you what we found that doesn't work.

When I first started, we did one-day and two-day seminar retreats on business development and creating business development plans. Generally, we were pretty good in getting the audience and the participants excited about it. The program ended and we left, and not surprisingly, on Monday or Tuesday, whenever they came back to the office, there was a reversion to business as usual, with little or no behavioral change.

We've changed over the years. We spend much less time doing workshops and much more time with individual, one-on-one coaching sessions. The procedure that we found helpful is the following: first, we don't do one-offs, just one attorney at a firm. We do groups. My organization, similar to Akina's, has three or four people that do coaching. Generally, we'll go into a law firm and coach 10 to 15 attorneys at a time. We find doing it this way provides a couple of benefits: One, when you have 10 or 15 attorneys and you've got three coaches, this allows you to make the best mix and match of personalities and practice areas to locate the most compatible coach for the attorney. Two, it promotes a peer support group for people going through the program. Whether they're in the same office or different offices, we encourage people going through the program to meet on a regular basis to talk about what's working well either with their coach or with their business development activities, or any obstacles that they have. We find that peer support continues the momentum and effectiveness of the coaching.

We have found that four to six months is probably the right time period for follow-up one-on-one coaching. Some may need more, in which case we're flexible. Lawyers can generally develop the skill sets, perhaps attitudinal shifts, and shifts in frame of reference, for how they approach business development after the four to six months of regular support, follow-up, and accountability.

Years ago, somebody got up after the kickoff workshop that we had and stood up and said, "Peter, everything you said was great, but, respectfully" – and when we hear "but respectfully" from the attorney, we know the hammer's coming down. Usually these are litigators who stand up and say that. "But, respectfully, you haven't told me anything I don't know." I said, "So, okay, you're right. You're absolutely right. I take your point. I probably haven't told you anything you don't know, but I probably have told you a lot of what you don't do." He laughed and said, "I take your point."

> If you can make friends, you can develop business.
>
> —*Peter Johnson*

Much of what we teach is common sense, but it's not common practice. Our job is to take what for the most part is common sense and make it part of their daily routine: to open their eyes, grow their antennae, to recognize where business development comes from and recognize their strengths, recognize what they're good at, and recognize that there's no magic. It's all about relationships. If you can make friends, you can develop business.

Coaching: The Johnson Technique: "Getting Started," Part 2

(Peter Johnson)

The first step we take in getting started with a business development program is research. We also conduct a short survey. We ask managing partners and practice group leaders how they think we can be helpful. We also ask the actual participants to tell us how they think we can be helpful along with a whole series of questions to get us prepared for our meeting with them. All of this is done in advance of meeting the group to be trained and coached.

We require a kickoff reception the night before we start the program, particularly with firms with multiple offices. The reason for that is at least twofold: One is a very selfish interest. I want the opportunity to see these people relate, to see them talk, to watch them in a social situation, and to start to develop a rapport with the attendees before we meet them formally. It also gives the firm attorneys, particularly from different offices, a chance to meet each other. Typically, they haven't been communicating with each other as effectively as they could, and it starts the cross-selling process by getting to know people in different offices or even people in the same offices. Immediately, they start talking about what they do. It's an excellent way to get them in a good mood, hopefully, before the next step, which is the workshop the next morning.

The other benefit is when they walk in the workshop the next morning, they've already met each other and they've met us – and so that when we start our program we begin with some degree of familiarity and rapport. Without the warm-up reception the prior evening, if I walked in at 8:30 in the morning to attorneys whom I've never met, before I can say "hello," they've got their arms folded. They're all from Missouri, the "show me state," and they're already saying, "It's 8:30 in the morning. I've got work to do. Why am I here?"_

By having the icebreaker the night before, they already know me. As an example of how micromanaged my planning goes to help assure success, I don't have a sit-down dinner. I have high-top tables, so, it gives me and everyone else a better opportunity to mingle with each other.

When we start the business development program, it is generally based on what they want to learn and on what we understand to be their goals and objectives individually and as a group. Most of it is talking about what gets in the way of business development and how to overcome those obstacles and challenges. We do that in a group.

One part of the agenda, which is somewhat unique, is we ask the business development and marketing professionals to be part of the workshop. Too often lawyers don't know the resources that are provided in their own law firms. We like to support and showcase the firm's excellent business development resources. The marketing department comes in for 15, 20 minutes and gives either a refresher—or to some it's an introduction—as to here's how you should use us, here's when you should use us, here's how you contact us, and here's what we can do for you.

After the group meeting we have a lunch. Following lunch, we break out into individual meetings where we sit with the attendees and get to know them better, one-on-one, and take the information that we've gathered and start to either develop their plan if they don't have one, or take a look at their plan and revise it. After their post-lunch meeting, they're back at their office, so, they will get some work in during the day, and they're not thinking that it's a gone day. Then we start the post meeting follow-up process, which is by phone. We have had much success doing the remainder of the program by phone as we have by going and meeting with them face to face. It is less expensive and just as effective.

We schedule calls for the first couple of months, every other week, and then it goes to every third week until the end of the program. Of course, in between calls, they are encouraged to contact us if there is a situation that they want to discuss immediately. They need not wait to schedule a call to have that conversation. We're on duty and available to them as needed.

The end of the program is the transition. Now that they have completed the program, the focus is put on a transition plan. Specifically, what are they going to do in the next three months to six months? What are the implementation steps? This information is also shared with one of the business development professionals at the firm. The firm is responsible for the program and ongoing work with what we call the graduates.

Now, we stay there because we're meeting for approximately an hour and a half with each of them afterwards. That's when you draw down to the one-on-one.

It's set up that for the second half of the day. We have a brief meeting for about 90 minutes where they bring their calendar and we set up the follow-up appointments. Then they are off to their work day.

They bring their calendars, and before they're done we schedule our first call and set some next steps and action items. We also provide a couple of different variations of tracking sheets that we use in order to see the initiatives in which they've been involved between our calls. Whether it's our tracking sheets or their own way of tracking their activities, we put the action items into different categories, such as existing clients, targeted potential clients, enhancing reputation, networking, etc. They plug their business development actions into each of those categories so that between phone calls they send it to us and we know what they've been doing. This allows us to either ask which ones that they've gotten the traction on, or which ones they want to discuss.

Keeping track of activities is similar to tracking calories. It makes you think about what you do and what you eat.

We're very fortunate that most of our clients are repeat clients. We have graduates of the program mentor and work with the incoming class so that it keeps the graduates on track and it gives the new participants another mentor as they go through the program. We also ask graduates of the program to participate in the workshop for the new class, providing suggestions and guidance as to how the new class can maximize the potential of the coaching resource.

Coaching: The Johnson Technique: Follow-Up: Accountability and Strategizing

(*Peter Johnson*)

Accountability and strategizing are key elements of the follow-up one-on-one coaching. Depending upon where the lawyers are on the business development persona scale, some coaches will say, "Did you do what you said you were going to do?" Okay. For others the approach is, "Okay, let's strategize. You're now going to have this lunch. Let's talk about the right way to make 'the ask' for business. How are you going to close it?" It's more strategy. It depends where they are on that business development learning curve. That's key. We help them outline a strategy to make the pitch, "the ask," or help them identify the next step to take to the upcoming meeting, based on whatever stage they're in with this new or existing client.

Coaching: The Johnson Technique: The "But For" Test

(Peter Johnson)

During our four to six month business development coaching program, we evaluate how we're doing by the "but for" test. We ask them, "What's going well, and how can we be doing better?" We ask them to finish the sentence, "But for the coaching, I wouldn't have done X. I wouldn't have gotten Y result. I wouldn't have said Z." Then we have them expand on this. It holds us accountable too. Last but not least, we do ask the people who are in management or the CMOs to check in monthly with the participants, not to necessarily say, "What specifically are you doing, business development-wise?" but to make sure they report that they're continuing to benefit from the program.

> We have a "But For" evaluation of our coaching results. We ask the attendees to finish the sentence, "But for the coaching, I wouldn't have done X; I wouldn't have gotten Y result; I wouldn't have said Z."
>
> —*Peter Johnson*

My philosophy is that 10 percent of the population have business development genes, and you only need to feed them and open the door and let them out. Ten percent, regrettably, have a recessive gene, and you shouldn't let them out. Eighty percent, though, are folks that have potential to develop business, and you maximize that potential by discovering which set of actions are best suited for their interests and abilities. Some people are very good at speaking. Some people are very good at networking. Some people are very good at writing. We work with them to maximize their strengths, overcome some challenges, and, yes, get themselves out of the comfort zone, but not necessarily transform who they are. We don't change who they are; we do change what they do.

> My philosophy is that 10 percent of the population have business development genes, and you only need to feed them and open the door and let them out. Ten percent, regrettably, have a recessive gene, and you shouldn't let them out. Eighty percent, though, are folks that have potential to develop business, and you maximize that potential by discovering which set of actions are best suited for their interests and abilities.
>
> — *Peter Johnson*

We've had 14 years to define, retool, and make appropriate revisions. It's a program that works for us, but we're not the right people for everybody.

Coaching: The Johnson Technique: The Three Challenges

(Peter Johnson)

Lawyers face a variety of challenges. We categorize challenges in three different ways: One is *internal*, that is, what's going on in the law firm that may be an obstacle or challenge? It could be a compensation system. It could be partners that don't like to share client relationships. It could be that the firm doesn't reimburse you for client expenses. It could be any number of internal firm-based issues. Then you have *external* challenges: what's going on in the marketplace, the predatory practices of competitor law firms, a changing environment with convergence, consolidation, bankruptcies, etc.

The third category of obstacles is the *personal*, between the two ears, what I call the "head trash" category, the Groucho Marx category. I wouldn't join a country club that would have me as a member. I'm not worth this amount of money. I wouldn't hire me, why would anybody else?

Code Your Clients

(Sally Schmidt)

One business development strategy that we have found successful is to code your clients. It is unique for each practice, but the overall approach is similar. For example, if you are an estate planning attorney, we might code your contacts and clients as accountants, trust officers; current clients, former clients, referring lawyers, and other categories. Each coded group might have a little different need in terms of information. So if you put together an alert or an advisory, you could easily pull up a list of folks who could most benefit from the information and who would most likely appreciate receiving it. One informational alert might be best suited to send to the accountants who have sent me business or who work with my clients. The other thing is that you could, if you have them categorized, create a list of the target folks with whom you want to make sure that you stay in regular contact. This list should be reviewed annually. And, it might change every year, so you start with the list of accountants and you tick off five and say, "These five, I want to make sure I see at least once a quarter" because, to a certain extent, it's about being in front of people and staying top of mind and talking to them about things that you're doing and things that they're doing. So, again, it gets back to that discipline piece, that activity habit . . . creating consistent, habitual behaviors that actually make the business development process so much easier . . . and more fun. When people thank you for the informational alert, it feels good, you've become more top of mind and you've deepened that relationship.

Compensation: Is It Helping or Hurting Collaboration?

(Bill Mooz)

Over the course of my career, I have experienced a number of situations where law firm compensation systems did not incent their lawyers to collaborate and work in teams.

Compensation: People Do What's Measured and Rewarded

(Peter Johnson)

I used to chair our firm's Compensation Committee, and generally, people do what's measured and rewarded. The corollary to that theory is you can't change behavior unless you affect compensation. If you're rewarding billable hours, and you ask people to also volunteer as a mentor, they've got a choice. They've got college tuitions to pay, and if they mentor, they don't get paid for that time. With the pressure to bill and the rewards geared to billable, what are they going to do?

I am frequently asked about compensation and how to properly reward contributions that the firm wants to emphasize. We're finding that compensation systems that reward overall contributions to the firm and are not necessarily solely based on objective data sometimes can affect people's behavior.

An existing partner of mine, when he was a managing partner in a law firm, changed a totally objective system in which you got a percentage of what you billed to a totally subjective system in which there was a teamwork bonus for people who worked effectively and collaborated. It's not the right compensation system for all firms, but it has to do with setting expectations. My belief is that all lawyers need to be required to spend non-billable time for the benefit of the law firm. They need to be accountable for that, and the value of that time needs to be good value.

Compensation: Sharing Origination

(Silvia Coulter)

Most firms today will share origination credit. There are still firms that don't, and if you haven't even made that jump yet where you're allowing people to share origination credit, right there you have a dead stop. What is going to facilitate team behavior? Some people are good guys, and they'll do it anyway, and they know that ultimately the whole firm is going to benefit if they operate as a team. But many lawyers don't think that way. People behave in ways for which they are rewarded.

Here's an example. I'm a lawyer with a good contact. You're a lawyer in my firm with some expertise. So, we team up. We go out. We talk to the prospect or the client. We get the work. And I take all the credit because it was my contact. At some firms, for some partners who had the expertise required to secure the engagement in order to get any origination credit they actually have to have a conversation. "Frank, let's talk about this. It was your contact, but there is no way in the world that you would ever get this business without my skillset. I'm a scientist, and I'm highly specialized in pharmacology science. And unless you have that expertise you are not going to get this business." I had a similar conversation with a partner just yesterday.

If you want some credit, ask for it. Otherwise, you may not receive it. You can't be upset about the things you don't receive (like credit) if you don't fight for it.

Compensation: We Do What We Get Rewarded For

(Silvia Coulter)

Partners are pretty blunt when they're in meetings with us. If I don't get paid for this, I'm not going to do it. We've heard that a thousand times. We'd never share an individual's opinion with firm management, but it's the truth. We do what we get rewarded for, and so does the firm leadership, by the way. They can say "team" all they want, but if leaders are not modeling the behavior and compensation isn't supporting activities then there is a lack of alignment between firm strategy, messaging and compensation/reward.

Competitive Environment: Now More Lawyers Open to BD Training

(Allen Chichester)

Turning skilled attorneys into skilled rainmakers is not as hard as it used to be. When I first got in the business—it's been 15 years now since I came over from advertising—sales was not something that was easily accepted by attorneys, and certainly pipelines were things that carried oil, gas, or water. So, times have changed. The increasingly competitive environment has forced law firms to really step up in terms of how they do business. The audience (attorneys) is more willing to listen now than they have been in the past. The winds of change are upon us in this field. It was happening before the great recession, it was happening with the increasingly competitive nature of law firms, but it was certainly accelerated by the great recession and nowadays it's an accepted part of every partner's responsibility.

Consumer Advocacy: Succeeding as a Consumer Advocate

(David Boies, Wayne Hogan, Gil Purcell)

Three attorneys who are considered amongst the best consumer advocates in the legal field all agreed to answer the question, "How would you respond to a person who said, 'I would like to go into law and help people like you have. How can I become a successful consumer advocate attorney?'"

What was fascinating to this author was that all three of these nationally respected attorneys gave virtually the same answer.

First, get a quality legal education. Second, decide where your passion is in terms of helping people and what aspect of consumer advocacy you prefer. Third, find a well-experienced law firm that tries cases in that subject, and work there, learning everything you can about that field of practice and the trial of those matters. Fourth, once you are skilled in this particular area of law, and you've had a chance to be the lead attorney on a number of occasions, find that special case where you can do the most good in terms of the advocacy that speaks to your heart – the case where the quality of the trial lawyering can make all the difference.

It is also interesting to note that each of these attorneys all have become generous contributors with their time and financial resources to support various social causes that speak to their hearts.

Content Marketing: Essential to Stay Competitive Online

(Larry Bodine)

The Internet is the number one way that consumers look for a lawyer, according to both the 2014 Hinge Report "Beyond Referrals: How Today's Buyers Check You Out" and research at LexisNexis. While 80% of consumers check out an attorney online, only 55% rely on a referral. The second radical transformation in legal services marketing took place in 2014 when Google changed its algorithm. In a single update of Google's algorithm, all the sites that curated content, i.e., placed another party's content on their site, went to the bottom of the search results list and, as a result, they lost much of their organic traffic. It is clear that Google prefers original, frequently-updated material. That's where *content marketing* comes in.

Now more than ever, if you want your website to produce clients for you, you need to update your site two or three times a week. Google considers around 300 words to be an article; anything shorter is not considered an article. The longer the article the better.

I'm very happy about this development because I started writing my blog in 2003—and I've gotten more than one million visits Every blog post I wrote was completely original.

I remember colleagues of mine would laugh at me and say, oh, why are you putting so much effort, you could just curate content or put in snippets and then refer to somebody else. I said, well, people are coming to me because they want to know what I think. They're not coming to me because they want a reference to what somebody else thinks.

The content marketing approach of using information sourced from a third party is really the old fashioned way of doing things. Today, you must come up with something original. And you must write more than a typewritten page. If you understand that providing original material is a must, you're going to be found by Google.

Another issue is you have to engage the person who's coming to your site. You want them to spend time on your site. You want them to be interested in your article in a way that they retain you as a lawyer. That's where good story telling comes in. Picture grandma sitting around a bunch of young grandchildren telling a story. Those are the ones you remember because you loved them so much. When you think about it, it makes sense, because telling a story is one of the best ways to communicate. People remember stories. Everybody says, hey, listen to this, I just heard this story. This happened to this person and then he ran into this obstacle and then he overcame it and here was the result. People just naturally remember stories and when people hear the story or tell it, they feel the emotions that happened. A story causes you to feel the same emotions as the people in the story. The emotion is the hook. That's the hook. People think logically, but they make purchases emotionally.

It starts when a law firm puts something new up on their website. I'll give you an actual live example.

I update the National Trial Lawyers site one or two times a day and what I'm looking for is a good story, so I found a press release by a law firm in Maryland and the headline was, "Maryland Personal Injury Attorneys Obtain $1 Million Dollar Settlement."

When I read that, I thought it was probably the worst way that you could tell the story, because it was all about the lawyers saying "we're so great, look at what we did." There was no mention until you got into the press release about who the client was, when it happened, or any description of the accident.

I went to the extra trouble of calling up and asking, "This $1 million dollar settlement is great, where did it happen, when did it happen, how did this affect the person who was hurt?" It turned out the story was about a $1 million dollar settlement for a man who was riding a motorcycle late at night in Baltimore and another driver who was in a company-owned truck. The truck driver was operating without very much sleep and ran a red light. He hit the guy on the motorcycle, put him in the hospital, caused him to have numerous operations, and completely devastated his life. He couldn't work. He couldn't do the things he used to do with his family. So, I published the story telling all of that and it got 1,400 page views in the first 24 hours. And all I did was tell a story.

I don't think Google cares which page you put your new content on, but I prefer to put the headlines of the new content stories on the home page, as I do for the National Trial Lawyers website, for example. Google doesn't care how important you think it is. What Google is looking for is something that answers the question, "Is this unique and is this fresh . . . is this something that was just put up?" Because many visitors to your website are going to go to the home page, that's the place you want to have a series of these stories that illustrate your practice.

It works in the business context, too. I'm always on the prowl for a story and I found one that was called, "Contractors Beware—Be Careful in Settling a Construction Defect Claim Without Your Insurer's Prior Consent."

I looked at the article and it summarized a Fourth Circuit Opinion and it was 14 paragraphs of some of the densest text you can possibly read about . . . the terms of an insurance contract and the different lines of coverage and all of the complex details about the problem with the construction. It was one of the most complicated things that I have ever read.

I boiled it down to six paragraphs. I figured out that the dispute involved the construction company that built the Gaylord National Resort in Maryland. The developer discovered the hard way that to get reimbursed for a lawsuit settlement, they should have told their insurance company first. That's really what the whole story was about.

The key to writing is you have to hone in and identify the mistake. What was the precise error that happened that led to all of this? It could be the guy fell asleep and he ran a red light and hit a guy on a motorcycle.

It's that little piece, the little detail that he fell asleep at the wheel. When somebody retells that, you make sure to mention that point. But for that, there's no story in the classical sense of real people with real problems that call up real emotions. You could have simply said, well there was a collision, Driver A was injured, recovered $1.5 million dollars. Nobody's going to tell that story. It's too dry.

Or if you say that a contractor got into a dispute with an insurance company, you put everybody to sleep. But if you include the detail that it was the

Gaylord National Resort in Maryland, something that people around there are all real familiar with, you get everyone's attention.

Many of us have been to a Gaylord Resort. So, it's the kind of research I love doing—finding out what's going on and then really drilling into what was the one mistake, what was the particular point of negligence that made everything else happen. It always boils down to a tipping point. There could be a hundred factors, but one of them is going to be the tipping point.

The facts covered many other things. There were many smaller side issues, but for my story, I left all that out. For people to remember a story, it's got to be pretty simple.

To reiterate, you want to refresh your website two or three times a week. I update The National Trial Lawyers and Personal*injury*.com sites one or more times a day. Here's the other thing. The more you blog, the more business you'll get. There's a direct correlation. Two or three times would be good, but every day is better. [See also *Online Marketing: More Critical Than Ever.*]

Content Marketing: The "How-To" with Blogging Examples

(Larry Bodine)

There are three law firms for whom I write stories under my own name. The stories are about their practice areas. I update these three sites, once a day, Monday through Friday. So, for one firm, it's public. We're not doing any ghost writing here. I'm writing under my own name. For example, I write about medical malpractice, vehicle accidents, wrongful death, brain injuries—I will write about how 18-wheeler truck accidents are increasing and becoming more deadly in California. Or that in Washington DC, the most common cause of medical malpractice is a failure to diagnose properly. Or for a firm that does business litigation, I found the story about the contractor that built the Gaylord Hotel and lost the dispute with its insurance company, which cost them a great deal of money, $26 million dollars. What Gaylord did was put their insurance company on notice, but only after the settlement had been concluded. Gaylord then filed all of the paperwork to be reimbursed. The insurance company said, no, we have to be involved from the beginning and must approve the settlement.

For the plaintiff firms and for the defense firms, I'll write about employment discrimination, insurance dispute, and employment disputes.

I read a 35-page opinion about ERISA Plan Fiduciaries who were in charge of a 401k plan. They removed a top-performing fund from the plan and, as a result, the employees in the plan lost a great deal of money. The crux of the issue was whether the fiduciaries acted prudently. So that's the question, what is prudent? That makes a compelling business story. The warning was that if you're on a pension board, you could be personally liable. So, that went in the headline—if you're an ERISA Fiduciary, you can be personally liable if you're not prudent.

You can just imagine all of the people that are on these boards going, "What, you mean that I'm going to be second guessed and I'm going to be second guessed in a lawsuit?" And if you're individually sued, you have to hire your own attorney. The only thing you can do is act prudently . . . and not just rely on the board's attorney.

That's another key to hooking people. You need to go into detail about how this affects people. So, for instance, in a personal injury case, I'll always go into as much detail as I can about the extent of the injuries. For example, were both ankles broken, was it the left one, how many ribs were broken, how long was the scar on the guy's face?

In the best stories, you identify the emotional element within the content and you put the spotlight on that, and that's what people will remember. They'll be driven by the emotional trigger and that then triggers the details of your article.

When you ask me, how do you tell someone to create or develop or bring that out? How would you tell them if they were going to put these pieces on their website, update their website, two, three, four times a week and put something that has some emotional element to it? I tell them imagine you're telling your kids about it over dinner. How would you express it? And you have to do it in just a few sentences.

Cool Staff Titles

(Melanie Green)

- Chief Talent Officer
- Chief Market Leader
- Chief Operating Partner

Creating Rain: A Case Study from Cades Schutte

(Roger Epstein)

My activities in China are starting to really blossom into what I expect will be a seriously good niche for Cades Schutte LLP, to work on inbound Chinese funds to Hawaii and the US.

If I were to share my experience with an associate, newly minted partner, or a partner who has been practicing for more than 30 years (like me) on how to establish a new source of revenue for the firm I would say:

Foundationally, I am defining "rainmaking" in my example as a brand new source of revenue for the firm that can eventually support many lawyers within the firm once the specific new revenue niche has been properly established. This kind of rainmaking takes patience and dedication and because it will take a concerted effort over a period of time, possibly many years, it will reduce hours available for other billable activities. It definitely requires a risk–reward analysis. Also, as part of my foundation in asking the firm to back my rainmaking idea is that this is a tax-based business development concept and I have had a successful and respected career as a tax lawyer.

So, it goes without saying, first, you must be excellent in your area of practice before asking the firm to back your idea and before asking new clients to trust you.

Second, decide that this is what you want to do. Your heart has to be in it, so, you need to find your source of desire and passion to pursue the type of clients and client matters that you want to bring into the firm (for fun, to be become partner, to become an equity partner, to provide greater financial security for your family, to be a trailblazer in a new area of practice for the firm, professional recognition, whatever it is you need to find your personal driver that feeds your spirit like your original desire practice law).

Third, get an agreement from the firm that this is what they want you to do, as well, and an arrangement for compensation that is mutually agreeable. This plan would allow the attorney to focus on rainmaking, i.e., creating a new stream of substantial revenue, and take pressure off of billable hours and collections for the individual lawyer while working to establish an entirely new client base.

Fourth, analyze the area or targets for rainmaking and verify they are within the skillset of the attorney undertaking the new task.

Fifth, make a clearly defined plan to turn potential clients into actual clients by: a) undertaking client relationship development activities including individual meetings/meals, presentations to existing clients, public speaking, etc.; b) reviewing the targeted clients or areas on a regular periodic basis, e.g., quarterly or semi-annually (in my case, I decided to take semi-annual trips to China and review progress at the end of each trip); and c.) making adjustments to plan, as you see what's working and what's not.

Sixth, narrow your focus and eliminate the chaff, after some period of more broad brush marketing efforts; and hone in on those that make the most sense for you and the firm.

Seventh, continue to do this until it proves successful, or you and the firm decide there are better opportunities elsewhere for your skillsets while remembering no risk, no reward.

And finally, do these kinds of rainmaking activities until it stops being fun, or you retire.

Critique Style: Using Humor While Being Direct and Honest

(Adam Stock)

I find that criticism can be virtually painless by using humor. In my role as mentor and manager I refined the skill of critiquing within a humorous context while at the same time being honest and direct. I rely on this leadership technique of balancing direct feedback tempered with humor and self-deprecation.

Maybe because of my East Coast New York background, I think if you're direct and honest with people, even if it's not the best information that they want to hear, that actually shows that you care. And I find that to be true in California especially, and it's also true with Midwesterners. People will oftentimes take offense with someone if they are not very direct with them.

Being direct moves things ahead and it causes engagement and is not easy at times, and so deflecting with humor really helps. And frankly if you don't say what you mean, it really causes a lot of issues in relationships. If you don't really address the meta-issue, if you are trying to work with someone and they're doing bad work or they're communicating in a strange way, then, it's much better to say, hey, you know let's talk about [XYZ topic], and make a joke out of it, but address it. That's what I find that I do and hopefully not too many people take offense, but that's really what it's about. I find that self-deprecating humor is one technique that I use. That's almost always the most important one because then it's not like you are insulting the person. Together, we are insulting all humankind. We are feckless human beings. We are full of blemishes, mistakes, and we muddle along.

CRM: Data That Makes Me Look Brilliant

(Jeanne Hammerstrom)

For our Client Relationship Management (CRM) we use Interaction from LexisNexis. I have a CRM specialist who really is awesome and very analytical. So, I don't even go to accounting anymore. Whenever I have a client team meeting, he can get me all the financials. He's a wizard with Excel, pivot tables, and all the related info. Allows me to go in those client team meetings looking brilliant.

CRM: Here's Six, Depends on Apps You Desire and If You'll Actually Use It

(Stephen Fairley)

There are a number of good CRM programs out there, but the problem is that most of the CRM programs either, number one, they're not utilized properly, so all they do is warehouse a lot of data. A CRM is only as good as the information you put into it, and it's only as good as the way that you actually manipulate that data to get things out of it. You've got to be able to push the boundaries of your CRM. Most companies, in fact, who do CRM implementations end up getting rid of it down the road because they don't use it. You've got to make sure that you're willing to use it and in order to use it effectively, you need to make sure that you're putting good information into it.

So, I think there are a number of CRMs out there, there's certainly Salesforce, there's ACT, there's SugarCRM, there's Infusionsoft, there's Marketo, there's Pardot. I'm familiar with several of them. It really depends on the application and it depends on what you want to do with it and what purpose the CRM is supposed to serve.

CRM: Marrying CRM to BD for Opportunity Analysis

(Shanda Zavalsky)

I have worked with some terrible CRM programs that cross referenced in correct data. So, after quite a bit of searching, we found one for our firm. It's the Thomson Reuters Elite Business Development Program. And what's great about it is, it will help us not only track people and efforts but also help identify opportunities. If I'm sitting next to someone at an event who is a potential client, I can reach out to my marketing department and ask for the profile of this person's company and other general background. We can quickly provide current relationships, work history, and past marketing efforts. It is necessary to provide our attorneys with a clear snapshot of who this company is and our firm relationship with that company so that we are not duplicating efforts and looking disconnected.

We marry our CRM data with our business development research. We have a team member who focuses solely on business development research.

She can provide a list of targets based on a specific set of criteria, we can drill down to the most viable and create an in-depth opportunity analysis to identify areas of need, past relationships, legal needs, industry trends. Our attorneys should never attend a meeting without having in-depth knowledge about the organization and the people they are meeting.

CRM: Perfect Solution is Tough

(Steve Bell)

CRM is a struggle for the entire legal profession as far as I can determine. Whenever chief marketing officer people get together, they go over CRM options in great detail and I don't know of any solution that is satisfactory.

CRMs: Buy What You'll Actually Use

(Sally Schmidt)

Periodically, clients ask me about Client Relationship Management software programs, CRMs. They say, "Is there one that you like or that you recommend?" Well, to a certain extent, most of my clients have dabbled in something and most of their experience has been less than successful. So, it has been tricky. There are some very nice programs out there available to law firms and specifically for law firms. The key is that you don't want to buy more than you need. And that's what I find firms do. They'll invest in some six-figure CRM and it's only being used by the marketing department. Many firms are like that. The CRM is just being used to generate lists for materials that go out for seminars and activities like that. The whole point of CRM is for everybody to manage their relationships. But if that's not happening then I think it's not worth the money. Otherwise, if the firm is really committed to it, I think it's great and, as I said, there are several very good ones for law firms. There are some individual lawyers, who just download applications they find online and track their contacts that way too. The point is to find a CRM system that you'll actually use to track your clients, and manage key information about your clients and client-related activities, as well as the potential clients on your target list.

Cross Selling: We Call It Cross-Serving/ Baker Donelson

(Adam Severson)

Today's competitive environment requires us to ask, "How are we getting the lawyers to think about cross-selling?" First, we call it cross-serving not cross-selling. This allows our lawyers to have a greater open mindedness to the sales process and think about providing a cross-practice service as opposed to selling. Because what I feel happens when people talk about cross-selling is they try to go sell litigation when the client might not be buying litigation. Cross-serving implies a greater understanding of the client's needs and a stronger understanding of the client's business. In which case, we're simply doing them a favor by making them aware of some capabilities within our firm that could be advantageous for them. Many times they'll take us up on the idea of using additional firm resources. Our cross-serving involves two approaches. The first approach is through direct client interaction to develop a keen understanding of the client's business and their needs. Then finding the right resources within the firm to present the solution that both makes substantive sense as well as economic sense. The second approach would be based on research that we do where, while we may have a strong relationship, we may not be as intricately familiar with the internal issues of a given client. So we supplement our client knowledge using external research services. We will do a gap analysis of our firm's share of the client's overall expenditure on legal services. The gap analysis is based on firm financials as well as on third party research that we acquire from Lexis and Westlaw tools. This allows us to more fully understand the breadth and specific areas of their legal activity. This allows us to engage and ask questions of our client about that activity and explore if there might be an opening for us to have a more explicit conversation about a different area of legal need beyond what we are already providing. [Read more: look up *Severson, Adam* in Index.]

Cross-Selling: "I'll Be There."

(Matt Taylor)

At our firm we're not territorial with our clients. We truly consider all clients "firm clients." I think an important role for me as a leader in the firm is to be there for my partners and associates for major pitches. They might have a pitch, and they'll say, "Matt, can you come with me?" Absolutely, I'll be there.

Cross-Selling: Client Teams Done Right Make It Happen

(Mark Usellis)

Some people will give lip service to the benefits of cross-selling but are not actually doing it or aren't doing it very well. We found that if you're going to have a cross-selling program, client teams, done right, really do work.

I always urge people to include clients on the client team because a big part of the client team's mission is centered on your service delivery model. It's going to be much better if the client is giving you real time feedback on what works for them rather than you sitting in a room and trying to decide what you're going to do for the client.

As with anything in business development, they've got to come from a mindset of generosity and concern about the client's well-being as opposed to individual profit maximization. Client teams are something you do "with" a client, you don't do "to" a client.

From the cross-selling standpoint, if you approach it from a mindset of "I want to help them solve problems, so I'm not going to sell them based on where we have lawyers who need work or where the highest rate work is, but where can we best help them?" That's going to work better.

The client teams that have been successful have primarily been successful based on the quality of the client team leader. Even outside of a client team, if in a relationship you have a lawyer skilled in needs assessment evaluation and a mindset of, "How can I help them?", then cross-selling will naturally take place as those needs arise for the client.

> Some people will give lip service to cross-selling, but are not actually doing it. We found that client teams done right really do work. The client teams that have been successful have primarily been successful based on the quality of the client team leader.
>
> —*Mark Usellis*

Most people approach it from, "Does this person need what I do?" That's just wrong and ineffective.

For example, you don't approach the conversation, absent any knowledge of need or interest, saying, "Hey, I'd really like to introduce you to our real estate lawyers."

Because that's an imposition on the client. They're giving up time and then it's going to be awkward if they don't want to use your real estate lawyers. Put yourself in the other person's shoes and think about what would be effective. Ask them about the company's priorities and challenges.

And, if they say, "Oh, we've got these real estate problems."

"Oh, really? Well, how do you handle those?"

"We have this firm that's been doing it."

"Well, do you like those guys?"

"Well, yeah, I like them, but the problem is, they don't have enough depth."

"Oh, well if you have overflow needs, let me introduce you to someone and we don't need to displace this firm that you like, but if they have depth issues, we could be a second source."

Something along those lines shows sensitivity and is a whole different conversation in the client's mind than one where you push a legal service before establishing a need.

Cross-Selling: Cross-Market to Win Work

(Jeff Berardi)

Well, we've come a long way. At one time, using the term "sales" in a law firm environment was considered pretty crass. You didn't want to use that word. You used the euphemism of "business development." I think we are much more comfortable with the idea of cross-selling and cross-marketing and really that's why we've grown this platform to a global stage - so that we can do more work for clients across practices and across offices. So, the terms "sales" and "cross-selling" are something that the firm's attorneys are comfortable with hearing and it certainly is a message delivered from the top with our chairman and global managing partner, Pete Kalis. He very much conveys that this is something you do at what we call the retail level, rather than just the institutional level, and that means that our lawyers need to be directly engaged in it. So, it's not, "Just go out and sell." That's not the message. It's that we've got to win work in the marketplace and that means cross-selling or cross-marketing your clients to others in the firm and sharing work and conveying the value proposition to the best of our abilities using the resources we have internally to do it.

Cross-Selling: Fast Forward Supports Cross-Selling

(Jill Weber)

Our Fast Forward program naturally leads to cross-selling. It's the trust. First they need to meet the person and build the rapport through the training sessions and meeting them regularly and then they say, "Oh, I trust this person. I trust that he or she is going to treat my client the way I do. Gosh, I'm a corporate attorney, and I need somebody in real estate, so, therefore, I'm going to call Gina and see if she can help me with this real estate matter." Whereas before, that attorney might have sat there and thought, "I'm not sure who to call in real estate." Now, having been through the program, I might say, "Hmm, I'm going to call my Fast Forward colleague Gina and start with her first." The program naturally builds relationships across practice areas. They become more aware of the services that are being offered, because even in the lunch-and-learns or breakfast-and-learns, I don't just say, "Okay, it's 8:30, we're going to start right in on the session." There's time for them to chat and talk about what's new and what's going on, and then they learn, "Oh, I didn't know we had that practice. I didn't know we did that." So, it's built into the program because we always start with a little opening intro discussion of "What's new?" Those discussions naturally lead to cross-practice awareness, cross-practice trust, and cross-practice sales.

Cross-Selling: Green Space Analysis

(Shanda Zavalsky)

We definitely have issues in the cross-selling area that we're trying to address. Currently, it's a slow process to bring some on board. For many, it's about the credit, the way that attorneys receive credit. The billing credit is a huge hindrance and something that firms don't like to openly speak about in many cases because it is a hindrance to teaming and working together. I'm trying to work around that, but that is definitely an obstacle for us.

I try to make it easy to visualize where there is opportunity. One example is that I created our version of the green space analysis. When I was at another firm our CMO was a technology whiz, and he created this database that allowed you, access the client profile view via the firm's intranet. You could retrieve data by client, or pull up all of the Denver office clients, or all of the IP clients.

By accessing the database and looking at a specific client profile you were able to see all the work we've done for that company. Maybe it's JP Morgan. We can see we've done some litigation for them; some corporate M&A work; and we have also done some lobbying. But we haven't done any real estate, and we clearly have a great relationship with them, and we have an extremely talented real estate practice group.

> I find that our green space analysis leads to improved cross-selling
>
> —*Shanda Zavalsky*

As a real estate attorney, I might easily conclude, "Oh, I should look at that." Or perhaps as an IP lawyer, if we've done some corporate work for them, if that IP space is open, I probably should ask for an introduction, or at least do some research on this company.

As of today, we haven't been able to create a fully functional database, but I do create a spreadsheet where we can see some of those gaps which gives people, especially when they're new to the firm, a starting point. I give them that sheet and they can identify companies it would be worthwhile having an introduction to.

We just hired several new IP folks, we went through a process where we determined what their dream clients looks like. We then determined our current clients that met the various criteria of that dream client. This list provided us with a hit list for internal introductions and a good list of cross-sell opportunity. We then began making introductions and highlighting our substance through client alerts, personal meetings, and speaking opportunities.

Another example from the recent past was to identify areas of overlap between our State and Federal lobbying practice groups. We sat down and created a list of those areas of overlap. We will go through that list at about ten a month and discuss the history. Here's where there might be opportunity. Here's who we should introduce to the other group.

And then lastly, it's really about the message and how you introduce someone. Our attorneys are trained well at speaking about their expertise, but they are not good at educating the other attorneys on how to introduce their expertise with their client without sounding like you're trying to upsell them. Instead, highlight the fact that we have additional resources to help them achieve their goal, the key is knowing your peers and their expertise.

I'm trying to educate them to educate attorneys how to spot the red flags of opportunity. For example, as it relates to the IP group, if you hear your client has a new product, they have a new idea, or they're worried about a trade secret, those would be red flag comments. That's where they might need an IP attorney. That's where you could easily say, "Hey, you know what, I should hook you up with one of our IP guys, or Jane Smith. She would be great. Here's what she can do for you."

By doing it this way you're making it more natural to cross-sell, because everyone wants to help their clients. We just don't always know how to approach them and we don't want to seem like we're trying to sell them services they don't need. The other practice areas can educate us on how they motivate a potential client without sounding like a hard sales pitch.

Cross-selling practice areas is no longer just a good thing. It's a necessity. Because in today's world if you aren't looking out for the client's needs and staying one step ahead of trying to connect them with the right people, other attorneys are trying to reach them and give them that same information. Receiving legal services from another source might cause the client to go a different direction and you'll lose the client altogether. So, the more you can try to be helpful and stay one step ahead of them, the more clients you're going to keep, and you're going to keep them happy. You have to assume that your client is being approached and building new relationships.

Cross-Selling: Incentivizing the Attorney to Cross-Sell

(Author David King Keller's discussion notes with a law firm staff member)

I think you need the incentives in place to make cross-selling occur.

Our firm is set up so that our lawyers really do benefit from sharing work. If they introduce a client to another lawyer and we end up getting engaged in a new matter and even if they are not working on that and our colleague is in another office, they get credit for that. So, we have this system in place to assess just how involved they are at sharing work across the platform. We have great incentives in place to maximize the power of the cross-selling platform. The incentive is only based on the results. It is not on making introductions and setting up a lunch with someone else and going out and getting 10 business cards and sitting down.

It's not about the work involved. It's about how it ends up and, certainly, our most productive partners are the ones who have maximized the power of the platform because there are incentives in place to share work and there is only so much one person can do. So they are able to have a client that they originated and they have got people all over the place doing work for that client. That's really going to boost their overall numbers way more than if they had a client that they never shared, and just spent their time working head down at their desk constantly.

So, that's the system we have in place. That's something that's an institutional difference, I think, with our firm and some others. That is we really have something in place that makes sure that people get it. And that by sharing work it is going to benefit you. If you don't have that you can talk all you want about it's great for the firm and a rising tide floats all boats and such, but if they don't see it really affects them directly, I think that's a tough sell.

It helps me in my job to ensure that people get it and want to do it because, otherwise, I think you have to incentivize. And it needs to be an ongoing revenue stream. It's not like it just ends. If that person is still providing work to the firm, the person who originated the client would get credit for that. You can't duplicate credits which means that if you originated the client and you did the work for it, it's not like that doubles up. But if you originated the client and someone else did the work, you both get credit. It's kind of simple that way. It's just a calculation to try to understand what value and benefit those lawyers brought, in any given time period, and the incentive is recognized on an annual basis.

We have had this in place for as long as I have known. It pre-dates me and it's something that I think is kind of an institutional quality about the firm. I think it is a great idea. So, there are three different buckets: the client originator, the matter originator, which could be a different person, and then, it's the people who are working on the matters.

Cross-Selling: It Can Be Difficult, But Shouldn't Be

(Scott Kessler)

At many firms, cross-selling is hampered by the way compensation or origination credit is set up within the firm. I've heard many lawyers push back when I suggest cross-selling other practice groups because they "won't get any credit." The problem is that lawyers view cross-selling from their own, "what's in it for me" perspective rather than from the clients' "how can you help me" perspective. Lawyers should want to cross-sell because it's good for the client! And when you do good things for the client it strengthens relationships with the client. And strong relationships lead to rain! It's the Macy's Santa saying, "We don't have it, but go on over to Gimbles." That's what builds relationships!

The fact that you may not get compensated directly for cross-selling shouldn't have any bearing on whether you do it. What's most important is meeting the client's needs; that's what matters. It's good practice. It's your career. It's your life. It's who you are. Cross-selling is so much more than telling the client that your colleague can help you with their issue. It's telling them, "I hear you and I want to help you." Why would you not want to do that?

Cross-Selling: It's Now Essential to Keep a Client

(Silvia Coulter)

You have to do cross-selling today to keep the client. Because if you're allowing a competitor access at a high level, and the competition has a good relationship with the client, you're betting that you're going to hold on to what you have. And that's not a good bet. That's especially true if you've got an aggressive person on the other end with some great expertise to sell, and a dynamic system that rewards that behavior.

The other big piece of cross-selling that, quite frankly, may be even more important or as important is relationships at the firm. There are two sides to this. If you're a rainmaker and you really know what's going on with your client, then go out and meet the other lawyers at your firm and at other offices so you are comfortable recommending them when you know the client is using competitors. On the other hand, if you are a lawyer who could do environmental work for DuPont, for example, or another firm client, you might then go to the DuPont lawyer or go to the responsible partner for a client that might use your services and build a relationship with that individual. We're building the relationship, and at some point I'm going to be comfortable enough to say, "Mike, ultimately what I'm hoping we can get out of this relationship is that you know me a little bit better. You know some of the clients I've worked with at my practice, and that you and I can go to DuPont together and talk to them about XYZ."

Currently, I would say cross-selling is being mostly driven by the sales professionals in firms.

Cross-Selling: Partners Caring About Fellow Partners and Client Needs

(Louise Muldoon)

I tend to also think about the sociological dimensions of business development. We have partners that genuinely act as partners and care about the welfare and businesses of their fellow partners and, in recent times, I've seen a real uptick in the activity of partners proactively introducing fellow partners to their clients. They say, "You know, I've just been talking to my client and I can see that they've got this particular requirement, and I instantly thought of you, Lawyer X. I'd like to introduce you to them if you think you're the best person. Here's my thinking on it . . . Are you the best person or is it someone else on your team?" In other words, a lot of cross-selling happens organically across the partnership, and we're seeing that increasing as we're improving our cross practice awareness. Communication is a big part of this. Our lawyers will happily respond to that type of call from the partnership provided that they're armed with the information about others' practices. So, we've spent quite some time disseminating information about what different people are doing, what they're working on, any skillsets that we've brought to bear in the firm, and other cross-practice awareness activities. We're also very proactive about it as a business development function. As we're improving communications across the business, cross-selling is improving. We also regularly analyze our client base. We assess the services we're providing to particular clients. In areas where we're strong, if we're not providing that service, we start to ask questions about that. We are increasingly looking at being much more proactive about both approaching people who might not have thought about us providing that service to a client and then proactively suggesting it to the client. It all goes back to being very close to your client's business and trying to anticipate what they might need. So, we see cross-selling growing organically the more closely our attorneys align with all of our client's legal needs. We're quite proactive and deliberate about it and it goes back, again, to business intelligence. If we go out and interview a client about our service in one area, quite often they'll talk about a need in another area, and this frequently can lead to new business.

Cross-Selling: Partners Mentoring Partners, A Pilot Program

(Melanie Green)

We pilot a lot of ideas. You just don't know which idea will become the next big thing. One of the new programs we're starting to pilot here is what we're calling Client Collaboration Groups.

What generated this idea was our talking internally as a team about how we always encourage our lawyers to kindle external lead and referral sources. For example, we might tell an associate, "Stay in touch with your banker, accountant and financial planner friends and share ideas with them. When you can, refer business to them. Keep reminding them about your work and the firm's work and periodically ask for any leads from these external sources." So, how do we take that external lead group concept and turn it internally to those who are managing client relationships? How do we get these client managers to share information about what they're doing to manage that client relationship in a way that might spark ideas for others?

That is to have our client relationship managers come together and collaborate on various aspects of their work: challenges, successes, questions, etc. You might call that a partner-to-partner mentoring activity.

We piloted the Client Collaboration Group concept. As we thought about lawyers having conversations with clients about rates, we wanted to learn from them. What's the real-life application and experience around the vital topic of talking to clients around rates, fees, and value? Who has done it well? What experiences have they had? What can they share with their partners? We hosted opportunities to come together and talk about that. We got pretty low attendance, but the people who came benefited. So, that was step one of the pilot.

Even though the groups were small, they did share information. You could see that they enjoyed sharing information with each other. We then took it to the next level. Okay, if small groups work, why don't we look across our top, say, 100 clients, identify the client relationship managers, and create about 10 collaboration groups with five or six managers. We looked at linking managers into a group if their clients were within a similar industry. We also linked managers that had clients who generate significant revenue in multiple areas of service. They're managing a different kind of client–practice mix.

So, we sliced it and diced it quite a few ways to come up with how to pair people. And we've introduced it. We've gotten it approved through the lawyer leadership, and we're starting the meetings. It really came from that initial look at how people came together to talk about something tricky like rates. Lawyers don't like to talk about that at all.

We can write memos all day long and send out marketing tips of the day about a rate discussion, but they're going to look at us and say, "You've never done this."

And even if we have done it, it's not going to be in their context. How do we get people talking to each other? Then we also put a member of our client relations team in those conversations to add a tip or two along the way. I have two team members who divide up amongst the group meetings.

I call those meetings a type of mentoring, or quasi-mentoring. Partners advising partners. And we'll see how that one goes.

I guess our concept here is trying to find a way for lawyers to learn from each other— but have it set up in such a way that it doesn't feel overly structured. We have to create an environment where they will talk to each other, where there's an opportunity for insertion of somebody else's viewpoints and ideas, and where somebody can be brought in to help facilitate that conversation.

The facilitator in the beginning will probably be the client relations staff. For instance, they would say, "Well, now, Joe, you did 'X"—because many will be reluctant to talk to each other right?—"Now, Joe, you did something with so and so, didn't you? How did that turn out?" That'll get Joe talking. And then if Joe says something and somebody else didn't hear Joe the same way, I heard Joe. Then I'd say, "Well, I just want to make sure I have that right. Because I heard something slightly different."

So, that's the facilitator role. We're not telling them what to do. We're bringing out concepts through that conversation.

We're going to schedule them for 45 minutes. We're going to try to make it very informal. We're actually going to have the first meeting, with some topics that we think would be helpful for them to discuss, and then let the first meeting of every group allow them to get to know each other. What clients are they representing? And then form a discussion around, "Hey, what would be really helpful to learn more about?" Again, this is based on that high autonomy; we're not directing it, we're facilitating it and shaping it. I think each one of these groups may take a different course. But then, our client relations team can come together and say, "Here's what this group talked about." and share it more broadly.

I'm hoping this will be of great interest to them because they'll like to talk about what they're doing. We went to the top 100 clients. So, these client managers, the people we're starting with, are people who have had a good deal of success, though not all of them want to tout it. There's a lot of skepticism and hesitancy in our firm about patting ourselves on the back.

So, there's a mix of people who are more comfortable about sharing, and then those who are doing great things but don't say a word. To increase motivation and participation, we couch it in terms that we're really trying to serve our clients better, and knowledge sharing/best practices is an important piece to that. All of you are successful in servicing clients in different ways. Wouldn't we benefit from learning from the different approaches? And you can take aspects of that approach to apply to clients you work with. At the end of the day, one challenge that law firms face is that almost all of these client billing managers, not all, but almost all, have come up to be in that position of managing the full client relationship based on the work that they do in a specific practice area. If they're an IP lawyer and we've grown our IP work for a client over a number of years and that's successful, then that's really what they know.

They know IP, and they know what works for the client for IP, and they know IP preferences for that client. It's a really different thing to say, "You now manage the entire client relationship and you need to grow it, cross sell it," however you want to phrase it. And that's not something they've ever done.

Our Chief Operating Partner, Tom Froehle, has a phrase, "We need people to build a practice bigger than themselves." That statement works in the traditional sense that a lawyer builds a practice so large that the work spills over to senior associates and even junior associates in their practice area. But also from a client development perspective, a lawyer needs to build a practice bigger than their one practice area, so, that the relationship expands into other services of the firm.

Cross-Selling: Peer Groups

(Allen Chichester)

When we get in to the training seminars, the best thing that happens is when attorneys share their experience, and it's in those shared experiences where connections are made. It is where, "Oh, I know those people, have you thought about this, have you thought about that"- ideas grow and develop in terms of prospects or ways of approaching prospects that we couldn't hope to teach or provide as staff. It really is in attorneys working together where a lot of the magic happens.

Also, one of the things we are working on now is trying to create peer groups within the firm to self-coach and also cross-sell. We look for any opportunity to try to facilitate. We think of it as analogous to those who belong to running groups. People get together and run together. In some cases, you show up because your buddy is expecting you to show up-he or she is going to be there and you don't want to let them down.

In some cases, cross-selling and general collaboration is better in the smaller offices. There have been peer groups running our smaller offices for a while because the attorneys in these offices are able to easily get together on a regular basis and simply talk about what's happening. Business development discussions are a natural part of that. In the larger offices, it's more of a challenge and you have to look harder for commonalities. What we're doing is taking on people who have been through our sales, we call it the "Build Your Book Seminar," and as a follow-up, we're offering to get them together with other people who have been through the same seminar as a type of business development peer group where they get together by phone conference and share experiences and share success and seek advice. Honestly, we're just in the early days of this and we're hoping for good things to come. Lawyers are busy, and you have to make sure these things benefit them, otherwise they're just not going to show up again.

We take advantage of any and every opportunity to create branded "BT Law Academy" training events. We will host lunch-and- video conferences, we'll do webinars, we'll do virtually anything, but the particular one that we found works best is a live conference.

Cross-Selling: Requires Trained Practice Group Leaders and Obstacle Removal

(David Freeman)

The siren song in law firms with complementary practices is cross-selling (which, hereafter, we'll call cross-serving, reflecting the notion that these activities are all in service to the needs of the client). However, while there is no shortage of exhortations to internally cross-connect to pursue new work, many firms have not developed the skills and processes necessary to maximize their opportunities.

It all begins with your leaders. An Altman Weil survey of 81 managing partners at firms with 50 or more lawyers revealed that the majority of the practice groups were not very good at cross-serving. The survey uncovered three major factors for improving group performance: provide training for practice group leaders; get practice group leaders to spend over 250 hours per year on group leadership, and engage in a formal practice group planning process. The following are some approaches to take with your leaders to help them drive more, and better, cross-serving activity:

Provide training for practice group leaders so that they can:

- Teach (and continually remind) their lawyers to overcome the common obstacles to cross-serving.
- Encourage communication and relationship-building throughout the firm.

- Become effective business development mentors and coaches.
- Develop proper goals, measures, and tracking systems.

Get practice group leaders to spend over 250 hours per year on group leadership:

- Establish clear roles and responsibilities relating to leading cross-serving efforts.
- Track and reward time spent executing leadership responsibilities.
- Encourage complementary group leaders to meet to plan cross-serving activities between their groups.

Engage in a formal practice group planning process:

- Get group members together to develop a collaborative plan for cross-serving.
- Drill down to specific strategies, goals, measures, action steps, personal commitments, and timelines for completion.
- Provide regular reminders, measure ongoing progress, and make implementation a top agenda item at meetings throughout the year.

To further master the art of cross-serving, firms must see it for what it is: a rewarding exercise in team building and obstacle removal. Once key barriers are reduced, work can flow more easily between lawyers and practices.

A few of the more common obstacles to cross-serving are:

- Lawyers who don't want to sell a different practice area.
  Everything we do should be focused on the best interests of the client. I shy away from the phrase cross-"selling," since "selling" centers more on the firm than the client, thus making many lawyers reluctant to engage in these activities. Clients don't want sales pitches, and relationship lawyers don't want to be perceived as pushy salespeople. When the activity is reframed as cross-"serving," however, with a focus on introducing clients to firm lawyers who can serve their needs, your lawyers become more comfortable making cross-introductions, and clients become more interested in hearing from these other lawyers.
- "Can I trust other firm lawyers to protect and not endanger the relationship I've worked so hard to create with my client?"
  While a bit harsh stated this way, it is a realistic concern—will other lawyers do anything to hurt my relationship with my valuable client? Will they deliver the kind of service this client demands? Will they try to take fee credit that should come to me? The key

here is to foster excellent internal communication and relationship-building. Get cross-group lawyers to know, like, and trust each other. Encourage them to discuss fee split expectations and how to best manage their ongoing working relationship.

- The compensation system doesn't reward cross-serving behavior.
  This is an ongoing refrain, to which there are a number of responses. First, often there *are* mechanisms that recognize cross-serving behavior, but they are poorly understood by the lawyers in the firm. Leaders must do a better job of constantly communicating these elements of compensation throughout the firm. Where there are no direct comp rewards, lawyers need to recognize that cross-serving benefits the entire enterprise by raising all boats—the more money coming in, the more there is to spread around. Finally, studies have shown that cross-serving can be a great client retention tool—the more practice areas a client uses in a firm, the less likely they are to leave and go elsewhere.
- Not understanding the needs of the relationship partner.
  The relationship partner is the gatekeeper, so the cross-recipient must make it as easy as possible for the relationship partner to make an introduction. To that end, consider the following:
  1) Provide the relationship lawyer with probing questions they can ask to identify whether any needs exist in the cross-practice area.
  2) Provide the relationship lawyer with "gifts" of added-value activities they can offer the client, ways to make it easy to get in the door, such as a no-charge review of their term sheets, employee manuals, or other documents. Perhaps they can offer in-house presentations on topics of interest to the client. In all, it's about offering real value and making it very easy for lawyers from other practice groups to get in the door so they, too, can begin to develop a relationship with the client.

> The more practice areas a client uses in a firm, the less likely they are to leave and go elsewhere.
>
> —*David Freeman*

So many firms are looking for ways to develop a more robust culture of business development, and few efforts can yield better results than an effective cross-serving campaign. By mastering the art of cross-serving, your firm can enhance your culture through improved client loyalty, higher revenue, and greater internal collaboration.

Cross-Selling: See also *Industry Marketing*

Cross-Selling: With Staff and a High Tech Tool

(David King Keller)

Did you catch the Legal Marketing Association's webinar featuring RelSci.com? Talk about 3 degrees of separation from a "named" individual on your ideal client target list. RelSci created a new connectivity data base backed by SalesForce.com and other venture capital resources who have invested over $100 million in RelSci technology. A number of AmLaw 200 firms are already taking advantage of this platform.

Do you have 500 LinkedIn connections? RelSci has over 4 million and growing, mostly high level decision makers/influencers. For example, every board member at a major public company or large nonprofit_has been entered into the RelSci data base. Every major organization that a law firm member belongs to has a Board. Those Board members sit on other Boards. Apparently now with RelSci you can see which other Boards your Board members sit on. And those other Board members sit on Boards. You may only be a second or third generation away from being introduced by someone who knows you to someone who knows your ideal target client. You need to research the value to the firm to have a connectivity tool this robust. For serious big league players only. Matters you are targeting should be in the 7 figure plus range in order to justify the 5 figure plus investment annual usage fee. For a one-pager on RelSci for law firms contact david@kbdag.com.

[See also: *Targeted Clients: One New Fast Way To Connect: RelSci.* Author's note and disclosure: If you contact RelSci please use my name or use this URL: http://go.relsci.com/DavidKeller. I saw RelSci as an up and coming resource and I was able to establish myself as a referral partner for RelSci potentially eligible for a referral fee for introducing an eligible new client, which fees, if any, I will use toward my pro bono work. I can introduce you to people at RelSci, or you can connect using the RelSci URL above. More details available upon request at david@kbdag.com.]

In a related activity I've often thought that everyone in the law firm, yes, including the most important "first impression" person, the receptionist, should fill out some type of informational sheet to set up a confidential firm-based intranet, a firm-centric "LinkedIn." This would help the firm "see" 2nd and 3rd generation connections of its members, attorneys and non-attorneys. If the questionnaire is designed properly you may find out that the receptionist has an uncle who plays golf with the CEO of your target client, but nobody ever asked her/him, "Hey do you have any friends, family or contacts that might know (target's name)?" Possibly, something like a confidential firm-based intranet set up like LinkedIn. Maybe some of the CRMs have this function. The ultimate cross-sell, your admin staff's connections.

Culture Shift: From a Few Rainmakers a Ministry Firm of Rainmakers

(Dave Bruns)

If you have a strategic plan and you have a strong firm culture, then people can assimilate and get on board with business development. This allows them to become part of the firm culture and part of a greater good. They understand their role and, therefore, they're happier and will spend more time focused on their role within the firm's overall goals and culture. If they have embraced the firm's culture, they're not going to be looking outside the firm to fulfill their legal career ambitions. They know what their purpose is. They have a connection to the common goal and they're harder to pull away. Everything's better when you have a strong culture.

You're not going to have good business development if you don't have a good culture. If your culture isn't positive and people are not on board with it, then you're at risk of being poached.

Whether it's associates or partners or entire groups, or offices. If you have an office in Picket City and it doesn't feel like it's integrated into the culture of the firm and isn't part of the firm, you're at risk of losing one or more attorneys. And lateral hiring is expensive.

We realized that we needed to have more people making rain than what we had. It became a cultural issue for us. In the past Farella, like most law firms that have been around forty years or longer, succeeded wildly with the idea that if you do good work, more work will come in the door. We also received quite a bit more referral work when a firm needed Bay Area representation. Now, the Bay Area is one of the most competitive marketplaces in the world for legal services. Almost every firm has an office here, either in San Francisco or somewhere in the Silicon Valley. They have boots on the ground in our nine county region.

With the heavy increase in competition, we determined that we needed the entire firm and each attorney to be more focused on rainmaking. We looked at our culture and said, "How do we make that culture shift? How do we change to get people to realize that, you have to do good legal work *and* you have to provide good client service, *and,* you have to be building a relationship that can bring in more work?" While service partners are needed, we can't have a firm of only service partners.

We worked with a consultant and came up with a plan where we trained the partners in cohorts of 10–12 on client service skills and client development skills, using the same model. Not only did we train those cohorts, but we took that same training and we did "all attorney" events, whether it was lunch or some other function. We also worked within practice groups. We worked within the affinity groups of the firm. We extrapolated the lessons learned and presented them in different mediums within the structure of what we had going on at the company.

Everybody involved with new business was getting the same message. Some people were getting it more intensely. Others were getting more of a cursory review. It gave us the ability that if somebody was going out to meet a client, they could have a conversation with another lawyer, with me, with their consultant, with their manager or with their department chair. They were using the same lexicon and the same process.

> Today, the Bay Area is one of the most competitive marketplaces in the world for legal services. We realized that we needed to have more people making rain than what we had. It became a cultural issue for us.
>
> —*David Bruns*

Everybody was on board. We didn't have opposing thinking or different ways of approaching important firm matters. When we sent out a team, they knew what they were doing. They had a similar goal, set of tactics, steps that they were going to take, and questions they were going to ask. It seemed to work extremely well. That organized process altered the firm's culture. Now, most of the partners have been through that process. We put some associates through that process. We are now on the back end doing the implementation of the action plan, the action items, and the next steps that were developed as part of that process. Now, Farella incorporates strategic planning and planning, generally. The firm has a plan. The practice groups have a plan. The partners all have a plan. Those all work together.

> Here at Farella we implemented strategic business development planning at all levels. So, now the firm has a plan. The practice groups have a plan. The partners all have a plan. Those all work together.
>
> —*David Bruns*

Our clearly defined culture has helped our client relationships. Clients want to understand what your culture is. You might say that clients tend to, whether consciously or unconsciously, culture match. It's probably unconscious, an unintended bias in the area of emotional intelligence. Clients are going to work with lawyers that they like. That touches on the loyalty issue, as well. You're going to be loyal to that law firm that has the culture that mirrors what you're trying to emulate within your own firm.

Culture: Building a Business Development Culture Within the Firm

(Allen Chichester)

I am actually fortunate because I was hired for this job about five years ago to help build a business development culture within the firm. That was the stated primary purpose of the hire. Naturally, I have to make sure the mail gets delivered. I have to make sure that things get done. There's a lot of "to-do's" on the list, but at the same time the over-arching responsibility is for me to help this firm drive incremental revenue. We do that by helping create a culture of business development and that involves a lot of different things, a lot of activity, and a lot of initiatives.

Personally, I believe in big hairy goals, but I do not believe in big hairy programs. I don't think there's a one-size-fits-all solution for how you build a law firm or how you build a book. We take the point of view, and I'm sure you've heard this before-that sales pipelines eat business plans for lunch. It's good to know where you're going, otherwise you won't know when you get there. And when you're working with a group, they all have to work off the same plan, but the real bread and butter of business development is managing the pipeline, whether you call it a prospect list, whether it's simply a list of five names that you keep on your desk in front of you or a sophisticated CRM program where you actually manage, the focus is turning your prospects into leads and your leads into clients, and if you're not driving towards that, then you're not making things happen.

We took the point of view that in order to get things moving, we needed to have some type of-let me call it, institutional cover-to start engaging the attorneys. We created what worked for us, something we call the "BT Law Academy," which is an institution for business development and professional development training.

Culture: The Law Firm's Culture

(Jeff Berardi)

A firm's culture, to a large degree, determines the average attorney's mindset when it comes to marketing the firm's resources and a lawyer's individual practice. Essentially, we need to be out there in the marketplace. Our lawyers are the ones on the ground doing these things and engaging in these client development activities directly, and we in the marketing department are trying to train them and give them the tools to do it. We've got 100 people in the marketing business development team, but we have 2,100 lawyers out there. So, if we can engage the lawyers, and if they really embrace the brand and the value proposition, that's a pretty powerful force out there. If you don't have that, if people don't really get it and don't really want to engage in active client development efforts, it's going to be hard to make much of a difference in the marketplace. And, I don't want my team to be the go-between, the liaison between the client and our lawyers. I think it's really important that our lawyers are comfortable making the outreach directly to clients or prospects. Sometimes my team members do, in fact, accompany the lawyers on pitches or sometimes make the introductions, if that situation is appropriate for them to do so, but I'm not really a sales department guy. My business development team may exhibit certain sales-like behaviors, but at the end of the day, I think the true salespeople need to be the lawyers. They are selling their expertise and their services – that's the talent that we have and experience that we have – rather than something my marketing team can offer.

At the end of the day, I think the true salespeople need to be the lawyers. They are selling their expertise and their services. That's the talent that we have and the experience that we have, rather than something my marketing team can offer.

—*Jeff Berardi*

Dialogue Project Management®: A Client-Centric Approach

(Karen Bell)

Our client-centric culture is supported by a program we designed called Dialogue Project Management®. We believe that no one knows what matters most to our clients better than our clients themselves. So we ask them. "What are your objectives?" That is a big part of the dialogue. Some of our clients have told us they are looking for more predictability and control of costs. We've responded by mobilizing our people and our resources to enhance our project management capabilities. In an economy where budgets are constrained and costs scrutinized, it became evident that we also needed to systemize our approach to project management. The basic premise behind our approach is that to give our clients what they're asking for, we must manage their mandates as projects. That is, legal mandates must be completed while managing the constraints of cost, time, and scope— without compromising quality. Working together as a team with our clients, we identify and plan around these competing constraints.

We made a substantial investment to develop our Dialogue Project Management® system, which is based on the general principles of the Project Management Institute (PMI); and it is supported by proprietary tools and techniques developed for use by our lawyers. These include customized work plan templates to help in developing detailed plans for mandates, a firm-wide database of professionals to help ensure we bring the best resources in the firm to each matter, estimating tools and best practices to help in developing realistic budgets, and techniques and processes to help identify and account for project risks.

The support program for our attorneys includes in-depth demonstrations of our Dialogue Project Management® tools and detailed training using customized project management templates relevant to each attorney's specific expertise. One-on-one sessions with a project management support team are available to attorneys to assist them in the development of project plans for clients.

We have built and are continuously improving our firm's processes and tools to deliver better results and a better experience for our clients and our people. Enhancing our project management capabilities is another way we demonstrate of our commitment to responding to our clients' needs.

Coming from the training side—the education side—we have a client development curriculum that provides skills development that complements the project management approach. Included is training or development around communication skills and development around one's business acumen. In the communications area, the fact that you need to be an active listener is emphasized, and there is a focus on framing a message so that it's cast as a leader's message. On the business acumen side, we look at the industries that we serve, making sure we're as expert as we can get to be a player in the industry – whether that's financial acumen or economic acumen. In different industries like energy, oil and gas, mining, you need to know the lingo. You need to know the process to put your insights into the context that the clients then truly value. And, learning how to articulate that, as they say, it's not about just being concise and having good grammar—this is about persuasion and thoughtfulness and being able to, whether you've thought about it for an hour, a day, or a minute, articulate a message that's compelling and clear so that you're effective. So, that's the skills development that we layer onto the more classic business development programming along with our client service that looks at expectations and client experience. We're working to create that unparalleled client experience.

Directors of Business Development: Need to be a Sponge

(Dave Bruns)

Constant learning is a commitment that people in my role must do. As I've evolved in my career, I've learned from people, books, magazines, blogs, Facebook, conferences, mentors, you name it. You've got to be a bit of a sponge. To understand your work you need to get a variety of training. You need to get some training on understanding personality tests, whether it's DISC or Caliper or I-Speak or Myers-Briggs. You don't need to be an expert at it so that you can give those tests, but you need to understand the concepts behind them. You need to understand emotional intelligence. You must commit the time and energy for formal learning. If you become a CMO, an MBA makes a lot of sense. I did mine in night school. How to critically think in those business areas is very important. I also think that when you're working with consultants, if your consultant's not teaching you how to do their job, they're not a very good consultant and I would fire them.

> If your consultant's not teaching you how to do their job, they're not a very good consultant and I would fire them.
>
> —*Dave Bruns*

You're never going to supplant what the consultant provides to your firm, but you can certainly learn from them and implement their lessons because if you're not learning those lessons, then whatever you're spending on that consultant is wasted money.

We are the implementers of what the consultants bring to the table and if we don't understand what they're talking about, if we can't work with them side by side, we're not going to be able to implement what is being presented or suggested. Every firm is a little bit different. What works at one firm may or may not work at another firm. If you can provide the political and contextual hurdles that you're fighting to the consultant, and they can then tweak their program a little bit to match the needs of your specific firm, your success will increase.

The answer to "Where do you learn?" is everywhere. I would also suggest getting a mentor. I've got several. Sometimes you grow out of a mentor and you need a different one. Sometimes, you have mentors for different aspects of your life, whether that's, "I need somebody to help me on purely management issues because I'm dealing with a team now and how do I become a better manager? Or, I've got this problem and how do I deal with it?"

You need somebody that you can reach out to on any given issue. Maybe you have somebody that's a more of a sales coach and you're able to say, "Hey, I've got this issue, how do I deal with that? Or, did you ever deal with that?" You need peers and mentors that you can trust enough that you can have those critical conversations and they can help you out.

Diversity

(Wayne Hogan)

The world is diverse. Clients are diverse . . . and, today, to win a client's business, law firms are expected to be as diverse as the communities they serve. Law firms need to be able to bring lawyers with diverse backgrounds into the range of legal services required to meet a client's locally diverse and globally diverse needs. This is why our Florida State University College of Law Summer Program seeks a range of undergraduates from an ethnically and socially diverse background.

Elevator Pitch or Verbal Business Card: It's Knowing How to Introduce Yourself

(Allen Chichester)

Lawyers will ask me about the verbal business card, or the elevator pitch or the water cooler pitch. We try to make it a part of all of our training activity. For example, if we're doing a networking training program, we will emphasize part of the networking is knowing how to introduce yourself in a way that people can relate to and understand and is interesting enough so they may ask you a question about it, versus a long, boring explanation of what you did that no one's likely to care about from a networking perspective.

In a "Build-your-Book" seminar, we may apply it from a slightly different perspective as always having or needing to be able to describe what you do quickly and easily. So, it's definitely still a part of what we do, and fundamental.

Elevator Pitch, aka the Verbal Business Card Answers Four Questions

(Sally Schmidt)

To develop your elevator pitch, it helps to write down the answers to four questions. First, who do you work for? What types of clients? Not necessarily the names of clients, but describe them—they're wealthy people, startup businesses and entrepreneurs, executives at major corporations, energy industry regulators, etc. Second, what are you doing for them? And by that

I mean, what are the benefits that you're bringing to the table? Not just general terms such as "litigation" or "M&A" or whatever, but helping to find buyers for a company if they're selling, or whatever you do to help your clients, specifically. The third question would be, do you have a point of differentiation? Is there something you can say that you do differently? You've done more of them. You have a certification. You have a specialized degree. For example, someone that might have spent two years as a human resource manager before going to law school might say, "As a former H.R. person, I've been in my client's shoes." Something that you can say that's different. And then, the fourth and last thing you need is a "for example"—Something you can just throw in at the end and it might be similar to something they've read about in the paper. "So, for example, when Casey Kasem died and they were fighting over his estate, that's the kind of thing I do. Disputes with trusts and estates." So, it's who do you work for, what are you doing for them, what makes you different, and, then, one "for example."

Elevator Pitch: A Custom-Tailored Idea

(Nancy Kostakos)

I like the idea you raised in our interview where we ask a number of rainmakers to record sound bites on the various ways they introduce themselves and describe their practice and the firm. Then we could share those recordings with the associates and other lawyers. That could become part of our knowledge base and training toolkit. If you can't get that rainmaker into a room with the associates when you're training them, at least you would be able to play that recording. Our rainmakers would certainly be amenable as we tape them frequently on a variety of topics.

Elevator Pitch: A Pre-Set Script Is Not Flexible Enough Within Every Setting

(Jeff Berardi)

My issue with having a highly-defined elevator pitch is that it somewhat oversimplifies the challenge. We are not selling a tangible product, we are selling a concept of what this law firm is all about. That concept is really hard to describe in just a few words. I don't know how I would do that in two minutes and, frankly, I don't know that I want our lawyers to be that aggressive about it. This isn't to suggest that there is no value in having the lawyers figure out better methods for describing themselves and what they do. Developing active listening skills, keeping their comments concise and focused, and so on.

I think that our lawyers need to work on the longer-term play, and building strong relationships with prospects seems to go way beyond just an elevator ride. It is sometimes important to educate the lawyers on how long the sales process can take. You may meet with someone ten times before you actually get their business or maybe you pitch them three or four times and you don't win the work until the final time. It can be months, years. It's not a week-long program and it certainly isn't a ride up the elevator with someone.

I want to make sure that our lawyers get that this is a long-term play. You've got to work it and you have to have a pretty thick skin about it and not be so worried about hearing "no" or getting no feedback at all and just move on and look to other opportunities. So, I suppose I've gone against the grain there in terms of this idea. I think certainly they need to understand the value proposition of the firm, but what we have done is provide an umbrella strategy and positioning statement for them that can work in a lot of different ways.

We point out, for example, the six things that we feel are important about the firm. Here is how we position the firm and how we differentiate it at the global level. Then, it's up to the lawyers to say, "Okay, maybe three out of six works." We don't want them to go completely off script and talk about something totally different from our value proposition, because that might be confusing to the client who hears something from our institutional branding activities that is at odds with what they are hearing at the local level or personal level. But, maybe certain elements of the broad value proposition don't work in a particular setting. So the lawyers then need to mix and match based on the situation.

I'd rather give our lawyers the framework and really have them understand how you've got to be adaptable and pick what fits in any given situation, rather than say, "Here's what you say when you go up an elevator," because I think that they'll then pick that one statement and use it as a script and it's not going to be effective.

We need to build in some level of managing expectations, because I have seen some lawyers who get frustrated after a few tries at it. The response is, "Well, you know this takes months and you've just got to keep working at it and learn from what didn't work and keep going." It's not like you just try it and move on. It's a long game. Because there is such a range of backgrounds and experiences, I think it's easy to fall into a trap, and develop a tendency to feel like, "This is just too hard and I can't do it, it hasn't worked yet and it won't ever work." Well, just try something different, or just feel confident that this is the right thing and it will happen over time.

We have seen that it can be a multi-year process to win work and it's pretty great when you do it. It's not all that unremarkable, though, that it can take that long, because we are dealing with very sophisticated decision makers. We are dealing with people who usually have established relationships in place already with other law firms. They might be happy with their current firms. They have a lot of options. It's not a quick determination. They're not usually the only player involved in terms of making decisions, so it can take a long time.

Elevator Pitch: A Verbal Business Card: Essential Elements

(David King Keller)

You need to have a very brief but engaging answer to the question, "What do you do?" This has been traditionally referred to as the "elevator pitch."

"In my 30 years as a lawyer," stated one senior partner, "I've never met someone on an elevator who became a client by the time we got off the elevator."

Two great qualities of an attorney are the ability to be direct and interpret the literal meaning of the words being used. This is an exception. The expression "elevator pitch" is a metaphor, an allegory. Few communication coaches expect you to actually make a pitch in an elevator. It's a metaphor to address the question, "In a very brief encounter with another, what can you say that might lead to a second conversation, which, in turn, might lead to a relationship with enough trust and appreciation for you and what you do that would cause that person to give you business or refer business to you?"

The qualities of the ideal "Verbal Business Card":

(1) *Brief*: within 30 seconds or less (remember, companies sell billions of dollars worth of products using 30-second TV commercials. This is your verbal TV commercial.)
(2) *Memorable*: something you said will cause your remark to be remembered.
(3) *Value Offered*, sometimes called the Value Proposition: this answers the question "Why should I, or anyone, care?" What specific value are you offering to them or someone they might know?
(4) *Advances the relationship*: somehow a next step is created that moves the relationship forward, known as an "advance." Some call this creating a "hook" that hooks the interest of the person to want to know you better. Some call it a "link," something that can link you more closely with that person.

Next time someone introduces herself to you, look for these four elements.

The verbal business card can follow a fill-in-the-blank formula behind two key words, as suggested by Scott Kessler. Start your description with "I help ______________."

Opening phrase:

"I help attorneys win malpractice cases."

"I help entrepreneurs and venture capitalists come together to realize their dreams."

Complete message:

In answer to the question: "What do you do?"

"I help attorneys win malpractice cases. I just helped an attorney save his career, his home, and his marriage. If you know any attorneys, please accept my card as an invitation for a free consultation. If you personally ever need legal assistance for any reason, I can probably refer you to three great lawyers to select from. And what do you do?" [24 seconds]

"I help save companies millions of dollars before, during, and after mergers and acquisitions. I recently saved a Fortune 500 corporation $10 million in acquisition fees of an overseas company. If you know any decision makers at large companies, please accept my card as an invitation for a free consultation. And if you personally ever need legal assistance for any reason, feel free to call me and I can probably refer you to three great lawyers to select from. And what do you do?" [30 seconds]

Any rainmaker will tell you to get the upper hand by finding out about your audience before you launch into your verbal business card. So, one answer to the question, "What do you do?" might be, "I would be happy to respond, my work is quite fascinating. But may I first ask what you do, so that I might put my answer into a more personal context?"

An elevator pitch training idea:

Go to the top rainmakers throughout the firm and record their answer to this question, "When you talk about the firm, what do you say? Or, when people say to you, 'What do you do? ,' how do you respond?" Get that on tape, and then with their permission, distribute those responses around the firm or within that rainmaker's practice group as a little example for others to listen to. "Oh, this is how Frank does it. This is how Helen does it."

Elevator Pitch: Always Start With These Two Words

(Scott Kessler)

How do you reply to the question, "What do you do?" I always start with two words, "I help." That's your purpose for being a lawyer. "I help companies become more profitable." "I help people get through difficult times in their lives." "I help people fight battles that they can't fight on their own." The goal is to receive the follow-up question, "how do you help them do that?" That's when you can mention that you are a lawyer and dive in deeper in to the work you do. But it's best to only go there after you explain how you help. After you get that first phrase out, what's going to happen is, the person you've just met walks out of the elevator, goes down the hall, goes to some event later that night by themselves, they are out there and they hear someone mention that they're going through a divorce. Or, they hear someone mention that they're going through a bankruptcy. Or, that their company is looking to do a merger. Alright. What's the first thing they're going to remember? They're going to remember you because they can connect their need with your purpose to help, "Oh, I just met a guy who helps people/companies do that. Here's his card."

Elevator Pitch: Ask the Pros

(David King Keller)

Record the elevator pitch of your top rainmakers. Include at least one for every practice area.

Play these recordings back to associates and other partners in a BD brainstorming session during a retreat or other opportunity. [See also: *Elevator Pitch: A Verbal Business Card: Essential Elements*]

Elevator Pitch: Coaches Review as Part of Business Development Plan

(Jill Weber)

The coaches primarily work with our lawyers on the elevator pitch as part of their individual business plans. In our newest Fast Forward program, we've used our first meeting as an opportunity for the participants to share their elevator pitches with each other. It is a great way to practice and also to promote their expertise to one another.

Elevator Pitch: For Example, How Do You Describe Yourself at a Cocktail Party

(Erin Meszaros)

I actually like to help the attorneys come up with something unique that defines them.

Some get nervous about the "elevator pitch." They will ask for a definition or example. I will often reply, "When you are at a cocktail party, how would you describe yourself?" Make sure you define yourself in such a way that your audience wants more. Make them ask another question. Intrigue them.

Elevator Pitch: I Think There's a Better Alternative

(Stephen Fairley)

When it comes to the elevator pitch, if you don't already know, I'm a bit of a contrarian. Everybody follows the herd and there's a lot of copycat marketing out there in the legal industry and all that does is emphasize how much of a commodity you've become when you market yourself like everybody else, so this is another way. I used to teach attorneys how to come up with a really good elevator pitch. I don't do that anymore. You know why? 'Cause it's a waste of time.

You can have a great elevator pitch, but the whole thought process behind an elevator pitch is, if you walked into an elevator with your perfect client and you only had several floors to get your point across, what would you say to them that would be so compelling that they would want to talk to you again? Right? That's BS.

It's complete bullblip. The people that are teaching elevator pitches are doing a disservice, I think, because it basically goes into the whole interruption-based marketing. I don't normally talk to strangers on the elevator. Do you? No.

So, basically, you're saying you're going to interrupt me in my little world, because that's where I'm at when I step onto the elevator. I'm either going to an appointment, coming from an appointment, or going to lunch or something else. So, I'm not in the mode of wanting to talk to a stranger on an elevator. What you say is irrelevant. It's the questions you ask that show me whether you're an expert. By the questions that I ask you, you can determine in a matter of minutes whether or not I know what the hell I'm talking about or whether I'm just another sales guy there to sell you something. Right? So, it's the intelligence and the intellect behind your question-asking that makes a huge difference. It's not the 30-second pitch that you're going to give. It's not like these attorneys are sitting in front of venture capitalists and they have two minutes to make their point. No. We're talking about potential clients, and people don't care about what you tell them. They care about the questions that you ask and how much you listen to them. That's Sales 101. Yes, you have to know your product, yes, you have to know your service, but if you don't know the questions to ask, then how in the world can you sell that?

It's the old example that many people have used over the years: sell me this pen. And any idiot can say, well, it's a good pen, it's a good price, and we're having a sale on it today and it's a two-fer. It's a BOGO, buy one get one free. Right? Any idiot can do that and that's what a lot of attorneys are doing . . . they're commoditizing their services by selling on price. Your weakest step, your weakest positioning statement is to sell on price. When you don't have any other way to differentiate your services from any of the other 10,000 or 100,000 other attorneys who do exactly what you do, you go to price. Right? Anybody can do that.

The decent salesperson will say, well, it's a great pen. It's blue, it's blue ink, so it stands apart from all the other black ink out there. It's got this great grip on it, it's rubberized so even if your fingers are slippery, you'll still be able to hold on to it, but if you press real hard, how you get finger cramps, that won't happen on this pen, because it's got this great rubberized grip on the front and it's a clicker, so you're not going to stick it in your pocket accidentally and get blue ink all over it and it's a gel pen, which is very different from all the ink pens out there. It's a gel pen, so it flows better and has a better angle to it. They can talk about the benefits and the features. That's a good sales person. Not a great one, but a good one. Right? The real sales person, when told, "sell me this pen," will respond with, "why do you need a pen? Tell me if you need the pen and I can sell it to you." See, the questions are the answer.

Elevator Pitch: In Plain English and Readily Comprehensible as Being Valuable

(Louise Muldoon)

So, we do think about the elevator pitch, and, essentially, it's trying to distill down what your offering is with a brief comment that's in plain English and makes it readily comprehensible that something of value is being delivered. In fact, we're looking at it now and it has been part of a branding exercise that we did. The premise of the elevator speech is, "When we're making a brief introductory remark about Baker & McKenzie, what do we say?" There were a number of people across a number of jurisdictions who worked with consultants to develop an elevator speech which was distributed to all lawyers. One component of that speech was "Baker & McKenzie defined the global law firm in the 20th century and is redefining it to meet the challenges of the global economy in the 21st." You need to do something that everybody looks at and is able to respond to, which is a big task when you're talking about 77 offices.

What we do well is taking something like the elevator speech and then spreading it very effectively right across our network. The elevator speech was then widely socialized, a series of presentations were prepared, which were delivered by the managing partners in each office and people were given hard copies and really encouraged to make it part and parcel of their daily activities. We're looking at that and we're revising it, but it's definitely a tool that we have used.

Elevator Pitch: It's Contextual

(Steve Bell)

Lawyers understand that they need an elevator speech. They work hard to fashion it. They sit down and they experience intellectual angst about it because they know it can only be about 30 seconds long. So, they sit down and they try to jam pack all this meaning and nuance into 30 seconds and it comes out to be so artificial and stolid. It's just a bunch of baloney. What I aspire to, and I can't say I've succeeded, is to recommend that your introduction be done in a contextual way. Introduce yourself in the context of the person you are talking to. Who are they? What does who you are matter to them and where they're coming from? I don't think you can write it and rehearse it.

So, if you're talking to a custodian on the way up to your floor, then who you are and how you introduce yourself is different from the president of a company or the head of intellectual property. So, it's all contextual. It's having the frame of mind, "Who is this person and how can I help them?"

I know who I am, but what part of me would relate to them in a way that would be helpful to them. Many people who spend a great deal of time intellectualizing their elevator speech, they end up with one elevator speech and one size does not fit all. My guidance is, think about who you are talking to, and for a second contemplate what might be of interest to them about you or what you do.

Elevator Pitch: It's Not Just for Elevators

(Despina Kartson)

It's important to prepare concise, compelling, and credible elevator pitch. Let's say you go to a cocktail party and someone says, "What do you do?" Do you say, "I'm an immigration lawyer for Law Firm X," or do you say something more memorable like "I focus on the needs of individuals and small businesses" or "I help people with immigration law and related issues. I am working on the sale of a business by an owner moving outside the US. I have another client fighting deportation attempts and am representing her in immigration court."

It's important to speak in laymen's terms and offer an interesting and memorable 30 second sound bite.

Elevator Pitch: Know Your Practice and Know Your Firm

(Matt Taylor)

It's important to know how to effectively and efficiently answer the question, "Well, what do you do?" That goes back to what I think I said earlier on in our interview: "You better pay attention about what's going on in your law firm," because if you don't, then you're really not going to have much to say in your elevator pitch. Let's say you're a young associate in the trial group and you're really happy working for our big software clients, or our big medical device clients. And you're billing 2,200 hours a year. You get a big bonus and life is good. Well, guess what? That's not really practicing law. That's not being a member of the firm. You have to know what your unbelievably talented IP lawyers are doing. What are your healthcare lawyers doing? What are your energy lawyers doing? You have to wake up. So, you're never going to have an elevator pitch. Ever. Unless you know what's going on.

So, I can't really help anybody unless they are going to invest the time and the energy to learn about what's going on in your firm. Be a member of the community. Go to the firm functions. When the firm's having a charitable event, sign up and go. You have to put time in. You can't just be a numerical unit of a law firm and expect that you're going to be someone that's able to sell that law firm. You have to volunteer for the associate's committee. Volunteer for anything you can. Learn about the firm so that when you're in a situation where someone would like to know about the firm, or you would like to tell them about the firm, you have a something to say.

Because you're all smart. And so, next time you're at a picnic and your friend's cousin shows up and he's a CFO of a fracking company or a drilling company, you can say, "Hey, Jack. I'm with the law firm of Duane Morris. We've got an unbelievable group that knows all about fracking regulations." "Oh, really? Wow. Give me your card." Guess what? That may never lead to anything, but it might. So, you're never even going to get there unless you're aware that you have a group of energy lawyers in your firm that has expertise in that area. You might not know everything, but you can at least talk and then go educate yourself more. Say you'll send him some materials. Branding is just not that hard. People get all wound up about it like it's the hardest thing in the world. It's just not that hard.

So, the associates, from day one, need to be trained to learn about your firm so that you can easily refer to that information in your verbal card or your elevator speech.

You remember Lenny Bruce? His big line was: "Always have 15 minutes of material." And Lenny Bruce always had 15 minutes of material. You have to have something. Now, that gets easier as you become a more mature lawyer and you really do know the firm. But right off the bat, if I'm a first-year associate, I am looking at our firm website. I am learning everything about every practice group leader. You have to invest some time.

Elevator Pitch: Not For Elevators, Apparently

(Adam Severson)

A portion of our pitch workshop helps folks craft their elevator speech. First it tells them that it's a misnomer and that it doesn't necessarily happen in an elevator. Years ago, at one of the first trainings I did for a group of attorneys, a very senior litigator who literally had practiced law for longer than I was alive said, "I have been practicing for more than 35 years and I have never gotten a new case in an elevator." I explained that the "elevator pitch" is essentially answering the question, "So, what do you do?"; and ensuring that you say something interesting in response while also looking to be *interested* in what the other person individual has to say. The goal is to engage them in some way or another. The elevator speech is designed to spark a conversation. It is intended for somebody to hear what you have to say for three sentences and then, if engaged, stick around as opposed to walk away.

We go through the exercise where we talk about differences in how you can describe your work. One of the examples we use is how you say what you do. For example, you might say, "Well I research case law related to personal jurisdiction and subject matter jurisdiction." We might recommend you say, "We help the client to determine the best play to sue a former business partner." The preference is to use layman's term because even the lawyers that are in-house counsel – while they are still lawyers – most of them are business people first and lawyers second.

They craft and write down their elevator speech. We then go around the entire room. Everybody has to practice and then we critique and provide refinements. Once you say it out loud you are inherently going to be at least 30% better the next time. It might still suck, but at least it will be better.

Elevator Pitch: On Target and Memorable

(Shanda Zavalsky)

We address the elevator pitch in the "Ready, Aim, Fire" personal brand piece. This is the "ready" part. Once you are clear what you want to be known for, then we work with you on how to describe that and identify relevant successes. We determine what the audience needs to know specifically. Once we have that message, we're able to help develop a better elevator pitch or introduction. You want to be remembered. I don't think you want to give your introduction thinking they are going to love me so much they will hire me, right here on the spot, but you do want them to remember you. So the key is introducing yourself in a way that you'll be remembered.

Elevator Pitch: One of the Two Most Important Conversational Skills

(Tasneem Goodman)

The "elevator pitch" is one of two essential conversational skills I think lawyers need to have. There are lots of other ones, but the elevator pitch is in the top two.

And the reason I say that is because we all get asked that question, "What do you do?" so often when we meet people. The ability to answer that question well is an essential business development skill. I see too many lawyers answer the question, "What do you do?" with, "I'm a lawyer," or "I'm a real estate lawyer," or "I'm a litigator," or "I'm a business lawyer," or whatever it might be. But at the end of the day, what do you do turns into "I am a blank kind of lawyer."

Although that answer is true and accurate, unless the person you're speaking to is also a lawyer or is very used to being around and talking to lawyers that response tends to be a conversation-stopper instead of a conversation-starter. I often find when you respond with, "I'm a lawyer" when the person listening is not also a lawyer or really familiar or comfortable with lawyers, they'll say, "Oh, great, so, seen any good movies lately?" Or, they'll say, "How about that baseball game last night?" They immediately change the subject because it's really hard if you're not a lawyer and you don't know a lot about the law to engage in conversation in response to, "I'm a lawyer."

What I often recommend to my clients is, in addition to communicating that they're a lawyer, talk about who you help and what you help them do. What kinds of people or organizations do you serve, and how do you actually help them? At the end of the day, as lawyers, we're helping our clients get from where they are to where they want to be, whether that's out of trouble, or into more opportunity, or making more money, or whatever type of legal help they need. That's what our job is, and so we're in many ways a means to our clients' ends. If we can talk about who those clients are and what it is that we help them accomplish or avoid or achieve, people can then connect with that. They can listen to what you've said about how you help these kinds of people or organizations, and they may say, "Oh, wow. I know about that. I worked for a company like that. I am a person that fits into that category. I have a neighbor who is a doctor, and you're a lawyer who helps doctors" as one example.

Or, you can talk about the specific issue that you helped them solve. Get out of trouble, make more money, expand their business, or whatever it is, and now people can say, "Oh, I've read about that in the newspaper." Or, "my company has done something like that." Or, "the company that I work for has had a similar situation." "My friend has a business that's going through that very same thing." Or whatever it is. Now they've started to connect their own personal experience or their own set of circumstances and what they know with what you've just imparted to them in a way that then, hopefully, starts a conversation. And that's all it is. At the end of the day if business development is about building a relationship, the building block of relationships is conversation. And so if you answer the question, "What do you do?" with "I'm a lawyer," and that's a conversation-stopper, you just ended your business development opportunity. If you answer the question, "What do you do?" with "Here's who I help, and this is what I help them make happen," now, hopefully, you've started a conversation.

And I often tell my clients that it's got to be quick. It's got to be able to roll off your tongue. So anytime you start to list things, I tell my clients, "Okay. You're probably not being quick anymore." Any time it starts to sound like a list of anything or a brochure it's no longer quick, and so now it's probably starting to seem contrived. It's got to be able to roll off your tongue. So, in part, your response to "What do you do?" that elevator pitch, it's not always going to be entirely comprehensive. There's too much that you do. You've got to make it simple because your answer to that question, "What do you do?" is not meant to be entirely comprehensive. It's just meant to start a conversation. And similarly, it doesn't even have to be entirely 100-percent accurate. It just has to be close enough. You know, "I help CEOs stay rich and out of jail." (Laughing.) Whether or not that's actually what you do in your practice, if it's close and it gets somebody chuckling, or remembering you, or thinking, "Okay. Tell me more about that. How do you help them stay rich and stay out of jail," it starts a conversation, and that's all it has to do is start a conversation.

I started this by saying the answer to "What do you do?" is one of the top two conversational tools. The other one, number two, you've got to be able to answer the question, "What's new?" or "What's up? What's happening?" in a way that's not, "Same old, same old," "Nothing much" or "I'm so busy." And that, I think, is an opportunity for conversation that comes up every day, often with the people that we're trying to develop business with, or from. And most of the time, we answer that question with, "Same old, same old. "Nothing much." or "I'm so busy." And those are, again, conversation-stoppers, not conversation-starters. And so, if you come back to business development is about relationships and relationships are built through conversation, then you can't answer the question "What's new?" with "Nothing much" or "I'm so busy." You've got to answer with something that's actually new. And it doesn't have to be groundbreaking, and it doesn't have to be a

10-minute answer. It can be a 10-second "I'm about to go to Italy next week" or "We just had this great win for a client."

And I usually tell my clients to have one personal and one professional "What's new?" message. That's usually because a professional contact will ask you what's new and you give them a professional "What's new?" message, and that's what's appropriate. And by the same token, sometimes you'll have a personal or social contact ask you what's new, and you want to talk about your kids, or your vacation, or a book you read. But sometimes it helps to criss-cross those. Sometimes we've got a client who asks us what's new, and by sharing something about our family or our personal lives, it warms up the relationship a little bit. And by the same token, sometimes we have a personal or a social contact who asks us what's new, and if we share something about what we're working on, it gets them seeing us in a professional way, oftentimes in ways that allow us to create opportunity in a social or personal relationship where otherwise bringing up professional or business matters might feel uncomfortable or contrived as self-serving.

It's just everyday conversation. And I think those are the two questions that come up the most that you've got to be able to answer well. Otherwise, there's other things you've got to be able to talk about, you know, why you and why your firm, and those kinds of things, but that's business development 2.0. These are the basics. You've got to be able to answer the question, "What do you do?" and you've got to be able to answer the question, "What's new?" in a productive way if you want to have good conversations with people. And then after you're done with all of that, having good business development conversations requires shutting up. (Laughing.) And asking good questions and then actively listening and demonstrating interest in what people tell you and asking good follow-up questions. I'll tell you, most of the best business development conversations that my clients tell me they have are ones where they say very little, ask thoughtful and insightful questions, demonstrate an interest in what the person is telling them, and let them talk.

Elevator Pitch: Tell Them Your Value

(Karen Bell)

The elevator pitch is part of the training. Or, the water cooler speech as it used to be called. Each generation has its reference. Our coaching programs have group sessions and that's part of it. We do that in junior associate programs as well as in partner programs. That's where we bring in

LinkedIn as a form of elevator pitch to expand the concept because some of them will say, "Well, we're not supposed to talk in the elevator." Now we talk about how to develop your introduction. Not to say, "I'm Karen Bell. I'm the Senior Director of Professional Client Education." Instead, say, "Hello. I'm Karen Bell and I lead the educational initiative for a large national firm, for our professionals as well as our clients." "Oh, really? What does that mean?" I'm telling people what I do rather than my title. That's the idea. OR for a practitioner, that you're not just an attorney in the tax department, but that you help clients, for example, manage the complex regulations relevant to crossborder transactions. The point is to focus on your value.

Elevator Pitch: Two Different Approaches

(Hans Haglund)

The elevator pitch? That's simply a matter of practice. Industry groups and associations relevant to your practice provide a great environment with plenty of opportunities to describe your value to potential clients. The elevator pitch needs to be personal. It needs to include the problems you solve, value you bring to companies, versus the firm and practice overview. You can talk about your firm, but show your personality and ask questions. The other way is story-telling. Have two or three successful client stories that you can talk about. Tell them in a way where you are not beating your chest, but allows you to show your approach and how you work with people. It should be something with a positive and engaging message, but make sure it is relevant. Relevant to the person you're talking to.

When meeting someone, start by asking questions* and get to know them. Again, it's that 70/30 rule. 70 percent listening. 30 percent talking. Make sure a large percentage of your 30 percent is spent asking open-ended and directed questions to allow you to further get to know them. Now you have a better understanding of who they are and how to make your professional description relevant to their world.

> The elevator pitch? That's simply a matter of practice. Networking within your practice or within your industry will provide a great environment with plenty of opportunities to describe your work. It should be something with a positive and engaging message, but make sure it is relevant. Relevant to them.
>
> —*Hans T. Haglund*

[*Author's note: For some of the questions you can ask go to Exhibit 1: *Five Good Questions Upon Meeting Someone*, and Exhibit 2: *Twenty Questions You Should Ask Current and Prospective Clients*.]

Elevator Pitch: We Call It a "Business Introduction"

(Mark Usellis)

We call it a "business introduction" which seemed to have a better connotation and caused lawyers to cringe less than the phrase, "elevator pitch." We made "business introduction" training part of the partner and associate program because, clearly, everyone has a need for that since they will be going to a networking event, speaking at a CLE, or some other function.

We would do an exercise and give them some tips and have them create their business introduction. Then, at the beginning of the next class, each of them would give their business introduction. When they were done, we would ask the group, "So, did you like any of those? Which ones do you remember? Which ones resonated with you and why?" When they would go into coaching, those people who needed some extra help would work with the coach on that.

Emails: Online Marketing Tool

(Lisa Salazar)

People are so used to turning out emails that sometimes they don't fully consider the power of an email, especially in online marketing. It's definitely a craft. And it's not just the writing. It's about formatting, tone, targeting your audience and properly laying out the email. When talking about online marketing and email marketing, it's important that the writing is carefully considered and then what appears above the fold and what appears below the fold. Also think about frequency, how often emails are sent, and whether to use a professional mailing system rather than using just Outlook, AOL, Yahoo! or Gmail. Unfortunately, people are using these email systems. Also be sure to use a reputable email newsletter system. There's a number of vendors that provide this kind of service.

Another factor is how the email looks. Emails need to be eye-catching. If your firm doesn't have an email marketing expert, then consider hiring a consultant to develop one.

When people ask, "How should an email be sent to a client base?" the answer is that it depends from market to market and sector to sector.

I've discovered this working at a global firm, in the United States we have to be very loud because it's such a competitive market, whereas in the

United Kingdom it is a smaller one. It has been a learning curve to learn the different markets and what their throttle is. It's been interesting learning what their expectations are and what the marketplace is like as far as social media. The key is to look at metrics and measure how clients are contacted. Make sure that different people in the firm aren't sending multiple emails to the same person. Make a coordinated effort.

In response to the question, "Should these be personalized like, 'Dear Frank,' with a personal signature line? Or are people okay with a generic update and so just identify the firm's name and contact information?" It depends on what you're sending. If it's an invitation, it's important that it's personalized. If it's an update, I think people are getting so many emails that you just want to get to the top line.

Events: Partnering: Introvert With Extrovert, Newbie With Veteran

(Dave Bruns)

Not everybody is super comfortable walking around a room, shaking hands, meeting people, engaging in conversation, small talk, and doing face time. Some people love that. Those people that hate it, you partner them with somebody that is more comfortable with it, someone who has more of an "in" with the organization so they know more people. That approach makes it a little bit easier for the one who is less social.

Maybe someone is a writer and a great content generator, but they're not comfortable speaking. On the flip side, you have somebody that hates writing, loves to speak, but in order for you to get to be a speaker and be seen as that expert, you have to have some base of content that people can refer to and say, "Yeah. This guy is an expert and we'll put him on the dais." So, you're going to have to write a little bit of content. How do we figure that out? Maybe we associate you with that guy that loves to write, and you jointly write content for articles, blogs, etc.

As we all know, you get work from face-to-face meetings, so we try and push people into that face-to-face discussion. But we also try and allow the lawyers to take advantage of the activities that they like to do.

Somebody in my role needs to have a strong understanding of personality traits and communication skills so that they understand how to push people a little bit. They understand when they're getting pushback, where's it coming from, and how do they overcome that.

It's very important that you spend time understanding the characteristics, demographics, and differences between a "boomer" and a "silent generation" and a "millennial." You need to know what you can expect from those people and how you can leverage those skill sets. Maybe you put your "millennial" with your "silent generation" so that they can work together on a social media effort.

It does take insight. Longevity with your firm helps, too. You can understand the politics and the people. You have to understand body language. You have to understand how people are communicating and when they get into an uncomfortable place and think, "Okay, I just put this person somewhere uncomfortable and is it uncomfortable in the good sense of uncomfortable, a healthy stretch, or is it uncomfortable in the sense that they shut down and you've lost them, and do you need to back out? How do you back out of that in a way that keeps the momentum of what you're discussing or what you're trying to get them to do moving forward in a space that keeps them comfortable? "Comfortable" is the right word to use. Literally if they're not comfortable doing the act that they say they will do, they're not going to get it done no matter how many times you put it on a task list, how many deadlines you put down, and how many penalties that you exact. You want them to get to a point where, "Yeah, I'm comfortable doing that. Okay." Then, it's going to get done.

Facebook and Twitter

(Lisa Salazar)

When lawyers ask me, "Do I really have to be on Facebook? Should I create a Twitter account and be active on it?" I tell them that I think that's a personal decision. Some of our lawyers really like Twitter, and they do it on a personal basis. Speaking for just the general legal public at large, I would say that if a lawyer is comfortable in that arena, they enjoy it, they could certainly benefit. It can't hurt.

If they're not comfortable and don't have the time or inclination, don't force it. And the same would go for Facebook. I think there's a lot of younger attorneys who are quite comfortable on Facebook and have been doing it since they were in college, and they want to continue with their Facebook pages. A lot of rewarding networking opportunities arise from being on Facebook. I don't think it's something to turn my back on. I think for the sake of a lawyer who grew up on those sites, just be aware, again, that you are an officer of the court. It is a public forum and you need to act as if it is a business email or a business transaction. Think not once, twice, but thrice before you post something. Don't be negative. Be positive. And remember, your Bar rules are going to be different from state to state. Of course, don't be misleading or breach client confidentiality, and pay strict adherence to all the Rules of Professional Conduct.

Fast Forward: A Formal Business Development Program: Part 1: Background

(Jill Weber)

The Fast Forward program is where our formal training program for rainmakers began. The program launched at legacy firm Leonard, Street and Deinard in 2003. The purpose of that program was to take young partners with business development potential, enhance their business development skills and expedite the growth of their practices, with the focus primarily on revenue generation.

So, the first program started out with, "let's pick a group of people who we think have significant business development potential [and] have not achieved it yet, but we think they could grow their practices half a million dollars over a two-year period."

All of these were younger partners who had never had a book of business over $1 million, so $500,000 was a fairly significant jump. And so that idea was posed to me by our then managing partner when I was interviewed for this job in 2003. So, I said, "That's a great idea," and he said, "Fine, figure it out." That was it.

He said, "I want to take 20 attorneys and grow their practices half a million dollars each over a two-year period. How do we do it?" So, I called a lot of peers. I did a lot of research in our industry to see what people did. And what I found was a mixture of different pieces of the puzzle, but not the full puzzle. For example, many firms offer coaching. There are a lot of people in the industry who are coaches. Each coach tends to have his or her own coaching program with a defined way of approaching it with periodic check-ins, whether they be weekly, biweekly, or monthly. Here is the plan template. Here is how I approach it. Here is how it works. And it's usually for a very discrete period of time. The challenge I found with that approach is that these programs often don't have built in accountability to the leadership team for what they are to achieve during their coaching sessions.

A second thing that firms do is group training. For example, we used the Flannery training here. There is some value in getting that sort of one-to-many communication, but I don't know that it [alone] changes behavior.

Then, we saw that some firms use individual business plan templates and then it's up to each attorney to implement the plan. Most of these plans, though, weren't client-focused. I looked at all of these different pieces and decided to create a program that stitched them together and that was branded. The program was briefly called the "Top 20 Attorneys" program, but as you can imagine, since we are very egalitarian like most firms, the idea that we would identify anybody as being in the top 20 to the exclusion of others just didn't go over well. So, I worked with a copywriter and designer to create a brand. We literally created a logo and named it the *Fast Forward* program because the program goal is to "fast forward" business development efforts.

Fast Forward is an integrated program, and that's what primarily differentiates it, I think, from what's in the market. So, it includes some of the components I mentioned. First, each person has an individual business plan. That plan has to be put in writing and has very specific components that include revenue goals, practice goals, clients, prospects, referral sources, etc. It is very specific and very detailed; and those plans need to be submitted to a coach and to me. It provides accountability and oversight, someone actually saying, "Did you write it, and is it current?" I review and give feedback on the business plan. The second piece is an outside coach. We strongly believe that, for true accountability, you must have someone outside the four walls. I prefer to hire people who are experts. I mean, as CMO, I have to be jack of all trades, master of none. That's the intent of the job though, right? We are supposed to be able to handle everything and know the right resources. It is [a] little bit like a relationship partner where they might say, "Yes, I'm a corporate attorney, but my goal is to provide the full range of legal services to the client." So, we incorporate the outside coach along with a training curriculum because we didn't feel the attorney should just operate independently in implementing [his or her] plans. That's a lonely place.

We determined that we needed a monthly training curriculum to bring the attorneys together because these are common topics. We design the educational curriculum after the participants write their plans so we can identify certain common themes that emerged from the different plans. With that information we and work with the coaches to say, "I am consistently seeing 'delegation' as a need in the business plans. I am consistently seeing they are interested in learning more about alternative fees and pricing." We learned over time that doing that training over breakfast or lunch tends to work best. People tend to show up. It's only about an hour, and we feed them. In fact, I just had a Fast Forward program this morning. We called it, "The Wind-Up and the Pitch. Effective RFP Strategies." And some of the attorneys come in and say, "Well, I don't receive RFPs." We tell them it is not just RFPs, it's pitches. We ask them, "In the last year has a client asked you to come in and discuss the firm's capabilities, and did you know that they were also interviewing other law firms?" Everybody says, "Yes." We say, "Okay, well then, that was a pitch and these tips are important to you." So, Fast Forward has that pitch training piece. It also has a discrete timeframe that I think is longer than most coaching programs. I have interviewed a number of coaches and their programs range, on average, from 6 to 18 months. Fast Forward is a two-year program.

Fast Forward has accountability. I actually work with our finance department to track their financial results, and I report that to senior leaders in the firm. And the attorneys know it's getting reported. They also receive the monthly reports from finance. The report is not just showing them how many hours were billed, it's also: "Here's your top client list." "Here are your fee receipts this year to date and compared to prior years." Their coaches receive this report as well. And the attorneys will meet with their coaches monthly to discuss these reports, along with other topics.

And the final thing, and this was the most controversial, I included incentives. I am married to someone who is very good at sales and I have been on president club trips, which is a reward for a job well done. So, I put incentives into Fast Forward. If you achieved the half million dollar increase over [a] two-year period, this was for the first program, you got an all-expense paid three-night four-day trip with your spouse because my feeling was that the spouse was sacrificing as well. Because, to achieve that goal, there are going to be a lot of late nights and early mornings and a lot of time away from home to get this done. It's an all-expense paid trip to any Ritz Carlton in the United States. We offered tiered incentives. So, if you didn't hit the half million but you hit $300,000, then you got a trip to a northern Minnesota golf resort.

We tried all this out. We positioned it as a pilot program. The other key element is that you could not nominate yourself or request to be part of the program. We had specific criteria to be selected. You could not have a book in excess of "X," but you could not have a book less than "Y." You had to be at a certain stage in your practice in terms of years of experience. What we found is that younger partners, those who have been partners less than ten years, tend to be the sweet spot. I often speak to the (younger) partners, partly because they are trainable because they haven't created bad habits yet; and second, they are very eager to try things; and third, most of them in that time period enter what I call the Valley of Despair.

Fast Forward: A Formal Business Development Program: Part 2: Milestones

(Jill Weber)

The "Valley of Despair" is when a fairly new partner thinks to him- or herself, "I have been a wildly successful associate. I have had work handed to me. My title is associate, therefore I can be assigned this work. The partners love me. Now, I've become partner and all of a sudden everyone has abandoned me. I get no work assignments because I have a partner title, because my billing rate is higher, and because the client needs a senior associate, not a young partner, to do the work." These are the "Valley of Despair" partners who form "the sweet spot" for business development training.

All of a sudden reality hits them. It doesn't matter how often you tell him or her as an associate, "you need to build business development skills to be successful," and we do provide business development training to associates, but they don't really get it until they feel the pain. And usually it's about year two of being a partner. There is this trough. What happened to their billable hours? It is the Valley of Despair. They talk about it all the time, and they really get the meaning of that phrase. It is so true. And so, they are in a position where you are handing them a lifeline, so to speak, and they are very eager to try what it is that you are putting in front of them. So, we came up with criteria which said that to be part of the program you had to have a book of at least "Y," but not more than "X." You have to be "X" number of years out in practice, and other criteria. Our business development committee actually looked at a list of all the partners who met those criteria and then picked the 20 for the initial program. At that time it was somewhat controversial because people wondered, well, isn't this sort of creating an exclusive group? Our response was this was just a pilot, and we have no idea if it's going to work. We said, if it works, then we promise whatever we learn that is a best practice, we will share with others. And we have. It has informed our associates' business development training because one of the key outcomes was the question, "Why didn't anybody teach me this when I was young enough to do something about it?"

> Suddenly the senior associate becomes partner and the work assignments stop. This is the Valley of Despair, the sweet spot for business development training.
>
> —*Jill Weber*

So, the pilot actually informed other business development training. The other thing that I think was really critical, and I say it often, is that you never get a second chance to make a first impression. The invitation to participate in the program came from our business development committee chair and me. We both went and personally invited each person. We did not use an email. We did not use a letter. It was eyeball to eyeball. We went and sat down with each person. And it took a lot of selling to put together that first group because they didn't know what it was. They thought, "I am going to be scrutinized and am I going to get billing credit for the hours that I spend in the program? What if I don't make the target numbers?" So, there was a lot of skepticism. The lawyers asked, "Is this in my best interest? Am I just putting myself under the spot light in something I don't want to be part of?

In the end, all of them agreed to participate. We let them know it was a pilot. But having that face to face, I think, is critical, and it had to be an attorney who is a senior leader in the firm and me explaining everything. Then, we gave them a letter of invitation that came from the president. We then hosted a kick-off meeting at a private club in downtown Minneapolis. The firm leadership was there. We explained the program over cocktails. I'm a big believer in both cocktails and competition. The combination gets their attention.

> At the end of two years, the first Fast Forward pilot group had grown their practices by seven and half million dollars.
>
> —*Jill Weber*

With our first group, at the end of two years when we measured and reported on all the things that I said we would measure, that group of 20 had grown their practices by seven and a half million dollars. And the firm's out-of-pocket investment, including all the training, the coaches, the incentives, was about $150,000.

> A $150,000 investment in Fast Forward returned $7.5 million. That ROI got a lot of people's attention.
>
> —*Jill Weber*

A $150,000 investment for a $7.5 million return is a very good ROI. That got a lot of people's attention. To me what is more important is what I call the behavior modification that comes out of the program, and that is, we want to permanently change how they think about business development. If I look at that first group of 20, none of them had a book over a million, now nine have sustainable multimillion-dollar practices. To me that is more important because we have created an annuity for the firm. They are also, I think, much more engaged. In other words, they have become leaders in the firm. They have become more engaged in cross-selling. One of the big barriers to cross-selling is trust, and we intentionally create these Fast Forward groups where trust is dramatically increased among the different practice groups.

I am now on my sixth *Fast Forward* group here at the firm. We have narrowed the criteria, so that, as I mentioned, we are going to younger partners. They are also really engaged. Like at my training session this morning on RFPs, I think I maybe spoke for half of it, and the other half they were sharing their own war stories, or asking questions of each other. I see that the people who have been in this program, they go on to continue to cross-selling, and it just builds this level of trust between them. We have continued to monitor and measure the Fast Forward program, and consistently the attorneys in this program have revenue growth that is between 8 and 10 times that of their peer group not in the program.

> Consistently, the attorneys in this program have revenue growth that is between 8 and 10 times that of their peer group not in the program.
>
> —*Jill Weber*

We have really specific metrics about Fast Forward. I am, as you can tell, really passionate about it. I really believe in it. Plus, I have seen it work so many times. It wasn't a one and done. It is institutionalized here at Stinson Leonard Street. It was a Leonard, Street and Deinard program. Now we have merged with Stinson, and it's a Stinson Leonard Street program.

Following our merger, we actually saw Fast Forward as a great way to help integrate the two firms by bringing together these young partners who will be the future of this firm. The program allows them to understand each other's practices, so that they are focused on business development. It is very client focused. Even though we say the goals are revenue generation, it is not like sell, sell, sell. It's all the good principles of client service.

Part of the training is we set them all up with Manzama. They get daily client and client industry news feeds. As soon as we get their business plans it goes to our business analyst and she sets them up on daily news feeds to help them monitor and keep up to date on their clients' industry and business. It is a way that we institutionalize good client service practices that we want everyone doing, and because they are part of the program they say, "Oh, I have to do it because it's part of the program." As opposed to, if you were to approach them outside of the program and said, "Can we set you up on daily news feeds?" they might shrug and pass on it. But if you are part of [a] program you start to institutionalize these good best practices.

> Part of the training is we set them all up with Manzama. They get daily client and client industry news feeds.
>
> —*Jill Weber*

In our last group of 10, in the first year, 4 of the 10 who have never had books over a million hit over a million in their books. Honestly, it was the best group I have ever had here at the firm. They are really outstanding. They follow through. They're really just engaged in the whole program and they ask good questions. And it gives us, as a business development team, good insights into what their challenges are and what help they might need, so that we are properly staffed and have the right services and capabilities.

One emerging thing that came out of it, probably two programs ago, was the need for social media support. They were struggling with LinkedIn. As a result, we found a local LinkedIn consultant who is just exceptionally talented at helping them. We piloted that LinkedIn training within Fast Forward. We said, "Let's work with this consultant with these 10 people and see if it works." Well, they were all raving about the LinkedIn training. We rolled it out within the firm, so that people could work with the consultant one on one. You spot these needs that they have that you may not necessarily hear directly even if you are working with attorneys all the time. It's the collective that allows the themes to emerge from those attorneys in the program.

> In our current group of 10, in the first year, four of the 10 who have never had books over a million hit over a million.
>
> —*Jill Weber*

Fast Forward: A Formal Business Development Program: Part 3: Candidates

(Jill Weber)

We wanted to bring up people who had business development potential. That is still something that we look at, but that is the subjective component. You can have objective measures: does the person have at least "X" amount of book? Subjectively, you look at how they've demonstrated great client service as an associate or a very disciplined approach or they've been proactive in approaching partners with questions about business development.

They've demonstrated some level of interest or skill. We look at experience both internally and externally, meaning they may show great client service in how they are treating the partner and being responsive, and, therefore, we know that's going to translate outside the firm in terms of how they're treating the clients as well, or they've demonstrated a willingness to step up to the plate for internal projects. I'll use a phrase I heard from a peer at another firm, which is you're looking for the people who are "scrappy." His comment was "Scrappiness is vastly underrated in recruiting at a law school." I think that's absolutely true. It's a great phrase. It's so intangible, but it's so accurate.

We usually set our educational program as a lunch-and-learn, which is great, because you can get people to eat and listen, but for one group, we couldn't find a common lunchtime that worked, so we changed it to a coffee. We'd take them down to the Caribou Coffee store and buy them whatever coffee they wanted, and then go back to a conference room for the educational session.

Our goal is diverse representation on a variety of levels – gender, race, geography, practice. So, if we have 10 people, we try not to have three from the same practice group. On the other hand, if they're three of the best people, we might do that. We don't want to be so regimented that we aren't taking the full picture into account, and pick someone who may not qualify just to meet some predetermined practice group participation criteria. We just say, this may not be the year for that practice area. Let's say it's a smaller practice group, and there's no one in that group that fits our participant criteria. This is just not the right year. We wouldn't say, "Oh, but we have to have somebody from Practice Group X."

Fast Forward: A Formal Business Development Program: Part 4: Mentoring

(Jill Weber)

We incorporate mentoring. We are constantly tweaking the *Fast Forward* program as we go forward. The program today has evolved. There are things that we tried that we didn't continue. For example, in the first program, we identified more experienced, typically senior, business generators to serve as mentors to those in the program. We found that the participants didn't take advantage of that resource. I don't know why. You would have thought it would have been a great feature of the program, but I think people were hesitant to demonstrate their lack of knowledge in business development to someone more senior. As a result, we no longer offer formal, assigned mentoring as part of the Fast Forward program. I would say that more of their advice is coming from the outside coaches, which is not to say that they don't ever rely on an internal resource, but I think that mentoring has been more effective when it is relevant to a specific client opportunity. For example, a younger partner says, "I finally have the bite. I want to go make the pitch." And my phrase in that situation is, "You've got to bring in the big guns." Don't do it alone. Sometimes they may worry about billing credit, but I remind them that if they don't get the help they need, 100 percent of zero is still zero. Most senior business generators are supportive in helping younger partners grow their practices. It's not going to become some kind of financial debate. With this approach, they are actually getting the mentoring on the job, so to speak, as they are preparing for the pitch and then they get to see the more experienced partner role modeling active business development and how they're making the pitch, and how they're preparing for the pitch. In this way, the mentoring becomes a more natural development as they actually implement their business plan and seek help within a very specific client situation, as opposed to formally going to a senior partner and saying, "I am now going to review my business plan with you and I want your input." That feels more stiff and forced. [See also *Mentoring: BD Mentoring = Yes; Formal = No; Case Study Based = Yes.*]

Formal Mentoring: As part of our associate program, we do have a more traditional, formal *professional* development mentoring program. Within the context of Fast Forward, we do not assign formal *business* development mentors to each attorney. Instead, we tend to bring in mentors on an as needed basis to support and advise the Fast Forward attorneys in the context of an actual business development scenario. If an attorney needs help and advice with a business development opportunity, that's where we bring in an experienced business generator to serve as a "mentor" in that situation, but we don't position it as formal mentoring per se. [*Author's note:* Jill Weber provides situational "mentoring" without calling it formal mentoring. It occurs in the context of just-in-time support. That's a great distinction. I appreciate the fine-tuning that this brings to the discussion.]

Fast Forward: A Formal Business Development Program: Part 5: Tracking For 2 Years

(Jill Weber)

When they go into the Fast Forward program we help them develop the clear mindset that "I'm going to be tracked for two years."

After two years, there is still formal tracking. I continue to financially track their results, and that's where we've gotten some of the performance data that I shared with you. We don't formally report that up to leadership; that's just for my own tracking purposes, so I can share those results with leadership on more of an aggregated basis.

Within the Fast Forward program we're providing these templates, like the business plan template. We also have a business development committee. I work very closely with them. The business development committee is separate from our board of directors. We have eight members from different offices of the combined firm. They are key business generators from a variety of disciplines. We meet once a quarter to talk about business development initiatives. I think it's particularly going to be important in our merged firm in terms of sharing best practices. One of the outcomes of our first meeting was that they have high regard for Fast Forward and they asked me to implement it in the combined firm within the coming year, so we're working on that strategy. It's very exciting. Whenever I talk about it if I'm in any of our offices, I immediately get partners who are coming up to me and asking, "Can I be considered for the program?"

It's very exciting. We've got more and more who are graduates of the program. I think the people who have been through it feel that it has given them the right tools in the toolbox to be successful in their practice.

Fast Forward: A Formal Business Development Program: Part 6: Results

(Jill Weber)

Fast Forward: Quantitative Results

- Over two year period, fee receipts increased by 80 percent
- Growth rate ten times that of peer group
- Over four year period
  - Net incremental fee receipts growth of more than $20 million
  - 9 attorneys with sustainable practices over $1 million

Fast Forward: Qualitative Results

- "It keeps me focused on the most important and achievable marketing objectives."
- "This program should be sold as the 'inevitable' steps for having a successful practice, not an option."
- "It facilitates and encourages cross-marketing better than any other activities I've seen the firm undertake."

- "Participation has caused me to focus on existing clients . . . has allowed me to gain a better understanding of client needs and has encouraged me to actually ask for opportunities to expand our current client service."
- "Fewer seminars; more one-on-one contacts."
- "I have more regular contact with potential clients and opinion makers."

Fast Forward: Top 10 Takeaways

(1) Think long-term.
(2) Think team.
(3) It's a marathon, not a sprint.
(4) Create a memorable brand.
(5) Provide incentives.
(6) What gets measured gets done.
(7) Facilitate feedback.
(8) Create a pilot program.
(9) Be prepared for the "Valley of Despair."
(10) Praise efforts, not only results, publicly.

Fast Forward: A Formal Business Development Program: Part 7: For Sale

(Jill Weber)

The last thing that I will say about Fast Forward is that I presented it to the Legal Marketing Association conference in Chicago 2006 and it was a standing-room-only breakout session. All these people kept coming up and asking me questions, and then a lot of people called afterwards saying, "Could you help to implement the program at my firm?" and I thought, "Why am I giving this away for free?" So I approached our board of directors with a business plan and proposal. I said, "These people are trying to replicate it and I think we could sell this because I have it all packaged. I have the letter. I have the criteria for hiring coaches. I have the financial report. I have the business plan template. I have written the educational curriculum." I mean, that's all the stuff that any CMO gets stuck with, right? It's that blank white page starring at you. How do you do it? So, the ink on paper is so much better. I approached the board, and a couple of partners were reluctant. They said, "I think this program is a great asset," and I said, "Yes, but all of it is how you implement it." I mean, I am here implementing it. I know it in depth. And it's great that people can buy things, but the key is having the right person implement it. We did package it, and we actually sold it to six firms. So, it's actually generated revenue for the firm in that way as well. I don't actively go out to market Fast Forward. It has primarily been through word-of-mouth. We have learned a lot from those sales because I have picked up some really good best practices that we have implemented here from what people do at other firms. It's like, "Oh I never thought about that, now that's a really good idea; we should try that."

Fear: Success In Many Cases Involves Fear: One "Secret" To Overcome Fear

(David King Keller)

Who said, "Everything I ever did I was afraid to do"?

United States Supreme Court Justice Sonia Sotomayor.

A group of senior executives from the U.S. federal government met and to the one they all agreed that every step forward in their career was preceded by some heart-in-the-throat action.

Most of my presentations address fear. In fact, I have one "lunch and learn" presentation and overcoming fear is the entire topic. Many people, including attorneys, are shy and introverted. I'm able to help most advance their career despite that challenge. Sometimes it is "simply" a fear of taking a step into unfamiliar territory. During my presentation I put up a couple of slides of over 100 famous people who were documented as being shy or introverted, e.g., Eleanor Roosevelt, Albert Einstein, Tom Hanks, and Sally Fields. Fear can be a career killer. Fear can also be a signal that this is something I must do in order to advance.

Fear can stop an otherwise very good business development action from ever being implemented. Most lawyers, like most intelligent people, have a fear of "looking bad," of making a mistake. Of course, I'm not talking about actual physical danger. We're talking about the day in and day out fears. Fear of making a call. Fear of presenting an idea. Fear of joining a group of strangers at a networking reception. Fear of asking for someone's legal business. The extreme discomfort of stretching oneself into unfamiliar territory in order to make progress, to grow and to expand one's practice and career.

Here's one secret to overcoming fear and to overcoming shyness and introversion. Whenever you feel that fear, tell yourself, "This feeling means this is something I *can and must* do." Take the fear from in front of you and put it behind you while turning that fear into a very large hand pressing against your back pushing you forward.

Fees: Alternative Fee Agreements (AFA): Project Management Profile Approach

(Karen Bell)

When it comes to Alternative Fee Agreements, we engage in a very open discussion with our clients. We have a working relationship with them that allows us to have the broader conversation about costs without them having to worry about the clock running.

The leader of our pricing group encourages our attorneys to engage in active listening. When a client says, "Well, I'm concerned about hourly rates or volume discounts," or whatever their specific issue is, we say, "Well, let's talk about pricing." You have to build in room for flexibility and take the scary factor away. Not all clients are ready for it, though. There are clients who are change averse. It's taken a long time for alternative fee arrangements to take root.

Alternative Fee Agreements, for us, were born out of the firm's commitment to project management made many years ago. Our firm leadership adopted Six Sigma and the Six Sigma Lean approach, and we started educating our clients about it and we created teams who were dedicated to it. One of our partners also co-wrote a book on the subject called Project Management for Lawyers which was published by the Ark Group.

We now have a Client Service and Innovation team in place that works on client matters and prepares a project management profile or plan for each matter. You have to have a profile in place before you can entertain alternative fees because you now have a structure on which to base pricing and not just quote hourly rates. You're saying, "What are the requirements? How long is this going to take? Who are the right players?" Only then can you talk about pricing – when you know what you're going to price and you do this by dissecting the pieces and the processes. This way you may end up advising a client along the lines of, "Well, maybe we don't need this part of the process." Ultimately, our project management approach facilitates client discussions that are so necessary for alternative fee agreements to work.

Firm Culture

(Despina Kartson)

It's important to develop a business development culture and a business development mindset within a firm. Approach every encounter as one that could lead to a new business opportunity which means everything that you do should be considered as a potential business development opportunity or one in which you're representing or reflecting the firm.

Firm Leadership: Top Down Support Essential To Build Rainmakers

(Hans Haglund)

It was the leadership of the firm that said to me, "Yes, that's what we want. We are going to support your business development strategies. This is how we think, as well, and we are going to help you push this out firmwide." As a result, I had the active support of my practice group leaders, my department chairs and, most importantly, my chairman and managing partner. All of that together can equal a big success on moving the needle into greater participation by those lawyers that are being encouraged to become a rainmaker . . . to build their business. There is no way I could have the success I think I've had without that. You can do it bottom up, but that requires brute force. I have done it that way before. It is a tough slog, but it's better if it is both, bottom up and top down, and I know most would rather have full top down support from the outset.

Flannery Rainmaker Training: Part 1: Mentoring

(Bill Flannery)

Let me give you an off-the-cuff comment that has to do with my experience in training people and mentoring people. The mentoring model in law firms has failed dramatically with regard to rainmaking. Here's why: the mentors grew up in a different buying environment than exists today. They all grew up with this relationship experience that good old chaps treat other good old chaps in a certain way. These good old chaps were the owners, founders, and CEOs of companies. The reality is that a lot of work today is being pushed to the functional units that need to buy this legal services such as purchasing, environmental, and HR – and that's not where lawyers have good old chap relationships. Lawyers don't even want to see those people.

> The old mentoring model in law firms has failed dramatically with regard to rainmaking.
>
> —*Bill Flannery*

First of all, how can a 55- to 65- year-old white male mentor a 31-year-old African-American woman to do business development? There's no models for mentoring these various diverse minorities because the vast majority of seasoned attorneys don't have the same life experiences. A related reality is the fact that many firms are not giving these young women a chance to build a book of business because they don't give them any opportunity to work with the key clients of the firm. If you look at the vast majority of the key clients of the firm, they are represented by white males. If a women wants to break into that business development arena, the firm is going to have to give them key accounts. They are going to have to give the accounts to them. That's what they did in the commercial industry world. I actually participated in that process at IBM in the 60s, and 70s. IBM didn't have any choice because of the fact that the company was doing business with the federal government.

Is this too brutal? I have strong opinions about this. I've been around a lot, abused a lot, yelled at, and a lot has been thrown at me. Not doing more mentoring and giving client assignments to talented minorities is a shame because there's an implied promise that when skilled minorities are hired they are going to get help.

Flannery Rainmaker Training: Part 2: Coaching versus Training

(Bill Flannery)

There's an American Lawyer magazine article where the partners are asking for training and not coaching. Because the coaching thing has failed also. And you know why? You can't coach people you don't see play.

> "You can't coach people you don't see play."
>
> *–Bill Flannery*

It is so fundamental. Think of any great sales organization and your coach is the person that goes out with you on sales calls. Typically, your immediate supervisor. In the legal world this would be your practice group head. For example, I just met with a few attorneys, these are veteran guys who have been practicing law for 15 years; and they were telling me that they don't have a clue on how to do business development.

Then, it got worse. I did some actual run-throughs, which meant that I said, "Okay I'm somebody you just met. Here's what we are going to do. I want to know why is it I need to hire you?" This guy was speechless. He had nothing to say. So what they need is true training. Training means that you run simulations of various business development events and put them in the caldron. First, give them the necessary information. I believe the hierarchy is this: data, information, knowledge, and wisdom.

In coaching, you are just giving them the data and information. The way it becomes knowledge and wisdom is if they use it. In order to use it in a safe environment, you have to run simulations. You have to bring in true buyers. You can imagine a 60-year-old white male pretending to act like a general counsel, who, in the real world, is a 45-year-old African-American woman, like Paula Boggs, general counsel of Starbucks. There's no way that 60-year old white male can pretend to be Paula Boggs.

Many CMOs are afraid to hire me because I run real-world simulations where I bring in actual general counsel. This is like a soldier going through live fire training. This is what really sets us apart; and this is why typically CMO's will reference me but won't hire me because they are scared to death. I bring in in-house counsel, current and former in-house counsel, and I video tape lawyers in a business development mode using a sophisticated case study, one-on-one. Then I play the tapes back. This is just like classic IBM and XEROX sales training. You get videotaped over and over again. You actually put people under the gun where they have to perform, but it is one-on-one, so, the only failure is the failure they experience personally. But, that's how you learn.

Every great invention came out of failure. Consider the light bulb. Ten thousand failures before success. Here's an example, the Dyson vacuum cleaner. A man with an Irish brogue comes on TV and says, "I made 4,999 of these bloody things. All failed. Number 5,000 worked. Now I have the most popular vacuum cleaner in the world!"

Think about anybody that is in athletics. Especially, anything that's measured, like weight lifting or the 100-yard dash. If you come in second, you don't train to come in second again. You train to win. And the reason you do that is because you fail.

Weight lifting, as another example, you take it all the way to the point where you cannot lift that next 10 pounds. So, failure is the best teacher here. However, we don't like failing as lawyers. Because a loss in this "safe" training environment still feels like a loss in court. But, in fact, for you to be successful, you have to try things that didn't work.

IBM and Xerox taught us that the best sales teacher is failure in a safe training environment. However, and here's the challenge to every law firm business development trainer, we lawyers don't like to fail . . . under any circumstance.

> IBM and Xerox taught us that the best sales teacher is failure in a safe training environment. However, and here's the challenge to every law firm business development trainer, we lawyers don't like to fail . . . under any circumstance.
>
> *Bill Flannery*

Most of the huge law firms keep putting new lawyers in the mix by adding laterals. Usually, there's no integration strategy. So as I'm talking to these guys, they're saying, 'we have not been trained in business development but that's what we're charged to do."

Most huge law firms don't have a culture. They have a climate. IBM has a culture. Xerox has a culture. Spain has a culture, not law firms.

Flannery Rainmaker Training: Part 3: Don't Waste It on a Poor Next Step

(Bill Flannery)

> Most of the huge law firms keep putting new lawyers in the mix by adding laterals. Usually, there's no integration strategy. As I'm talking to these guys, they're saying, 'we have not been trained in business development but that's what we're charged to do.
>
> *—Bill Flannery*

After Business Development Training, Then What? Don't waste business development training going after new clients. Look at the statistics.

Okay, so we train them. Then, you know what the law firms do? They take these young associates and these young partners and they send them out to get new clients. Well, that's crazy. Look at the statistics. You ready for this?

The market share of total legal billing that most of these law firms have within their top 100 to 200 clients is less than one percent. So, why would you train a lawyer in business development and then send her to somebody who doesn't even know you when you could send her to a client who does know you and has the potential of reallocating to you some portion of their remaining 99% legal portfolio? So, you do what Xerox and IBM did, and you set up key account teams. This is what the accounting firms did with great success. They hired trained Xerox and IBM salespeople to help grow their key accounts. Not to sell for them, but to manage the business development process. For example, the head of the Austin, Texas office for Ernst & Young is a former Xerox representative. So now these guys from Xerox and IBM are adding a critical skill set that the accountants don't have – key account planning. They're running the old Neil Rackham key account planning program. Neil was the single-most influential person in all of Xerox training. He wrote the book on SPIN selling: **S**ituation, **P**roblem, **I**mplication, **N**eed-payoff. [Author's note: To expand on SPIN. SPIN can help you approach your client/potential client with discovery questions that will generate awareness of key issues in your mind and that of the client/potential client, i.e., S-Situation Questions, P-Problem Questions, I-Implication Questions, and N-Needs Payoff Questions.]

So, many people think that the law firms should adopt or adapt this accounting model to selling. They could adapt it. They can't adopt it because at an accounting firm you're selling an audit. An audit is almost a commodity, it's not judgment. You start exercising judgment in audits, you'll go to jail. So, law firms need to consider adapting their own customized form of the key account model.

Don't teach people to sell, teach them to understand what motivates the buyer.

> Don't teach people to sell, teach them to understand what motivates the buyer.
>
> —*Bill Flannery*

Flannery Rainmaker Training: Part 4: Marketing: Law Firms are Not CPA Firms

(Bill Flannery)

What you want to do is to train the people to understand what motivates the buyer. This is different from selling, as I use the term in this example. "Selling" in this case means pitching their skills versus finding out what motivates the buyer. Teach people to determine what the buyer's blatant and latent needs are.

Here's another distinction. Some consultants focus on the pitch. What makes you different? Well, nothing. You're not different. So once you get past that, you go, okay, so what is it that we need to do? You need to understand what motivates the buyer and then take what you're offering and figure out what it is that they need. Now, the old way was doing solution selling. Remember that phrase?

Okay, the problem with solution selling is that because of the web and because of all of the information that's available the buyers already know their needs. So if you want to make rainmakers, you have to train them and give the people who don't have key accounts, key accounts – so they can work those accounts instead of hoarding them, which is what these senior partners are doing. In many cases leadership objects, saying, "There's no way I'm going to tell these senior partners that they need to share their clients." Then you send untrained lawyers in, and they've got this fistful of practice group descriptions. And the untrained lawyers say, "Well, let me tell you what you need." And the client responds, "You know what? Tell me something about my company and our business for which there are legal implications that I don't know I have."

These are the undiscovered needs. Flannery calls them "latent needs." And there's a great scene in the movie Wall Street when the stock broker, Charlie Sheen, walks into Gordon Gekko's office, the Michael Douglas character, and says, "You need to buy this airline's stock. This is a hot one, and . . . " Gekko says, "Wait a minute. Stop. Tell me something about my company I don't know."

You need to answer that question to distinguish your firm from the others. You need to point out the undiscovered needs, the latent needs, of the client or potential client. Because, at the end of the day, how many other law firms of exactly the same size, in exactly the same area of geography, offer exactly the same practice area and offer the same "look at me" approach? Well, stop. Stop doing it the same old way.

> "Wait a minute. Stop. Tell me something about my company I don't know." You need to answer that question to distinguish your firm from the others.
>
> —*Bill Flannery*

So, now, we [at WJF Institute] train people instead of mentoring them. We hunt in packs, focused on key clients. We measure what it is we want, because compensation is not the answer.

> So, now, we [at WJF Institute] train people instead of mentoring them. We hunt in packs, focused on key clients.
>
> —*Bill Flannery*

I have a compensation consultant. His name is Napoleon Bonaparte. What Napoleon said about law firm compensation is that people will not lay down their lives for money. They will lay down their lives to pin a medal on their chest. So, Daniel Pink, who is a former Washington Post reporter and a lawyer, wrote a book called "Drive." He said that most compensation systems incent all the wrong things: how to exploit the client, how to shove work down their throat, how to overbill – and he said at the end of the day, if you want people to really strive for goals, you've got to give them passion. You can't pay for passion. You can see it in some basketball teams. They have the skills, but not the passion. So, their game is lacking. With passion you can have a bunch of guys that are playing better as a team than they would individually.

> I have a compensation consultant. His name is Napoleon Bonaparte. And what Napoleon said about law firm compensation is that people will not lay down their lives for money. They will lay down their lives to pin a medal on their chest. Daniel Pink, who is a former Washington Post reporter and a lawyer, wrote a book called "Drive." And he said that most compensation systems incent all the wrong things. If you want people to really strive for goals, you've got to give them passion. You can't pay for passion.
>
> —*Bill Flannery*

So now we have these teams. That's where we send these young partners that have been skilled and trained, not mentored. So they're not told you need to smoke cigars, drink Scotch, and play golf. And she's saying, you know what? I don't do any of those things. Now, isn't that terrible? Those poor people. I feel sorry for them. And then we're going to measure you for hours, which is – and you can quote me on this – timing the high jump. It's the wrong measurement system.

Some firms use the wrong performance metric. It's like timing the high jump.

> "Some firms use the wrong performance metric. It's like timing the high jump."
>
> —*Bill Flannery*

So what do you do to get these lawyers to perform? Well, you give them deadlines, you let them set their own goals, and then you measure against those goals. People will do what's measured. Look at the reality TV show, "The Biggest Loser." They're not getting paid money to lose that weight. They're having to stand up there in front of the nation and get weighed on a scale. They will lose the weight.

Flannery Rainmaker Training: Part 5: Metrics: Inspect What You Expect

(Bill Flannery)

The Marines have a great phrase: "Inspect what you expect."

So now we have measurements. We have trained people. We're using these resources at the highest point of value in the law firm - key clients.

We're incubating their skills over time by not forcing them to go out and try to close a big deal. They can close a lot of little deals, and if I get ten people working on Wells Fargo and they're all closing little deals, our market share – the other thing we need to measure, not hours, market share, of the profitable work in Wells Fargo—goes up over time.

Smart firms don't reward seniority, and don't reward based on past achievement. This is all about future forecasting, and that's the other thing that's missing. Firms don't forecast. All they do is measure what happened last year, and spend up to seven months in the new year doing comp reviews related to the prior year. The real activity should be centered on the question: what is your potential future work at Wells Fargo? Now, Wells Fargo knows what the work is because they have a budget that they did late last year. So you're seven months behind the curve.

According to WJF Institute research: law firms are out there selling (meaning pitching their skills versus finding out what motivates the buyer and what the buyer's blatant and latent needs are), and they're doing seminars. They're doing all of the soft stuff. According to our surveys, the average partner in most major law firms in the U.S., Canada, South America, Far East, the U.K., and Western Europe spend only **30 total hours a year of face-to-face discussions with clients and potential clients. That is really, really low.**

So, as a practical matter, if you want to make rain, train, focus on the key clients, give the people an opportunity to excel, measure what they're doing, track face time.

[Areas to measure: the firm's market share of available legal work at a given key client and key client face time. What do you do to get these people to perform? Well, you give them deadlines and you let them set their own goals, and then you measure against those goals. People will do what's measured.]

> So, as a practical matter, if you want to make rain: train, focus on the key clients, give the people an opportunity to excel, measure what they are doing, track face time.
>
> *Bill Flannery*

Flannery Rainmaker Training: Part 6: Team, Resiliency, Rewarding Failure

(Bill Flannery)

Now, let's add just a couple more things, and we have a pretty good picture of what is going to help these law firms and lawyers make rain.

We're raised individually through grammar school, high school, law school, and then subsequently to act as individuals. We're measured by our own grades, not on the grades of all the people in our group, whatever our group might be. So team work is totally missing. There's very little collaboration. And it's all based on how we achieve success along the way. So, in the meantime, the client is forced to create a virtual law firm by putting together various lawyers from different places with their different specialties. Whereas, if the firm helped them do that by marshaling all of their needed legal resources, putting them together, and saying to the client, "I have a team here, and we're <u>not</u> going to charge you to meet internally and discuss what it is that we need to do to help you find and address those latent needs. That's part of the value that we bring as against our competition." What client wouldn't accept that?

Today, clients are managing a virtual law firm they've had to create with all of these different lawyers from different firms from all over the world. In essence, the client is acting as a managing partner of all of these diverse legal resources.

The clients may say, "I buy lawyers, not law firms." Well, of course they did. But, when that client is faced with major litigation: What do they do? Well, they probably hired a top-tier firm to handle everything. So, don't listen to what clients say; watch what they do.

For a law firm to consistently make rain, they need to adopt the following policy: reward success, reward failure, and punish laziness and inaction. So, I'd rather see somebody go out and visit a client and not get the work than not visit the client at all. What many lawyers will do is they'll nail their right foot to the floor of their office by saying, "I'm not going to go out there because I wouldn't want to see people like me."

A key dimension behind this reluctance is that, in many cases, the lawyer sees himself as a lawyer in a law firm measured by billable hours as a determining factor as to how worthy he is of the buyer's work. That is not the buyer's view of the world, and a lawyer viewing himself through that lens is looking through the wrong end of the telescope, everything looks small and unimportant.

> "Reward success. Reward failure. Punish laziness and inaction.
>
> —*Bill Flannery*

With that perspective a lawyer may give up before beginning by saying, "Okay, I have low resiliency. I'm not going to get the business. I can't stand the idea of failure. Why try?" Then there is classic lawyer skepticism adding to the whole dynamic of recalcitrance to engaging potential clients described humorously by lawyer-psychologist, Dr. Larry Richards, who summarizes a lawyer's skepticism by saying, "Lawyers are so skeptical they smell the roses and, then, look around for the coffin."

If you do what everybody does you'll be treated like everybody else. Don't spend your money on branding. Spend it on performance.

Flannery Rainmaker Training: Part 7: Replace Branding With Performance

(Bill Flannery)

Law firm management skepticism will say, "Why bother to do this kind of business development? Let's just do what everybody else is doing: branding." Doing that gets you lumped in with all the other people that spend all their money and time on websites, seminars, written articles, speeches, hoping to snag somebody out there. Branding – I love that phrase. That one is really the worst. Are you ready for this? Your brand is defined by your clients, not by you.

> Your brand is defined by your clients, not by you.
>
> *—Bill Flannery, JD, WJF Institute*

Most branding is ineffective. I'm living in Texas right now. Brand cows, not lawyers. Yeah, and they go, "Well, look at Skadden. They have a brand." Skadden doesn't have a brand. Look at all the branding they did. They did nothing in branding. You know what they did? They established a long-term reputation for performance. That's a big difference. Now, not to say you shouldn't have some way of identifying your firm. For example, in my case, yes, I have developed a brand, but it wasn't really me. Our clients develop a brand for us, which they always do. The clients – they're the ones that give you the definition of who you are, not who you want to be. So, for example, clients who have been through Bill Flannery's training will say they have been "Flannerized." Like Google, my name has been turned into a verb. I am flattered. I say you know what? That is our brand. It's considered to be a change of behavior, which is what we're seeking, and that's what they're seeking, and this is the one-liner that sums it all up: You're seeking to get a change in the behavior from the buyer. So quit buying from your competition. Quit doing it in-house. Quit not doing anything and buy from you. Well, in order to do that, the only way to do that is to build trust and go see them and understand what it is they need to change, which leads back to what do you have to do? You have to change your own behavior.

Flannery Rainmaker Training: Part 8: How Do You Change Attorney Behavior?

(Bill Flannery)

Here's the question, "How do you change attorney behavior and build their new rainmaker skills?

You have to change the attorney's behavior. And how do you do that? You do that by running simulations with current and former in-house lawyers in a sophisticated case study that requires them to do a couple of things: pitch a flat fee for all the work in this hypothetical company, and use project management and systems analysis to manage the entire legal affairs of the client. All I do is I put out this fax, and say, "Ok, here's what I want you to do. I want you to go to see these hypothetical buyers tomorrow. We will videotape you. Just present a solution the following day. Then come back and tell me what you learned from this whole process." Usually, they will say, first of all we learned that taking literature up there or going up there and telling the company what their needs are doesn't work. Developing enough rapport to understand what their hidden needs are and needs that they don't know they have is clearly the best way to do it.

You learn by doing. So, the best way to build rainmaker skills is by running no-risk live simulations where the attorney interacts with a current or former in-house counsel. Followed by feedback.

> You learn by doing. So, the best way to build rainmaker skills is by running no-risk live simulations where the attorney interacts with a current or former in-house counsel. Followed by feedback.
>
> *Bill Flannery*

Let's review the things I gave you. We don't need skills. We don't need to be organized. We don't need to give opportunity and power to what is now the disenfranchised. We need to continue to reward these senior rainmakers who in another five years, ten years, are going to be dead. We can fire the CMO again. Or we can just beef up our website. I had this one guy who didn't have a book of business. He argued with me vehemently that everybody reads brochures. Well, they don't read the brochures. He was designing a 28-page energy brochure.

Why? Because that was his only way of justifying where he was spending his time in business development. He didn't have any work. He thought his energy brochure was going to have a huge impact. Well, of course it didn't. So, I said why don't you ask the former general counsel of Chase and the current general counsel of Live Nation, who will be here tomorrow, and they will be teaching the rest of this workshop and ask them what they think. He said, no, I know I'm right. Huh? There's no amount of genius that will overcome their skepticism.

Oh, I get that from about 80 percent of the lawyers.

What they're using is lawyer logic, not market logic. So, they create these systems of thinking and their actions feed into their behavior. They like brochures so they assume clients like them too. I tell them, you're not the client. They are the furthest thing from you possible. Whatever you think, they are thinking 180 degrees differently. So, that's a great way of understanding what it is you need to be doing.

I said the test is not what I'm telling you and what these people do in this simulation. The test is to go out and try something that you're not doing now and see what happens.

Flannery Rainmaker Training: Part 9: A Synthesis of Methods to Achieve Results

(Bill Flannery)

I've got a new book coming out on business development and the way that the market has turned on lawyers. They don't know what to do. I address a new direction we're taking in the legal field, which is one that I don't want to call it a confrontation, but you have to challenge the buyer, because if you don't challenge the buyer, then the buyer will say, "Look, I'm happy with the law firms I have now." Well, of course *you* are. Somebody in your organization may not be, including your CEO. And maybe I should be talking with him or her instead of you. Make sure you are talking to one of the company's stakeholders because a part of their brain is always open, at least for a quick moment, to explore a change that can make a significant positive difference.

The bottom line is to get to the people that really have their jobs and future on the line, the people who know that there are dire consequences if they don't have the right lawyer from the right law firm on critical legal matters. Make sure you are meeting with key stakeholders and answer their unspoken question, "Will this lawyer make me look good to my boss and help me succeed in getting a promotion and a bonus?"

Everybody is discounting. I talked to one lawyer who said they have 30 different pricing schemes for their work. I said how do you keep track of that? He said, "Well, what should I do?" I said try this. I want a discount. What are you seeking with a discount? Well, lower cost. Well, of course you are. Okay. To what extent is discounting helping to provide the in-house lawyers with lower cost? The answer is, it hasn't. The litigation bills in this country the last five years have gone up $5 billion dollars in payments to outside counsel. So it obviously is not working.

Flannery Rainmaker Training: Part 10: Associate to Partner Transition

(Bill Flannery)

I commonly get asked about the classic situation when you've got an associate going to partner, and his 2100 hours as an associate is now down to 1500 because of all the non-billable new responsibilities she's doing. Other associates are getting the work that she used to get because the client will only pay associate-level fees on those matters. And she says, what do I do? She's also trying to have a life. So one response is to forget about it. You're not going to have a life. If you want to be a partner, just forget that.

Well, there're a couple of answers to what she needs to do. One, have her go on Amazon and buy both of my books. Then have her call me. I tell you what I'm going to tell her. They are, to a large degree – right, you are going to have to put more hours in, but then the question becomes if you're putting in hours at $700 an hour with a 98 percent realization rate versus $400 an hour with a 84 percent realization rate, which is where most people are, then what does that tell you that you need to do?

Number one is to find the highest quality work, and that means not milking the asset. That means thinking outside the box and doing new things that stretch your legal skills and experience. Second thing is do the best you can to come up with ideas that get your sponsors in-house to look good. In the legal department what that means is saving money. The best way you can save money now in these companies is to help them to reduce the number of outside lawyers they're using and concentrate more work with you. Well, that's almost a self-eating watermelon. Those are the type of things you want to do, and business development, albeit valued, is looked down upon in these organizations. In fact, many people will tell you I'm a great lawyer, but I don't have the book of business he has, but he's not a very good lawyer. He's got a big book of business, but he's not a very good lawyer. I love what one of the lawyers at Doherty Rumble & Butler said when the firm collapsed. He said we were great lawyers. We had great collegiality, etc, etc, all the usual platitudes. He said the only problem was we just didn't have enough work. That's why they need to be Flannerized.

Formula for Success

(Silvia Coulter)

A high volume of activity across a broad group of individuals within your targeted audience is always going to get you feedback that can be converted to leads, then prospects, then clients. It's a proven formula for success.

Future Trend: New Opportunity: New Risk

(Sally Schmidt)

I believe it makes sense to align yourself with other professional service companies that don't do what you do, but do what a lot of your clients need.

So one way to form a market-centric group is to align with other providers and go after that market in a united effort. I don't see a lot of this now. In fact, I think in the future there'll be more opportunities to form associations, informal or formal, with people outside the legal profession. For example, if you wanted to have a startup company or a tech-company practice, you could bring in venture capitalists, someone from a bank, a CPA from an accounting firm and go at it together.

I find that a lot of clients like one-stop shopping. Now, I'm not talking about the general counsels at giant corporations where their job is to go out and find these specialists all the time, but for the vast majority of clients—middle-market companies, smaller companies, growing companies—they don't actually understand where the accountant leaves off and where the lawyer begins. So, a law firm seeking business from these types of clients might consider forming alliances with various other professional services and offer a one-stop shopping experience. Many companies would appreciate a one-source solution to various common business needs. I think it could be a very smart move.

I can give you an example. We did a focus group for a client of mine who does a lot of a middle-market company work. We had a number of companies in the market participate and they were not necessarily clients. It was interesting because they basically said that they don't care where they buy their legal services. They don't care if they are offered by an accounting firm. They like the idea of simplicity. So, as we see more people dip their toe in the legal market, it could be scary if we aren't thinking ahead of them.

General Counsel, GC: See In-House Counsel

Google: Pay Per Click

(Erin Meszaros)

We don't use it.

Hiring a CMO

(Dave Bruns)

When you're looking to hire somebody in my role, what is it that you need? How do you find that person? A good search consultant should help you in that process. They should be asking questions such as, "What is it that's going to make this job a success? What do you expect this person to do in 6 months? What do you expect them to do in 12 months? What's their goal in 5 years?" This way you have a real understanding of what skill sets you're looking for.

Without having a true understanding of what your goals are, you may hire the wrong person. You may need brand awareness and you hire somebody that's a sales manager. Or, somebody that wants to be out doing sales themselves as opposed to training others to do that. Well, that person is going to fail because you didn't hire the right person and it's not that person's fault. You hired the wrong skill set.

Industry Marketing: Cross-Selling Occurs as a Matter of Course

(Sally Schmidt)

Another opportunity for firm-wide revenue growth that I love is industry marketing. You may review your clients and find 10 that are in the food and beverage industry. So you need to ask, "What are we doing to use them as a platform to get more business in the food and beverage industry?" Or, hospitality. Or, energy. Or, whatever industry grouping may apply. Law firms traditionally haven't been very good at looking at their clients that way; they tend to look at them from a practice group standpoint and try to market tax or try to market real estate as opposed to what the clients need. So, a lot of times, we'll help a firm set up an industry-focused marketing group, for example, create a new sports law group or a new hospitality law group—and it's interdisciplinary. There are usually very good opportunities, because we might have a contractor that we're doing litigation for and it's a family-owned business, but we have never talked to them about succession planning. So, you start to bring lawyers from different practices together around client types. The idea is to get the firm to think "client types" and "industry types." This creates a cross-selling mechanism right within the structure. In fact, you don't even have to talk about cross-selling if you have the right people on the team. Put it together prospectively, thinking about, for example, what any life sciences company needs—from patents to product liability to whatever—and then have all of those people on the team.

Information Aggregators: We Use Manzama

(Jill Weber)

We use Manzama. Client and potential client research happens at two levels. One is at the company level, and that could be a client or prospect, so you can put in searches, so it pulls up any news or any mention of the company in a blog post. That's the way Manzama works. It aggregates these news articles. I benchmarked it against Google Alerts, and Google Alerts are useful, but (A) you have to have a separate alert for every company, and (B) it doesn't always catch the breadth of what I find through Manzama, and so they are aggregating it from all kinds of publications. It's a subscription service. They cater to the legal industry, and then you can also pick specific industries if you want. So, if you want to track information, say, on Minnesota healthcare insurance companies or healthcare insurance nationally, you can track on specific industries if you're just trying to keep up to speed on those kinds of things. You can also track competitors, so if you know that you compete a lot with Law Firm A, or against a specific attorney, you can set up a news tracker to see any time he or she is quoted. I find it useful because Manzama pulls not only from news sources but also from the Web sites themselves—Google Alerts is not going to pick up a news release posted on a law firm Web site. For example, I was tracking a local competitor in Manzama, and found a news release they posted announcing a series of employment seminars in different cities in the Midwest on a specific topic. Well, that's really helpful information if I'm an employment lawyer and I'm competing in that same market. In addition, Manzama tracks Twitter posts about companies, so if you have a key client you want to monitor—granted, you can do that separately on Twitter, but most attorneys don't have a Twitter account—with Manzama you can have the news stories and the Twitter feeds all in one place.

Information Aggregators: Internal and External

(Steve Bell)

I feel good about what we're doing in the information aggregation realm. It's a combination of resources. I'm not saying that this is the only combination that would work, but we have a very fine information staff internally. They are not librarians exactly. It's information services and they bring a great deal of resources to the table. They don't particularly analyze the resources. The information that is compiled. We use an outside service in Buenos Aires, Argentina, called Latin Brains, and they do competitive business analysis for us. They do a tremendous job.

We have also acquired a tool called "Manzama," which is a listening platform. Manzama is a good way to fine tune the other information that we learn from the raw information the information staff puts together along with what Latin Brains puts together. That information is fine-tuned with blogging, social media, and other news posts using the search features in Manzama. It's a confluence of those three that provides a reasonably rich understanding—as much understanding as you can get without actually talking to somebody who's on the inside and knows what's going on.

We add in the information sources from LexisNexis or Thomson Reuters information along with the business and competitive analysis from Latin Brains, and the absolutely to the moment information from Manzama.

At that point, somebody from the firm needs to sit down and say, "Okay, so here's what we know. What does all this mean with respect to Womble Carlyle and its capabilities and service lines? Based on what we know about this company, what's the intersection between what's going on there and what they need and what we can do?" I feel very good about what we're doing in the area of information aggregation.

Information Aggregators: Manzama and Others

(Hans Haglund)

We have a CRM system and other ways to look at getting that big picture overview of any given client. The firm's historical experience provides us a profile based on internal data, and then for external information, Manzama is our work horse, and our day-to-day way to get a lot of information. The Manzama algorithm is such that it can get very granular. You can search for something very specific and anytime that hits across any external information Manzama serves it up, then pops it into our data base. We are always looking to try to get that one nugget of information that, "Oh, hey, this is relevant and actionable."

Manzama is our work horse, but there are many additional and very specific resources to aggregate data about a client or industry. For example, legal complaints, tracking, and really diving into the courts. Steve Bell probably knows that better than anybody. You are digging in to find out what kind of litigation companies are facing. That's critical to know. There are different tools. There is Lexis and Thomson house products that do that. Monitor Suite is the Thomson one. Then there are more specific feeds that may be more suited for intellectual property, or mergers and acquisitions. For instance, Merger Market and Debtwire are tools that get to information that is more proprietary, where their people interview a CEO that says, "Yeah, we are looking at five mergers in the next 24 months," and they pass that on to us. It's very challenging. The way the world is today, there is so much information. It's hard to get to that nugget, but that's where we want to get to. That's what our research and our CI, our library, and our business developers are searching for, that gold nugget. What is that relevant chunk of information that is going to matter when we go meet with them or call them. We are always seeking to find out if there is an issue that the company needs to know about. Because the ideal is that we're ahead of the curve. That's the ideal. Getting ahead of the curve and knowing . . . trying to track anything that could be a risk or opportunity to one or more of our clients, or a potential client that we are targeting.

Information Aggregators: Using Third Parties for Critical Research

(Jeanne Hammerstrom)

I used to have a person who did almost all the competitive intelligence for me. I've now outsourced that. I outsource to Chris Fritsch and her Clients First group who use the suite of tools that I designed for our law firm. I use ShiftCentral's capabilities to help us with the aggregating of information and industry trends and information of that type in certain industries, like for healthcare, shale, shale and energy, and private equity. We invest a lot of money in those resources.

The aggregation work is done by Data Fusion or Business Intelligence. So it lays on top of our Thomson Reuters' Elite system. So, if we want to find information like industry trends within our clients, or where we are losing clients, or what industries we're gaining in, it's all there in our own client data base to tell us.

These program help us decide where do we want to invest? Why am I putting so much money in this industry or practice group when we can look at the trend in the last ten years? This is business intelligence software that allows all the attorneys in our firm to have that information on their desktop, so, they can see it anytime, where they are, where the firm is, and other timely and relevant information. This is a pretty open firm as it relates to financials and other information that will help our attorneys and practice group leaders have as much insight as possible to what's important to them and their practice. It includes information like realization rate and other data immediately available on the firm's intranet. It is comparable to Redwood, the business intelligence and analytics software from LexisNexis.

Author's note: In summary, some of the providers used by Jeanne Hammerstrom for information research: Chris Fritsch/Clients First; Data Fusion or Business Intelligence; ShiftCentral, per their website, "is the leading provider of outsourced market intelligence services for major organizations across the globe. The agency provides actionable insight." URL: http://www.shiftcentral.com/; Thomson Reuters Elite system whose website states, "Save valuable time by researching WestlawNext or Westlaw directly from the ProLaw desktop. From within the context of your specific cases and matters, ProLaw helps you get the information you need by automatically searching relevant WestlawNext or Westlaw databases." URL: http://www.elite.com/prolaw/in-context-legal-research/; the firm intranet which is similar to Redwood Analytics Business Intelligence software from LexisNexis can be used to improve performance and uncover hidden risks. LexisNexis URL: http://www.lexisnexis.com/intelligence/redwood-analytics-BI.page

Information Services Staff: A Gold Mine to Those Firms Who Have Them

(David King Keller)

An interview with numerous CMOs and BDOs has indicated that an information services staff is a gold mine. One firm converted a library staff person to this task.

In-House Counsel Addresses How You Can Impress or Turn Off

(Casey Flaherty)

Well, let's just say I've become much more cynical on this question. I was outside counsel and I had all kinds of assumptions about in-house counsel that have since been exploded. Here's my advice to outside counsel: first, treat the corporation's money as your own; second, think in systems.

Lawyers are trained—for the most part—to think in cases; to think in one-offs. So, the most important thing to a lawyer is whatever it is they happen to be writing at the moment. This motion, this deposition notice, this whatever. And the good lawyers see the case holistically. They understand why they're doing this motion and that comes with maturity, but it's also . . . somewhere between a talent and a skill, because not everyone learns it.

You have a much better document reviewer if they understand how it fits into the bigger case and, even better, if they understand how a particular document is going to be used. If they know that it's going to be an exhibit to a motion for summary judgment or if they know that it's going to be presented to a witness at deposition, they can think holistically about the case. What I thought the best in-house counsel would do is take that up another level and not only think holistically about everything the legal department is doing, but think holistically about the company.

I remember being involved in a very, very large . . . It was a mass action, not a class action. They didn't seek class certification, but there were hundreds upon hundreds of individual cases consolidated. And it became clear to us that the wrong entity was being sued. The entity that should have been sued didn't really have any assets and in many ways, making this clear, would have gotten them out of the case in any meaningful way.

They said "no" because they understood to make that case, they would need to reveal their overall structure in discovery and that that specific information was more valuable to them as a business than this one case. To us, it was an enormous case. There were nine figures in damages. The attorneys' fees were insane and we thought we had come up with some lawyer magic. At the time, I did not understand it, but I have come to understand . . . it's about winning the war, not the battle.

I really expected to encounter those two things—treating the corporation's money as your own and thinking in systems—when I moved in-house. Yet, many in-house counsel mirror the outside counsel they used to be. They're very, very focused on individual cases. They don't tend to think strategically or holistically. They don't think in systems. They're not nearly as interested in the business as they should be and the people they are closest with are their outside counsel—not their internal clients. For them, just like outside counsel, the size of your book of business is a big point of personal power.

For in-house counsel, the size of your budget is a point of personal power because the more money you have to spend, the more outside counsel kisses your rear end. That was actually one of the hardest things for me to get my mind around. All my jokes are funny now and we had someone recently come in-house and ask, "What's the biggest transition?" I said, "Well, other than not having to track your time and no longer thinking in billable hours, which is amazing, it is whether you want to admit it or not, that my four-year-old could take your job and his insights would be treated just as brilliant as yours." "I went pee pee on the potty." "Oh, that's great! No one's ever done that before. Tell me more." And, if you didn't think your jokes were funny, you wouldn't tell them. So, it's really easy to believe that people are laughing at them because they're funny. And so, you get a big head. You have pride in having a big budget and you want to focus on the case at hand and don't bother me with all that other bullblip. And there's way, way, too much of that. I used to think that the biggest impediment to performing in the legal market was large law firms. I am now thoroughly convinced that law firms will do whatever clients tell them to do. And that clients are the number one impediment to change.

What is it? One of the 48 laws of power: "Talk about change without doing anything, because that maintains the status quo." The status quo is really comfortable for the most part for in-house lawyers because in a lot of respects, we aren't accountable for anything.

People like to go on and on about the billable hour, well, we could have done away with the billable hour 30 years ago. We haven't. But, think about what the billable hour does for in-house counsel. It is easy. It is familiar. It is flexible. The only thing that you have to worry about with the billable hour is the kabuki theater of rate negotiation. That's it. And it helps you foster this illusion of unpredictability that not only insulates outside counsel from accountability, but insulates you from accountability. When you start going to fixed fees, you have to do a whole lot more work. You have to have a handle on your data. You have to be able to price matters appropriately. You really have to do a lot of additional work on the front end and then you can be held accountable on the back end. It's a lot more work and it's a lot more risk and why would you volunteer for that? I'm not saying people expressly think this way.

They're lawyers. Just like everyone else, they react emotionally and then explain and justify rationally and they're very skilled at the rationalization. So, I have become much more of a cynic than I was. There's definitely change and I think that, to me, the best symbol of that is the rise of "non-lawyer legal professionals"—they may or may not be lawyers, but their role in the department is not that of a traditional lawyer. And so, that's legal operations folks like Lisa Konie at Adobe or procurement folks, an example being Justin Angler at GSK. To me, that is the best sign of moving towards law departments becoming sophisticated purchasers of legal services. Right now, we are still very much locked into a credence good context where relationships rule. And there should be advantages to incumbency, but we've taken that to an extreme and utterly ridiculous degree.

And so, what I would say is that what you need to do is, first of all: identify your customer because they might be one type or the other. And, one type, it is relationships and it's really, really hard to break up a couple. You know, they've been together a long time. They're familiar with each other. They're comfortable. They like each other. Coming in as a mistress is a hard thing.

First of all, identify your customer because they might be one type or the other. One type is relationships and it's really, really hard to break up a couple. You know, they've been together a long time. They're familiar with each other. They're comfortable. They like each other. Coming in as a mistress is a hard thing.

—*Casey Flaherty*

The only marketing piece I've ever written in the *ABA Journal* had to do with using the offer of free hours. Normally, free hours is really just a hidden discount. "Well, yeah, you have to assign us a matter and the first hundred hours are free." Well, that's great, but it's going to be 1,000 hours, so you're just telling me you're giving me a 10-percent discount. Discounts are fine as far as they go, they're just not compelling. So, what I recommend to both inside and outside counsel is, to help with all those things internally that in-house counsel wants to clean up but doesn't have time to get to. For example, there are so many policies to be written, templates to be revised, processes to fix – do that. [Offer to do it for free.]

Because there's a real value there as opposed to, "Okay, this person I don't know, I'm going to give you the case that is least important to me; and I'm not going to pay attention to it; and it's probably going to go away quickly; and I'm not going to have much of an opinion of you." If you come in and fix something that bugs me all the time, you're going to get more face time with me. I'm going to think better of you—assuming you do a good job. And when something comes up . . . let's say you fix a contract template. With that particular contract where you revise a policy for us, related to that policy, you're the first person I'm going to think of. So in terms of my advice on marketing, I would say the best advice I have for the traditional relationship—which I would say is still by far dominant—is building upon that relationship. And it really depends, then, on the person. They're just personalities and for some of them, it is, "We went to law school together," and that's kind of it. Or, "We've been friends for a long time." Others, it's "Well, we like the same football team and we go to games together." Others, it's "Are you going to take my spouse and me out to really nice dinners?" And, "Our kids are about the same age." Very rarely is it about the work. It's about the personal relationship. It's not that they don't care about the work, but at a certain point, quality is no longer a consideration. I wouldn't be talking to you if you weren't good enough to do the work. So, now we need to talk about other things, including, "How well do I get along with you?" "Do I trust you?" "How easy is it for us to communicate?" And so, those relationship matters are still the most important and if you have a hard time establishing relationships, you'd better be really freaking good. And not only really freaking good, but do something that differentiates you in a way so that everybody knows you're good.

If you want to do something to get my attention, what I recommend to both inside and outside counsel is, is to help with all those things internally that in-house counsel wants to clean up but doesn't have time to get to. For example, there are so many policies to be written, templates to be revised, processes to fix – do that. [Offer to do it for free.] And when something comes up – let's say you fix a contract template – with that particular contract where you revise a policy for us, related to that policy, you're the first person I'm going to think of.

—*Casey Flaherty*

And so, maybe you write *the* "go-to" blog on a very narrow issue. Or, you are forever speaking on a very technical topic so that people recognize you as *the* expert in that area, because if you don't get that separation, if you're just a commercial litigator—and a fairly good one—why choose you as opposed to the 1,000 others? And, it's not that there aren't people like that, there are just very few of them and so much more often, it's relationships. "We're going to narrow it down to people who can actually do it and then we're going to choose among them with quality no longer a factor," What we're talking about here is top-line quality, really. The relationship partner.

In the credence goods context, prices tend to converge because you don't really have a good ability to differentiate on quality. In the perfect competition context, prices tend to converge because the outputs tend to be substantially similar. We've got a lot of price convergence in the legal space, and I would say that when it comes to the billable hours, and when it comes to flat fees, it's the similar product issue. Sylvia Hodges wrote a case study of GSK's reverse auction—the use of reverse auctions for selecting counsel. And the thing you get there is a very high degree of price convergence. So now, all of a sudden, you're looking at firms who you've already pre-screened for top-level quality with similar prices.

So, how do you differentiate among them? Do you just fall back on relationships? Or, do you start looking at metrics? And so, when you look at my testing of outside counsel, that is one metric, because you and Lawyers A and B are offering substantially similar prices. Is it because they're doing it exactly the same way, or is one better at knowledge management and using technology and leveraging their prior work product? While the other just throws a lot of low cost, low value resources at it?

We are just getting into a space where we can start differentiating firms using metrics and I consider what I'm doing just one small piece of a much larger metrics puzzle, but that's the language that people like Lisa [Lisa Konie, director, Legal Operations of Adobe Systems] and I speak. Metrics, turnaround time, coming in, on, or under budget, those kinds of things, because those are all measures of quality and, look, not all qualities are legal quality, but we care about data security. In a sense, that has nothing to do with the quality of your legal services. That doesn't make you a good or bad lawyer, whether or not your firm has proper data security protection. But, again, it's part of thinking holistically.

We don't buy legal services; we buy solutions. And, we need to make sure that we're not also buying additional problems.

So, appealing to the second kind of buyer, is where you can start. If you can start quantifying things, then you can start a conversation. You can have a conversation that many of your competitors can't have because they come from a "Well, let me take you out to dinner" background, and that works on everybody to one degree or another, but once you introduce metrics into the equation, all of a sudden, you have that accountability I talked about and you have to justify those decisions.

> And, we need to make sure [when we hire outside counsel] that we're not also buying additional problems.
>
> —*Casey Flaherty*

You referred to the non-holistic, non-360 approach as the "less sophisticated and less informed old ways" that firms used to approach clients like us. But I wouldn't call them "the old ways," because it is still the dominant paradigm, by far. By far. I consider them less sophisticated. I consider them inferior, but I have not considered them old, because they are dominant.

You asked me, "How can outside counsel improve their 'C-Suite awareness'? Should they take an MBA course, take some finance courses, or take something like a C-suite awareness course?" Well, so are you talking about them being good lawyers or getting business? Because I actually totally agree with you that they will be better lawyers if they take a C-suite awareness class . . . But, in-house lawyers especially, do not like to be held accountable. One of our biggest fears is when our outside counsel has to interact with our internal clients, because what our internal clients think of us is very important and to the extent we can keep it all separate, we've got that priest mystique, Oracle at Delphi type of reputation where we can say, "Just leave us alone because you wouldn't understand what we do, but it's really, really important." And we like to maintain that and where it gets dangerous is when the business people, especially at the higher level, have to interact with our outside counsel. That really scares us. We get very, very concerned about that and a lot of the C-suite folks don't automatically assume that the lawyer is the smartest person in the room. Strange as that may be. The lawyer, of course, assumes that the lawyer is the smartest person in the room, but there are executives who actually think they're smarter than lawyers. [Laughter.]

And so, it is extremely important to us and for us that certain outside counsel—it depends on the role—are able to represent us well internally and a huge part of that is being able to speak the language of the common man, or the language of the business. And the language of the business tends to sometimes be very specialized. There are a lot of acronyms and abbreviations that are unique to the business, but, in general, it's the language *of* business. It's the language *of* financial statements; the language *of* PR; the language of marketing; the language of sales; and that's where, if they are able to sit there and converse with some fluency in the language that the business person speaks, the business person will come away with a much higher opinion of them than if they retreat into the cant of legalese. Because at a certain level, the C-suite people know that anyone who can only speak in their own jargon, like an IT person, is only of so much use and can only be trusted so much, because they don't ultimately understand what's going on, what's at stake. And so, I would say that is . . . That's extremely important if you want to get that repeat business. How you interact with the business folks and how business folks react to you. Much of that is based on fluency in the language that the business people speak.

In-House Counsel Tell Us How to Get Their Attention

(David Keller and Jeffrey Silber)

The following remarks are by counsel from Adobe, NetApp, and AOptix.

In a meeting billed as the "In-House Counsel Summit" on Wednesday afternoon, a panel of three legal leaders from prominent Silicon Valley hi-tech companies moderated by David Bruns, director of client services at Farella Braun + Martel LLP, spoke to an audience of over 50 attendees about "Rising Above Your Competition—What Today's Tech Industry General Counsel Expect From a Law Firm." The Garden Court Hotel meeting was hosted by the Bay Area Chapter/Silicon Valley City Group of the Legal Marketing Association and emceed by Monica Kuniyoshi of K&L Gates and Jill Stolarik of Morrison & Foerster.

Creativity, flexibility, innovation, thinking outside the box, skilled in project management, and "lawyers who listen to us and know our business" were just some of the key factors a law firm should present to impress Lisa Konie, director, Legal Operations, of Adobe Systems.

Michael Haven, senior litigation and operations counsel for NetApp, Inc., illustrated Konie's point. "When we were running short on funding for a matter, I called our law firm and explained the situation. Within an hour they called back and told me they were able to restructure the project and approach it in a different way so as to work within our remaining budget. This firm showed flexibility when we needed it, and sensitivity to the pressures we face, and gained a lot of our loyalty by doing so."

Needless to say, fee and billing approaches are critically important. In fact, two of the panelists said they were moving away from the billable hour model and prefer alternate fee arrangements, while one panelist stated, "I am actually mixed on billable hours/AFA. I think the latter is appropriate in some situations and prefer billable hours in other areas provided there is appropriate communication about expectations." Some even said they would not work with a law firm that did not offer fixed fees on some matters. The panelists said in many cases they know what the value of a given specific matter is and one panelist stated, "Law firms find ways to become more efficient when they are on a fixed fee." All emphasized that a firm must demonstrate efficient use of their company's time and money. "We are not willing to pay for 20 hours of training for a first-year lawyer on a basic commercial transaction," emphasized one panelist.

Haven said in some cases he likes to work with a 10-percent collar around a fixed fee. That is, if the actual cost is within 10 percent of the agreed fee, his company will pay the agreed-upon fee. However, if the real cost is more than 10-percent higher, he will entertain renegotiating the fee upward. Similarly, if the actual cost is more than 10 percent lower than the agreed fee, he also wants to negotiate a reduction in the fee.

The panel agreed that they expect outside counsel to be extremely knowledgeable about their industry. "And it's a big bonus to the relationship," added Haven, "if the law firm is buying and using our products and services. It's like reverse selling." Konie agreed that using Adobe products can help build rapport.

It was universally agreed that diversity is important and desired in the law firms they work with, but on any given RFP, it is not the primary deciding factor when choosing outside counsel. Yet diversity is primary in some situations. One panelist stated, "A law firm representing them who puts three older white men in front of a young diversified jury would not be rehired. It's important that the trial lawyers mirror the jury as much as possible."

The panel was divided about dealing with a partner from one of their preferred law firms who switches to another firm. Jan Kang, vice president and general counsel of AOptix, said, "We work with lawyers, not with law firms" and would be in support of following the switching partner to his/her new law firm. On the other hand, Konie noted that, having labored long and hard to create a panel of preferred law firms, having whittled 1,000 law firms down to 30, she would be hard pressed to deviate from her panel.

On the other hand, all agreed that, other than the rare outside expert, building a relationship was paramount. For example, one panelist pointed out that it would be better to pitch to someone on the in-house team with whom you have a pre-existing relationship rather than the GC with whom you have no prior relationship.

The panel agreed that trust is an absolute essential component when working with or selecting an outside law firm. The panelists agreed that "Building trust was everything." And one way to build that trust is for outside counsel to demonstrate that they understand that the GC and the GC's legal team have to answer to a CFO, a finance committee, and others. Lawyers who make it clear that they are sensitive to and appreciate the pressures on the in-house legal department will further endear themselves to in-house counsel.

All three panelists like their outside counsel to provide value-added services. Examples would be: training their legal personnel as to what they can and cannot do in a given legal area, sending them relevant information on changes in the law that the in-house legal team may have missed including any pertinent cases, doing free research for them, and sending them memos, at no cost to them, which may have been prepared while working on another matter elsewhere, but would also be of interest to them.

One panelist explained that "We are contacted by many law firms offering to help us when they see an action has been filed against us. That alone does not get our attention. But when we are contacted in a different way, such as 'I saw X law firm filed an action against you the other day. Did you know that they also filed the following actions that same day?' Or the lawyer offers some special insight into the firm filing against us, or suggests some special legal tactic that might be considered. That value-add will get our attention."

As to providing information, they agreed that they don't generally read blogs, but they like e-newsletters that have direct relevant information that they can use. On occasion, one panelist offered, they will start to look at a video related to a topic of interest, but if the spokesperson in the video is not captivating, that ends the review and reduces the likelihood that the panelist will look at another video by that provider.

A MarCom note: Marketing leave-behinds are not reviewed by these three panelists. They just don't have the time. Sorry.

When a new law firm approaches a potential in-house counsel client, they should take the long view. For example, Kang said she is very disappointed when a lawyer makes an enthusiastic pitch for a particular matter, but if turned down, acts like they've been hurt and their enthusiasm for the relationship has suffered an irreversible set-back. Kang said, and the other panelists agreed, they like to work with lawyers who are in it for the long haul.

In-House Counsel: Secrets to Gaining Their Trust and Their Business

(David King Keller)

Go to: *In-House Counsel Tell Us How to Get Their Attention.* Also go to Chapter 3: *Avoid These Disasters* and learn how to do great work and get fired by unconsciously alienating in-house counsel.

In-House Counsel: Take This Tech Test to Demonstrate Minimum Tech Skills

(Casey Flaherty)

My in-house counsel colleagues and I have been burnt too often by inefficiencies and, because our budgets are limited, we will not tolerate an attorney charging us for two hours when the task could have been done in

10 seconds. I created a tech audit to validate claims of efficiency and see if my lawyers possess certain fundamental skills that will save you time and make you more efficient.

Go to leagaltechaudit.com at http://legaltechaudit.com/ and watch the three-minute video, then take the LegalTechAudit (LTA) test for a small fee to prove to in-house counsel that you possess minimum requisite tech skills, for example certain Word and Excel skills, to help assure them that you've invested in your craft and can function efficiently within minimal parameters, and will not be billing for time simply because of your tech skills ignorance. The website provides a brief Q&A about LTA.

> What is tested in the LTA?
>
> The first release of the LTA requires test takers to perform a series of discrete tasks that commonly arise in practice. The tasks are part of a series of assignments that constitute a single, continuous workflow. The test takers will finalize a redlined investors' rights agreement (word processing). They will then be given data on dividend payments to investors to investigate whether payments were made equally to all investors (spreadsheets). Finally, they will prepare an e-filing attaching the agreement and spreadsheet (PDF).
>
> Can you provide more detail about what is tested?
>
> Yes. We're not going to give you the exact workflow. But we are also not playing a game of gotcha. The LTA assesses core, labor-saving features of common software. A list of features that may be on the LTA are provided through links on the website, but suffice it to say there is a one-page list of skills tested for each of three programs: Word , Excel, and PDF.
>
> Who should take the LTA?
>
> Timekeepers and staff who spend an appreciable percentage of their time working at a computer should take the LTA to ensure they utilize technology to deliver accurate, efficient client service and do not waste their own time on unnecessary tasks that can be handled more efficiently by technology.
>
> How is the LTA scored?
>
> The primary metric is time. The time taken on each assignment will be compared to various benchmarks—target time, average time of all test takers, median time, etc. Accuracy is also assessed, and if a task is performed incorrectly (or not at all), the test taker is assessed a time penalty that roughly equates to how long it would take the slowest user to complete the task (generally about 16 times the time it would take for a skilled user to perform the task).

Who can request the LTA?

Almost anyone. Law firms and legal departments can purchase the audit to assess the proficiency of their own lawyers and staff. Further, clients can request the scores of any of their outside timekeepers.

Why request LTA scores?

The information provided by the LTA can be used in many ways. For example, law firms may want to use the results as part of annual reviews or as a way to incentivize technological efficiency and lower costs. Strong results can be marketed to clients and improve a law firm's bottom line. Clients may want to use the information when selecting law firms for particular types of legal work or when negotiating appropriate hourly rates.

So you are just going to release my score to anyone who asks?

No. We will release your score to whoever registered you (i.e., your firm or company). For anyone else, we will send you an email identifying the requester and asking your permission to release your score. Some law firms may choose to have all such requests go to a single person rather than the individual timekeepers. And some firms may even allow for a general release of all scores requested by a particular client. Otherwise, you will have control over who sees your score.

How is the LTA administered?

We send login credentials to registered timekeepers. Test takers will be asked to take the LTA using locally installed software (i.e., software installed on the test taker's own computer or on a computer provided by the test taker's firm/company). In the future, we hope to provide an option to take the LTA on a virtual desktop that is preloaded with common software.

Introverts: Rainmaking for the Introvert

(Larry Bodine)

Even if you are introverted, you should be able to go up to somebody and ask them five good questions about what's going on with them, what's happening in their business, what challenges are they facing, what are they going to do about it, and what would happen if they didn't do anything? It very quickly leads to people telling you their problems.

Laterals: Culture Integration Is Critical

(Dave Bruns)

Lateral integration gets to that culture issue. Especially when you're lateralling in a large number of people, you need to be able to integrate them into your culture. Otherwise, you lose culture, and that's one of the things that is the glue. We talk about our glue here all of the time. The things that make Farella Farella are really important. All firms have that same need and, when you lose that glue, either through lots of mergers that are not fully integrated or through a great deal of lateral hiring or office openings and not a great of synergy, you start to lose why the firm is the firm. You start to move into a place of risk, because people don't know why they're working for you versus another firm. If you have a strategic plan and you have a strong firm culture, then people can assimilate and get on board with what that is and then they become part of it and then they're part of a greater good, they understand their role and, therefore, they're happier and going to spend more time focused on being a part of something larger and they're not going to be looking for something else. They know what their purpose is. They have a connection to the common goal, making them harder to pull away. Everything's better when you have a strong culture.

Laterals: Needing Clients and Requiring New Skills for a New Market

(Silvia Coulter)

Rainmakers who have built enviable books of business sometimes find themselves lateralling over to another firm and some of their clients aren't going with them. Now they've got to build part of their practice all over again. As some firms find out, gee, this person isn't living up to what we thought he or she could do. Part of that is because the lateral may have been managing some old client relationships for a long time and they are not aware of changes in the buyers in today's market. It's no longer necessarily the guys at the golf club or whatever worked when they built their practice. It's new faces, new names, new buyers, educated buyers, and very savvy competitors. All of those factors come into play. Why are they trying to make the square peg from yesterday fit into the round hole of today? Again, it's making sure that we help them understand how to reach potential clients and communicate to these new buyers in their language. Otherwise, those clients whom they think are loyal but in reality are not loyal, will stay with their existing firms.

LinkedIn Training: Invite Both Associates and Partners?

(Jeff Berardi)

I will say that when I am talking about digital communication activities, such as how to use LinkedIn and other social media that has been—more so than probably any topic I have discussed in recent years—more universally interesting to both associates and partners. With that topic we don't seem to experience the same kind of issue with attendance. I think it may be that whereas our younger lawyers are probably savvier about social media, they also haven't been focused on it from a business perspective, having viewed it more as on a personal basis. On the other hand, some of our older lawyers haven't been doing so much with social media even though they might be very established in their careers, therefore they don't have as much of a digital presence, which doesn't really fit with their market recognition more generally in the marketplace. So, I think it's interesting that for whatever reason, the social media topic has no challenges in blending the two groups together.

LinkedIn: Do You Need 500 Connections?

(Lisa Salazar)

LinkedIn. I think most lawyers are comfortable or have accepted the fact that they've got to be on LinkedIn. When I am asked, "Lisa, should I try to get to 500 plus connections," I tell them I don't think it's necessarily quantity but rather quality of contacts. It's very easy to accumulate a hundred. I think, after somebody builds their profile, within a month, most people have a hundred. And then after that point . . . I don't think it should be an ambition or a goal to amass a large quantity of contacts. It will just naturally grow, and after four years, a lawyer probably will have 500 plus connections if they're active in the legal community. It will happen naturally. They don't have to go out and look for that.

LinkedIn: Encourage Use: Individuals and Firm

(Karen Bell)

We encourage all of our lawyers to be on LinkedIn. We are not policing it. We offer training around it and we have a firm presence on it. We also strive to change some misplaced attitudes about this social media communication vehicle. The goal is not that everybody has to be on it—but it's awareness around the real power of it as a tool. We encourage all of our lawyers, especially our associates, to develop a LinkedIn profile and to understand the various ways LinkedIn can be used as an effective way to network. I consider LinkedIn as another form of elevator speech where you're encouraged to create a brand and, in the space of a few sentences, to really nail down what your value proposition is and what you offer in terms of a business opportunity.

We really woke up to the value of social media working with some external folks—one fellow in particular, a couple of years ago. Certain partners grab it and run with it and do really well. It's not for everybody, but we've certainly built a lot of awareness as a result. LinkedIn was the obvious choice for our business. I really looked at it to see what it does and what it's about, my favorite thing being about the connections. As our associates become more mature and are much more active in relationships, it's a way to find out how to meet people. You almost never need to have a cold call. If someone in the firm doesn't know somebody you want to meet, then you go and look at connections and you find someone you know who knows who you want to meet. I love that "six degrees of separation" element of the tool except it is whittled down to two or three levels instead of six.

Litigation: The New Norm and Adjusting for It

(Erin Meszaros)

Litigation is, in my opinion, taking a different turn, and it's becoming more of a commodity, and people are holding more litigation in-house. To me we have to figure out what is the new norm for litigation. It seems the new norm for litigation is you've got three tiers - very high dollar cases – companies who are using the big law firms that everybody knows they won't lose their job even if they lose. The second tier is what I call "middle of the road," which is the steady stream of litigation that might be considered commodity work, and then you've got the 25 percent that the smaller firms do, and do it much more efficiently than we could. What has been happening lately is a massive amount of firms of our size and bigger are going after that middle of the road litigation, which ends up being more of a consulting type practice, with young people handling the actual day-to-day tasks on the commodity side while the partners turn to more of a consulting approach, for example, how do you stay in compliance and avoid litigation in the future? How do we streamline things? What is happening with Cyber Security? What pitfalls do we need to be aware of that we haven't thought of? The challenge is trying to change the mindset of the litigators who love to be in court.

How do we go after the new litigation norm?

The idea is to help our litigators understand the new norm, so they can do what they love, but also understand that it means they can't always be in the courtroom. What is in the best interest of the client in some cases is that the client just needs a good consultant to help them oversee the work of some of their lower priced in-house attorneys, but they're willing to pay for that consultant in order to be in compliance, and apply the most successful tactics and strategies; and other related issues that only a senior, experienced litigator would know about.

Market Environment: New Climate Requires New Approaches and New Solutions

(Karen Bell)

The market has changed. Expectations have changed. I think it relates to what the business demands are and whether you're dealing with the general counsel, and his or her team, or the C-Suite because, our connections can be one or both of those groups. They have pressures and so we are trying to make sure we're listening so that we are responsive and can help them address the pressures. The old way to respond typical of when I was practicing was reactive. You get a call. The client has a problem. You're the lawyer so you deal with the legal problem. You give them the legal solution and you're done. You send them a bill, which was probably very large.

Now, the approach must be more proactive. You have to have worked hard to earn the right to advise and you're invited to the table to help figure out how to solve the problem which is not just the legal problem. Your response needs to address the larger business context. It has to be done in half the time that the lawyers might like to have to peruse it and it has to be done within a certain cost parameter. It can't be done assuming a blank check; and it can't be qualified with terms like, "Well, I can't predict this, so I'm not sure what it's going to be." Because that's not how businesses work today.

Instead, it's really being more open to understanding the challenges as a client and then being prepared to work with them to address them all and not take such a narrow view that perhaps lawyers historically did.

But, all of our clients are more sophisticated these days. So, the expectation is that we all have to be more sophisticated. It doesn't mean that we don't have a number of highly specialized practitioners, but we do need attorneys who are doing a good job of keeping up-to-date on what's going on with the clients; their business; their industry; and taking the insights they have about the legal environment and then putting it all together as a package that's practical for the client.

Market's New Reality: Requires an Age-Old Approach to the Solution

(Mike O'Horo)

In the legal world there was a bright line reset in 2009, when the legal profession shifted to a buyer's market after 25 years of being a seller's market. That meant the order-taking era was over, permanently.

It's time for law firms and lawyers to deal with the world that their clients have faced for a long time, characterized by declining demand and increasing competition, both of which require real marketing and sales skills. Because nobody is born as a good salesperson and there are no "naturals," that means you have to actually get good at marketing and sales, which in turn means: understand what it is, learn how to do it, practice to get good at it, do it often enough to become experienced, and get objective feedback and coaching so you can improve and approach the "artistry" level.

You'll get good at business development the same way you got good at lawyering. So, let's start by no longer calling it "business development" and, in recognition that the five activities above represent an investment and progression over time. Hereafter, call it business development *practice.*

Marketing Audit

(Sally Schmidt)

In many cases a law firm will ask us to review their new revenue-generation strategies. I call it a "marketing audit." In general, in a marketing audit, I look at everything that they are doing marketing-wise, their budget, and their activities. I interview people. In my final report I say, "Here's what I think you're doing well. Here's what I think you should stop doing. Here's what you should be doing that you're not doing," and a number of other marketing-related measures. Much of the firm's new business development activities will flow out from that marketing audit.

Marketing Climate: A Sea Change in 2014

(Larry Bodine)

We hit a turning point in 2014, when a company called Hinge Marketing inquired into how an ordinary person finds an attorney. For the first time, looking someone up on their website became the number one approach. I was at LexisNexis earlier and we found the same thing in our research. Up until then, people would find a lawyer by talking to colleagues and friends and neighbors, but that fell to the number two way that people look for lawyers. That's a huge change.

When you think about it, it makes sense. You could go to a neighbor and say, I need a divorce, but that's going to be pretty awkward. Or you could go to somebody at the office and say, "I just got arrested. Do you know a lawyer?" That's also going to be awkward. People prefer to conduct their research privately. That's why the attorney referral source changed.

All of the strategies that I described before about keeping your name out there are going to make you the first person that they search for. Ideally, clients will search for you by name. But, failing that, they're going to use Google. So, now it's extremely important that you have a really good online presence.

Marketing Communications

(Allen Chichester)

Another group we have that's very important is Marketing Communications. We tend to centralize this group because it's easier to engage across departments, across offices to support communication needs. Within communications, we have a digital group, a brand group, and our PR group. These are all the people with specialized ability and responsibility to support all of our written or digital activities. We have about 540 attorneys and we have about four people in the marketing communications group, which seems to be enough. They also manage the relationships with PR agencies, ad agencies, and graphic agencies.

Marketing Environment for Legal Services

(Jeff Berardi)

Let's start by taking a look at the business development function within law firms, and how it has grown in importance over time. I think a lot of it has to deal with simply the fact that the world has changed and, obviously, law firms are a much different place than they were 10 years ago, 20 years ago.

The reason there is more attention paid to business development is really due to demand from clients for greater value from law firms and increased competition within the legal industry. So as the availability of high-quality legal services has grown there's just more sensitivity on price and value. The clients are the decision makers, always have been—perhaps now clients realize more than before they have the decision-making power in the relationship and have lots of choices.

I think now the onus is on lawyers and on the firms to really deliver and communicate that value proposition, and the way you do that is through effective business development; and by strengthening client relationships. In essence, that means making sure that the client really understands what the differences are between particular lawyers or between law firms, and describing what they bring to the table, beyond just the legal knowledge.

A huge shift has occurred. We have gone from completely focusing on building the lawyer skills to now include the need to build business development skills, as well. When you are in a situation where, let's say, a client or potential client is considering 5, 6, 10 law firms, and everyone involved in the discussion considers each of the firms to have very good lawyers, that's a given at that point, now what you're really talking about is that the client is making decisions based on overall trust in the relationship and how comfortable they are with that lawyer, or the law firm more generally. So, it often comes down to the business and client development skills that set apart the firm or the lawyers.

> When you are in a situation where, let's say, a client or potential client is considering 5, 6, 10 law firms, and everyone involved in the discussion considers each of the firms to have very good lawyers, it often comes down to the business and client development skills that set apart the firm or the lawyers. I think now the onus is on lawyers and on the firms to really deliver and communicate that value proposition, and the way you do that is through effective business development.
>
> —*Jeff Berardi*

That's the background of all this and, frankly, I don't think our lawyers have been taught those requisite business development skills. They didn't really learn them in law school and that's not necessarily what they've been rewarded for in the past. In fact, it might even be the opposite. We've gone, I think, within the business development department over the last decade or so, to explaining, "Here's what we can do for you and why" to now keeping up with a high level of demand from our lawyers for strategic business development support.

It's part of the reason why we've developed different business development training programs. This is a big part of my job. It's a big part of my team's job. This business development coaching, training, almost behind-the-scenes work that you do and you don't always get a lot of pats on the back for it, but it, I think, is making the difference in the market for clients. And because of how competitive it is out there, any bit of an edge can really help. If our lawyers are better trained and understand how to go about business development and feel more comfortable and they practice, I think they have a better opportunity to then actually deliver that win for the client engagement.

Marketing Services

(Allen Chichester)

Marketing Services is the third leg of the stool. We have a director of marketing services and a number of locally based marketing service representatives and coordinators. Marketing services is our answer to the need for lawyers to have someone next door. Our marketing services staff tend to be event focused because event marketing is a large part of what we do. We invest in staff who understand how to plan and manage events In our system, when you get to be a certain size of an office, usually 25 to 30 attorneys, we'll put a full-time marketing services person in that office. If you're in an office with less than that number we tend to share a person or the office administrator takes on that role and then we parachute in as needed to provide support as needed. Marketing services are responsible for local event activity, as well as local initiatives, community relations activity and office budget support. They help manage each office's local budget. This is actually one of our larger groups because we have 12 offices, and someone is designated in each office.

Mentoring: BD Mentoring = Yes; Formal = No; Case Study Based = Yes

(Jill Weber)

In the first [mentoring] program, we identified more experienced, typically senior, business generators to serve as mentors to those in the program. We found that the participants didn't take advantage of that resource. I don't know why. You would have thought it would have been a great feature of the program, but I think people were hesitant to demonstrate their lack of knowledge in business development to someone more senior. As a result, we no longer offer formal, assigned mentoring as part of the Fast Forward program. I would say that more of their advice is coming from the outside coaches, which is not to say that they don't ever rely on an internal resource, but I think that mentoring has been more effective when it is relevant to a specific client opportunity. Mentoring is more formalized in the professional development side as opposed to the business development side. We do have an active mentoring program with the associates. It's simply that formalized mentoring within the component of Fast Forward—what I call "mentor assignment" did not work within the context of this program, but the more case-study mentoring with specific business development opportunities was effective. [Read more by Jill Weber on mentoring in ***Fast Forward: A Formal Business Development Program: Part 4: Mentoring.***]

Mentoring: Different Types: Adjusting to Market Pressures

(Marian Lee)

The economic pressures work against natural mentoring. Many years ago, partners typically were very proactive about taking an associate under their wing and mentoring them in all aspects of the practice and the business. Today, depending on the size of the firm you're with, billable hours are everything. The industry is so competitive now. Now partners are pressured to bill hours, bring in new business, manage the firm, and take care of many other responsibilities. I feel the billable hour is largely to blame for incentivizing partners not to mentor and train as much. Although, many partners, to their credit, will still find some time to do it.

In some cases, an associate will gravitate toward somebody and a chemistry develops over time, but in today's economic environment you can't count on that happening with everyone. You need to create those relationships, to some extent, to help people get the mentoring they need.

There are some partners that still love it and they will still take the time, but there aren't enough of them like that. There's a little bit of an artificial push that we have to make to get our associates the attention that they need in order to really grow properly. We do that in both a formal and an informal way. Different firms have tried different things. I've talked to lots of my colleagues about mentoring programs, and there's a lot of them. Some firms will say, "We don't want a mentoring program. Those things don't work. They're artificial. It just has to happen. The associate just has to go get themselves a mentor. It'll just happen." And that's just not quite true.

We created a mentor program where every new associate gets assigned to a mentor, ideally, a couple levels above them. So, a Level 1 associate would get a Level 3 associate, a Level 2 would get a Level 4 associate, and a Level 3 or 4 would get a partner. And so, we apply our best judgment and make the assignments.

We ask the new associate to fill out a questionnaire about their goals and the kind of person they'd like to work with. And then we do the best we can to make a match. Obviously, some of them click and some of them don't. But what we tell the associate is, "We don't expect this to be your sole mentoring relationship. This is just a start for you. You're getting into the firm. Here's a person to get you started, a resource. Maybe this connection will take off and you guys will be best buds or work together, and great if that happens. But if not, don't worry, within the next few weeks and months, you're going to start building other relationships. So, it won't be as critical that this one works out. Over time, we expect you to have informal mentors as well as your formal mentor."

We rotate the mentor assignments every couple of years. This happens when an associate moves up a level, and they are assigned a new mentor. We tell them, "The idea is that, yes, you still have your informal relationship with the outgoing assigned mentor, but now you are adding more people to your "board of directors," if you will, as you go through your career. So, ideally, among all of those folks you've got some good people to go and talk to for help."

And if we survey the associates, we'll find some who aren't getting as much out of it as others. There are certainly proactive mentors who do a lot and some who don't do as much. When we hear about one that's not going so well, we try to help by making a new assignment. But usually, the associates are pretty good at making their own relationships. So, they're not utterly dependent on that formal mentoring program for very long; it's really most critical for the new associates who are getting acclimated to the firm, getting integrated, and getting started.

And we're not just talking business development here; we're talking about the whole gamut of practice development, getting accustomed to the firm's culture, and a mixture of important experiences. Some of the mentoring relationships also have a supervision component. So, sometimes the mentor is the associate's supervisor. So they talk directly about work assignments in addition to big picture items. And sometimes the mentor is somebody they don't work with very much. Different associates have different desires, and we try to accommodate them.

We don't define the mentoring relationship very strictly. We leave it open to the pair to decide what it is they want to get out of it and what is going to be the scope of it.

The mentor, when they're assigned a mentee, is given some guidelines for the program that tells them the philosophy, what it's trying to achieve, what they should expect to communicate about, etc. We really don't give them strict time requirements. We say, "You should get together at least once a month, ideally more, as opportunities come up." And then our firm tries to encourage more contact by organizing various activities. Sometimes, we'll have mentoring events, like a happy hour or something like that where mentors and mentees come together. Even informal mentoring pairs can come to the event.

And then, sometimes, our firm has tickets to sporting events and if they're not being used for client entertainment, the next priority down is for mentors to take their mentees. So, we try to incentivize that. We pay for lunches and coffees. So, we encourage the mentor and mentee a lot, but we don't require a certain amount of meetings per month.

Mentoring: Done Through Professional Development Department

(Jeff Berardi)

We have a formal mentoring program, but we also encourage this to happen on an informal basis, too. It is really meant to make sure that we have our more senior lawyers working with more junior lawyers and to convey the sense of the fact that it's really important to be focused on their career development as well as their client development skills. This is something that is done through the professional development department rather than through the business development department. We do have a program, there's some link to business development, but then if they are looking for business development training, then it transfers over to this other program that we would have, which is more of this professional development/business development mix. Whereas, I think the mentoring is really focused on career development and there is an aspect of business development in there for sure, but it is much more of focused on one-to-one training in career advancement. It really depends on the lawyer who is doing the mentoring and how savvy they are with these things.

Mentoring: Essential for Success

(Daniel Kloke)

Regardless of our own desires and expectations, being a skilled legal practitioner does not (necessarily) translate to rainmaking. Training, practice, and old-fashioned hard work must necessarily be focused on to develop legal skills. The same is true for rainmaking—however, different training, practice, and old-fashioned hard work is required to succeed in business development.

A mentor may be the difference between unfocused struggling to market yourself (or losing sight of the ball entirely) and winning new clients. I have been very fortunate to have worked with excellent mentors both within the workplace as well as with a law firm business development consultant (a coach). My mentors know successful techniques and approaches to business development, but, more than that, they have the ability to help adapt those techniques and approaches for my particular professional environment (my market) and my particular business development skills. I will often work with my mentoring co-workers to uncover networking opportunities, pitch new potential clients, and work on existing client management. My business development consultant is a great resource because of his outside perspective, experience in working with others who are at a similar stage of their careers, boundless positive energy, and dedication to my development.

While it is true that there are no short cuts to a successful career, I find that developing rainmaking skills, like legal skills, is best with a team. The best rainmakers I know share at least two things in common. First, they treat business development as necessary for success. Second, they actively find others, internally and/or externally, in order to learn and refine their business development skills.

Mentoring: Every Partner Has a Responsibility to Mentor

(Matt Taylor)

I think every lawyer should be given the opportunity and trained to find out whether they are a potential rainmaker or not.

We have a very formal mentor program where every associate and, frankly, every new partner is assigned a mentor. It's like anything else. Some mentors are more involved than others, but clearly, in my view, most young lawyers have multiple mentors and most of them happen organically because you're working closely with them or they just happen to be next door. But, yes, we have a formal mentoring program, which, I think I'm speaking correctly, has been very well received by our associates. But, again, that's another cultural thing. I think every partner has a responsibility to mentor every associate, whether they are your mentee or not. Much of the mentoring happens organically, as well. But, yes, we have a formal program which is monitored.

Mentoring: Formal and Informal

(Melanie Green)

As to our mentoring programs, some of them are formal and some informal.

For new partners who come in, we have new partner orientation. We do have a group that I rely upon or I go to get feedback on things worth thinking about. And they're not necessarily like a marketing committee. There are a group of people who have been successful, and we kind of draw upon them for various firm business development programs. We call upon that group to see if there's anybody who will be willing to be a mentor or a coach to a new partner in their first year of being a partner. We put hardly any structure around it because each relationship is formed in a different way. What we say is if we find out who wants to be the coach and we pair them up with a coachee based on personality styles, and with other information that we know about them, we try to get them off team sometimes in a different office. So, it gives them a chance for a new partner to have a different perspective, but again, thinking about that personality alignment so we're not completely shooting in the dark.

We talk to them about the program. We say "Hey, we're going to pair you up. What we want you to do is have an initial phone call and talk about you as a new partner, what questions you have, what would be helpful to you in that coaching relationship, and then build what makes sense for you in this first year." We, then, check in a couple of times to see how it's going. There have been times where we have changed coaching assignments.

But generally, we're trying to let them have that autonomy in that case by putting people together and finding their way and not saying, "Here's the three things that you guys need to talk about when you meet."

We give them autonomy and flexibility; and yet, we want to make sure we're getting feedback throughout that process.

Mentoring: Formal Mentoring Tough to Coordinate

(Jonathan Fitzgarrald)

In response to your question, "do we have any formal or informal mentor-mentee relationships for business development?" No. We considered it, but found it to be too difficult to coordinate logistically.

Mentoring: It Can Work and It Can Be Formalized

(Peter Johnson)

Mentoring works. Some come together organically. Some are part of a formalized mentoring program. Others recommend forming mentoring relationships, but they don't strong-arm people. They encourage it. They don't say, "Okay, A, you're working with B for X period of time, and you've got to have at least one meeting a month over lunch or dinner."

Formal mentorships are great. It's like having internal coaches. As part of their responsibility, practice group leaders should—depending upon the size of the firm—wear the hat of the mini-CMO, and in their practice groups they should devote a portion of every meeting to business development and educating the newer folks about how to do it.

The firm's Compensation Committee must determine a way to financially compensate non-billable contributions to the firm that the firm has deemed important to the firm's culture and success.

A lot of firms have a bank system where someone, as an example, has spent a considerable amount of time drafting a detailed a mentorship program on paper and started to implement it. Well, that attorney receives some special recognition by way of compensation, part of a bonus. Some firms have the firm contribution bonus. What have you done? Then, the lawyer says, "Here's what I've done and here's why I should share in the contribution bonus."

Mentoring: Organic Is Best

(Silvia Coulter)

I think mentoring happens organically. I haven't seen it work well if there's been formal assignments for business development. The partners don't have the time.

Mentoring: Largely Depends on Senior Partner Culture

(Mark Usellis)

Mentoring has historically, as with most firms, been random and haphazard and opportunistic. A few years ago, we created a formal mentoring program. This is my personal opinion. I don't think arranged marriages are the best way to do things.

Some senior partners, honestly, aren't very good mentors. On top of that fact you create this artificial intimacy, where they may not have the skillset or the interest. Having said that, mentoring is critical. We conducted a very interesting study that relates to this mentoring issue. We did a large survey of our associates and received about an 85-percent response. When you boil everything down and you talk about what really mattered to their job satisfaction and retention likelihood, there were three results that stood out. One of them was the general work life. It would be great—I have kids—if I have to work late, if there were a taxi service or if I had a gym here. Those are easy to do. Two other factors really mattered, too, which should be of no surprise. One, was that they had sufficient amount of interesting, challenging work; and second, that they felt like there was at least one partner in the firm who actually cared about whether they succeeded or failed. I'm not a professional development person, but I think the terminology for the relationship the associates are seeking is not mentorship, it is sponsorship, which goes beyond mentorship. But there's the feeling that is almost parental in a way of, "I really care about this person personally and I'm going to go out of my way to make sure they succeed." There's an intensity and purposefulness and an emotional individual commitment to it. When we spoke with many of the most successful lawyers in the firm, they realized, once they thought about it, that nearly all of them had somebody like that when they were coming up.

To me, what's important for mentoring is to reignite that sense of commitment among the more senior partners and it becomes more of a cultural experience rather than a programmatic one. You do it because it's the right thing to do, not because there's a program and someone is telling you to do it.

Mentoring: Make it Personal

(Hans Haglund)

Mentoring can be very helpful. I have never seen a formal program for mentoring work in the case where relationships are assigned. If you were my mentor, our families need to know each other. You would know my kids' names. You would know what I deal with on a regular basis. You would know my strengths and weaknesses. All of those qualities that go into a much deeper relationship. You need to have those elements to really make progress, and you cannot force people into those deeper mentor relationships. In my past, I selected a mentor. I approached him. We had a good meeting and I stayed in touch, asked questions and showed a strong work ethic. Fortunately, he took me under his wing. Lawyers need to seek out potential mentors, stay on top of the relationship, and make sure there is a good connection. If no single person emerges as a mentor, you might develop a number of relationships where you get periodic feedback and support. It is up to you to make sure you are always following up and you are developing those relationships, and having those lunches and swinging by their office and saying, "This is what I'm working on and how have you approached this in the past?" Never stop continuing to build those very helpful one-on-one mentoring relationships.

Mentoring: Needed: We Encourage Formal and Informal

(Despina Kartson)

It's important to have a mentor, someone who can guide you, lead you and help you along the way. It doesn't even have to be a formal mentoring relationship, but you should talk to other successful partners and ask them how they did it. What did they do? What worked for them? What are some tips that they would offer? While it isn't formal mentoring, you could gain valuable insight, wisdom, and guidance from conversations with other rainmakers. For example, just stop by a partner's office—a key rainmaker's partner—and ask if you could have 20 minutes on their calendar. Could you go for coffee and say, "I really respect you and admire how much you've really built a great book of business. What's on your top ten list? What did you do? What guidance could you give me?"

Mentoring: New Partners

(Melanie Green)

As to our mentoring programs, some of them are formal, and some informal.

For new partners who come in, we have a new partner orientation. We also have a group of lawyers I rely upon or go to for feedback on key issues that come up. They're not a formal marketing committee. They are a group of people who have been successful, and we draw upon them for input into various firm business development programs.

We also call upon that group to see if there's anybody who would be willing to be a mentor or a coach to a new partner in their first year of being a partner. We put hardly any structure around it because each relationship is formed in a different way. We find out who wants to be a coach and we pair them up with a coachee based on personality styles and other information. We try to get someone not within their immediate team, sometimes in a different office. It gives the new partner a chance to have a different perspective. But again, factoring in the personality alignment ensures that we're not completely shooting in the dark.

We talk to them about the program. We say "Hey, we're going to pair you up. What we want you to do is have an initial phone call and talk about you as a new partner, what questions you have, what would be helpful to you in that coaching relationship, and then build what makes sense for you in this first year." We check in a couple of times to see how it's going. There have been times where we have changed coaching assignments.

Generally we try to let them have autonomy. We don't say, "Here's the three things that you guys need to talk about when you meet." At the same time, we want to make sure we're getting feedback throughout that process.

Mentoring: Pilot Program Builds Momentum

(Melanie Green)

We pilot a lot of things. Because you just don't know sometimes what will work long term. So, one of the things we're actually starting to pilot here shortly is what we're going to call *Client Relationship Manager Collaboration Groups.*

We have our client relationship managers come together and collaborate on various aspects of their work: challenges, successes, questions, etc.

What generated this idea was our talking internally as a team about the fact that a lot of people form lead groups externally. So, we might tell an associate, "Oh, stay in touch with your banker friends and your accountant friends and your financial planner friends and share and refer contacts and information." So, how do we take that lead group concept and turn it a little bit internally to those who are managing client relationships? How do we get them to share information about what they're doing to manage that client relationship that might spark ideas with the others?

We piloted Client Relationship Manager Collaboration Groups. As we think about lawyers having conversations with clients about rates, what could we learn from each other rather than our business development marketing team putting together their talking points? What's the real-life application? Who has done it well? What experiences have they had? What can they share with their partners? We hosted at the end of last year some partner opportunities to come together and talk about that. And we got pretty low attendance, but the people who came really benefited. That was step one of the pilot.

That's a mentoring activity. That's a type of partner-to-partner mentoring.

Even though the groups were small, they did share information. And you could see that they enjoyed that sharing. And so, this was taking it to the next level. Okay, if small groups work, why don't we look across our top, say, 100 clients, identify the client relationship managers, and group them into groups of five or six and think about creating 10 collaboration groups? And we looked at it from the perspective of, are there clients within a similar industry? Are there clients that have a larger portion of revenue and multiple areas of service? So, they're managing a different kind of thing.

So, we sliced it and diced it quite a few ways to come up with how to pair people. And we've introduced it. We've gotten it approved through the lawyer leadership, and we're going to test that. But it really came from that initial look at how people came together to talk about something tricky like rate.

So, really hard topics are addressed—lawyers don't like to talk about rates at all.

We can write memos all day long and send out marketing tips of the day and various other memos. But the lawyers are going to look at us and say, "You've never done this."

And even if we have done it, it's not going to be in their context. And so, how do we get people talking to each other, and then we'll put a business development manager in those conversations to add a tip or two along the way. I have seven managers who would divide up amongst the group meetings. I also have some coordinators who work with the managers, and some of the more senior-level coordinators can probably help along the way as well.

I would call those kind of a mentoring, quasi-mentoring capacity. And we'll see how that one goes.

I guess our concept here is trying to find a way for lawyers to learn from each other but have it set up in a way that doesn't feel overly structured and have a way to create an environment where they will talk to each other, where there's an opportunity for insertion of somebody else's viewpoints and ideas, and somebody to help facilitate that conversation taking place and continuing to flow.

The facilitator would be a senior partner, or in some cases I'll ask the business development manager. So, in one case, the facilitator would say, "Well, now, Joe, now you did"—because they won't talk to each other right?—"Now, Joe, you did something with so and so, didn't you? Like how did that turn out?" That'll get Joe talking. And then if Joe says something and somebody else didn't hear Joe the same way, I heard Joe. Then I'd say,

"Well, hey, I just want to make sure I have the right information. Because I heard something different."

So, that's the facilitator role. We're not telling them what to do. We're bringing out concepts through that conversation.

We're going to schedule them for 45 minutes. We're going to try to make it very informal. We're actually going to have the first meeting, with some topics that we think would be helpful for them to discuss, and then let the first meeting of every group allow them to get to know each other. What clients are they representing? And then form a, "Hey, what would be really helpful to learn more about?" Again, this is based on that high autonomy approach; we're not directing it; we're facilitating it and shaping it. I think each one of these groups may take a different course. But then, as BD managers, we can come together and say, "Here's what this group talked about. Throw this idea out."

And what we don't know yet is if we'll have one lead partner or not, because I think that'll get tricky if we try to do that.

I'm hoping this will be of greater interest to them because they'll like to talk about what they're doing. We went to the top 100 clients. So, these client managers, the people we're starting with, are people who have had success of some level, though not all of them want to tout it. There's a lot of skepticism in our firm about patting ourselves on the back.

So, there's a mix of people who are very vocal about it, and then those who are actually very good at it and don't say a word. And so, if we're really trying to serve our clients better, and all of you are successful in servicing clients in different way, wouldn't we benefit from learning from the different approaches? And you can take aspects of that approach to apply to your relationship, because at the end of the day, the challenge that law firms have is that almost all of these client billing managers, not all, but almost all, have come up to be in that position based on the work that they do. If they're an IP lawyer and we've grown our IP work for a client over a number of years and that's successful, that's really what they know.

They know IP, and they know what works for the client for IP, and they know IP preferences for that client. It's a really different thing to say, "You now manage the entire client relationship and you need to grow it, cross sell it," whatever you want to call it. And that's not really what they've ever done.

Mentoring: Some Come Together Naturally, Others Formally

(Nancy Kostakos and Karen Febeo)

Some mentoring relationships come together naturally and others are formally invited to work together. In the latter case, we initiate those formal pairings. Honestly, we prefer to have the pairing develop in a more organic way. Assigning people to each other does not always lead to the kind of bond and level of trust we are hoping to establish. You can encourage it on both sides, but the two sides have to gravitate towards each other. Nevertheless, we did try this as part of our revenue generation program. We worked with our department leaders and others to identify those who had current working relationships where we could leverage what already existed and other areas where we wanted to introduce attorneys we thought would connect well and hopefully be able to identify synergies in their practices. We had mixed results. Some pairings made immediate connections as soon as they met. And we have seen some of those relationships continue because there was an organic reason for them, others, not so much.

Mentoring: The Lesson That Saved My Career

(Jonathan Waldrop)

So in 2006, I left Kilpatrick to go to Greenberg Traurig, Atlanta, to work with a guy who was building a patent litigation practice at Greenberg. It was a great situation because I was going there to try cases. I was going to be his partner's right-hand guy. We would try cases together. It was what I wanted. A small group. We were going to build something together. That's October 2006. By May 2007 he had left the firm, and the whole IP department at Greenberg, Atlanta, disappeared. That was my seventh year. You could imagine the seventh year, I had a big trial. My career was in front of me. I thought I was going to become a trial lawyer, and within seven, eight months the whole department's gone. He's gone. He went to another firm, took a junior associate with him. Couldn't take me because where he went to they didn't have the budget for me, and I didn't want to go there. So I find myself as a seventh-year lawyer working in the commercial litigation group in Greenberg Traurig in Atlanta after I had been a patent litigation associate for years.

It turns out . . . the best thing that ever happened to me. So at a moment where most people would say, "Your career is over. You're finished. You're done. You're at Kilpatrick. You leave for a new patent litigation practice with a new firm. Now it's gone. You're done." It ends up being the best thing that happened because I ended up working for Ernest Greer who had just become the managing partner of the Atlanta office of Greenberg Traurig.

And he was a guy who looked like me. He was a black guy, and he had millions of dollars of business. He was about 40 years old and he gave me the game. He taught me how to do it. His style was not my style, but it was the first time I'd ever met someone who looked like me who was extremely successful, and built it himself, and was doing the work, getting the work, and managing the work all at the same time.

I spent two years there, 27 months. The best 27 months of my life. It changed my life. Literally, I saw him say, "Look, we're going to get this client." I saw him prospect it. Working with him, I saw the life cycle, the whole life cycle of how you meet someone, and grow that connection into a client. And he'd say, "Look, Waldrop, we're not going to get anywhere with that guy for a year, but we're going to keep doing it." But his game was a drinks game, an after-work drinks game. He'd say, "I go out at 5 o'clock. I buy all the drinks. I hang out late at night. I get in the office at 7:00. I leave at 5:00, but from 5:00 to 10:00, I'm out hanging out. I'm meeting with people. I'm taking people to drinks. I'm going to dinner." He was an entertainer. And that's not my style. That's not how I do it, but it was great to see it and just to see it work. And he was the guy who taught me: "Waldrop, you've got to ask for work." And maybe you don't ask the first time. He always equated it to dating. He's a very smooth character. He said think about what you would do in dating. Are you going to do certain things on a date? The first date, there's some things you do, some things you don't do if you want a second date. And that changed my whole life—I met him at a time in his career when he was building something. There was another associate. We were about the same year. We helped build his practice for him.

That partner gave me and the other associate opportunities to run cases. He provided us with experience which in turn gave us confidence in how to grow and build a practice. Now, it may take a long time, but the confidence was there.

His big thing, too, that changed my life was that most lawyers are transactional, but this business is relational. You have got to move from being transactional to relational because all lawyers are skilled in transactions. I do this, you do that. But business development is relational. Sometimes in a client relationship, you may give, give, give, but it's going to all equal out. At the end of the day, no one's going to be behind. That partner gave me that, and it changed my career. Best thing that ever happened to me.

I saw him not long ago. We had drinks together and I told him that he changed my life. He gave me the game. Best two years of my life. I then left Greenberg. Went to work with Jeff Toney at Southern, and then skyrocketed. That was five years ago. It was like a light switch. But I had to spend two years in a place where most people would think "you're screwed," you know? You're done.

I saw how the game was played and that put me light years ahead. Even though I hadn't done the things that I wish I had done, like building a network. And I had friends. And I was social, but because I got that mentoring

I was able to advance, accelerate myself. Want a better life? Change it. Change it.

Mentoring: Use Graduates from Business Development Training as Mentors

(Peter Johnson)

We've been very fortunate that most of our clients are repeat clients. We have graduates of the program mentor and work with the incoming class so that it keeps the graduates on track and it gives them another mentor situation as they go through the program. We also ask graduates of the program to participate in the workshop for the new class, providing suggestions and guidance as to how the new class can maximize the potential of the coaching resource.

Mentoring: We Have Both Formal and Informal

(Dave Bruns)

In regards to mentoring we have both an informal processes and a formal process. We have mentoring circles that are cross-practice and cross-level led by a partner. Every associate belongs to one, as do many of the partners. They meet on a regular basis and talk about everything. Some of it is business development. Some is about how to make partner or I need to take a vacation and how do I do that? We have a women's group, a parent group, and a group that's focused on women on maternity leave or going on maternity leave that helps them onboard and off-board. Each associate, gets a senior associate as a "buddy." So, there's quite a bit of informal and formal mentoring and we encourage it on a regular basis. We also encourage it in specific situations. Our senior partners who are working with junior partners or associates are encouraged to be an "on-the-spot" mentor. "This isn't working." Or, "That was fabulous what you just did." Or, "Why are you going down this road? It doesn't make any sense. Let's try . . ." or "When you didn't call me back until Monday, this is what it caused . . . " So they can understand what's going on. A great deal of mentoring goes on at Farella.

Mentors: External Mentor Needed To Supplement Internal Mentor

(Jeffrey Silber)

As a trained business development coach and certified personal Life Coach I can spot characteristics in a person's personality that might be holding them back that an internal mentor may not be able to spot. The mentor may be trying for a one-size-fits-all approach. The role of a trained business development coach and certified Life Coach is not just to be a cheerleader, but sometimes to confront and challenge our coachees about some wrong paradigms they hold, which are leading them to incorrect behaviors when it comes to attracting new clients.

For example, one of my clients did not know how to listen. When I'm talking to him, he's thinking of his answer. His eyes are wandering, he's looking everywhere, and I know that is how he behaves in front of potential clients. He's not visually demonstrating the slightest bit of interest in what the potential client is saying. And as you know, potential clients want to be the center of the universe. You should imagine that every potential client has an invisible sign hanging around his or her neck and it says, "Make me feel important."

It's not only about you impressing the client with your legal acumen. They want to feel important and you do that by stressing a human connection with them, by asking them a million questions about themselves, their families, and their work. The distinction between a mentor and a Life Coach, is that the mentor may not be trained to recognize paradigms and belief systems that do not serve the mentee's career goals and revenue-generating activities. The mentee may be unconscious of behavioral traits that are sabotaging golden opportunities when he/she is actually in front of a potential client.

Working only with an internal mentor can also create problems because mentees may not want to reveal personal things about themselves such as their weaknesses, fears, or doubts about being an attorney in the first place. People in a law firm have their images to maintain.

Being a successful lawyer requires devoting your life to the profession and making tremendous personal sacrifices. That is why it is important to work with the individual lawyer, finding out what he or she really wants to do with their life and build on the passion that led them into the legal field in the first place. How does what she/he is doing now fit into their life goals? These, typically, are not areas where a mentor can take the conversations with the mentees. In fact, if the mentor is not trained as a personal life coach, their recommendations may be downright inappropriate. This is life coaching territory.

Sometimes the successful rainmaking mentors may have forgotten some of the skillsets that they had developed 20 years ago when they were just starting out. And perhaps they forgot the importance of things like their home life, the relationship with their mates and their children. And again, this is where a coach could help the associate open up and say, "I'm having trouble at home. My wife/husband and my kids are wondering where I am and I'm afraid to talk to the firm about it because I don't want them to think that I'm being distracted." This is where they could have a confidential conversation with a Life Coach.

I was brought into a partners' annual retreat of a law firm in New York City which had 113 partners. One of the partners raised his hand and said, "I'd like to make a proposal that we bring in 20 percent more partners; that we work 20 percent less; and we earn 20 percent less, because I'm married to my third wife. If I don't do something different soon, I'm going to be .looking for my fourth wife." That became one of the big issue that we discussed over the course of that retreat. His proposal was rejected.

The Life Coaching lesson is: What good is it to be the most successful lawyer in the firm with a fat bank account, if you gain the world and lose yourself? So, these are very serious issues and that's why it's important for a Life Coach to be involved with the younger lawyers. [See also: *Mentors: Internal and External: Both Needed, Mentors: Work-Life Balance: Requires Three Types of Mentors, Mentors: Limitations of An Internal Mentor, and Mentors: Work-Life Balance Expert Can Make A Difference.*]

Mentors: Internal and External: Both Needed

(Jeffrey Silber)

During a coaching session one of my attorney clients received a cell phone call from his wife. When he hung up, he started crying. So I asked, was it bad news? He said, "My daughter's getting married," and I said, 'Well, that's good news isn't it?' He said, "I don't know who she is! These last 22 years passed like a minute. I was devoted to building my practice. Now, she's getting married. And I'm never going to know who my daughter is."

This is an example of when an external mentor-coach who is a veteran certified life coach is fully capable to address a situation like this, whereas an internal mentor may not be.

Mentors: Limitations of an Internal Mentor

(Jeffrey Silber)

In a mentor –mentee relationship, what worked for the mentor in his or her own business development efforts over the years may not be compatible with the personality of the mentee, or compatible with the market environment that the mentee finds her/himself.

With exceptions, in general, the mentor can only create a clone. So, if he or she is a successful attorney, they might tell the mentee, "Look, this is the path to success in this law firm that I took. I think you need an LLM like the one I have, you should hitch yourself to this particular power clique, you should be friendlier with this particular managing partner, and try to play golf with partner "X" on the executive committee. These would be the best ways to succeed around here." The mentor might impart whatever he/she knows about the firm, as well as certain technical aspects of being a lawyer. That's clearly an excellent role for the mentor, but he/she should respect their limits when it comes to guiding the mentee. That is, someone may be the world's best dentist, but you don't go to her to set a broken leg.

The mentor can only teach what he or she knows, and not everybody is the same. Because I have worked with over a thousand lawyers in my twenty years as a professional business development life coach, I can introduce the mentee to many different approaches successfully utilized by hundreds of different rainmakers, not just one or two.

A mentor knows only what has worked for him or her. Who knows if that's going to be suitable for the mentee? If the mentor's advice does not resonate with the mentee and the approach to building a book of business does not come from the mentee's heart, the mentee will not use the approaches that worked for the mentor.

For example, if a mentor's main practice development tool has been public speaking and his mentee is just no good at it, he can pound on the mentee as much as he wants, but it is not going to be an effective tool for him/her. As a Life Coach, I am able to guide that person into an entire series of other tools and techniques that were not in the mentor's toolkit. Perhaps, this person should be on the boards of trustees of various charities. Maybe he/she needs to write articles or join industry organizations. The point is that if it doesn't come from the mentees' core values, they are just not going to do it.

Doing individual marketing is like wearing a custom suit. The mentor can't say, "Here is my old suit, put it on and go out and do some business development work." What if it's too big or too small? The mentee would look ridiculous and so would his marketing efforts. I make custom suits. I make sure they go out wearing the right suit for the job they have to do.

So, I know what I'm good at, and that's where I try to confine my professional activities. The same thing should apply to all mentors. There are borders to be respected. Mainly, the coach and mentor should know that it can never be a one-size-fits-all approach to business development.

It's clear if the mentor has been a successful lawyer that is why he/she is a partner. She has a certain skillset in practice development. There is no doubt about it. It is unreasonable to say she doesn't know how to do that. However, the issue is, how does she transmit that knowledge to the mentee while allowing and encouraging the mentee to explore and grow in areas of business development areas which the mentor has never considered teaching because the mentor has never done them?

Let's say a mentor introduces the mentee to the GC in charge of litigation and the mentor might say to him, "Hey, Bill, how's your wife, how are those kids of yours?" and if the mentee is not made aware of the value of that, he might think he's just saying hello to a client and not understand the true significance of what appears to be a trivial conversation.

The main element of building trust is the human connection. A great many law firms can deliver high-quality legal services. They never let the client down. They are definitely credible and reliable, but the true distinction is the human connection. The client can really relate to you when you say, "Hi, Bill, how's your wife and your kids? How's the mathematical genius son of yours doing over at MIT?" That is worth much more than talking about what cases you have had recently or your firm's new practice areas. If the trust-building value and relationship-bonding value behind those words about the client's family are not called to the attention of the mentee, he or she may not realize the enormous value of that kind of salutation at the beginning of the lunch is more important than anything else that follows. [See also: *Mentors: Internal and External: Both Needed, Mentors: Work-Life Balance: Requires Three Types of Mentors, Mentors: External Mentor Needed To Supplement Internal Mentor, and Mentors: Work-Life Balance Expert Can Make A Difference* by Jeffrey Silber.]

Mentors: Work-Life Balance Expert Can Make a Difference

(Jeffrey Silber)

In 2012, the secretary of a client of mine in a Century City firm came to him and said, "I'm taking six weeks off this summer. I'm going to Europe. It's my dream and I hope you keep my job open for me, but if you don't, I will understand. But, I'm going in any event." So, she went and he did keep the job open for her. He said to me, "Jeffrey, I make 20 times more money than my secretary. I cannot afford to take off six weeks and go to Europe, so between me and my secretary, who's rich?" Just think about that. If you were an extraterrestrial in a space ship and you look down and you see the secretary on the Champs-Elysees sipping a Cappuccino enjoying a lovely summer day and you see the partner working 12 hours a day on contracts under fluorescent lights, who would you think was the rich boss?

In that Century City case, the lawyer loves being an attorney, that's not the issue for him. Working with him, I was able to have him create a better separation between his personal life and his work life. He's bought a sailboat again and he is doing a better job making a clear distinction between the personal and professional parts of his life.

There are many good illustrations of when it's good to get a Life Coach involved in the process. That doesn't mean that the young lawyer is going to suddenly throw up his hands and storm out and say, "I can't stand this life!" But, he or she has to find the balance among family, personal life, and the firm. If they are not happy at home, it will be difficult for them to be successful lawyers and even more difficult for them to be successful rainmakers.

Mentors: Work-Life Balance: Requires Three Types of Mentors

(Jeffrey Silber)

Mentoring can take many forms, internal mentor, external business development coach, and external life coach. Life coaching should be considered as an essential work-life balance form of mentoring. Even better is a certified life coach who is also a business development coach. The best business development coaches are also trained in the internal dynamics of the human personality. These are skills that can help a lawyer determine how to achieve "reasonable" or "acceptable" work-life balance along with uncovering and addressing any personality traits that might limit the attorney's ability to develop and grow client relationships.

Internal mentors, besides guiding their mentees in developing their legal knowledge, are able to teach their mentees skills related to specific internal issues of the law firm that external coaches may not be aware of, such as internal politics and policies and the nuances of the best career path within the firm.

External mentor-coaches, are in a unique position to help a lawyer in ways that an internal mentor may not. Sometimes, it's as simple as a personal issue the attorney will not discuss with anyone associated with the firm for fear of their career path being impacted, yet is holding the attorney back professionally in some manner. A confidential life coach with business development expertise in the legal field has developed the "ears" to listen inside what a lawyer is saying in order to pull out and address core issues that may be interfering with a lawyer's progress, and therefore impacting firm progress, as well.

Internal mentors and external mentors in the form of a business development coach and a certified life coach are all essential for optimum results for the individual and the firm.

There are many essential aspects of the law and the politics of a given law firm that a Life Coach will not be expected to know. That is why an internal mentor has an important role to play in developing young talent in a law firm. Keep in mind that a mentee under the wing of one mentor will frequently become very similar to their mentors because the mentors only see the world through their own experiences. That is why some mentees can end up as clones of their mentors.

> You need both internal mentors and external mentors. The external mentor should be a business development coach and a certified life coach. Both types of mentors are essential for optimum results for the individual and the firm.
>
> —*Jeffrey Silber*

[See also: *Mentors: Internal and External: Both Needed, Mentors: Limitations of An Internal Mentor, Mentors: External Mentor Needed To Supplement Internal Mentor, and Mentors: Work-Life Balance Expert Can Make A Difference.*]

Metrics: A Very Clear Set of Expectations

(Louise Muldoon)

Yes, we have a very clear set of expectations and metrics. We expect people to have achieved or be able to perform X, Y, and Z at certain levels of development. As an example, things like presenting at conferences. One of our objectives is to make sure that every attorney understands his or her business development metrics and how often we will review those with them.

Metrics: Areas to Measure

(Bill Flannery)

Areas to measure: the firm's market share of available legal work at a given key client and key client face time. What do you do to get these people to perform? Well, you give them deadlines and you let them set their own goals, and then you measure against those goals. People will do what's measured. [Read More: Go to Exhibit 3, *How to Hire a First-Year Associate Who Has Rainmaker Awareness.*]

Metrics: Business Development Training

(Jeff Berardi)

To the extent that metrics can be used to measure the success of our business development training, we certainly want to do so. We measure as much as we can. We get as much feedback as we can as to what the lawyers want to hear and learn about. They're not easy judges, you have to have a pretty thick skin, but we always, always ask for feedback and send out the questionnaire right after a business development training activity and encourage honest feedback, both good and bad. I feel every program we do gets better because we tweak it a little bit. We try to take into account what they are saying and our business development educational programs have evolved over time. So, we struggle with it just like other firms do, I am sure. My view is the more of this you do the better it gets. And the fact that more and more lawyers are embracing business development and asking for more is a good sign.

Metrics: Financial Numbers and Activities

(Sally Schmidt)

When I work with individuals, we always have metrics and they take the form of both things that are very objective—numbers—and things that are more actions. For example, with most lawyers, I try to help them figure out what type of a practice mix they want in the future. "You're doing this, this, and this. Is that what you want to be doing five years from now? If not, what do you want that to look like?" Products liability is 50 percent of their practice and they'd like it to be 30 percent, and that type of thing. We'll try to set some numbers. We'll also set some origination numbers, or, dollars in the door or however they measure it in a particular firm. We always set the financial numbers. Then, the other things are activities. It might be, "We're going to try to get out three alerts this year." "We're going to try to have a lunch every two weeks." I try to get the lawyers to have some measurable objectives, but they're not things that are necessarily ways to measure business. If we've done a good job of figuring out that they're the right activities, then they're good things to measure too.

Metrics: Metrics and Accountability Are Molded Together

(Erin Meszaros)

In terms of metrics, when talking to an attorney about business development, it's really important to customize it for each individual. Yes, it includes metrics like X number of calls, X number of lunches, X number of this, and X number of that. For example, I had a young partner the other day say to me, "How much time should I be spending on business development?" And I said, "Well, it's not a matter of me giving you an amount of time. You need to identify, one, how much time you have and then, two, realistically how much time you will actually commit to follow through." If you tell me you have two hours a week but you know realistically you're only willing to do 30 minutes, then just tell me you're only willing to do 30 minutes. I will then take that 30 minutes and show you how to use it effectively so your efforts will drive successful results.

We have individual business plans where the coordinators and the managers meet with each member of the team to develop their plan. The leader will then have his/her own group goals. The leader will use the information from the individual plans as well as the group plan at his/her monthly Practice Group meeting to hold folks accountable. For example: "We said we were going to talk to these five clients over the last five months. I see here from InterAction*, our activities tab shows we've only talked to two of them. How do we approach the other three and who was identified as being responsible to do so?" And so accountability and metrics are molded together. [*Author's note: InterAction is a LexisNexis CRM designed specifically for law firms.]

Metrics: Tied to Business Plans

(Nancy Kostakos and Karen Febeo)

We establish business development targets on an individual, business unit, and firm basis. When an attorney goes through a coaching program, they put together business development plans that they need to execute. Each metric doesn't necessarily tie to a set revenue expectation because some of these activities take a longer time to bear fruit. It depends on where the particular participant is in their understanding of business development. Many are just taking their heads out of the law books for the first time and figuring out how to warm up their network. We're not expecting that we're going to have new revenue in the door next month in these instances, but it's still important to start the process.

The bottom line is we're trying to get everyone the skills they need and get them all to be more active than they currently are in business development, and that will bear fruit. Some of them are much closer to the revenue than others just because of how their career has gone. The program itself is not really tied to a specific revenue per lawyer target, but as a department or as a business unit, each individual does have a responsibility to contribute to specific revenue targets in one way or another.

It does get down to specific tactics. We're taking them through a process. The first step in the process is to figure out who is in their network. The next step is to really qualify all those contacts within their network and identify somebody they can reach out to that might have work now or who's someone they should just generally stay in touch with. Ultimately, this is about learning to ask for business once they've identified that there is business available.

We can also connect the dots where they can't sometimes. In some cases, our marketing and business development team has a broader awareness of what's going on with all of the clients and prospects than individual practitioners do. It's our job to facilitate business development by making those connections and arming our lawyers with well-crafted, targeted pitch materials and messaging.

Metrics: What to Measure to Make It Rain

(Bill Flannery)

- Face Time: track key client face time
- The firm's market share of available legal work at a given key client
- Let attorney set own goals with deadlines and then measure results against those goals.
- Reward Success. Reward potential client contact face time that fails.
- Reduce Fear of Failure: with simulated run-throughs with former inside-counsel
- Increase BD activities by rewarding success or failure in front of targeted decision makers.
- Reduce Fear of Failure: Suggestion: Give 50-percent billable hour credit for face time with identified client target decision makers.

> People will do what's measured.
>
> —*Bill Flannery*

Middle-Market Companies: They Want Simplicity and "One-Stop Shopping"

(Sally Schmidt)

I recently conducted a focus group for a client of mine who does a lot of middle-market company work. We had a number of companies in their market participate, not necessarily clients, and it was interesting because the companies basically said they don't care where they buy their legal services. They don't care if they're offered by an accounting firm. It's because they like the idea of simplicity. So, maybe there'll be a few more people dipping their toe into the legal market. I don't see a lot of this now, but that could be scary, if we aren't thinking ahead of them.

Mindset: A Lawyer's Mindset Toward Business Development

(Nancy Kostakos and Karen Febeo)

Lawyers are excellent negotiators, and they exude great skill and confidence in developing legal opinions. Yet they often have a hard time asking for business and communicating their value. While some lawyers may tend to be a bit more introverted, and thus less comfortable with sales, we really think it's just a lack of practice (and not something many lawyers thought about doing when they decided to go to law school). The lawyers we work with are incredibly smart and know how to stand behind their legal opinions, so we just need to teach them how to stand behind their own qualifications, and those of their colleagues, when they have the opportunity to explain their potential value to a prospective client or referral source. Our firm thinks it's important to give them the tools, resources, skills, and coaching to help them further develop and practice this skill.

Minorities: Creating and Finding Business Development Introductions

(David King Keller)

Lawyers of minority and socially diverse backgrounds should form or seek out organizations that support your efforts to meet clients hiring skilled lawyers of diverse backgrounds such as the California Minority Counsel Program (CMCP), whose executive director, Marci Rubin, brilliantly implements CMCP's mission to promote diversity in the legal profession by providing attorneys of color with access and opportunity for business and professional development. Women and LGBT also benefit from CMCP's efforts to infuse diversity throughout the legal services profession. In one example, a coaching client of mine, a patent litigator, following this advice, joined me at a CMCP San Francisco function where I was able to introduce him to the general counsel in charge of litigation for Wal-Mart who, in turn, at my request, introduced my client to his head of patent litigation.

Motivation: 5 Strategies That Motivate Lawyers to Pursue Business

(David Ackert)

When seriously at-risk heart patients are told by their healthcare practitioner that unless they radically change their habits around diet, exercise, smoking, etc. they will die . . . 1 in 7 follow their doctor's instructions.

> When seriously at-risk heart patients are told by their healthcare practitioner that unless they radically change their habits around diet, exercise, smoking, etc. they will die . . . 1 in 7 follow their doctor's instructions.
> Robert Kegan in "Immunity to Change"

Motivation is not a lawyer problem, it's a human problem. The fact is that people are reluctant to embark on difficult tasks, regardless of their profession. But if you examine lawyers' inconsistency with business development, despite the fact that it has become an intrinsic part of the profession, according to the Altman Weil lawyer personality profile, most lawyers tend to be risk-averse. This trait plays out to their detriment when it comes to business development, which requires a considerable tolerance for rejection. But the profile also shows lawyers to be highly practical, analytical, prudent, articulate, and competitive. These traits can be leveraged for better business development results.

(1) Trait: Practical. Strategy: Play to Your Strengths

Not all business development activities are well-suited to every lawyer. An introvert might prefer to author a substantive article whereas her extroverted partner might prefer to present CLE. Match the tactic to the lawyer's personality so that they can operate within their comfort zone.

Extrovert	Introvert
• Group networking • Panel discussions and CLE Presentations • Social dinners • Media interviews	• One-on-one networking • Writing articles or blogs • Social media • Analyze client needs and propose solutions that cross-sell the firm's services

There is no guarantee that an extrovert will be drawn to the activities in the first column or an introvert to the second. The point is that the lawyer should consider the activity that matches their natural talents so that their approach is effective.

(2) Trait: Analytical. Strategy: Use Data to Prove Outcomes

Because of their risk-averse nature, lawyers often rely on evidence and precedents to make decisions. They prefer empirical data and indisputable facts over hunches and theories, so appeal to their analytical side. For the skeptical lawyer who doesn't like the uncertain results of business development, consider sharing the following ratio, developed from interviews with hundreds of lawyers:

The Referral → Meeting → Matter → Revenue Ratio

Example:
1 Matter = Average of $50,000 Revenue
3 Meetings = 1 Matter
5 Referrals = 3 Meetings = 1 Matter

Given these numbers, a lawyer seeking to originate $50,000 of revenue will require at least five referrals, $200,000 will require at least 20 referrals, and $1,000,000 of revenue will require at least 100 referrals.

The formula should be adjusted according to a given lawyer's practice area and effectiveness with prospective clients, but it demonstrates to the analytical lawyer that, in order to reach their monetary goal, they will need X more referrals than they currently generate. Once they realize this, they will be more likely to spend their non-billable time on networking, CLE presentations, article writing, and the other tactics listed earlier.

(3) Trait: Prudent. Strategy: Tie Business Development to Monetary Incentives

Lawyers at all levels are motivated by money. Sure, they are motivated by other things too, but business development initiatives unilaterally fail whenever firms expect their lawyers to originate without reaping some of the benefits personally. If the comp system at the firm does not reward originators with some type of bonus (especially at a non-equity level), a prudent lawyer will likely use that as a reason to forestall business development altogether.

(4) Trait: Articulate. Strategy: Change Language to Change Culture

Is "sales" a dirty word at your firm? Do the lawyers prefer to mislabel it as "marketing"? Culture changes when new language protocols are introduced into the lexicon. Think about it—our society has made great strides toward equality by shunning the use of racial and sexist terms over the years. Even derogatory lawyer jokes are less common than they once were. So examine the language used at your office and ask yourself what kind of culture it is fostering. If it isn't a sales culture, perhaps it's time to start using the words that will encourage intended attitudes and behaviors.

(5) Trait: Competitive. Strategy: Use Technology to Measure and Report Comparative Progress

"Gamification" principles work well in the context of business development. When another practice group at your firm is scoring more client lunches than yours, you will find yourself pursuing clients more aggressively than you would without the friendly challenge. There are myriad technology platforms (e.g., a simple Excel form, Practice Pipeline, and many others) that can track performance. By using a friendly competitive scorecard to spice up business development activities, you appeal to the competitor that exists in most lawyers.

So, as you engage in business development, play to your attorneys' strengths. Chances are most are some combination of *practical, analytical, prudent, articulate*, and *competitive.* Leverage these traits to turn what may be one of their least favorite activities, into one of their most effective.

Motivation: Mine

(Hans Haglund)

I love what I do. There are numerous practices, e.g., appellate, securities, IP, estate, litigation, etc. With each practice you have to get into the individual's specific circumstances because practices are different and this is why I think my job is so interesting. Some of my friends who are serial entrepreneurs would say to me, "You're in a law firm and you are dealing with lawyers, how is that? You used to be an entrepreneur with startup companies. What the hell are you doing? This makes no sense." What I love about what I do is digging into the uniqueness of every lawyer and every lawyer's practice that I work with. You have to get down to that individual level because of the complexity of the circumstances. It's not cookie cutter at all and that's probably true across the board. For example, when you deal with someone on the defense side of white collar, it's more of a pure marketing approach and networking, getting in front of people and telling them what issues similar companies are facing. You tell them what they should look out for, and preventative measures that can be taken today to prevent a disaster tomorrow. What I do takes all the energy, focus, business knowledge, creativity, and enthusiasm that any successful entrepreneur must possess, and I love it.

Motivation: My Personal Motivation

(Louise Muldoon)

I think, if you're going to be an effective business development professional, you've got to give the lawyers things they can take and use in the most effective and efficient manner possible. Or, put another way, I see every single lawyer in this whole organization as my client and I want to give them the same value I tell them they've got to give to their clients. We're going slightly off topic now, but the thing that keeps me in the law firm is that you get to work with very smart people. I am surrounded by very smart, very thoughtful, often incredibly socially aware, people. I really like that environment. I work with a lot of people, for example, that spend a good chunk of their time on pro bono, on projects such as writing constitutions for developing countries, the legal rights of homeless youth and that type of thing. It's a fantastic environment to work in.

Motivation: The Opportunity Analysis

(Shanda Zavalsky)

We help motivate attorneys through individualization of approach and a presentation that provides a clear picture of next steps and possibilities that can win new business.

One action generator that can excite an attorney into taking a new business development step is our green space analysis which identifies cross-selling opportunities. The hurdle is not as high since we already have a relationship with the client (so it is less intimidating) but there is opportunity because the client is not using a particular practice area.

To support our attorney's with key client information before making a call we use a full-time business development research specialist on our staff. She generates what is called an "opportunity analysis." This enables us to identify areas of need and relevant solutions. We are diligent and concise with the product we provide, it is short and contains analysis on people, past legal needs, firm preferences, industry trends, firm connections, past work, past marketing efforts along with recommendations of where there may be opportunity.

Network and Networking

(Matt Taylor)

I always tell the associates, "Start day one to be a networker. Do not wait." One, it's fun. It makes life interesting. You're staying connected to the people that you already have something in common with. People you went to college and law school with. Stay in touch and network. I always tell them this, "You don't have to be a snake oil sales man about it, just be interested in people and just ask them what they're doing." And then, at some point, as you develop that relationship, you have to ask for the business. They always ask me, "What's that mean?" Because when you're a young associate, you really don't know what that means. So, we provide plenty of training on what asking for the business means and how to do it.

> Associates need to get real about rainmaking. Some old-school thinking was, "Young man, or young woman, when you come to our firm be the best lawyer you can be and everything else will take care of itself. Don't ever worry about marketing." Well, that's just not real. That's just not the reality of this world. You must network from day one.
>
> —*Matthew A. Taylor*

Network, Network, Network

(Michèle Silva)

As executive director of the Association of Business Trial Lawyers, Northern California Chapter, for many, many years, my first response when asked what is the primary trait of a rainmaker was, after being a damn good attorney, it's being a great networker. To all associates and new partners out there, I say network, network, network! I don't think most attorneys are good networkers. At our events, I have to push them on each other to talk and get acquainted. And I hardly ever meet attorneys at networking events, e.g., chamber mixers, association meetings, leads groups, etc. I guess they prefer to be logging those billable hours or spending time with family versus using their personal time to network, but, since many young associates don't have families yet, I think they could be stars if they would go out and meet non-lawyers in networking situations. Like John Siamas of Reed Smith says, "it could be years before the incremental business manifests," so, ya gotta plant those seeds now.

I certainly agree networking is key, but I also believe that there is a "prerequisite" for networking.

New Partner Orientation: Half Day Meeting Includes Business Plan

(Marian Lee)

In the last year or so, my focus has been to spend more time with newer partners and on promoting their growth and development. And, of course, business development is a big piece of that. I know something about business development, but I am not the expert. Shanda Zavalsky, our Business Development Director, is the expert. She and I will partner on various new associate and new partner discussions and meetings. For example, next month, we are going to organize a mid-year meeting of our new shareholder class. We're going to bring them together for an afternoon and do some business development training. We use Tracy LaLonde of Akina Corporation. She's awesome. She's doing some different things for us this year. We'll bring them together for a half day orientation. We tell them to bring their business plan. They will talk to each other about their business development actions and goals. "How are you doing on revenue generation goals? How are things going with acquiring new clients and new client matters? What's working? What's not?" And, "What's it like to be a partner, so far?" We then provide some additional tips on business development.

In this upcoming session, we will focus on making "the ask," doing the pitch, how you can use the marketing department, and what you should be doing right now. We will ask them, "What are you doing in the area of leadership?" We remind them, "You're transitioning from that associate doing your job for a partner, to being the partner, running a practice, and being responsible for the well-being of the firm as a whole and the people around you."

Newsletters: That We Send to Our Lawyers

(Adam Severson)

We have created a newsletter that we distribute every other week to the broader group of the firm's attorneys that focuses on trends and the business of law. It is essentially a compilation of different articles with a synopsis of those articles to let our lawyer leaders be smarter about the practice.

Niches Lead to Riches: Specialization Can Narrow Market and Increase Revenue

(Stephen Fairley)

One of our clients is a criminal defense attorney. When he first came to us, his business was generating about $300,000 to $400,000 per year, which is about where most criminal defense attorneys peak out. What he wanted was to build a multi-million dollar firm. He knew he had the technical skills, he just needed the marketing and management help. Over the course of the next four to five years, we helped him break through the seven-figure barrier and build a $3 million dollar firm! One of the ways we did this was to help him niche his firm and differentiate himself from all the other criminal defense attorneys.

One of my favorite sayings is, it's the niches that lead to the riches. So, he heard me talking about this and he said, well, how can I niche, I'm a criminal defense attorney? I said, well, what about DUIs? He said, well DUI, there are attorneys that just do DUIs. I said, well, how profitable are they? He said, "Well, first-time DUI, you're probably talking about $3,000 to $5,000, but it's highly competitive in California where I'm at," which is true. Being a DUI lawyer is incredibly competitive. Through the course of a number of different situations, what we decided to do is to niche him, or to niche his practice, in not just criminal defense, not just DUIs, but DUIs for healthcare providers, licensed healthcare providers. Why?

Well, because if you're an EMT, a physician, a nurse, a pharmacist, an ambulance driver, all of these people are licensed to perform it and they all have access to drugs. Okay, prescription meds. The medical industry has an issue with prescription drug abuse, just like the other industries have, but here's where he became knowledgeable.

He educated himself about all kinds of rules and regulations and come to find out, a very common issue is that you have a first-time DUI, they're an upstanding member of the community, and you don't want to send them to jail, so you do a plea bargain. You plead it down. That's very common. So, these DUI attorneys are pleading down their clients and then three to six months later the client gets a letter from their state licensing board saying we have suspended your license because you pled guilty to this misdemeanor. Whoops. Nobody knew it.

So, he made himself the go-to attorney to avoid this disaster. He studied to become an expert in all the licensing regulations for all of these different medical health professionals and now he is the go-to expert for any medical health professional in his area in California that gets a DUI because he knows what you can plead down to that won't impact your ability to make a living and keep your license.

And by the way, he now charges $10,000 to $15,000 for a first-time DUI, which is three to five times more than anybody else.

It's the niches that lead to the riches. People don't understand. They think, well, yeah, but I could be a litigation attorney for any kind of business. I'm a small business owner running a multi-million dollar company. I don't care if you know any kind of business. I don't want to know that you know professional services, because that's completely different from making widgets. It would help me if you knew something about marketing and business development and SEO. If your idea of marketing is having a website that your high school kid built five years ago, I'm not interested. You're not credible to me. There are plenty of experts in the marketplace. I want to find one that knows something about me because the marketplace, because of the nature of the beast, 1.2 million attorneys in the United States today to give you some perspective, that's one attorney for every 300 people, man, woman, and child included.

And there's somewhere around 30,000 new law school graduates every single year. So, there's an oversupply and an under-demand. And what happens when there's an oversupply in the marketplace according to Economics

101? The prices go down. Why do you think it is that the average attorney made $85,000 before the recession? Since the recession, the average attorney in the United States makes $65,000 a year. Now, average is a misleading statistic, as you know. Because 50 percent make more, but 50 percent make less. And we're not just talking about people in large law firms, we're talking about an associate, a first-year associate or a second-year or a third-year associate of the small to mid-size law firm and by the way, over 65 percent of all lawyers in the United States work at small law firms.

Objection to BD Activity: "Executives are Too Busy to Want to Talk to Me."

(Silvia Coulter)

I had a partner with whom I worked a couple of years ago who spent 400 hours a year blogging. He was a big rainmaker in the heyday of the tech rise. Then his practice fell off. And he wasn't all that open to business development. But I said, "You know what? Get out there and connect with these people directly." Sometimes when I say that, people will say, "Silvia, you don't understand how busy venture capitalists are. They don't have time to meet with people like me. They don't want to hear from me." This guy was really a struggle for me. So, I just picked up the phone and called five venture capital firms and said, "This is what I do, and I just want 10 minutes of one of your partners' time to brainstorm so I can give my audience feedback that I spoke with five venture capital partners at five different firms and this is what they said."

I don't generally do that, but I said to this reluctant attorney, "You know what? I talked to VC partners from firms A, B, C and D." And he knew all those names. I never mentioned the firm's name, obviously. I just said, here's their feedback. "Yes, share some insights with us. We'd love to hear from you. You guys do more of this than we do. You guys touch more clients than we touch. And what are you seeing in the markets these days?" I don't talk to very many clients who aren't interested in sharing their insights. But it's got to be something of value. Get out and talk to people! Don't make assumptions that they don't want to talk with you and they're too busy, because that's just a bunch of hogwash. Anybody who's a good business development coach has probably heard that. If they don't hold the lawyers' feet to the fire, then they're not going to be as good a coach as they could be.

> Don't make assumptions that people aren't going to want to talk to you.
>
> —*Silvia Coulter*

So, don't make assumptions that people aren't going to want to talk to you. The only issue is, some clients will come back to us and say, "We're willing to talk, but the question is, are the lawyers listening to what we say?"

Objections to Contacting an Old Classmate: "We Haven't Talked in Years"

(Silvia Coulter)

Lawyers, they'll throw up all kinds of objections to conducting business development. They'll be very speculative about everything. They'll say, "Well, they're going to know why I'm calling, aren't they?" Well, what's wrong with that? What is wrong with the fact that you want to connect with them? Remember, you're not going to call somebody whom you haven't talked to in seven years and ask them for business. You've got to build the relationship again. There's a timing to all of this and a balance. "Well, I don't want to bother them. They're really busy." Well, you don't know that you're bothering them, and most people are happy that you're thinking of them. I'm always trying to bridge it to their world. I'll say, so you haven't talked to somebody in a long time, and they were a law school classmate or your law school roommate, and then, out of the blue, they call you and say, "Hey, David, I was just updating my contacts, and ran across your name. And it's been way too long since we connected." You're not going to think, "Oh, what does this guy want?" You're going to think, "Hey, it's great to hear from you. Thanks for calling." Most people have enough of an ego that they're happy to hear from you because it's about them.

You have to get out of lawyer mode. Stop analyzing why this isn't going to work and just do it. Just do it and try it, and usually the lawyers are super energized by the results.

Origination Bonus to Non-Working Attorney

(Erin Meszaros)

In an ideal scenario I would recommend having a bucket of money that you could use for bonuses at the end of the year. I would have teams rewarded for cross-selling from associates all the way up.

Origination Bonus: A Serious Motivator

(Shanda Zavalsky)

When I am asked, is the origination bonus a motivator? I say, "Yes, absolutely. It's a primary motivator." Our firm will bonus an originating attorney even if that attorney is not the billing attorney.

Passion and Motivation: Find the Source of Passion First, Then Motivation Follows

(David King Keller)

Call up passion and motivation within your trainees/coachees before beginning the business development training.

Don't make this mistake when conducting business development training or coaching: many business development coaches and trainers make the mistake of teaching to the program as opposed to teaching to the individual attorney. A training program is only good if it is implemented effectively and with enthusiasm. So the first order of business in any coaching or business development training program is to ignite the passion and motivation within the individual attorney.

The way you do that is to invite the attorney to remind himself or herself of what motivated him or her to get into the practice in the first place and what additional motivations have been discovered and added since then.

To optimize the learning experience that is being provided with coaching and training is to optimize the mind that you are seeking to engage; and to do that you need to create an enthusiastic mental attitude on the part of your coachee/trainee. The way to do that is to support the attorney in getting into a mental state and frame of mind to passionately embrace what you are about to confer.

The following 10 questions can help achieve that goal. The first six can be used in a group training session. The last four questions are best done in a 1:1 coaching session.

10 Questions for Every Lawyer Before Starting a Coaching or Business Development Training Program.

A trainer in a group training should break the group into dyads to facilitate quick and personal ways to answer the first six questions. If time does not allow the dyads, ask the lawyers to write the answers in their training journal.

(1) What motivated you to go into law?
(2) What is exciting about the legal work you are currently practicing?
(3) Who has benefited from your practice as a lawyer, and who will benefit in the future?
(4) Are there people who benefit from your law practice that are not clients and if so, who are they and how are they benefited?
(5) Are there people who benefit from your income as a lawyer other than yourself and if so, who are they and how?
(6) Describe three of your favorite law practice experiences.

(7) How would you change your practice to make it even more exciting and more enjoyable?
(8) On a scale of 1 to 10, with 10 being sheer ecstasy, what number would you give your average workday and how could you tweak your current work day to make it more of a 10?
(9) What, if anything, is missing from your work-life balance?
(10) Describe three ideal clients.

Personality Identification Tools

(Silvia Coulter)

I've worked with one of the very popular personality identification tools, and I think they can be valuable. I guess I'm fairly intuitive, and I can generally read my clients pretty quickly. So, do I need to use those tools? Not really. They can be beneficial, but where I find them most beneficial is having the lawyers think about the buyer and then self-select. I use a really, really simplified format. It, literally, is a one-page PowerPoint that describes various profiles, and it's something easy for them to remember and relate to. Because they can take a Myers-Briggs, but unless they look at it all the time they're not going to remember all of those details and letter designations. I think Myers-Briggs is great, but, you can net it all out in a different way so it's memorable for people. It's not only about them. It's also about the buyer, because I could know all these traits about myself, but how I interact with the various people with whom I'm building relationships is also critical. I've got to figure out what *they* are like.

Personality Testing or Training

(Erin Meszaros)

I'm not thinking about using personality testing for our attorneys. I think I've, unfortunately, been through so many wringers that I can identify an attorney's personality within about 10 minutes of talking to them, and know what they're going to be like.

Pipeline Calls/Pipeline Meetings: For Attorneys Within the Firm

(Jeanne Hammerstrom)

Pipeline meetings. We have them every other week on Friday. And all partners are invited from every office, every practice group. And sometimes we'll get 20 on a call and sometimes we'll get five, but everyone's helping each other. One participant might say, "I know that person at ABC

Hospital. I can reach out to them." So they're helping each other, and it can be competitive sometimes. The calls are great. It's really collegial and very team-oriented.

Pipeline: see "Sales Pipeline"

Pitch Training

(Various)

See *Business Development: Guides, Forms, Templates* (Matt Taylor). "Our business development team has put together a very good guide on how to do a successful pitch and we turned it into an e-learning module that includes their insights. I have video of the team presenting the pitch material and we've found that to be useful."

See *Business Development: Overview* (Allen Chichester). "Of course, there are other business development functions that we have centralized. We have a small centralized group that work on pitches and proposals, mainly the large complicated RFPs. This is the same group that leads our competitive intelligence efforts, although all the BDMs are responsible for competitive intelligence and for pitch support."

See *Business Development Training: Client Needs Assessment Interview and Pitching* (Mark Usellis). "So, we focused on those two skillsets, needs assessment and pitching. Those were the two areas where people were weakest as a general rule."

See *Business Development: How Do You Turn Skilled Lawyers into Skilled Rainmakers?* (Jeanne Hammerstrom). ". . . We also have a two-and-half-day program that we use for business development training, finding client's needs, pitching, client development, client service, and related topics that all the partners and almost all associates have been through. It's a very expensive program. It's sizable. So, we use that program, and actually, I should tell you it's Bill Flannery's program out of Austin."

See *Business Development: Incentivizing* (Shanda Zavalsky). "If you're pitching a client, you want to give them a very clear picture of what it's like to work with you. How we are going to benefit them. We try to do that with our attorneys, too.

For example, when you're pitching, you want to say, "This is what it's like to work with our firm." For associates whose minds might be considering 16 different tracks of conversation, ultimately, one message must be, "This is going to be your experience if you work with our firm and work with me." And, in some way, allow them to experience your passion for your work."

Pitch: See also "Pitch" in the Book's Index.

Potential Client to Actual Client: The Connection Rapport Building Process

(David King Keller)

[Read more on this topic in the ABA book, *The Associate As Rainmaker, Building Your Business Brain* available at http://bit.ly/1dAxob6.]

Potential Clients: Connect Quickly with RelSci, a Type of LinkedIn on Steroids

(David King Keller)

RelSci may be a fast short-cut to finding someone the firm knows who can introduce you to that target client, who at the moment seems out of reach other than via a "cold call." Turn that call into a warm call via an introduction from someone who knows you and your client, but at the moment you don't know that connection exists. Relationship Science, RelSci, has an ever-increasing database of executives and board members, both commercial and non-profit that, at this writing, exceeds 4 million. It's like LinkedIn on steroids.

For example, a firm partner in your real estate department sits on a YMCA board. You would like to do some IP work for Intel. You plug in your firm contacts into RelSci in a confidential encrypted match-up that protects your information and keeps it private to you while you look for a link to Intel. It turns out that on that same YMCA board sits the VP of Intel. Your partner introduces you and you go from there.

For a one-pager on RelSci for law firms, contact david@kbdag.com. For more details on RelSci read: *Targeted Clients: One New Fast Way To Connect: RelSci.* Author's note/disclosure: If you contact RelSci directly please use my name or use this URL: http://go.relsci.com/DavidKeller. I have a referral relationship with RelSci. Read more at *Cross-Selling: With Staff and a High Tech Tool.*

PR: Free

(Despina Kartson)

Maybe someone knows who or what your law firm is and maybe they don't. But consider this – branded luggage tags on your roller bag. As you place your luggage in the overhead compartment of a plane, the firm's name is now dangling in front of other passengers and this is an example of an everyday life occurrence in which you are representing and reflecting the firm. If the lawyer with the branded luggage tag behaved badly and was being difficult, those who saw the firm luggage tag would certainly take note. That would leave a bad impression in the person's mind. When you consider developing a business development culture and a business development mindset, it means that every encounter that you have, both personally and professionally, has to be one that is a positive reflection on you and the firm.

Practice Development and Career Development

(Jill Weber)

I work with our director of professional development on associate business development training, because, as I mentioned, we promised we would share *Fast Forward* best practices with everyone. We have taken what we've learned from Fast Forward to include it in associate business development training, so one of the lessons learned was to start teaching associates about business development in year one, even though I will say to them, clearly, your number one objective is to hone your practice skills.

We are not implying that business development is on the priority list. What we will recommend is to stay in touch with their law school classmates and that they should be thinking about taking people to lunch or coffee, and here's how to think through what that visit should be like, but it is not an overt "I'm now at Stinson Leonard Street, and I want to sell to you." They may be at another law firm, but here's how you construct your conversation. You should come prepared to generally talk about one or two projects you're working on without disclosing the client or confidential information. You should be thinking about how you're talking about the firm and come prepared with two or three highlights of recent news. It's more about helping the young associates to think through how to do it so that they're prepared, because otherwise what we see is these people suddenly become partner, they weren't in touch with their law school classmate, and now that classmate is the general counsel of XYZ Company, and it's a little embarrassing to reach out then. "Oh, hello, remember me, your study partner?"

Mentoring is more formalized in the professional development side as opposed to the business development side. We do have an active mentoring program with the associates. It's simply that formalized mentoring within the component of Fast Forward—what I call "mentor assignment"—did not work within the context of this program, but the more case-study mentoring with specific business development opportunities was effective.

Pricing: Make Sure Client Knows You Have More Than One Hourly Rate

(Erin Meszaros)

Sometimes you have to ask for the lower priced work to increase revenue. [For an example, see: *Client Intelligence: Useful Information: Lower Billing Rate Can Increase Revenue.*]

Prioritizing

(Hans Haglund)

Prioritizing is the most essential component of what you must do to accomplish your goals over the next couple of quarters. I always try to take two big goals and get them done. This quarter we are going to start client assessment interviews. I need to implement that program. One of my other goals is business development training and a more comprehensive coaching program.

Professional Development Department Coordination

(Jeff Berardi)

This was the third year that we had our global associate symposium, but this is the first year that the programming was devoted almost entirely to business development training. We had a number of members of my senior director team and the marketing department who were heavily involved in the development. Just so you're aware, we do all this in conjunction with our professional development department. At a high level, we are working closely together on what the lawyer needs are and members of the professional development department contacted me and said that the associates are interested in client development, and maybe we should come up with a program devoted to it for this symposium. So we worked collaboratively on the agenda items.

My team is involved with the professional development directors and their managers and my managers work together, so it's definitely a joint approach. I certainly can't take credit just in the marketing and business development department. It's very much a concerted effort between the two administrative departments. The professional development department brings something to the table that we in marketing and business development don't and that is, I think they really know what the lawyers are looking for. They get that feedback more directly. They run many training and educational programs, not just business development. It's lawyer skills training. They have the logistical support and the process in place to really make sure it goes well. We usually work on the content with respect to business development, the execution and the actual presentations. So, it really is a good relationship and I think that it is critical to the success of any business development program that the firm wants to launch. I think the two functions need to coordinate pretty closely.

Professional Organizations: You Never Know Who's Paying Attention

(Wayne Hogan)

There's got to be substance and the ability to work with people. And, the other thing is, engagement in professional organizations.

Memberships in various organizations are, of course, also important. I've taken active roles in the Florida Justice Association, which previously was called the Academy of Florida Trial lawyers, and the American Association for Justice, which was previously called the Association of Trial Lawyers of America, as well as ABOTA, which is American Board of Trial Advocates, and Public Justice, which is known as America's Personal Public Interest Law Firm. Being involved in those types of boards helps you to develop relationships with lawyers city-wide, state-wide, and now, at least for myself, nation-wide. And so, it is one of those things that matters.

Now, some lawyers, depending upon the nature of their practice, they become deeply engaged in the sections of the ABA and I'm a member of the Litigation section of ABA. I haven't been a leader there because I've been a leader in other organizations, but others follow that track and they do awfully important work and of course, I'm just talking now in the litigation field, but there's a whole range of other fields where it matters, where people get to know you and know that they can rely on you and that you care about the same things that they care about.

One example was of a lawyer I met through the Public Justice Board, who lived in another state and had someone within an extended family who needed help in this state. The lawyer called and said, "This is the situation and I hope maybe you can be helpful to this family."

Obviously, substance matters. What I'm saying is: it helps to actually get involved in the organization, to actually get down into the nitty-gritty of the organization and the work that it does as distinguished from just being the lawyer that you see at the door as you go in and maybe you don't see after the presentations have been made.

My visibility and involvement with the community and professional organizations, as well as my reputation as someone who was skilled, acted responsibly, and could be trusted were probably some of the reasons I was selected to be on the governor's legal team to represent the State of Florida against the cigarette companies, and our settlement in favor of Florida.

Project Management: Six Sigma and Six Sigma Lean

(Karen Bell)

So, as you know, firms in the States started looking at Six Sigma and Six Sigma Lean a little while ago, and I believe we were the first law firm in Canada to adopt this approach. We even wrote a book about it called "Project Management for Lawyers" that was published by the Ark Group. Our firm's leadership took hold of Six Sigma and started educating clients and people within our firm about it, and had teams who were dedicated to it. Now we have a Client Service and Innovation team who work on client matters and prepare work plans using a Six Sigma project management profile. You must have that in place before you can entertain alternative fees, if you're going to do it properly, because you need to have a base or a structure so that you're not just quoting hourly rates. You're saying, "What are the requirements? How long is this going to take? Who are the right players?" Then you can talk about pricing, because then you know what you're going to price and you can do that by dissecting the pieces and the processes. Then you might realize "Well, maybe we don't need this part of the process." I had a litigation practice, and the first question I would ask is, "Why are we litigating?" A typical client answer was "Well, we want to apply some pressure." I would respond "How about we just take it this far and do this and this? We won't do that"; with that understanding you can price it more effectively for the client – and meet expectations and budget constraints.

Purpose and Passion

(Scott Kessler)

My passion has always been to find ways to help people achieve their goals, but now I am going deeper by helping them reclaim their life's "purpose and passion." I have found that by reclaiming those two "p's" everything else falls into place, i.e., achieving their BD goals becomes very easy because they can create incredibly powerful relationships. Once people become re-aligned with their authentic selves they get back on course."

Rainmaker Skills: Metrics

(Allen Chichester)

There's a simple measure to gauge the attorney's rainmaking skill and that's the size of their book. If they have a small book, they either don't care or are not very good at it-usually a little of both. If they have a large book, they may have brought these clients in on their own, or they might have gotten lucky and inherited a great client that they know how to keep happy. The latter method is really becoming less common these days. Even though institutional clients still exist, attorneys really have to scramble to build their books, and anyone who depends on one client for their book knows that they're taking a risk. Most rainmakers and most attorneys with large books of business diversify on purpose, even if they do have a strong large client that they manage.

Rainmaker Skills: Also see Rainmaker Traits

Rainmaker Training: At Colorado Law School Here's How We Do It

(Bill Mooz)

In today's world, making rain requires lawyers to be able to communicate a clear value proposition, and to do so in language that the C-Suite can relate to. This requires them to have a variety of skills that law schools traditionally don't teach – tech savvy, finance savvy, process savvy, and the ability to show how different legal strategies impact costs and revenues. These skills not only help lawyers make rain, they are also necessary for lawyers to transform their traditional doctrinal legal knowledge into a work product that delivers true value to the client.

We teach these skills today in our *Tech Lawyer Accelerator* summer program for law students at the Silicon Flatirons Center at Colorado Law. The *Tech Lawyer Accelerator* takes a select group of entrepreneurially minded law students, puts them through an intensive four-week boot camp and then places them with tech companies for internships ranging from ten weeks to seven months. The boot camp has four modules that are designed to provide the students with basic literacy in the economics of legal services, finance and accounting, process and technology, and contracting. During the internships, students use these skills to assist the companies with everything from contract reviews to template creation and management to M&A and securities transactions. The internships are paid and students are expected to generate positive ROI for their employers. We ran our first pilot in the summer of 2014 and 100% of the companies we invited back re-upped to take one or more interns in 2015.

Our goal is more to train people to do the work than to bring it in, but I think that doing work effectively and generating work effectively share a common foundation. This foundation starts with understanding your client's business, understanding your client's problem through that particular lens, and then being able to develop and deliver a solution to that problem in a way that optimizes the business result that the client is trying to achieve.

It's no secret that many law students across the country are exiting law school with massive amounts of debt and having tremendous difficulties finding professional employment. While lawyers undoubtedly are affected by economic cycles like everyone else, I also think that a big part of the issue here is that the training lawyers traditionally have received doesn't give them the full complement of skills that they need to deliver value in today's world.

In my experience, lawyers require three different types of skills to succeed in today's world. First, they need to have a strong base of doctrinal legal skills – knowledge of the law, legal reasoning, etc. Law schools, in my opinion do a good job of teaching these skills. This is table stakes.

Second, lawyers need to have the practical skills necessary to translate doctrinal knowledge into a product that somebody is willing to pay for. I can know everything there is to know about contract law, but if I can't draft or negotiate a contract, I don't have anything to sell. Historically, law firms provided this training on the client's dime, but those days are over. At Colorado Law we have sought to address this gap with an array of courses that include deal labs, clinics, etc. as well as externships and programs like the Tech Lawyer Accelerator and our DC Summer Scholars program that places students in technology policy internships in Washington, DC. These types of programs will never be a complete replacement for "time on the slopes" but they are a good start.

The big gap in my opinion really lies in the third area, which I call contextual knowledge. This area by and large has never been taught in law schools or law firms. The people who have it largely have learned it on their own and are quite valuable as a result.

By contextual knowledge I mean knowledge of areas outside of pure law that enable the lawyer to produce a truly valuable product. For example, I can know contract law, and know how to draft a contract, but unless I have the appropriate contextual skills, I am highly unlikely to draft a contract that yields the results that the client wants to see.

Contextual skills have a couple of different elements to them. First, you have to understand the client's business, which starts with understanding business generally. So if you are a transactional lawyer, you need to understand the basics of finance and accounting. If you are a litigator you need to understand the implications that different outcomes have on your client's financials, especially when they're public companies.

In addition to understanding business generally, you have to understand the industry that your client is in. This includes understanding the specific products and services that your client sells and how things like the rules around revenue recognition apply to them. It also includes understanding the industry norms around what documents get used, what market is on key terms, etc. There is nothing more frustrating to a client than having to explain the basics to their counsel other than perhaps having the counsel just not get it and push forward with an inappropriate solution.

Finally, you need to understand where your client fits within that industry and what their strategy is for deriving a competitive advantage. What is their position in the industry, how do they differentiate themselves competitively, what individual items are the crucial make-or-break items for this particular client? For example, both Gucci and WalMart participate in the retail industry but the make-or-break issues for each of them differ substantially.

If you look at the data collected by the Association of Corporate Counsel, year in and year out, one of the biggest complaints from corporations is that "my lawyer doesn't understand my business." The very best lawyers are exceptions to this, having gained this knowledge through their own efforts, and these lawyers tend to be in very high demand.

In addition to understanding the client's business, contextual skills also include understanding how to apply business concepts to deliver legal services with maximum effectiveness and efficiency. Many groups, including Finance, HR, and Manufacturing, are far more advanced than lawyers are when it comes to applying things like industrial process, automation, arbitraged labor, etc. to deliver a better result in a more efficient fashion. Lawyers historically haven't been taught to even consider questions such as, when does it make sense to standardize a process, build checklists and templates, and use arbitraged labor versus building everything custom? When does it make sense to move a particular type of contract to a "click accept" versus "wet ink contract," so that you fully automate the process and remove the lawyers entirely from the day-to-day process?

Even when lawyers do think about these types of questions, they haven't historically been taught how to do things like implement processes, drive effective change management, run an automation project, etc. For example, suppose you want to implement a contract management system. What law school course teaches you how to select the optimal tool, to determine whether the project will have a positive return on investment, and to change the impacted processes, implement the tool, and, most important, get the impacted people to buy into the new model?

Ten years ago lawyers didn't confront these questions and weren't expected to have these skills; today they are critical. Legal services now are out of the black box and get measured using the same metrics as other services – impact on profit and loss. Lawyers who understand this, who design their services through this lens, and can explain their value proposition to clients in these terms, stand to both provide value and be successful rainmakers.

We used this view of what it takes for lawyers to add value to clients to build our Tech Lawyer Accelerator program. We started with the premise that we had limited time to cover a lot of things and that we needed to be focused to have the greatest impact. Since students already have ample opportunities to gain doctrinal skills, and reasonable opportunities to learn practical skills, we focused predominantly on teaching contextual skills.

To build a broad contextual foundation, we developed a suite of lectures that cover a variety of core business skills such as finance and accounting, IT, leadership, sales, project management, etc. We then looked to tie all of these together through a series of team exercises. We felt that emphasizing team exercises was especially critical because law school historically has been a zero-sum gain environment. The better I do in my class rank, the better my chances are of getting employed. For me to do better means others have to do worse.

So even though the students at Colorado Law tend to be very collegial, we felt it was important to give them real training on how to work together collectively in teams. This isn't something that gets taught in a traditional Socratic class, but is something that they are going to have to do when they graduate. This is true in any professional environment. If you're working a big matter at a law firm, you need to pull together a variety of different specialists to deliver a complete product. If you're working in an in-house environment, you invariably will be interacting closely with clients and placed on cross-functional teams.

To provide additional focus, we structured our suite of lectures and exercises through the lens of a single industry – the tech industry. This allows us to go deeper into the industry-specific vocabulary and concepts, enabling students to hit the ground running faster when they start their internships with tech companies. Virtually all of these sessions were led by current and former industry executives. In addition to providing an industry perspective, a number of executives also talk specifically about how their companies fit into particular segments of the overall tech industry.

Finally, we spent a considerable amount of time in both lectures and exercises in educating student on how to use things like process and technology to deliver a better legal product at a lower cost. This included training students on technology and process generally and providing students with sessions on how to use specific technologies like Word and Excel to be more effective lawyers.

I have been overwhelmed by the response that we have received to this approach toward educating tomorrow's leaders among the tech industry. Over 40 senior tech company executives, including CEOs, CFOs, Legal Ops Directors, CMOs, etc. volunteered their time for the program. A full 100% of the companies we invited back from the 2014 program have signed up to hire intern again in 2015. And student demand for the program greatly exceeds the available slots.

Perhaps most gratifying are the stories I hear from students. For example, one of my students came in very excited one morning at the beginning of class and said, "Last night, I was over at a software developer and his wife's house with my girlfriend. There were several other engineers there and they started getting into geek speak and I understood what was going on. I could be part of the conversation." Think about how much more likely this student is to get hired by a tech company, either as an in-house lawyer or as outside counsel, than somebody who is sitting there with their eyes glazed over.

> The idea is that by obtaining focused training on contextual skills, and significant experience working in team exercises, the students will have a solid foundation when they start their internships. Students coming out of this program should add substantially more value to the tech clients and employers than students who go through a standard JD program and nothing more.
>
> —*Bill Mooz*

Rainmaker Training: Try the Just-in-Time Method

(Mike O'Horo)

Most rainmaking training programs suffer from poor adoption. Firms buy the programs, hire coaches, but lawyers don't participate. There are many theories why that's so. Mine is that lawyers don't really want training *programs*. "Program" smacks of continuous obligation, and continuous scrutiny, and lawyers don't like either of those.

When asked why they won't attend training programs, virtually all lawyers claim a shortage of time. Yet making time available is a function of priority. Everyone makes time for what's important. Getting a degree in rainmaking is nice to do, but not critical. Lawyers don't want a degree; they just want to do the thing they have to do now. Let them.

The only training or coaching that lawyers want is that which will enable them to succeed at what's immediately in front of them. Do they want networking training in the abstract? No. However, if they're scheduled to attend a networking event next Wednesday, would they welcome help making that more comfortable and effective? Absolutely.

This "Just-In-Time" approach lets lawyers consume only the training that's relevant to imminent needs.

The solution is a cloud-based video library, from which lawyers select a short video that relates to the specific circumstance that the lawyer faces. They get very targeted and specific training, which allows the lawyer to spend a few minutes to learn the specific skill that they need to apply to an actual situation in order to achieve maximum return on the attorney's investment in time.

One approach to this just-in-time training concept is called rainmaker virtual training, or RainmakerVT for short. Your chief marketing officer or business development director should be able to guide you to that resource, or you can simply Google the topic and go from there.

Rainmaker Trait: How the Great Ones Advance the Relationship

(Steve Bell)

The great ones advance the relationship by demonstrating something important. Every so often – every month, every six weeks – they do something to advance the relationship, just to keep it alive. Lawyers who are not automatically successful at sales are the ones who go out, have a good meeting, and deliver their sales report that it was a great meeting. Then nothing happens. Those lawyers are demonstrating that they're not good at client service, whereas the ones who advance the relationship and add value to it every now and then, every month or so, they're demonstrating that they are great client service professionals who are serious about relationships. They're actually demonstrating something important to clients. The great ones do that.

Sometimes a small opportunity emerges and the lawyers who are not successful at rainmaking turn up their noses at a thousand dollar matter in an area of practice that's not their own. The really great rainmakers say, "Here's my start. Here's my first opportunity to move this relationship forward at a deeper, more involved, level." They take that thousand dollar matter and they make it seem like it's the most important matter on Earth.

Client centricity is at the heart of it. Making that person feel super important, super special. The great rainmakers are advancing the relationship by being consumed with understanding what's driving and motivating the client. A client is an individual. A client is not a corporate entity. That's where the concept of trying to understand human beings, what's motivating them, and where they're coming from is integral. Every person is different. Every buyer is different, just as every seller is different. The great rainmakers have a passion for understanding what's driving and motivating these individual buyers.

> A client is an individual. A client is not a corporate entity. The great rainmakers have a passion for understanding what's driving and motivating these individual buyers.
>
> —*Steve Bell*

In my opinion, and based on research by BTI Consulting, four client service attributes distinguish law firms and individual lawyers: they understand the client's business, they demonstrate commitment to the client's success, they deliver value for the dollar, and they exhibit tremendous focus on the client and their needs. Lawyers who put these attributes to work for clients perpetually end up in the top of client-service ranking lists. When lawyers focus these same attributes on prospective clients, they end up with a lot of new clients.

Rainmaker Trait: Research Before You Meet

(Steve Bell)

It's so simple. It's painful how simple it is. The next step is to open the door. You are going to meet with an individual at a company that you've chosen as a prospective client. You have to be ready for the meeting. You can't just go in and bullsh*t. You need tangible, relevant content and spend the necessary time thinking about the company. The lawyers who are great rainmakers put some research and client understanding into their overview, so that when they have that conversation, which they may have engineered over some period of time, it's worthwhile for the person on the other end. It's not just baloney. It's something substantive and interesting. It demonstrates that the lawyer, who is pursuing the client, has made an effort and has put significant effort into this relationship.

This whole concept of understanding the client and client research cannot be overstated. I don't know that any lawyer or any person who works for a law firm anywhere, anytime has ever sold anything to anybody. It seems to me that what really happens is that the buyers of legal services have a need because there's a problem or because there's an opportunity and they buy legal services. So, what a lawyer or somebody who works for a law firm can do, is to be in that person's mind when an event occurs, and to make sure they educated that buyer about the skills and capabilities of herself or the law firm. What this implies is that you can't meet with somebody one time. As brilliantly as you may perform in a single meeting, you're going to have to keep that relationship alive. The successful rainmakers who I have seen take specific actions to sustain relationships and to advance them over time.

Rainmaker Trait: The Trick to Opening the Door to New Clients

(Steve Bell)

Lawyers who are successful at business development identify companies that they would like to have as clients. They actually write them down and say, "I'd like to have this company as a client. I am going to work on this over time. I'm going to think about how to open the door and get to know them." They successfully work out the equation of how to get the door opened. The bold ones just do it—just make the phone call—while others engineer it over time. That's a re-occurring quality of a rainmaker. They're intentional and work hard to get that door open.

Rainmaker Trait: They Think About It All the Time

(Hans Haglund)

A common theme for most rainmakers, is that they make business development part of their life. It's not something that they really think, "Oh, yeah, I need to do more business development." They just do it, and they make it part of who they are and what they do. They think about how they can help others and forge connections between the people they work with and their firm and their firm's skillsets. They think of relationship building and relationship enhancement all the time. They make it happen. Business development is incorporated into everything that they do in their life. Those are the people I see that are very, very successful.

Rainmaker Traits: A Short List

(David King Keller)

> What makes a rainmaker a rainmaker?
>
> It turns out that rainmakers have common qualities, traits, actions, and approaches that set them apart. Other attorneys will exhibit some or all of these qualities at some point. But a rainmaker will generally have these traits in play most of the time, not just sporadically.

> One trait highlighted by Hans Haglund is that rainmakers see business development as an enhancement to their own life, an opportunity to make new friends, have fun, and make money. It's not a boring chore, it's an exciting adventure. Rainmakers practice successful sales techniques (whether they call them that or not).

Other key traits and activities of successful rainmakers include: above average face time with potential and existing clients, passion for the business, extremely focused on identified targets and will engineer a way to connect with targeted client prospects, develops a personal as well as a professional connection with people, i.e., ability to connect on a person-to-person level that evolves to something akin to friend-to-friend relationship, exhibits and communicates a laser-like focus on the individual client in such a way that individual client feels like the center of the attorney's universe and that they are that attorney's number one priority whenever they have a need.

Rainmakers make clients feel super-special. Clients of rainmakers know the rainmaker "has their back." The rainmaker has become a valued business advisor.

The rainmaker is a closer. The rainmaker is perceived as a functional partner. Clients of rainmakers will say, "My attorney knows my business almost as much as I do and more than I do when it comes to my legal needs."

Business development is part of their day in-day out life. They just do it.

Rainmakers are tactical and methodical. They rank their contacts. They are great lead generators. They know how a client's executive team operates, their level of risk, and all of the key decision-making factors typically involved when addressing a legal issue. A client knows that their legal rainmaker has the attitude that "I will do whatever it takes to make sure that you succeed."

Follow the advice given by Bechtel's GC, Raymond Ramsey, and the former president of Northern California Association of Corporate Counsel who said, "I want to know that outside counsel has my back, and that they will make me look good to my boss."

Per Bill Flannery: If there is one rainmaker action that is arguably the single most productive activity with the greatest ROI, it's face time.

Following face time as a metric is client-centered conversations where the client or potential client does most of the talking and you ask the right questions that draw out their known and unknown legal needs. Sounds simple enough. But how much time, energy, and money is spent on activities other than those two?

It's also about taking the time to first identify who you really want as clients, and then taking the time to do the due diligence and background research on your desired clients.

The two biggest mistakes a law firm makes is: one, not knowing what percentage of the client's total legal billing you currently enjoy, and two, not taking a full-service approach to every client. Some partners have a client and don't want to share that contact with their other practice groups. The only problem with that is the fact that other law firms are taking a full-service approach to that same client which may get you bumped.

Rainmaker Traits: A Tactical Approach

(Hans Haglund)

I am more tactical, as are many rainmakers, in the way that they approach business development. For example: How many real viable contacts do you have? Do you rank them? How often do you connect with them? How are you building and enhancing that list? How often are you reaching out to make new viable contacts? A rainmaker works with their contact list to create leads. Their lead generation and their follow-up is very good. Some people do it naturally, but they all make it a daily habit. They follow up in a methodical way. They are constantly reconnecting with those individuals and trying to help them succeed and help them win and achieve their goals. They look for business opportunities for them, connect them with other people who can help them become successful. It is those kinds of value-add, that show people you care. You care about them. You can succeed in a strictly cold manner, such as, "All I care about is getting more business." Alternatively, a genuine interest in people and a genuine interest in helping people succeed is the goal. I think it is, ultimately, coming from that good place, when you are trying to help people. Revenue is not the goal, but a byproduct. Build the relationship, build the trust and, ultimately, you will be that trusted advisor. The process to get there is different for everyone but the commitment to the process/mindset is, I think, the most important first step to success.

Rainmaker Traits: Basic Activity

(Sally Schmidt)

Have a target list of the existing and potential clients that you want to make sure you stay in touch with. And, it might change every year. This is a foundational activity on which most, if not all, other business development activities follow.

Rainmaker Traits: Build Trust Instead of Annoyance

(Mark Usellis)

For any relationship, a lawyer needs to have the mindset of—and this is why needs assessment is so important—I want to understand what's going on in my client's business and what the related legal needs are and then think about how I can help them.

Most people approach it from, "Does this person need what I do?" And, that's just wrong and ineffective. Or some might approach the conversation as, absent any knowledge of need or interest, "Hey, I'd really like to introduce you to our real estate lawyers." But that's an imposition on the client. You're asking them to give up time and then it's going to be awkward if they don't want to use your real estate lawyers or don't have any need for real estate attorneys. Again, put yourself in the other person's shoes and think about what would be effective.

> Let's say you talk to them about their company's priorities and challenges and they respond with, "Oh, we've got these real estate problems."
>
> "Oh, really? Well, how do you handle those?"
>
> "We have this firm that's been doing it."
>
> "Well, do you like those guys?"
>
> "Well, yeah, I like them, but the problem is, they don't have enough depth."
>
> "Oh, well if you have overflow work . . . Let me introduce you to someone and we don't need to displace this firm that you like, but if they have depth issues, we could be a second source."

You could say something like this second example, which is a whole different conversation from the first example.

Rainmaker Traits: Calendar Business Development Meetings

(Matt Taylor)

I keep my calendar electronically like everyone in the modern world does. But I may be, I don't know, one in a million, that still keeps a big blotter, paper calendar. It drives my assistant crazy and I do it for a very simple reason. I'm a visual person and on my calendar, I put marketing type meetings, whether it's a lunch with a client, whether it's a Bar Association meeting, or whether it's any type of a networking related activity. A breakfast, a lunch, a dinner, golf, anything. In a different color. I put my appointments in one color and my law firm in one color and a different color on marketing events. For me, and I don't know why I started this, if I don't have five things on my calendar every month—five marketing things—every month– I feel naked. I think, "Uh oh. I've got to get something on that calendar." I tell the associates, "You have to be disciplined." If you think of this as "Well, geeze, Matt,

I'm so busy. Five things?" I say, "Well, it doesn't have to be five nights out 'til midnight. It could be a breakfast. It could be lunch. It could be a coffee. It could be anything, but you have to force yourself to schedule things in." I literally turn the page on my calendar and I want to see five things on my calendar every month. That's in marketing. I still do it and I think people are making a big mistake unless they are disciplined, to literally schedule things in. If somebody says, "no," well, call somebody else up and get something else on the books, because you'll never do it if you don't absolutely put them on your calendar. You will never do it. You can have fun at the same time, but you have to be disciplined and network. You have to.

Rainmaker Traits: Candor: Clients Want This

(Mike Haven)

A core value at companies like Mike Haven at NetApp and Lisa Konie at Adobe. Both commented on the high value placed on honesty and candor.

At NetApp (or Adobe) the personal review session has been eliminated because feedback is given in every interaction when appropriate.

Rainmaker Traits: Common to All Rainmakers

(Larry Bodine)

I've spoken to a very large number of people who are rainmakers and I've studied them all my life and try to discern what they do that makes them rainmakers. The bottom line is that these are people who have a lot of relationships.

Rainmaker Traits: Convert the Vendor's Sales Pitch into a Referral Source

(David King Keller)

Some lawyers make look busy with "outreach" because they're going to a lot of lunches, but it's because they're getting invitations and it might be brokers, insurance agents, vendors, and different people that want to see them, but not necessarily people that can hire them. If you find yourself in a meeting like this, convert the vendor into a referral source. Also, ask the vendor how she would sell your practice. Example: "Speaking of business, and because you know something about my work, I always like to ask brilliant and creative people like you a question about my business and I would be grateful for the answer. I know you haven't made a list of 10 people that can use my legal services right *now* . . . but who might be three or four people you could suggest to me that could use my legal services? Then, be quiet and listen.

Rainmaker Traits: Discipline

(Sally Schmidt)

Well, for people who are not naturals, which is, to be honest, probably the vast majority of the legal profession, I think there are still many things that they can do to become good rainmakers. Some can become great. Some might be good. Some might be fair, but they can certainly be better than they are. One thing that is important, and it sounds kind of process oriented, but it's true, is just some discipline. Successful routines and habits that are performed on a regular basis. For example, spend two hours every Thursday setting up client meetings and business development activities for next week and next month, sending personal notes to current and past clients, sending or drafting your next client alert, etc.

Rainmaker Traits: Empathy

(Louise Muldoon)

One skill factor that I think is important, which might not be the first that would spring to a lot of people's minds, is empathy. When talking to lawyers, one of the things that I often say to them is, you need to have a level of empathy with your client and you have to be able to identify the pressures your clients are under. Everyone talks about client "needs." I dislike the word "needs," which I think is a very simplistic word in this case. As a lawyer, you need to be aware of the client's business pressures, the politics of the environment in which they operate and thing holistically about the client's situation. So we spend—I spend—a lot of time talking to clients and asking them about these things in addition to the core question of, "How are we doing?" from a client service perspective. I spoke about this at a Legal Marketing Association session. The purpose of the meeting is really trying to identify for lawyers, what are the key things that are on clients' minds beyond the legal issue that may have initiated the engagement? Do our lawyers know enough about the client's business? So, we spend a lot of time gathering information about various industry sectors. Are they sensitive—and, again, this goes back to the empathy point—to the organizational influences on what the client is experiencing? Often our clients are working in pretty stressful situations. Do we understand how things are structured at the client's firm; what the culture is like; what the people are like that the client interacts with; what are the politics of the situation, etc.? So, we spend time thinking about all facets impacting the client relationship. And we take all of those different things and distill them and take them to the lawyers we're training and say, "Here are some of the component parts of how to be a successful rainmaker." It's not enough to simply give good legal advice anymore, although you do need to do that, of course. I don't think we should take the focus off that at all. We're very focused on legal training and that's a key element of making a lawyer a skilled rainmaker. They need to be very, very proficient at what they do, but it's the softer things that count, as well, and, as I say, the empathy element is very critical.

Rainmaker Traits: Habits: Calendaring BD Time Slots

(Despina Kartson)

I'm really practical, so I suggest scheduling business development activities on your calendar. Schedule when you have appointments for lunch, dinner, client meetings, and also schedule business development activities on your calendar. If you are making a commitment in your business development plan that you will spend a certain number of hours per week on business development activities, schedule that time on your calendar so that you meet the commitment.

I've worked with partners who schedule 15 minutes every day for business development which could be something as simple as sending an email to a particular contact or forwarding a link to an article about something of interest. Whatever you define as a business development activity, put it on your calendar. When people say they don't have time for business development, ask them, "Would you be able to find 15 minutes twice a week to do some business development activity at a minimum?" Chances are, they can say "yes."

Rainmaker Traits: Mindset: Every Encounter Has Potential

(Despina Kartson)

It's important to develop a business development culture and a business development mindset within a firm. Approach every encounter as one that could lead to a new business opportunity which means everything that you do should be considered as a potential business development opportunity or one in which you're representing or reflecting the firm.

Rainmaker Traits: Passion For One's Practice and the Firm's Capabilities

(Matt Taylor)

Rainmakers make selling the firm's abilities easy because it's like talking about a vacation resort you love, or about your favorite sport's team, or your child's accomplishments.

It's easy to have passion for something you love doing. The day never ends. You just got to do it. I love every minute of what I do. I really do. It's a lot of fun. "Okay. There's a lot of business out there. This other joker got business. I can get business."

Rainmaker Traits: Personality Research Shows Key Traits

Caliper personality profile research shows that a successful rainmaker will have *high ego drive*, empowered by positive emotions by successfully using persuasion; *high ego strength*, meaning high resiliency to set backs; and *high in empathy*, an ability to step into the other person's shoes. [Author's note: Some of this information on personality can be found in the article, *Herding Cats: The Lawyer Personality Revealed*, by Dr. Larry Richard, *LawyerBrain LLC*, at http://www.lawyerbrain.com/resources]

Rainmaker Traits: Rainmaker Mindset: Relationship Building

(Despina Kartson)

Relationship building is critically important to being able to develop business. It is an approach that needs to be something that is very much top of mind, whether it's the relationship with other parents out on your kid's soccer field, or someone that you're sitting next to on a plane, or anyone that you may come across professionally and personally. Think about how you are identifying people whom you think it would be great to have a potential business relationship with and then what determine what you are doing to cultivate that relationship.

Rainmaker Traits: Rainmaker Skills Start With Basic Lawyer Skills

(Silvia Coulter)

The skill sets to be a good lawyer are really the same skillsets to be a good rainmaker, the ability to negotiate. Sales is all about negotiation at some level. There are other traits a rainmaker demonstrates. You've got to sprinkle in other ingredients: like confidence, willingness to try, be a little bit of a trailblazer, and you've got to be collaborative. You have to know how to work around the political nature of your firm, especially in the larger firms. Successful people have figured out a way around the politics. There's plenty of successful people who have the same environments, and they've managed to do well. Emotionally you've got to have a lot of confidence to be good at whatever you do, and, especially practicing law, you've got to have a lot of confidence. So, you translate your confidence in your legal skills into confidence in your business development skills.

Rainmaker Traits: Rainmaker Skills: DNA

(Despina Kartson)

First and foremost lawyers need to do good work and deliver outstanding client service. Doing good work is the price of admission and it's an important one. It's key for client satisfaction and for referrals.

Rainmaker Traits: Rainmakers: Add This to List of Skills Needed

(Bill Mooz)

The first trait is you have to understand the client's business. This means that you have to understand business generally, including the basics of finance and accounting.

This is true not only for transactional lawyers but also for litigators who need to understand how different outcomes will impact the client's financials, especially when they're public companies.

Rainmaker Traits: Rainmakers: Must Speak C-Suite

(David King Keller)

To be a rainmaker you need to be tech savvy, C-Suite language savvy, and have a firm understanding of how a company can increase sales and reduce costs. Read about the Colorado Law Tech Lawyer Accelerator program for an example. [Read more at *Rainmaker Training: At Colorado Law School Here's How We Do It.*]

Rainmaker Traits: Responsive

(David King Keller)

One sure way to differentiate yourself from your competitors is to respond quickly to every call, email, inquiry, or request (expressed or implied) as close to instantly as you can. That's how you turn ordinary into a "wow."

I'll never forget a general counsel seminar where the inside counsel were talking about what impressed them about outside counsel, and the example given was the attorney answered his cell phone with a whisper. When asked why, the attorney replied, "I'm in court." That GC is now a raving fan of that attorney, who also happened to be extremely respected by his peers, as well. When I heard this story he was President of the American Business Trial Lawyers Association-Northern California.

Rainmaker Traits: Seven Rainmaker Practices

(David King Keller)

The time issue.

Follow these three rules. One: The two-minute rule. If it takes less than two minutes, just do it now. Don't put it off. You'll feel better. Two: The 10-minute rule. Pick one person a day, minimum, send an email, say "hello," mention something they're interested in, like a sport, a sports team, pets, or kids, and then say, "I thought you might find attached interesting." Attach some new regulation developments, court decision, industry news item, or, using Google Alerts and your business intelligence resources, comment on some recent positive news about their company. Three: Create an answer to this question every Tuesday at noon: "Who am I meeting next week for coffee, lunch, or drinks who can add a new matter, become a new client, or refer me to new clients?" Best times: before you open your email in the morning, just before lunch (let lunch be a reward), or before you walk out the door that evening (give yourself that extra pat on the back for "planting a seed for tomorrow's harvest."). Read the article: "Making the Impossible Possible" in my book *The Associate As Rainmaker, Building Your Business Brain*, an ABA best-seller available at http://bit.ly/1dAxob6.

Biggest Potential Opportunities First. Five minutes on $50,000 or $5 million? You decide.

Salespeople know that half the time success is determined by just showing up. In today's competitive market, you have to keep showing up, one way or another, over an extended period of time.

If It Pops into Your Mind a Second Time, do it now or calendar it. If you can follow the two-minute rule, do it now. If it's an opportunity that can't be done right now, calendar a time to do it and treat it with the same priority as a top-10 client. Because "you'll do it when you have time" never happens.

Prioritize and Follow The Next Step Rule. Steven Covey wrote in Seven Habits of Highly Successful People, "Put first things first." Ask yourself, "Is what I'm doing a 1, 2, or 3 priority, and what am I doing now or later today to secure new matters?" With every important lead, create a "Next Step." In sales it's called "an advance." You keep advancing the relationship by providing something of value to that person. Remember, it's always about the individual. What will help him or her achieve their goals?

Leverage. Leverage. Leverage. Leverage people. Leverage technology. Delegate. Use emails, blogs, Twitter, JDSupra.com, LinkedIn, public relations, video, YouTube, industry conference presentations, and other rocks-in-the-pond that ripple out your name to people you want to be popping in to their top-of-mind. You're a rock star. Let people know.

Organize and Track Your Leads. Use a system. CRM. Make notes quickly before you forget or run out of time. Governor Carter used to duck into the restroom and make quick notes on business cards he received. Then he became president. Note something unique about them that was mentioned, particularly anything where they showed passion. Stand out from the crowd and pop back into top-of-mind by sending a great-to-meet-you email that evening or first thing in the morning.

Build Your Business Development Muscles. Just like the law, the great ones practice, practice, practice. Same with rainmaking. Practice makes perfect and will delight you with results. Think of business development coaching and training as an annual MCLE. There's a reason all the best athletes have a coach.

Rainmaker Traits: Target Their Audience and Engineer a Meeting

(Steve Bell)

Rainmakers understand the fishing hole concept. Fish where you've already been successful. Rainmakers target their audience and find a way to engineer a meeting with that audience. It seems the great rainmakers have a passion for understanding what's driving and motivating these individual buyers.

Rainmaker Traits: The Whole Process is Experienced as Life Enhancing

(Hans Haglund)

One guy I still call on is with a major financial services firm. This guy is a deal person, and has advanced mathematic degrees. He's super bright and I just love talking with him and getting his perspective on market developments as well as pitch him on certain work that we do. We've become friends and he trusts me to take care of him when he sends me work. Again, I guess the thread is building it into your approach to relationships. Rainmakers understand that business development is life enhancing and they incorporate it into everything that they do. These people are very, very successful.

Rainmaker Traits: They Know How to Prioritize Prospecting

(Steve Bell)

Your best prospective client is a company that closely resembles an existing client with whom you have a fabulous relationship.

Rainmaker Traits: They Make It Part of Their Life

(Hans Haglund)

For rainmakers, a common theme is that they make it part of their life. It's not something where they think, "Oh, yeah, I need to do more business development." They just do it. They make it part of who they are and what they do.

Rainmakers think about how they can help others. They always ask themselves, "Is there any kind of connection that I can make between the people that I am working with and my firm and our skillsets? This is what they think about it all the time.

You can tell the best rainmakers see business development as something that enhances their enjoyment of life. Because it brings joy into their life, they think about it all the time. They make business development happen. Business development is incorporated into everything that they do in their life. These are the people I see that are very, very successful.

One major rainmaker I worked with had a mantra which was, "I call my clients every day, and I am their trusted advisor because I deeply care about their success and I know everything that is going on in their professional lives and even their personal lives. They became my friends and I go to dinner with them. Some of them I go on vacation with." He truly felt that these clients are an enhancement to his life.

> One major rainmaker I worked with had a mantra which was, "I call my clients every day, and I am their trusted advisor because I deeply care about their success and I know everything that is going on in their professional lives and even their personal lives. He truly felt that these clients are an enhancement to his life. They just think about it all the time. These are the people I see that are very, very successful.
>
> —*Hans T. Haglund*

I agree with him. A lot of people feel like developing relationships is a burden, not an enhancement. When I do business development and I go out and develop relationships, as I have been doing over the years, some of my best friends have come out of random networking events that I went to.

I have gotten business out of it, but I have also enhanced my life because I have gotten to know great people.

Rainmaker Traits: Translate Best Practices

(Steve Bell)

One can observe lawyers who are successful rainmakers, and while one can't transplant personalities from one lawyer to another, I think that one can translate best practices. I have observed that the great rainmaking lawyers who are innately successful may not know that they have a process or that they take successful actions repeatedly, but I think they do. What I have tried to do is to observe and describe those actions and help lawyers who may not be natural rainmakers to replicate them.

Rainmaker Traits: Value Rainmaker Training

(Allen Chichester)

One of the most interesting things about training is the value that people place on it based on their own seniority. We have found it is the people who are best at rainmaking that value rainmaking training the most, even though few of them really need it.

Rainmaker: Debunking a Myth

(Karen Bell)

Classically, the notion of the rainmaker continues to be the partner with the big corner office who's very extroverted and knows everyone and can call anybody you want to talk to on a dime. We're trying to debunk that myth. We're trying to ensure that our attorneys understand that everyone has a role to play and can be effective in business development, particularly if they follow the classic rule around focus, 80% of your time on current clients and 20% of your time on prospects.

Rainmaker: Description and Tactics

(Larry Bodine)

The climate for business development by lawyers has radically changed in some ways, but in a lot of basic ways, it's very much the same. So, for instance, I've spoken to a great number of people who are rainmakers and I've studied them all my life. I have tried to discern what they do that makes them rainmakers and the bottom line is that these are people who have a lot of contacts.

Rainmakers deliberately build networks and stay in touch with their networks for their entire lives. They also do several things that distinguish them. The first is that they visit clients. If there's a meeting to be held, they'll try to set it up at the client's office. They want to get in front of the client so that they can see the client's operation and get to know the client better. It puts the client at ease and they welcome the fact that a lawyer would actually come to their office or factory. It creates a perfect situation for the lawyer to see if there is any more work that he could be doing for the client and whether the client would be willing to recommend or refer the lawyer to someone else.

The second thing that rainmakers do is to be active in business organizations of their clients.

For instance, suppose a lawyer has a number of clients and they all happen to be in the manufacturing business. The smart attorney will go to meetings where there are a lot of clients and not many lawyers. That means, in my opinion, you don't want to spend a whole lot of time in bar association meetings, because you're just going to be standing next to people who are competing with you.

The smarter move is to go a business meeting of clients, get on their own turf, and participate. The advantage to that is at a trade association conference, there aren't going to be a lot of other attorneys, but you will find a large number of businesspeople who are thinking about business and it's an excellent time to find out the pressures clients face and how you can solve them with legal solutions or solve them with legal services.

The idea, of course, is for you to volunteer for speaking opportunities in one of these trade associations of clients. See if you can host a lunch or participate in some type of an industry study. Basically, weave yourself into the community and, if possible, see if you can get on the board of directors.

The advantage of being on the board of directors is that everybody in the organization will know who you are. That's the key spot that you want to be in. It's something I've done many times. You simply go to the head of the organization or the board and say, "I'd like to help out. Do you need help with a newsletter or educational programming or any type of a task or chore?" The only way that they can reward you is with an appointment.

I'm like a doctor who tests his own cures. I do this myself. So, if I'm looking for work from attorneys, I make sure I go to numerous conferences where attorneys are present. This has worked really well for me.

Part of it is you need to be credible, you need to be somebody who people can trust, and you need to be somebody that people can like. It's the marketing trio: people hire people they know, like, and trust.

So, I've always made it a practice. I've learned this from my dad. You've got to be completely honest in your business affairs and you make yourself known by just getting out of your office and you make yourself likable by just listening to people.

I once had a lawyer tell me or ask in a discussion I was leading, "How do I make people like me?" I said, it's pretty straightforward, you just talk about the other person's favorite topic, which is always themselves. "Tell me about what you're doing. Tell me about your business. Tell me about what's on your mind." If you come away from a conference or a meeting and nobody asked you any questions about yourself, you did it perfectly.

> I've learned this from my dad. You've got to be completely honest in your business affairs and you make yourself known by just getting out of your office and you make yourself likable by just listening to people.
>
> *—Larry Bodine*

Being a good listener helps tremendously. The more you know about what's in the other person's mind, the more ways you can see how you can help them with legal services.

It's important to get out of your office because last I checked not too many clients were sitting around your desk. You're not going to originate any work sitting in your office.

I have to say, much of this I learned when I was nine years old and I read Dale Carnegie's book, *How to Make Friends and Influence People*. His whole approach was notice things about other people, ask the other person about what's on their mind, and then listen. This way you've presented yourself as somebody who's empathetic, who's knowledgeable about the other person's problem and in a perfect position to help them. When I read this, it was like aha! See, the thing is, anybody can become a rainmaker. It doesn't require you to have inborn skills or to be particularly gregarious. You could even be very introverted. All your have to do is go up to somebody and ask them five good questions about what's going on with them, what's happening in their business, what challenges are they facing, what are they going to do about it, and what would happen if they didn't do anything? It very quickly leads to people telling you their problems.

> You're not going to originate any work sitting in your office.
>
> *—Larry Bodine*

Most lawyers view rainmaking as pitching. Yes, you have to have a good pitch or a good 30-second commercial, but I recommend worry less about your pitch and worry more about the questions you're going to ask. Anybody can ask a question. You don't need to be brilliant or handsome or loquacious.

So, I pointed out a couple of suggestions. One is to get out and see clients. The other is you've got to get active in some type of trade organization or business organization. Finally, you need to intentionally develop a referral network.

The way you create a referral network is, if you're a litigator, you look for people who are transaction lawyers or if you're a criminal lawyer, look for lawyers who practice civil litigation.

Anyone in a law practice is going to get calls from clients who have matters that the lawyer does not handle. So, if I am a real estate lawyer and somebody calls me up with a divorce case, I want to have right at the top of my tip of my tongue the name of a good divorce lawyer to refer them to.

It will be somebody that I have already met for lunch and we've gotten to know each other and entered into a referral arrangement. I will send all of my divorce cases to that lawyer, but then of course, that lawyer doesn't practice in real estate, and he's going to send any type of commercial leases over to me.

You need to prime the pump, because when you give another lawyer a file, and it's a worthwhile one, there's a little attachment that goes along with it and it's that sense of obligation that compels them to respond in kind.

It's a circumstance I run into all the time. People call me up and ask me to do things that are not a part of my practice, but I know everybody in the business who could possibly do it for them. That person will have been pre-screened by me and it will be someone that I have an arrangement with.

> Most lawyers view rainmaking as pitching . . . I recommend worry less about your pitch and worry more about the questions you're going to ask.
>
> —*Larry Bodine*

The arrangement has to be specific. First of all, you have to have a meeting. You have to meet your referral source in person. The key information you need to find out from them is what are the exact type of cases they would like to have referred to them. You don't want to send over cases that are close, but it's not really what they do, and vice versa—you need to make it very clear exactly what you're looking for. If you're in real estate, are you looking for individuals or are you looking for businesses that have real estate problems? So, you explain specifically the kind of real estate matters you want to be referred to you. The referral arrangements that I've seen work well are set up like that.

The one element that runs through all of this is that lawyers have trouble with what I call "making the ask"—asking for something.

It starts with meeting another lawyer, or it could be an executive or another professional, for example, an accountant. You have to be willing to ask for a referral.

With a current client, you have to be willing to ask for a recommendation. In most businesses, clients all talk to each other. The way you get work is through general counsel recommendations.

Even in cases where someone has told you that they have some type of legal need – and it's a legal need that you can solve – it requires that you ask for the business. Lawyers often choke on that. They become very uncomfortable. They don't know what to say. My advice is to practice. It could be as simple as something like, "I can help you with that. Why don't you come to my office on Monday, and we'll have you sign an engagement agreement?" Or some variation of that where you suggest, let's take the next step. "Let me handle this for you and we'll have a strategy session at my office on Monday."

The way that you make it easy is that in the course of asking questions, you get at the sense of urgency. So, you preface everything by saying, how has this affected you? What difference has it made in your life? Then you get into what would happen if you didn't do anything about it.

This is essential because the biggest objection that you're going to get is that the client is going to say, I'm just not going to do anything about it and that means that there is no sense of urgency. You really need to get at their underlying emotion and determine quickly how motivated they are. For example, you can say, well, how do you feel about this? How has this affected you? What difference has it made? If you can get them to say, "It's driving me crazy, it keeps me up at night, we've had to modify the way we do business, it's costing us a fortune," well, now you've just heard that there is a real sense of urgency.

> Lawyer referrals: The key element that makes it work is you have to give a file to get a file.
>
> —*Larry Bodine*

Then if you ask them, "What if you didn't do anything about it?" and they respond with, "Oh, I have to do something about it or we'll go out of business," then that's when you say, "Well, let me help you. Come to my office and we'll make you a client of the firm."

Determining their sense of urgency is a good way to avoid wasting a great deal of time with somebody who is only going to talk about their problem but aren't going to do anything about it. So, identifying if the matter is truly urgent in their mind is a good way to determine if they're going to do anything about their problem.

I recall talking to a partner in a Chicago firm and he represented a family business. The members of the family were complaining bitterly to him about the other family members and they were all fighting. He recognized what the problem was and he had a number of solutions, but they kept him hanging on for months and months because they just wanted to complain. They really didn't want to do anything about it.

The other thing that rainmakers do is keep a high profile. These are people who are speaking in front of crowds, they're writing articles that are published on the web and in magazines, they're officers or on the board of organizations. Some call it top of mind. Most of it is what they call thought leadership—which is writing articles, giving talks, just being active in an organization, and everything ties to your law practice. So, you're writing about your practice, you're talking about the kind of law that you handle and you're in a trade organization that faces this issue frequently. The idea is you want everybody to hear about you.

If you're the light under the bushel basket, no one's going to know you exist. That's another thing that lawyers are trained in – to keep client confidences and keep secrets – but they end up keeping themselves secret. You need to be out in public. Everything I've talked about was true 50 years ago, and it's all true today: talking to people (what I call relationship marketing) and networking in the right places. It all has to do with human nature; and the big change is marketing with technology and online.

Rainmaker: Not Everyone Makes Rain in the Same Way

(Erin Meszaros)

When having a business development discussion with an attorney, you're dealing with the individual. You want to be careful trying to use a one-size-fits-all, fill-in-the-blank action list. You have to avoid putting them in a box with pre-defined options, even though many will do it. While I may not believe every lawyer is destined to be a rainmaker, I do think every lawyer has a role in business development. You may be on the front lines with the client or you may be sitting behind the desk turning out the work. Turning out a superior work product is still business development, because if you don't have a good work product, you're not going to retain the client. Rainmakers build teams which leads to the successful landing and retention of clients.

I think you have to identify what role you play best and hope that you have a leader that agrees with that, and then you play your part on the team, successfully.

Through a recent client interview we discovered a client who launched a program to bring experienced working attorneys into local law firms that do not fit your classic rainmaker definition but add value and revenue nonetheless. This particular client established an effort to identify women with law degrees who had decided to take a leave of absence to stay home and be a mom for 3–5 years to participate in an internship program to ease them back into the law firm. What a great business development effort, to allow working moms to come back in the firm as a 9 to 5 person who's just cranking out the work and not someone responsible to develop the business. Seems this approach would also increase your diversity efforts as well, to hold five open spots every year for women who want to come back into the work force and work that 9 to 5 slot.

Rainmaker: The Power of Purpose & Passion

(Scott Kessler)

Creating a rainmaker is not rocket science. There's a really simple process to it. Where people get hung up is that they think that they need to do lots of things. They are given a list of "things to do" from their internal marketing people, they read books about things they should be doing to grow their business, and they see their colleagues doing things and feel like they should be doing those things too. Marketing professionals are paid to come up with initiatives that the lawyers can be a part of and then the marketers have trouble getting any of the lawyers to engage in the initiatives. A few lawyers might even sit down with their marketing manage and develop a plan, but then the plan falls by the way side as client work takes precedence. The fact is, most people – whether they are lawyers, accountants, or plumbers – just aren't going to execute on a plan. It's the same with diets and New Year's resolutions. So, what's the answer? Purpose and Passion.

I have spent most of my life trying to help people achieve their goals. Why? Because I believe that is my purpose and when I find a way to help, I become so passionate about it that my passion becomes contagious, which leads to "enrollment." When I have tried to launch a program without that passion, it dies a quick death. When I look at the people who have been able to make "rain," I see people with a clear "purpose" and people who can bring "passion" to the execution of their purpose. When purpose and passion are present, good things just seem to happen. The pieces fall in to place. Why? Because people who have 1) a clear idea of their purpose for doing what they are doing and 2) a true passion for how they are doing it can form incredibly powerful relationships. Relationships that are formed through an emotional tie are the strongest relationships. Once a powerful relationship is established, the "rain" follows. At their core, all people want to be helpful and they are going to be most helpful to the people they like and trust. It's the basic tenant of sales: "People buy from people they like and trust." You don't have to be the smartest lawyer to make the most rain, you just need to build the most powerful relation.

> Become a relationship maker and the rain will follow.
>
> —*Scott Kessler*

So instead of creating a business development plan that is likely never going to be executed, create your Purpose and Passion plan and start to communicate it to the world. You will enjoy the process, execution will be easy, and the rain will follow.

Rainmakers Eventually Retire: Next Gen Ready?

(Dave Bruns)

Each practice has a major rainmaker and they're all starting to get older and we needed that next generation to understand that the market had changed. The way in which work is obtained has changed. So we needed to start to get more people working toward generating some revenue. Bringing in their own clients, essentially, or expanding work for existing clients. We had identified that we needed more partners generating more work.

We took a look at our goals. What was our end game? What were we trying to do? One of the things that we identified four years ago was that we needed to decentralize or flatten the distribution of rainmakers. The old proverb, "All boats rise with the tide."

So, we needed to start to get more people working toward generating some revenue by bringing in their own clients or expanding work for existing clients. We needed more people, more partners, generating more work to secure the firm going forward.

Rainmakers: Four Things Rainmakers Do

(Larry Bodine)

There are four things rainmakers do. One, go out and see clients. Two, get active in a trade organization or business organization. Three develop a referral network. Four, keep a high profile. Rainmakers are speaking in front of crowds, they're writing articles that are published on the web and in magazines, they're officers or on the board of organizations.

All of these four actions are critical to put the rainmaker in a position to meet a potential client. Once a rainmaker meets a prospective client, the rainmaker will employ dialogue, discernment, and well-placed questions to determine if there is a potential for business. Then, the rainmaker will ask for the business by suggesting a meeting at the client's office or elsewhere to discuss helping them with a solution to their legal problem.

Rainmakers: Who Can and Who Can't: EQ versus IQ

(Stephen Fairley)

The very first thing that I would say is I don't really believe that every attorney can be a rainmaker. I believe that every attorney can do something to help them with marketing and business development, but that does not make them a rainmaker. I think it takes a certain skillset, a certain training, but most importantly, a certain personality, to truly be a rainmaker.

To me, a rainmaker is very different from an order taker. If I'm sitting across the table from a highly qualified prospect who has all the money that they need to pay me, and if I can solve their exact legal problem, have the background and experience to do so, and I can close them, to me that's not a rainmaker, that's an order taker. Right? There are certain attorneys out there who can't even take the order. To me there's a big difference between an order taker and a rainmaker. A rainmaker, however, is someone who goes out and proactively hunts down new business.

There are various types of people: the hunter, the farmer, the gatherer, and other types. I'm talking about hunters. There are certain people that are really good at it—they've got an existing client base and they can farm that client base to be able to get additional business from it. And then there's certain people who are gatherers. If you plunk down somebody, they're essentially an order taker. They'll take down the order if somebody wants to sign up, they can fill out the form to sign them up, but we're not talking about gatherers, we're not talking about farmers, we're talking about hunters.

People who go out and say, okay, we have a commercial litigation practice and we want to target companies in our geographical area or in our region that are doing somewhere between 10 million and 50 million dollars in revenue and I want to go after the general counsel, the vice president, or the CEO or the general manager of a division. I want to build a relationship with the goal of getting my firm in there, to get my foot in the door, to get them to give us some business. That to me is a hunter.

I think there is a myth out there that every attorney can be a rainmaker. I don't believe that. Over the last 14 years I've worked with over 10,000 attorneys nation-wide and a good one third to half of them will never be rainmakers and probably I'm being generous. It's probably much higher than that. It doesn't mean that they can't do business development. That doesn't mean that they can't do activities that typically lead to opportunities to generate business. But they don't have the mindset or they don't have the personality to truly be a rainmaker.

The second distinction that I would bring in is that it has nothing to do with being a skilled lawyer. In fact, some of the worst people out there in terms of business development and marketing are the skilled lawyers, because they take pride in being an excellent technician, and litigators are actually the worst. Some of the worst business development people out there are litigators because to be a great litigator, is almost the antithesis of being a great marketer. A litigator, you put your head down and you work on one issue, you're singular in your focus. You work on one issue or one client and you work, work, work, until the case is done. Then you lift your head up and look around and say, where's the next client?

Marketing and business development is a marathon, it's not a sprint. Litigators are taught to sprint.

So, being a skilled lawyer has absolutely zero to do with being a skilled rainmaker. In fact, some of the best rainmakers consistently that I have found come out of second- and third-tier law schools.

I've coached attorneys and consulted with attorneys from Harvard, Yale, Princeton, Stanford, University of Chicago, you name it, I've worked with top-tier attorneys who come out of top-tier law schools and they are brilliant people, they are very, very intelligent, but we're not talking about their IQ. We're talking about their EQ.

Referral Sources: Estate Planning Example

(Sally Schmidt)

Attorneys involved in estate planning already know that they need to focus on accountants as referral sources, as well as trust officers, current clients, former clients, and a whole range of referring lawyers. Each referral source might have a different need in terms of information. So, if you put together an alert or an advisory, you could easily pull together a list, for example, of the accountants who have sent me business or who work with my clients.

Referrals: A Specific Action Plan

(Stephen Fairley)

So, when you ask me to talk about how lawyers should think about referral sources, creating them, identifying them, rewarding them, growing them . . . the first thing I would say is that probably, if you were to ask most attorneys where they get most of their referrals from, they would say current and former clients. Also known as word of mouth. When an attorney says to me, I get most of my clients from word of mouth, what I typically translate that is, I haven't the foggiest idea where my clients come from, but I pray to God the phone doesn't stop ringing. I have no idea. It just happens. I get it, but you can't build a financially successful business long term by relying solely on word of mouth. Word of mouth comes, but it's not consistent and what happens when one of your major referral sources dries up or when one of your major clients goes away? All of a sudden, you're hurting for business. It's very difficult to rely on that consistently.

We work with an equity partner at Ropes and Gray. He's one of the most prestigious producers at Ropes and Gray. He alone is responsible for about 8 million dollars a year coming into the firm. That's not his team. That's him alone responsible for bringing that in, and by the way, he doesn't do all the work. Because he's a great technician. You don't get to become the partner of a major section of Ropes & Gray without being a brilliant technician and a brilliant attorney, but his primary purpose is to feed his team. Because that's the difference between a rainmaker and an order taker. An order taker only brings in enough business for themselves. A rainmaker brings in enough for themselves and everybody else. So, the number one place where you can get more referrals is from your current and former clients, and a lot of times attorneys don't look at their potential clients as real referral sources. It's foolish to me how little time they spend on cultivating them and they think taking them to a ballgame . . . it is so ridiculous what I hear attorneys and law firms spending their money on and labeling as business development and marketing.

We got a suite at the local professional football/basketball/baseball/hockey, whatever you want to call it, profession, because one of the equity partners or the managing partner loves football, baseball, basketball, you name the sport, and so they'll go out and they'll spend tens of thousands if not hundreds of thousands of dollars every year on getting a suite, right? They call that marketing and business development. No, it's not. Or, there's a law firm here in Phoenix Southwest that spent a half a million dollars a year on sponsoring their local Phoenix or the Scottsdale orchestra. And they call that marketing and business development. No, it's not. It might make you feel better about yourself and it's very philanthropic and altruistic that you're doing it, but don't label it business development. If anything, it's more about your ego. You need to stay in touch with your current and former clients on a consistent basis and it needs to be a meaningful touch, like giving them a seminar or inviting them to a webinar that you're giving or showing up at their trade association where you're speaking. Sending them an invoice is not a meaningful touch. That doesn't count. The fact that you communicate with them regularly every month by sending them an invoice, that's not a meaningful touch. It has to involve something that is meaningful to them and it doesn't necessarily equal money coming in to your pocket.

One of the easiest ways to stay in touch with them is through a monthly newsletter. Something that provides and adds value to them on a consistent basis. I'm amazed at how relatively few law firms out there are developing and sending out a monthly newsletter. I'm a big proponent of that. Send it to every single prospect, client, and referral source that you've got. We all know this principle and very few of us practice it.

Fairley: When it comes to sales and marketing: out of sight, out of mind. We know this. Let me ask you, David. Are you married?

Keller: Yes, I am.

Fairley: You are? How long you been married?

Keller: Seventeen years.

Fairley: Seventeen years. Congratulations. My wife and I just hit 19 years.

Keller: Oh, congratulations.

Fairley: So, that's fantastic. What's her name?

Keller: Carmen.

Fairley: Carmen. Do you love her?

Keller: I love her.

Fairley: How much do you love her?

Keller: I'm madly in love with her. I'm desperately in love with her. I don't want to live without her.

Fairley: I love that. That's fantastic. I feel the same way about my wife. Now, the next question is, how often do you tell Carmen that you love her?

Keller: Regularly.

Fairley: Okay, so the correct answer according to females that I've surveyed is "not enough." Right? Not enough. You can never tell your loved one that you love them enough, right? Now, David, what if I come to you with a little experiment and this is exactly the same dialogue I use when I'm giving a talk in front of a group of attorneys to illustrate my point. So, David, what if

I came to you and I said, we're going to do a little experiment and I'm going to have you tell Carmen that you love her, but we're only going to have you tell her that once a year.

Keller: Uh-oh.

Fairley: And let's say that we're going to say that you're going to tell her that you love her around the holidays. How do you think that would go over with Carmen?

Keller: I get it. Oh, no, no, it's not real. It's not sincere.

Fairley: Not very good, right? I mean she's going to begin to doubt your sincerity, she's going to—there's going to be all kinds of problems.

Keller: Yep.

Fairley: So, why the hell do we think that it's completely appropriate to tell clients that we love them by sending them a holiday card? And we think that that's sufficient. So you need to be in front of them on a consistent basis. Now, not only can you get referrals from your current and former clients, but you can also get referrals from non-client professionals.

Now, if I were to ask most attorneys who would be a good example of a non-client who is a professional that you could get a referral from, the very first thing they say is attorneys, which rarely is true. Attorneys are lousy referral sources. They are. They're not taught to think that way, they're not incentivized to think that way, that's not the way that they're wired. Now you could say there are exceptions in larger law firms and even mid-sized law firms where you get partial credit for referring an existing client over to another department or another division in your law firm. You can get partial credit for that and you might even get monetarily compensated for doing that. So, that's a little bit different.

In general, attorneys are terrible referral sources. In fact, I have attorneys who say, okay, so for my marketing plan this year, I'm going to go join my local Bar Association. [Fairley makes a buzzer noise]: Wrong answer. No, you don't join your local Bar Association because you're looking to get referrals. It just doesn't work like that. Or they'll say, I'm going to join the Environmental Section of the State Bar of California and that's my marketing. No, that's your peers. Your peers aren't going to refer business to you. You don't want to go after peers, you want to go after prospects, and potential referral partners.

So, if anything, that could be great for your professional development, but that's not marketing and that's not business development. Other attorneys will say, well, I want to give a CLE program to my local Bar Association or my State Bar Association or my National Bar Association to get referrals.

[Fairley makes a buzzer noise]: Wrong answer. You don't give CLEs to get referrals. You give CLEs to build your curriculum vitae. To gain credibility. You don't give CLE programs to get referrals. It doesn't work like that. All you're doing is educating your competition.

There are 135,000 trade associations across the United States. How do I know that? Because there is an encyclopedia of trade associations. Every single one of those associations could be a potential client or a potential referral source. So, if you're thinking about how to grow your referral base, you don't look to other attorneys; well, you can look to other attorneys, but certainly not in your practice area. You look to them in other ancillary practice areas, but then you look outside the legal industry, to whether it's CPAs, financial advisors, business brokers, real estate brokers, CEO Chairs of Vistage (Vistage International is a peer-to-peer membership organization for CEOs, business owners, and executives of small- to mid-size businesses), all different kinds of professionals out there who are in contact with decision makers at a variety of different companies, sizes, shapes, and geographies, and revenues, with different legal problems, and you build relationships with those people.

And there are a number of ways that you can do that. You can do that through trade associations, which are a great source because trade associations typically involve people who are looking for CEUs, Continuing Education Units, or they're looking to build their business, they're looking to network, they're more committed versus disconnected.

[To create a promotional niche, see *Niches Lead to Riches*; see also *Compensating a Non-Attorney Referral Source.*]

Referrals: Compensating a Non-Attorney Referral Source

(Stephen Fairley)

You just made the statement that when it comes to the ethics of compensating people who are non-attorneys for referring business to you, the big answer is that you can't—you can only compensate an attorney for referring business to you; and then you asked me if that was my understanding as well. No, that's not my understanding, because that's not really true. You can't compensate them financially, that is true. There's the key word, "financially." You can compensate them, it just can't be something of financial value. So, you can compensate them in other ways.

You want to give that referral source some positive psychological reinforcement, which may, hopefully, give that person some reason to perform that very valuable favor again. That's correct and many don't understand that the rest of the business world works like that all the time. If I do a deal with some company, I'm going to get a kickback or I'm going to get a cut, or I'm going to be able to white label it and sell it at $100 when it only costs me $75, but the rest of the business world works like that all day long, every day. It's kind of a holdover from, "this is not a business, this is a profession," and I understand that, but there are creative ways you can do that. For example, sending them a thank you card. And you can ask, well, what difference did that make? It makes a heck of a lot of difference, especially if it's handwritten. Or sending them a small gift, like a bottle of wine, and it doesn't have to be Dom, but it probably shouldn't be wine in a box either. Or, sending them a gift basket. Calling them and telling them thank you personally each and every time that they send you a referral and letting them know how much it means to you. There's one client that, every time you send a referral to their law firm, they put your name down and at the end of each quarter, do a drawing. Whoever gets drawn gets some type of gift, whether it's a day at the spa, or a set of new golf clubs. And once a year that same law firm does another drawing for anybody who has ever referred them business during the course of the year and sends them on a week-long cruise.

Now, you'll have some attorneys that will just flip a lid over that. They'll say, well, you're compensating that person. You're giving them a referral fee. Look, I get it, and some people will never understand that and they'll think that that is as unethical as the day is long. Quite honestly, I'm pretty comfortable with that because it's random.

It's random and it's not specifically related to the specific client or revenue. There's no direct relationship, like you said, it's random. And it's not based on the size. Right? Some attorneys are never going to be comfortable with giving even a small token of appreciation to a non-attorney referral source, so at least, for Pete's sake, send them a handwritten thank you note. Don't just do nothing. Don't just not even acknowledge it.

Relationship Building

(Despina Kartson)

Relationship building is critically important to being able to develop business. It is an approach that needs to be something that is very much top of mind, whether it's the relationship with other parents out on your kid's soccer field, or someone that you're sitting next to on a plane, or anyone that you may come across professionally and personally. Think about how you are identifying people whom you think it would be great to have a potential business relationship with and then determine what you are doing to cultivate that relationship.

Resilience and the Anterior Cingulate Cortex

(David King Keller)

According to PBS.org, "Resilience is the capacity to withstand stress and catastrophe."

According to the American Psychological Association, "Resilience is the process of adapting well in the face of adversity, trauma, tragedy, threats, or significant sources of stress—such as family and relationship problems, serious health problems or workplace, and financial stressors. It means "bouncing back" from difficult experiences." Read 10 ways to build resilience at http://www.apa.org/helpcenter/road-resilience.aspx.

People who experience trauma but do not develop PTSD, on the other hand, show more activity in the prefrontal cortex. In August, Kerry Ressler, a neuroscientist at Emory University in Atlanta, Georgia, and his colleagues showed that these resilient individuals have stronger physical connections between the Anterior Cingulate Cortex (ACC) and the hippocampus. This suggests that resilience depends partly on communication between the reasoning circuitry in the cortex and the emotional circuitry of the limbic system. "It's as if [resilient people] can have a very healthy response to negative stimuli," says Dennis Charney, a psychiatrist at the Mount Sinai School of Medicine in New York, who has conducted several brain-imaging studies of rape victims, soldiers, and other trauma survivors. [From URL: http://www.nature.com/news/stress-the-roots-of-resilience-1.11570]

A risk endophenotype included greater activation of cortical attention circuits. A resilience endophenotype included greater activation of the dorsal anterior cingulate cortex. [From URL: http://www.ncbi.nlm.nih.gov/pubmed/24369340]

Read about factors that contribute to resilience at URL: http://www.pbs.org/thisemotionallife/topic/resilience/what-resilience

Resilience: Mindfulness and Meditation Can Increase Resilience

(David King Keller)

My doctoral dissertation was on a very brief stress reduction practice that, in thirty seconds, can build resilience, and, based on published studies, can improve mood and increase productivity. In the research I include nearly two hundred studies published in peer-reviewed journal articles on the physical and psychological benefits of meditation.

The Harvard Business Review, in a stress-related article on January 08, 2015 titled, *Mindfulness Can Literally Change Your Brain,* states, "Recent research provides strong evidence that practicing non-judgmental, present-moment awareness (a.k.a. mindfulness) changes the brain, and it does so in ways that anyone working in today's complex business environment, and certainly every leader, should know about. This year, a team of scientists from the University of British Columbia and the Chemnitz University of Technology were able to pool data from more than 20 studies to determine which areas of the brain are consistently affected. They identified at least eight different regions. Here we will focus on *two* that we believe to be of particular interest to business professionals.

The *first* is the anterior cingulate cortex (ACC), a structure located deep inside the forehead, behind the brain's frontal lobe. The ACC is associated with self-regulation, meaning the ability to purposefully direct attention and behavior, suppress inappropriate knee-jerk responses, and switch strategies flexibly. People with damage to the ACC show impulsivity and unchecked aggression, and those with impaired connections between this and other brain regions perform poorly on tests of mental flexibility: they hold onto ineffective problem-solving strategies rather than adapting their behavior. Meditators, on the other hand, demonstrate superior performance on tests of self-regulation, resisting distractions and making correct answers more often than non-meditators. They also show more activity in the ACC than non-meditators. In addition to self-regulation, the ACC is associated with learning from past experience to support optimal decision-making. Scientists point out that the ACC may be particularly important in the face of uncertain and fast-changing conditions.

The *second* brain region we want to highlight is the hippocampus, a region that showed increased amounts of gray matter in the brains of our 2011 mindfulness program participants. This seahorse-shaped area is buried inside the temple on each side of the brain and is part of the limbic system, a set of inner structures associated with emotion and memory. It is covered in receptors for the stress hormone cortisol, and studies (DOI: 10.1146/annurev-med-052209-100430) have shown that it can be damaged by chronic stress, contributing to a harmful spiral in the body. Indeed, people with stress-related disorders like depression and PTSD tend to have a smaller hippocampus. All of this points to the importance of this brain area in **resilience**—another key skill in the current high-demand business world. These findings are just the beginning of the story. Neuroscientists have also shown that practicing mindfulness affects brain areas related to perception, body awareness, pain tolerance, emotion regulation, introspection, complex thinking, and sense of self. Mindfulness should no longer be considered a "nice-to-have" for executives. It's a "must-have": a way to keep our brains healthy, to support self-regulation and effective decision-making capabilities, and to protect ourselves from toxic stress. It can be integrated into one's religious or spiritual life, or practiced as a form of secular mental training. When we take a seat, take a breath, and commit to being mindful, particularly when we gather with others who are doing the same, we have the potential to be changed."

The Wall Street Journal in a June 19, 2015 article titled *Lawyers Go Zen, With Few Objections,* stated, "A Zen-inspired blend of meditation, breathing exercises and focus techniques are in vogue in corporate America—championed by blue-chip employers like Google Inc. and General Mills Inc. as a simple but potent mind-sharpening tool. Now, the movement is on the cusp of a more improbable breakthrough into the field of law . . . Scott Rogers, founder and director of University of Miami's 'Mindfulness in Law Program' noted students who take his mindfulness courses earn up to three credits toward their law degree. They all have waiting lists, he says, including the one in which students are instructed to lose an argument. 'It's not about losing a fight or giving up at all,' says Mr. Rogers. 'It's developing greater insight in the ways we lose touch' with our impulses . . . His law school is one of about two dozen across the country to incorporate mindfulness exercises into its curriculum."

In a report published on February 20, 2013 by the Nour Foundation, neuroscientist Richard Davidson states that meditation can help the amygdala, the emotional response part of the brain, calm down more quickly after a stressful event.

FYI: Don't call Adobe HQ between 3pm and 3:15pm, during their mindfulness time-out, you'll just go to voicemail. What do they know that you don't? Maybe nothing. Or, maybe something that can prevent a heart attack or a career crushing emotional outburst. Or, maybe they know something that can provide you with that calm rainmaker confidence that wins clients.

Revenue: Growing Firm Revenue: Job One

(Sally Schmidt)

When I receive a call and they say, "Hey, Sally, we want to increase our firm revenue by X," my first response is that I think business development happens at three levels. It happens at the firm level, it happens at either the niche or industry or practice level, and then, it happens at the individual level. At the firm level we want to start with existing clients. So, the first thing we'll do is go pick out the top 100 clients, and maybe others that are not in that group yet but could be if we did a better job of generating business. Then we create a game plan. For the top 10 clients, it might be some type of client feedback process where somebody goes out and talks to them and says, "What do you think of the firm? Are there other opportunities? Is there anything the firm could be doing for you that it's not?" From my experience over the years, about 50 percent of those interviews result in new business. So that, to me, would be job one.

Another opportunity for firm-wide revenue growth that I love is . . . [See *Industry Marketing: Cross-Selling Occurs as a Matter of Course* by Sally Schmidt]

RFPs and Pitch Training: See Pitch Training

RFPs: Not All Should Get a Response

(Erin Meszaros)

We evaluate all RFPs as to whether it is worth the time and effort by the attorneys and our team to respond. We have begun to weigh the pros and cons of responding to any RFP that does not come directly from a current client.

Sales Director: When Should a Firm Add a Sales Director?

(Steve Bell)

I would be way out of my league to even speculate when a law firm should add a sales director. Although, I would say this, if I were starting a law firm from scratch, maybe the second person I hire would be the sales director.

Sales Pipeline

(Allen Chichester)

Our point of view is that sales pipelines eat business plans for lunch. No doubt, it's good to know where you're going, otherwise you won't know when you get there. And when you're working with a group, they all need to work off the same plan. But, the real bread and butter of business development is managing the pipeline. Whether you call it a prospect list, whether it's simply a list of five names that you keep on your desk in front of you or a sophisticated CRM program where you actually manage the components of the pipeline, the focus of turning your prospects into leads and your leads into clients is the key. If you're not driving towards that, then you're not making things happen.

> Sales pipelines eat business plans for lunch.
>
> —*Allen Chichester*

Sales Process: "When Lawyers Get It, They Fly"

(Silvia Coulter)

Lawyers already possess sales skills. That's what I always say. When lawyers get it, they fly because sales is all about negotiation at some level. It's asking effective questions. It's being a good listener. It's being prepared. It's knowing when you go to a meeting you want a certain outcome to occur. It's facilitating questioning and facilitating discussion to that outcome. That's what lawyers do for a living. It's about understanding how to use their existing skills in a client development setting, which is the same thing as a sales setting, and understanding where they are in the client development process/sales process. That's why I say when lawyers get it, they fly to a whole new level.

It's making sure that you are driving the situation to a desired outcome, whether it's a desired legal outcome or a desired sales outcome. To get there, you've got to listen. You've got to be prepared. You've got to ask questions. You can't be reactive. You've got to stay in control of the communication process, the sales process. When we present it that way it helps to bridge the lawyer's relationship to us as business development and sales coaches. It's now working with your skillset and using it in a sales context.

Once the attorney has a relationship to work with, it's simply applying legal discovery techniques. You've got these contacts—not only clients, but prospective clients, referral sources. How are you going to work with these contacts to have an outcome? Once they have the contact, and everybody's got some contacts. Sometimes, they think they don't, but they all have contacts. It's just a matter of leveraging existing contacts to have introductions to new contacts, or it's developing the ones that you have. Once you have made a commitment to yourself that this is what you want to do and you want to be effective at it, then that's when the legal skills come in. Or the skillset that is certainly parallel to the legal skillset.

We align the skills they already have to building relationships. At some point you have to ask for business. At some point you've got to close the deal just like you would in a court room. You've got to ask the jury to vote for you. There are going to be good litigators, and there are going to be not-so-good litigators. There are going to be good salespeople and not-so-good sales-people, or people who are good at developing business and people who aren't good at developing business.

Emotionally you need to have a lot of confidence to be good at whatever you do, and in practicing law, you have to believe that you can practice law *and* you can develop business. You translate your confidence in your legal skills into confidence in your business development skills.

How does an attorney develop confidence in their business development skills? They've got to try it. We've talked for three months about the same thing. Pick two people, and let's put this into action. I've sat in rooms where I've said "let's pick up the phone, right now." Most people don't really want to do that. Once in a while they will, but you've got to make something happen here. What's standing in the way? I had someone respond to me the other day, after I asked "How did it go?": "This was so easy. I am so over being worried about this."

In summary, lawyers already have the skills, they simply need to apply them within the business development context.

Sales Process: Friendly Witness Interview Style

(David King Keller)

One person I spoke with likened the sales process to creating a friendly witness to win the case.

First, you need to find a potential witness (potential client), then you need to make friends by building rapport and gaining trust and confidence in you with them feeling comfortable that you understand who they are, their needs, and they need to believe you've got their back and can actually help them (use your trust building skills, see article on "The Neuroscience of Going From Stranger to Trusted Advisor" in *The Associate As Rainmaker, Building Your Business Brain*, my ABA best-selling book available at http://bit.ly/1dAxob6). You do this by asking open-ended questions, then listening to the answers. Demonstrate you heard their answer by repeating back key points of the answer, so the "jury," the decision maker, your potential client, hears that you understand, appreciate, and empathize.

Sales Process: The Three-Legged Stool

(Silvia Coulter)

There is a process called "the sales process." There have been loads of books written outside the legal industry on selling. Regardless of who writes it and which year it was written it's still the same fundamentals. It's assessing needs, understanding the buyer's needs. It's then bridging your solutions to their needs. You can say it in many different ways. You can put new spins on it. You can add social media to the mix. You can do all those things, but at the end of the day, it's about a relationship. It's about expertise and experience. The process doesn't really change. The process is pretty much the same. It all boils down to the three-legged stool: expertise, experience, and relationship.

Remembering relationship begins with understanding the buyer's needs, and demonstrating that the lawyer's skills match the buyer's needs.

Sales Skills: Necessary to Advance

(Steve Bell)

We do not have a different approach for associates and partners when it comes to supporting the acquisition of new business. My firm doesn't do that. There might be law firms that make a big distinction between partners and associates, when it comes to who can bring in new business. That's not true in the environment I work in. I don't have that particular challenge. It's possible for people who don't have law degrees to single-handedly bring in legal work – usually not single-handedly, but it's possible. So why isn't it possible for somebody with a law degree to do that? Associates are perfectly viable salespeople. They won't necessarily be able to sign the engagement letter which requires a partner's signature, but there's nothing that I do that an associate lawyer couldn't do. Bring on the associates if they're interested and they want to learn the art and science of client acquisition. They have to do this to advance these days. So I'm very interested in working with associates who are motivated to be successful in this area.

Currently, we do not incorporate a firm-wide formal sales training schedule. I've been here for a long time and we have done many types of training, both sourced from the outside and undertaken inside. I wish we did have a formal curriculum for all the attorneys. We keep thinking about it, but we don't have it. We provide individual and small group sales training, and I expect most law firms do, as well.

Sales Training: "Just-in-Time" Business Development Presentation Support

(Steve Bell)

We use an online "Just-in-Time" sales training and sales coaching program that's available to our attorneys. One resource for that training is Rainmaker VT, V as in video, T as in technology, with Mike O'Horo.

If an attorney in our firm needs sales support, then I am glad they want the help and I'll do everything I can to get it to them. We have myself and my staff. If it's midnight or we cannot be reached for some reason, we have outside sales consultants and business development consultants to help us.

"Just-In-Time" sales training is helpful, for example, if they're having a sales emergency at midnight and I'm asleep, they can go to this "Just-In-Time" site and say, "I'm giving a speech tomorrow, how do I transform it into a business development activity?" Or, "My neighbor, is CFO of a company, what do I do?" We have a number of resources. There are people here who like and who use our relationship development coach Mark Maraia, and LawVision's Silvia Coulter.

I'm interested in success. I am not interested in personally accounting for everything that happens around here that's good. I just want good things to happen. So any source I can find, provide, identify, leverage, bring to bear, that's what I want to do.

Sales: A Four-Letter Word? Yet, It's a Part of Our Daily Life

(Stephen Fairley)

This is the way that I talk about sales with attorneys. I'll stand up in front of an audience and I'll say, now, I'm about to cuss at you because I know in your vocabulary "sales" is a four-letter word. But, don't be too offended, because sales is simply this. It's the gentle art of persuading someone to do business with you. That's it. Then I'll ask, "How many of you have kids?" Most of them will raise their hand. I will then say, "When's the last time your kid tried to sell you on buying them an ice cream at McDonald's? When's the last time your kid tried to sell you on going over to their best friend's house for a sleepover? When's the last time your kid tried to sell you on buying them a new car versus that junker that you originally wanted to get them?" Everybody's in sales. You just may not know it or you may not be willing to admit it. So, I understand that you think that sales is for a business and you're in a profession. Well, I have news for you. It stopped being a profession about 15 to 20 years ago with the advent of the Internet.

You can't get away from it. The only way that you'll ever get away from sales is if you want to be a technician who is paid a flat fee or paid a set fee for the rest of your life. And there is nothing wrong with that. We all need good technicians. Or in the famous words of Miyagi to Daniel, we all need good dishwashers. There's nothing wrong with it. If you want to be a good dishwasher, that's great. But, I'm not here to talk to the dishwashers. I'm here to talk to the business owners. Until you recognize that, whether that means that you're a solo practitioner or whether that means that you're an equity partner, people don't become equity partners these days because they're a good technician. Technicians are a dime a dozen. They always have been, they always will be. You can make a lot of money as a technician. But the days of becoming an equity partner because you're a good technician are over.

In fact, you've seen that some of the larger firms have de-equitized partners. Not because they were not good technicians. The reason they got their equity taken away was what? Because they didn't bring in enough business. They were not producers. They were not rainmakers. As a rainmaker, you get to write your own ticket.

Sales: Asking for the Order

(Sally Schmidt)

When we work with law firms, sometimes lawyers will ask sales-oriented questions like, "What about asking for the order? Closing techniques?" How have you found attorney receptivity toward sales and sales jargon? How do you get the lawyers comfortable with sales, closing, and asking for the business?"

I've come around to the belief that there are many successful ways that generate a new engagement or a new matter coming in the door. There are lawyers who will pound the table and say, "What do I have to do to get some files from you?" And, there are other lawyers who are very good business developers who tell me they've never specifically asked for the business. So I'm okay with that. You have to get to is a point where you recognize a need that the client has; you've talked to them about your capabilities; and you're sure that they know that you'd like to help. And so, that could be tracking their cases and sending a note or email off and saying, "Hey, I saw there was something filed here in our courts. I'd love to help you with this." You have to express interest. Let me say that. You have to express interest. You don't always have to say, "I'd like your work."

Sales: Avoiding the Word "Sales"

(Despina Kartson)

We don't use the word "sales" or "selling" and prefer to talk about business development. We talk about asking for the business but we don't actually use the word "sales."

Additionally, using words like "coaching," are often received better by lawyers than "training."

These are important distinctions because you're dealing with a variety of personality traits and we need to be smart. Use words and phraseology that are more complementary to the personality you of the lawyer with whom you are working.

Sales: Careful with the Word "Sales"

(Barbara Lauterbach)

I sometimes laugh because I read all the business development books just like everybody else does. I buy them all. Almost all of these books are a rehash of what somebody else has said, but when you get right down to it, it's basic sales. But, you don't necessarily want to tell a lawyer that because many hold a very negative connotation of sales in their minds. It's finding a commonality and expanding on it. That's what a trial attorney has to do with a witness or an expert. That's where you have to start, finding that commonality, that connection, and expand the relationship from there.

It's a little like one of those language transcription devices, where you speak one language into it and the other language comes out. You're translating the sales process into a process that relates to the attorney's world and his or her experience.

Sales: Demystify Sales

(Melanie Green)

My goal is to demystify sales and make it not feel sales-ey, but really make it be about relationship and connection and providing something of value to our clients. Take a needs-based approach to the thinking. We always hear firms talk about cross-selling. And then we talk about the white space reports or green space, whatever the color is on the chart, where you pull the list of 50 clients and you line up your services and you say, "Here's where we do work. Here's where we don't. And shouldn't we be able to do X, Y, and Z work for these clients?"

> My goal is to demystify sales and make it not feel sales-ey.
>
> —*Melanie Green*

So, that's our traditional way of thinking about this. I personally feel like that's why we haven't been so successful. It's backwards. For example, what happens is this: let's say the labor employment group runs a report and sees the 50 clients of the top 100 that they don't do work for. They call the client billing manager and say, "We want the labor employment work of X." What's the likelihood of success taking that approach? That client billing manager is probably getting 4-5 calls from other groups as well and is paralyzed.

So, I talk a lot about the incumbent advantage internally. If we have a white space, we need to assume that there's an incumbent, another firm in that space providing that service. It's not like their labor and employment needs are just not being met. There's probably somebody doing that work.

We need to reverse this and try to get our client billing managers of those top 100 clients to do a better job of having those broader needs-based conversations with their client on a regular basis.

If client billing managers go out there first and expand the conversation beyond their area of service, building a practice bigger than themselves, and start saying, "Tell me more—I don't think I've ever asked you about some of the bigger picture topics. How are you staffed? What pressures are you under? How are you feeling about the services you're getting? From us? From other firms?" We can always learn to be better business partners with our clients by having those types of conversations. We can also learn if they're really happy with their X counsel. Do they love them, are they happy, or is there a real pain point there? Now we can align our sales approach to something that actually is solving a problem that they have. It becomes "cross-service" not "cross-sell."

So that's the mindset that we want to build the culture around. It is not just a pitch for pitch's sake. Not a "me too" marketing, we do it too, here's our pitch book approach. I think we really want to change that mindset. So, that's the baseline for what we're trying to do.

We have done it a couple of different ways. We have had group sales training, which I will call basic fundamentals, looking at the sales cycle, understanding the various stages of relationships, and trying to get a consistent nomenclature without being too jargon-y and losing them along the way. You want to have a consistent way to approach the conversation, "So, tell me where you are with this relationship. Are you early stage? You've understood their needs a little bit more. Are you positioning? Where are you?"

If we can get a standard nomenclature around "so tell me where you are," that would be helpful in our overall conversation. So, establishing a common and consistent language within the firm around selling and business development is one desired outcome. The group training has worked for that kind of fundamental training.

Additionally, we offer more customized one-on-one training for a select group of lawyers. We might pick 15 or so lawyers to go through a program at a time, and try to identify those who have the right combination of acumen, aptitude, and attitude, and will be the highest prospects to achieve success from this kind of program. Are they interested in gaining skills in business development, willing to try new things? Have they already had some success and we can help them take it to the next level? For this group, we do some group curriculum sessions and proceed with one-on-one coaching with an outside coach for a 12 to 24-month period depending on the program.

Sales: Don't Give It Away, Wait Until You have The Engagement

(Silvia Coulter)

Don't go into analytic mode and give away the store before you have the engagement letter signed. Stay in sales mode because what you're going to do is educate the prospect and give them some good legal analysis and answers. And I'm going to come in as a competitor and close the business. We have to teach people when to take their foot off the legal analysis pedal and put it on the sales pedal.

Sales: Getting Hired is All About YOU

(Scott Kessler)

I look at selling professional services like a job interview and as we all know, the smartest candidate doesn't always get the job. In fact, most people are hired based on the answers to internal questions the interviewers are asking themselves as they meet with a candidate: "is this someone I want to work with? Do I like this person enough to spend time with them? Do I trust what this person is saying?" Once these questions are answered in the positive, then, and only then, will the candidate be hired for the job. So, ask yourself, "Are you someone people want to work with? Do people like you? Do people trust you?"

Sales: Good Lawyers Already Possess Sales Skills

(Mike O'Horo)

This may not be intuitive, but if you look closely, you'll see that good lawyers already possess sales skills. "Lawyering" skills *are* sales skills. I've shown this to the thousands of lawyers I've coached, so they could see that they don't need exotic new skills that require them to be something they're not, and don't want to be. Take a look:

Practice Law	Practice Sales
In the law practice model you proceed logically, establishing foundation and earning the right to advance. The client is actively engaged at each step and advances with you.	Sell exactly as you practice law. As in law practice you proceed logically, establishing foundation and earning the right to advance. The client is engaged at each step and advances with you.
1) **No premature solution, advice**.	1) **No premature solution, advice**.

Practice Law	Practice Sales
2) Ask probing questions to understand **business situation** and the people involved.	2) Ask probing questions to understand **business situation** and the people involved.
3) Explore **consequences**, magnitude of problem: a) Strategic/Operational; b)Economic; C) Emotional	3) Explore **consequences**, magnitude of problem: a) Strategic/Operational; b) Economic; C) Emotional
4) Alert client/prospect re: **additional issues**/concerns based on your experience with such businesses, matters. Explore *Cost of Doing Nothing*. Test for *Decision Imperative*.	4) Alert prospect re: **additional issues**/concerns based on your experience with such businesses, matters. Explore *Cost of Doing Nothing*. Test for *Decision Imperative*.
5) **Confirm** agreement on expanded understanding of problem/situation.	5) **Confirm** agreement on expanded understanding of problem/situation.
6) Describe solution **options** (categories) and likely strategic, operational, economic and personal ramifications of each.	6) Describe solution **options** (categories) and likely strategic, operational, economic and personal ramifications of each.
7) Based on shared description of what seems best suited to situation and to buyer, **advocate** category option to pursue and why.	7) Based on shared description of what seems best suited to situation and to buyer, **advocate** category option to pursue and why.
8) Ask client/prospect: **agree** with analysis/advice?	8) Ask prospect: **agree** with analysis/advice?
9) Ask client/prospect what (s)he sees as sensible next steps re: solution action.	9) Next steps: Coach prospect: a) critical mass of internal sponsorship required; b) logical decision Champion among Sponsors.
10) Agree **timing and method** of next steps. Client's/prospect's self-interest drives process.	10) Agree **timing and method** of next steps. Prospect's/client's/buyer's self-interest drives process.

Both lawyer and sales executive will generally follow the same steps in order to optimally serve the potential client. As you see, in sales as in law you proceed logically, establish a solid foundation, and earn the right to advance. The prospect/client is engaged at each step and advances with you. In fact, the prospect/client is actually leading the process, determining the pace of advancement.

Neither professional would consider premature solutions or offer premature advice (Step 1). Both ask probing questions to understand in great detail the business situation, circumstances, or problem and all the self-interest of all the key stakeholders (Step 2).

Both salesperson and lawyer will explore the consequences and magnitude of the problem in four impact contexts: (1) Strategic; (2) Operational; (3) Economic; (4) Personal Emotional (Step 3). As a result of what they learn through this probing, and based on their experience, both will alert the buyer/client of additional issues or concerns that need consideration (Step 4).

In step four of the comparative table, each explores a version of the *Cost of Doing Nothing*, i.e., must the buyer/client take action at all? In many situations, doing nothing is the most prudent choice, as any number of lawyers have advised clients. "Yes, you can sue, but it's expensive, risky, disruptive and stressful."

Before proceeding further, both professionals will confirm that the client agrees with the problem definition, as expanded by the professional's added insight gained from addressing situations similar to this (Step 5). With this solid foundation in place, salesperson and lawyer alike will describe various solution options, and the relevant implications of each (Step 6).

At this point, most buyers and clients will seek the professional's advice about which option makes the most sense. A typical reply sounds something like, "Based on what you've told me so far about the situation and the principals involved, and your interests, it seems like Option #2 makes most sense because [reasoning based on analysis]" (Step 7). Both will ask the client if she agrees with their analysis and their assessment (Step 8).

With that agreement we advance to Step 9, both the attorney and the sales executive coach the client through a reliable decision process that identifies the stakeholders ("critical mass of internal sponsorship required") who constitute a critical decision mass, and the logical internal champion to make that process fruitful (the "logical decision Champion among Sponsors."). The Champion's role is to guide the sales initiative and provide reliable intelligence. Motivation is that the Champion already believes that the Cost of Doing Nothing is too high and wants to see some solution embraced and undertaken. It's not that the Champion loves us and wants us to win; s/he wants something done, and right now, we seem to be offering the best decision process. Finally, they agree on the timing and methods of implementing sensible next steps, with deadlines that enable timely follow-up (Step 10).

Skilled salespeople and lawyers are invested in the *legitimacy* of the decision, not its content. They're pursuing a *decision*, not a "yes." Integrity requires both not to care which solution option the client chooses.

Both recognize that no-decision is the enemy. In the salesperson's case, no-decision perpetuates cost-of-sales; for the lawyer, it perpetuates follow-up that delivers little value to lawyer or client, at meaningful cost. [See also: *Sales: The Worst Answer Is "Maybe"*]

Sales: I Don't Use the Word "Sales"

(Erin Meszaros)

When you ask about the word "sales," I don't use it. It's not because I think it's bad. I think every firm's going to be different. You should know the firm's culture and determine what will drive action and results. I am more focused on getting the best results and less about buzz words in the industry. "Sales" won't work at my current firm, so I don't use it.

Sales: Our Firm Culture Is Comfortable with Sales and Selling

(Jeff Berardi)

Well, we've come a long way. At one time the term "sales" was a word you didn't want to use. You used the euphemism of "business development." Today, we are much more comfortable with the idea of cross-selling and cross-marketing and really that's why we've grown this platform to a global stage, so that we can do more work for clients across practices and across offices. So, the words "sales" and "cross-selling" are something that the firm's attorneys are comfortable with hearing and it certainly is a message delivered from the top with our chairman and global managing partner.

Sales: Re-Framing Attitude Toward Sales

(Steve Bell)

Some people ask, "How do you help lawyers address this whole concept about 'sales?' Because some people think of it as a pejorative." That's fascinating because the word "sales" is more of a lightning rod inside of a law firm than it is in the world of commercial law. Inside counsel who deal with salespeople every day in every way understand what sales is. They think nothing at all of the term. They know what a sales person does, and they know that the salesperson helps the company and the company's clients. Whereas the word "sales" can have a negative connotation inside of a law firm.

The word "sales" or "sell" is shorthand for consultative selling. It's not really sales in the way people stereotype it. Sales is an intellectual and emotional process of understanding the needs of an individual buyer and his or her company and fashioning solutions that address those needs. So it's consultative sales that we are talking about – not hucksterism.

[Author's note: To support what Steve Bell is saying, the etymology of the word "sell" comes from the Old English *sellan* (verb), of Germanic origin; related to Old Norse *selja* 'give up, sell.' Early use included the sense 'give, hand (something) over voluntarily in response to a request.']

Sales: Send Them to Sales School

(Marilyn Klinger)

[See *The Solution: Here's How You Turn Skilled Lawyers Into Skilled Rainmakers*.]

Sales: We're OK With The Word "Sales"

(Allen Chichester)

Our lawyers are comfortable with the term, "sales." It's been a long time since I heard anybody complain that they're not salesmen, or salespeople.

Sales: The Best Sales Training

(Steve Bell)

Here's a comment that might be helpful to you. The very best rainmaker training takes place at the point of sale. If you have a sales professional in the room with a lawyer at the same time doing a sales event, that's where the best sales training can take place. For instance, the salesperson can actually demonstrate in a live-fire exercise what it means to listen or to let silence happen, or to ask lots of follow-up questions, to achieve true understanding.

> The very best rainmaker sales training takes place at the point of sale. If you have a sales professional in the room with a lawyer at the same time doing a sales event, that's where the best sales training can take place. The salesperson can actually demonstrate in a live-fire exercise what it means to listen, or to let silence happen, or to ask lots of follow-up questions, to achieve true understanding.
>
> — *Steve Bell*

The most successful approach, in my experience, is to have non-lawyer sales professionals in a professional services environment, teamed with a lawyer. A lawyer and a sales professional, or business professional, go into the same meeting and they look at the meeting with two different lenses and they bring different strengths.

A salesperson is obviously not going to bring much legal skill to the meeting, and most often a lawyer's not going to bring much sales professionalism to the meeting and that may be required. You put those two together, and you have a formula for success.

It makes complete sense. It's wonderful because it takes the pressure off both parties. The salesperson doesn't have to know the legal world. Of course, they can't. They don't. They can't pretend to. The lawyer can't pretend he or she has had 10 or 20 years of sales and marketing experience, because they haven't.

My card says "sales" because that's the profession that I'm bringing into the room. I'm bringing understanding of the room and the buyer, and the lawyer may be doing that, but they're also bringing legal expertise. It's not brilliant. It's just simple. It's just me observing the world. I didn't think of anything original. [Author note: Steve Bell's title is Chief Sales & Marketing Officer.]

We have 550 lawyers and in the best of all possible worlds lawyers would have become so good at selling, at least consultative selling, that outside sales professionals would not be necessary. Imagine if you had somebody who was a great lawyer and a great salesperson in one. That would be fabulous, but currently we need the sales professional support and when we're fully staffed we have six salespeople.

We have experimented with different models as to how we distribute our sales professionals. We started with a geographic distribution, we went to practice area distribution, and now we're back to geographic distribution. You could say that in the way that all real estate is local, I think all sales is local, too.

Sales: The Word "Sales"

(Louise Muldoon)

Well, in reviewing your list of questions, I had a bit of a reaction to the word "sales," and not in the context that you might expect. People like to say that lawyers hate the word "sales" and it's a dirty word; and I actually think it's an inadequate word. It's an inadequate word, because it doesn't address the relationship between a lawyer and a client. What I mean is all the things we've just talked about: the empathy element and the good legal advice, and the very close working relationship with the client, sure, sales is a part of that. No one denies that that's part of it, but I think to use the term "sales" in a legal environment can be somewhat simplistic because what we deliver goes beyond that. "Sales" is not adequately descriptive of what is actually taking place. You need to talk about all the different elements. Look at the relationship. As lawyers, you want to be very integrally involved in the development of the client's business. To the extent that you use sales, perhaps you're talking about client sales. Any salesperson of quality and high integrity would like their client to be successful. I mean, the relationship is such that a lawyer wants their client's organization to be successfully achieving their goals. And, if you want to boil it down to sales, then you might ask, "What can the lawyer sell, or more accurately, recommend to the client to increase their success?" It's a much closer link, though, for lawyer and client. I think lawyers are now much more integrally involved in their client's businesses than they used to be, and very often factoring in their client's overall success in every interaction and recommendation. But, to look at it as a simple sale of a service is overly simplistic and I suspect this simplicity might be a reason why lawyers may react negatively to the word. The way legal services are evolving, the word "sales" is a very inadequate term.

Sales: The Worst Answer Is "Maybe"

(Steve Bell)

Well, I'm from Missouri. I like things to be very simple. When I sit down with somebody, it's important for them to know why I am there, what I am doing, and what I'm trying to get done. I think that the person I'm conversing with appreciates it, too. By being straightforward, both parties know as soon as possible if there is a true opportunity to work together, and resolving that basic issue as quickly as possible is very important. The second best answer when you are dealing with a prospective client is "no." The first best answer is "yes." The worst answer, by far, is "maybe". The world of law firms and professional service firms is paralyzed by opportunities that aren't resolved. If one can resolve the opportunity, yes or no, you can move on to the next thing, but everybody's target lists are all jammed full of responses that are a "maybe." It's not resolved and it wastes time. It wastes resources. It wastes energy. Resolution is key to this business.

Sales: Yes, I Use the Word

(Hans Haglund)

Yes, I use the word, "sales." If it bothers people, that's their problem, that's not mine. So, yes, I use the word "sales." That said, you have to be careful, because sometimes "sales" sounds to some people as if you are saying, "I want you to put yourself in a room and cold call a bunch of people." Selling is much more than that, and maybe I have a deeper appreciation for what it means, and others don't, but, yes, sales or business development, means getting out there and developing a process and approach that leads to business development. I don't use sales methodology ever in my terminology, but you're developing that approach to get the pipeline filled and ultimately developing a new client or new matter.

Selling Was Easy

(Matt Taylor)

Selling was easy. The reason I say it was easy, first of all, I had some success as a lawyer and then, I had all of these incredible people around me that I could sell and it just, to me, was natural to go sell because if you're proud of your law firm, and you're proud of the people around you; then, I think, that makes it an easy sell. Whatever organization you're in, you've got to know the people. You can't sell people unless you build up your institutional knowledge. So, I took it upon myself to learn as much as I could about every lawyer that I could in the firm that I thought had some real substance to them.

Social Media: Use It Wisely

(Despina Kartson)

Use social media. Make sure that just like your bio, your LinkedIn profile is current. Consider tweeting. Not everyone's going to tweet, but if you're comfortable with it, consider tweeting. It's a good way to share articles and news of interest with those who would be following you.

Engage in simple networking. Make introductions. If you maintain a business development mindset, you are always thinking when you meet a parent on the soccer field who is a hedge fund guru and you think, "I should really introduce him to Lawyer "X" at my firm. I might be a litigator, but we have a great hedge fund practice and I think I should introduce him to this lawyer in my firm." Also, make introductions between clients. If you have clients who are in a similar or related industry sector and you think it would make sense for them to meet one another, make that introduction. Make introductions to professional colleagues, friends, and other lawyers.

Solutions-Based Marketing

(Karen Bell)

We are trying to move, as other law firms are, to a more solution-based model. We spend a lot of time saying, "Although we don't sell litigation specifically to a client, we can sell a product around it. It might be a focus on privilege or it might be a focus on e-discovery and any number of ways to avoid litigation." That's why having our client teams connected to all of our firm's diverse practices is a better approach to devise a client-centric solution rather than a firm practice area-based solution.

Staff: How Many People Do We Have Supporting the CMO and BDD Function?

(Jeanne Hammerstrom, Hans Haglund)

Two of the CMOs and BDDs I spoke with indicated an average number of staff for every "x" number of attorneys. In response to, "How many full-time people do you have to support you?"

Jeanne Hammerstrom at Benesch: approximately 6 for 180 attorneys, or a 1:30 ratio. Hans Haglund at Blank Rome: 20 for 550 attorneys, or a 1:27 ratio.

Staff: Sales: Do You Have a Dedicated Salesperson that Supports the Inside Operation?

(David King Keller)

At least three of the people I interviewed for this book believed that in the future we could see a dedicated salesperson who attends the occasional client call with the attorney; and that it was feasible that in the future law firms could have a dedicated salesperson who makes calls on clients or prospects independently.

Stress and Anxiety: Find Your Sweet Spot for Lowest Stress Business Development

(Despina Kartson)

Do what works for you and do what's in your sweet spot. If you don't have the time to go out and entertain clients three nights a week, then don't do that and add this stress to your life.

Stress Reduction: Optimum Brain Productivity Requires Breaks

(Don Joseph Goewey)

For day-to-day productivity, right after knowing your area of law, you need to manage your state of mind. Nothing can put you off your game more than an unhealthy level of stress. In my new book, *The End of Stress*, I presented two positron emission tomography (PET) scans from the Mayo Clinic that show the impact of stress on the prefrontal cortex. The prefrontal cortex is the brain region every professional needs to function at optimum in order to succeed. The first scan shows a brain beleaguered by stress to the point of depression. There were far more darks areas on that scan than light areas. It reminded me of flying at night and looking down from 30,000 feet over farm country, where the lights of towns were few and far between. Stress hormones had shrunk the prefrontal networks and broken the connections between them, leading to a serious loss of brain power. The second PET scan shows a healthy brain unencumbered by stress hormones. This scan is lit up and pulsing with activity. It reminded me of the massive array of lights you see when flying at night over a large metropolis. The contrast between the two scans was dramatic, revealing the significant decrease in brain power that stress hormones can cause.

You asked me, "How can a lawyer, in one of the most stressful jobs on the planet, cope with the ever present bombardment of stress?" There is one simple thing a lawyer can start doing right away. This one thing can reduce your level of stress and, at the same time, sustain you at the top of your game (http://www.nytimes.com/2012/06/17/jobs/take-breaks-regularly-to-stay-on-schedule-workstation.html?_r=1&). According to research, this simple step will also provide higher energy and a steady flow of creative insights and help solve problems and inspire new ideas. And on top of all that, it is also an essential step in achieving mastery in one's chosen profession.

Simply taking a 20-minute break every 90 minutes will give you all of those benefits. Just consider, for a moment, stepping away from the computer, leaving the smartphone behind, and going for a peaceful walk, preferably outside amongst the birds and trees and sky, allowing your mind to relax and your brain to refuel. (I'll explain the refueling part in a moment.)

Goewey said that in his seminars, when he tells lawyers about the powerful benefits a break every 90 minutes can achieve, many of them say, "Impossible. I can't stop every 90 minutes." Moreover, they find it hard to believe that something as simple as a 20-minute break could be the key to becoming a star performer.

It's all about the brain, he explained, and a biological cycle called the basic rest-activity cycle (BRAC), which recycles every 90 minutes. During the first phase of BRAC, brain waves oscillate at a fast rate, making you feel wide awake and able to focus your attention. Your mind is humming. Ideas flow more easily and faster. The ideas your brain produces during this phase of BRAC are usually better, and you tend to have more of them. Your memory is also better and your brain generates what is called "memory consolidation," which is essential for envisioning something novel or learning something new.

But in the second phase of the cycle, brain waves gradually start to slow down until, in the last few minutes of BRAC, you begin to feel tired and somewhat fuzzy. Ideas can dry up and it's harder for you to connect the dots. You start to experience minor but annoying memory lapses, such as looking for something and momentarily forgetting what it was you were looking for. These are tell-tale signs of brainwaves slowing down.

During the fast brainwave phase, brain cells use sodium and potassium ions to generate electrical signals. These fast brainwaves burn through these ions, which means your brain requires a period of rest to recharge with new ions. The restoration process requires 20 minutes of rest, after which your brain has the fuel to run fast brainwaves once again.

Goewey added that related research also found that the 90 minute/20 minute cycle was how musicians achieved mastery. This research focused on young violinists who had mastered the instrument. It was discovered that these virtuosos universally limited the rigors of practice to 90-minute sessions, systematically distributed over the day, followed by a leisurely break, and sometimes even an afternoon nap.

People don't take breaks partly because of guilt, partly because they are afraid it will cause them to fall behind, but mainly it's because we've been conditioned to keep our nose to the grindstone.

It's time we change our mindset and embrace 50 years of research, which shows that working non-stop is an unproductive way of getting things done, and a hopeless approach to excelling, innovating, or achieving mastery.

So, I coach people to monitor their mental energy and to take a break when it starts to bottom out (usually after 90-minutes of sustained effort).

Here's how to take a BRAC break. It's simple: Step away from your work. Leave your smartphone behind. Go for a stroll outside or simply look out a window. Gaze at the sky. Watch the wind blow. Smell the roses. Look at the people you pass with non judgmental eyes. Let your mind and brain relax completely. While on a break, keep your mind open just enough to catch a creative insight that might emerge.

You'll return to your office free of debilitating stress hormones. You'll feel mentally refreshed, eager to get to work, and have a creative idea or two in your head.

If you can't imagine taking a break every 90 minutes, I suggest starting out with a break mid-morning and another mid-afternoon. Do this for a couple of weeks, and the tangible increase in brain function you'll experience will motivate you to add more breaks to your day.

[Author's note: Research behind Goewey's comments includes: http://www.nytimes.com/2012/06/17/jobs/take-breaks-regularly-to-stay-on-schedule-workstation.html?_r=1&; http://www.hreonline.com/HRE/view/story.jhtml?id=534356144; Benjamin Baird et al., "Inspired by Distraction:

Mind Wandering Facilitates Creative Incubation," Psychological Science (August 31, 2012), 1117–22, doi:0956797612446024.; K. Anders Ericsson, Ralf Krampe, and Clemens Tesch-Romer, "The Role of Deliberate Practice in the Acquisition of Expert Performance," Psychological Review 100, no. 3 (1993): 363–406; "Basic Rest and Activity Cycles," Polyphasic Society, http://www.polyphasicsociety.com/polyphasic-sleep/science/brac/; Arielle Tambini, "Persistence of hippocampal multivoxel patterns into postencoding rest is related to memory," PNAS, Nov 26, 2013; 110(48): 19591–19596; Kleitman, Nathaniel. "Basic rest-activity cycle—22 years later." Sleep: Journal of Sleep Research & Sleep Medicine (1982). Vol 5(4), December, 311-317; Nathaniel Kleitman, (1895-1999) physiologist and sleep researcher who served as Professor Emeritus in Physiology at the University of Chicago. He is recognized as the father of modern sleep research, and is the author of the seminal 1939 book Sleep and Wakefulness; and http://www.sleepwarrior.com/brain-waves-brainwave-entrainment.]

Stress: Handling the New Norm

(Erin Meszaros)

How do you handle a high stress, high anxiety environment, especially with the stress of the new norm in legal services? The lawyers that I've created a bond with personally I'll talk to about the stressful environment they are in, but I don't have a formal program to help them deal with their stress or anxiety. I believe the best thing we can do is stay as positive as possible when they get down about any aspect of their career from developing new clients to servicing old ones. I will offer several solutions to explore in response to what might be causing them anxiety which I hope helps to alleviate some of the stress.

Stress: Three 10-Second Tricks to Reduce Stress

(David King Keller)

Rainmakers evolve techniques to reduce unhealthy distracting stress. One of the quickest ways to reduce stress according to a study of 21,000 people is to take six deep breaths. This will lower heart rate and can move your autonomic nervous condition from the fight-or-flight sympathetic nervous system mode to the more productive higher functioning parasympathetic nervous system mode.

A yoga master I met at the International Symposium for Contemplative Studies sponsored by the Mind and Life Institute while waiting for a keynote talk by the Dalai Lama showed me two five-second tricks to reduce stress. One is to place the palm of one hand close to your face in front of your mouth and blow into the palm, putting all of your attention on the breath and the sensation on your palm. It's very focusing and calming. The other trick is to hold the palms of each hand on either side of your face at eye level and try to look at both palms at once. The challenge is enough to distract the amygdala part of the "lower primal" brain that is "stressed" and place you into a calmer mode run by the higher functioning, executive decision-making part of the prefrontal cortex areas of the brain.

According to an 2009 Ohio State University study (DOI: 10.1002/ejsp.607) simply pulling your shoulders back will help to put you into a more positive take-charge frame of mind.

Research using high-frequency magnetic resonance imaging (fMRI) scans by Yale medical director Judson Brewer, MD, PhD showed that a person *feeling* the sensation of the breath in the body was sufficient to take the brain out of a random wandering default mode and place the brain into a higher functioning state of calm focus.

Stress: What Form of Stress Do You Have?

(David King Keller)

Rainmakers constantly strive to improve their discernment and detect subtle nuances that can make the difference between operating with "high octane" mental processes or losing productivity due to a sputtering mental engine.

Discerning the "type" of stress you have can improve your productivity. My PhD dissertation included a listing of more than 100 mindfulness-based stress reduction studies. The word "stress" may be too generic to serve the purposes of a successful rainmaker. There is healthy stress that comes from taking on a voluntary challenge, such as a competitive sport activity or working out at the gym. There is also workload stress created by having a hard deadline and a great amount of work to accomplish before that deadline.

Then there is anxiety-based stress, which is usually based on fear of a future outcome that at this point is non-existent and hypothetical. Fear-based stress is the easiest to deal with because it is a mental construct, where you simply have to change the architecture of your thinking. You take into account future possibilities and you act accordingly in the moment to address those and put your attention in present time. You simply label your anxiety-based "stress" for what it is, fear. You tell your brain that the feared future does not now exist and I choose to be in the present.

Since the fearful message is primarily originating from the amygdala primal reptilian "fight-or-flight" emotion-based part of the brain, it helps to know that the amygdala matured when you were two years old and you can generally distract the amygdala the way you would distract a two-year-old or a crying baby. Take three seconds and give it something else to do that is the equivalent to a bright shiny object. Imagine a traffic signal light in your left palm. See the green, yellow, and red lights. Place the number one on top of the green colored light, a number two on the yellow, and a three on the red. Then take your right index finger and press those numbers in reverse order: 3, 2, 1. By the time you press the number one on the green light, your amygdala has been thoroughly distracted and quieted down, and now you've turned off that annoying "noise," or significantly reduced it, and like with any green light, you're good to go on with being productive in the present moment.

Stress: Work Hard, Play Hard; Physical Therapists Give Neck/Back Massages

(Adam Severson)

I share the stress of the business of law along with everybody else. It is the nature of the beast. The benefit of the work that we do for our clients is that they turn to us when they have very sophisticated and challenging issues. Whether they are on the receiving end of a subpoena or trying to negotiate an acquisition of a target company, the expertise and experience in counsel provides involves very high stakes. With high stakes, high risk, and high reward naturally comes stress. We have various activities to address stress within the firm. In our Nashville office, we have a physical therapist that comes in every other week to give a neck and back massage. In some of our offices, we have yoga classes that occur in the break room from 10 to 11 o'clock. We try to provide outlets for folks to relieve that stress. We also have recess. Every other week, we have a recess activity that might be something as simple as going to one of our conference rooms and playing a bean bag toss game. In other instances, we use these bikes that you can rent that are in bike racks in various parts of the city. You slide in your credit card, pick out a bike, and go for a bike ride. Then drop the bike off at another bike rack wherever you want. We try to keep a proper perspective. For me I try to make sure that we work hard and play hard. Because we spend so much time together, we better do our best to make sure we have a little bit of fun, as well.

Succession Planning: When Relationship Managers Must Change

(Erin Meszaros)

Succession planning is extremely important. It's one of the rainmaker's responsibilities as they develop the client. Starting 3 to 5 years out we need to make sure that we have a plan in place to keep the client institutionalized and moved to the next generation of leaders.

Summer Program: Basic Training for Future Associates and Future Rainmakers

(Wayne Hogan)

Law firms from around the world should know about applicants who have had summer program training like that provided by FSU's College of Law; and law firms should support their feeder law schools to have a similar program. These summer program alumni, in many cases, have been given a head start toward a successful career. The program includes speakers like mega rainmaker attorney Wayne Hogan, who provides insight into how to establish a successful law practice.

The brochure for the Florida State University College of Law Summer for Undergraduates states:

Since 1992, Florida State University College of Law has hosted its award-winning Summer for Undergraduates Program, which brings to campus undergraduate students from throughout the country for a month-long immersion into legal study. The largest and oldest of its kind, the primary goal of the program is to acquaint students with the study of law and to assist them in acquiring skills that will benefit their undergraduate and future law school studies.

During the four-week program, students are engaged in activities covering three primary areas:

Classroom Experience—Daily classes are taught by law school professors and writing instructors. Lectures simulate first-year law classes and familiarize students with the functions of the American legal system. Writing workshops help students to develop their writing and communication skills.

Law School Admissions Process—Students are given the opportunity to talk to the admissions staff and committee regarding the important aspects of the law school application process. This includes practical workshops on completing the application, writing personal statements, LSAT preparation, writing resumes and cover letters, financing law school, and individualized career planning.

Careers in the Law—While the program is academic in nature, there are a number of exciting and enjoyable activities that take place outside of the classroom, such as: visits to the Florida Supreme Court and local law firms, moot court oral arguments, and visits from prominent attorneys in a variety of practice areas; and in many cases the program includes a Capital tour where they're meeting with governmental lawyers, whether they are staff lawyers in legislature or working in the various cabinet offices, the governor's office, and the attorney general's office.

Thanks to the continued support and generosity of Florida State Law alumnus Wayne Hogan ('72), President of the Terrell Hogan law firm, and his wife, Patricia, the Summer for Undergraduates Program has a financially secure future. In 2000, the Hogans designated part of a $2 million gift to the law school to endow the program. Their 2003 gift of an additional $1 million allows the law school to permanently maintain the size of the program at approximately 60 students each year.

Eligibility—College students enrolled at two- and four-year institutions, in all majors and from all backgrounds, are invited to apply following their freshman year. We particularly welcome students from groups historically underrepresented in the legal profession. Because one purpose of the program is to help students direct their remaining time in college to best prepare for law school, only rising sophomores, juniors, and seniors are eligible to participate. "We have a reception," stated summer program benefactor Wayne Hogan, "and it's such a fantastic experience to have them come up and obviously, they say thanks, but they engage in a conversation about the practice of law and they've got every question in the book. My impression from that, and I know it's the case, is that they have had multiple interactions with lawyers who are out there in the real world practicing and learning about what it takes to build a law practice, what it takes to be a good associate within a law firm, the kind of work that's required, the social skills, the interaction skills, they certainly had that with fellow students and their various classes over the years as undergraduates, but this helps them understand that the law is not just a dry thing that you get lost in the stacks in the library, that there's more to it than that. It's a very human kind of work, that it's a people business . . . They learn that you can be out there in a law firm and then become engaged in the community and that's the way that you become known to people and then, if they are in need of legal services, they'll know to call you, or at least they might potentially think to call you . . . and so built into the program participants are a variety of ways that they encourage the students to get out and really engage the people around them." [See also: *Business Development Training: Summers.*]

Summers: Training: See also: Business Development Training: Summers

[See Summer Program: ***Basic Training for Future Associates and Future Rainmakers*** by *Wayne Hogan.]*

Talking Business Development with Attorneys

(Barbara Lauterbach)

You've got to build your case first. I think this is essential when working with attorneys. It's a matter of getting them to see that the whole process is information gathering, gathering your evidence, organizing it, presenting it, and asking for action and asking for the right action. There's a timing to it and it varies from situation to situation just like it does in front of a jury or just like it does in front of a judge.

Targeted Clients: One New Fast Way To Connect

(David King Keller)

Can RelSci speed up your connection to a targeted client? The reasons are countless, but a universal cause of opportunities missed and clients lost is the failure of law firms to exploit one crucial asset: "relationship capital," the web of connections the most accomplished attorneys have cultivated and developed throughout their career.

Relationship Science (RelSci) is a technology solutions company that works directly with attorneys and their firms to create competitive advantage from relationship intelligence. The RelSci Platform helps law firms capture and leverage their relationship networks with the decision makers that matter to their success. Their legal clients use the platform's curated set of more than 1 million organizations and the 4 million leaders affiliated with them to accelerate client acquisition and expand current business. There's a reason why Salesforce.com and others have invested over $100 million in RelSci.

Specifically, RelSci helps attorneys in the following areas:

Relationship Capital Dashboard: Attorneys can discover paths from their relationships to people and businesses they'd like to work with in order to find opportunities for warm introductions. Attorneys can also strategize how to intelligently grow their business networks with a bird's eye view of the industries, locations, and roles in which they may have the most access.

Research Tool: The platform's dossiers include actionable, research-grade information about attorneys' clients and prospective clients, including boards they sit on, professional memberships, education, work histories, deals, mutual relationships and more.

News Aggregator: The platform provides real-time updates on news mentions and professional changes that help attorneys to stay on top of their contacts and give them a reason to reach out, whether for clients, prospective clients, or firm alumni. These updates can include employment and board changes, company layoffs, M&A activity, donations and more.

Travel Assistant: Travel-specific tools help attorneys make the most of business trips by identifying acquaintances, clients, former colleagues and prospects that live in the cities to which they're traveling. [For a one-pager on RelSci for law firms contact david@kbdag.com. Author's note/disclosure: If you contact RelSci directly please use my name or use this URL: http://go.relsci.com/DavidKeller. I have a referral relationship with RelSci. Read more at *Cross-Selling: With Staff and a High Tech Tool*.]

The Solution: Here's How You Turn Skilled Lawyers into Skilled Rainmakers

(Marilyn Klinger)

My response to your question, "How do you turn skilled lawyers into skilled rainmakers?" is send them to sales school. Now, my question for you is, "Is there a sales school?"

[Author's note: Great answer and great question, Marilyn! Hopefully this book will act as a primer for any law practice business development sales school, or as a valuable training manual for any law firm executive charged with increasing their firm's professional service sales. A number of law firm business development trainers, coaches, and sales executives, all of whom are excellent legal sales trainers, are mentioned within this book and provide some of their best sales tips within these pages. Most of them offer a program that can be considered a type of "legal sales school." One example would be William J. Flannery, Founder of the WJF Institute, who is a former IBM sales executive. In addition, a call or email to the executive director at the international Legal Marketing Association (LMA) headquarters in Chicago, Betsi Roach, would secure a referral to the Board President of the nearest LMA chapter in your firm's area, and that Board President, a legal marketing specialist, would surely have a number of recommendations. Here's Betsi's email address: broach@legalmarketing.org, or email LMA at info@legalmarketing.org. This book also contains tips I learned as a trained XEROX sales executive having been successfully certified during my four years with XEROX in Professional Selling Skills (PSS) and Need Satisfaction Selling (NSS). In one case, to satisfy a client's need, I used my engineering and design skills to invent an accessory for XEROX's quarter million dollar reprographic machine. XEROX marketing informed me that my invention to help one client ended up solving problems for an entire class of clients around the world, which increased XEROX sales by $98 million a year. I see this book in a similar role, to turn skilled lawyers into consultants who can decipher the overlapping intersection of two side-by-side circles; one circle, the firm's resources, and the second circle, the client's needs; and can sell to that intersection, and/or convert that personal connection into a business friend and a referral source. My goal is to convert my sales training, three law firm business development books, MBA, PhD, teaching experience, and love of education into an adjunct professorship at one or more law schools to bring the business of law and the skills of legal sales into the law school classroom. The result would be law school graduates who have a much higher degree of awareness when it comes to the art and science of acquiring clients.]

Time Management: Business Development

(Peter Johnson)

I recommend having a time management and special follow-up system dedicated to business development. I'm computer literate, but I still have a number of systems that I use to support my business development time management, I recommend that an attorney or firm use at least two systems to track time dedicated to business development – which means you always have a backup system. Other people teach time management. I help them with follow-up, which is critically important, and I will always verify that there are time management systems in place dedicated to tracking business development.

Time: A Response to, "I Don't Have Time for Business Development"

(Stephen Fairley)

What am I saying to lawyers when they say, I'm so busy with my legal work, I really don't have time to do business development? My go-to response is either you can make time now or you'll have plenty of time later when you don't have any more clients.

You could be like the client that I had that walked up to me after one of my talks at the State Bar of California, a white-haired gentleman who approached me after I gave a talk. He looked kind of down, so I asked him what was going on. To which he said, "Well, your talk really triggered something in me and . . . I wish I had heard you 15, 20 years ago." He then said, "Well, Stephen, my practice has been going great for the last ten years. I'm a solo practitioner and I was bringing in about $600,000, $700,000 a year pretty consistently with me and a part-time paralegal." I said, "Well, that's really good money." He said, "Yeah, but my biggest client, the Yellow Pages, just filed for bankruptcy. And now my practice has gone from $600,000 to $60,000 in the last 60 days. And here I am, about 65 years of age and I was thinking of retiring in the next year or two and now all of a sudden I'm scrambling and I feel like I'm starting over again." I've heard variations of that same story and that same theme over the years.

So, to each one that says they're too busy for business development, I say, either you make time for business development now or you'll have plenty of time for business development later when you don't have any clients and Murphy's Law strikes more often than not, the worst possible thing will happen at the worst possible time. Right? Business development is a marathon, it's not a sprint. You need to put systems, people, and processes in place to help you do that and either you need to do it, or you need to hire someone to do it, or you need to outsource it, and have it done for you. The final option is don't do it. Right? You have four choices. One, do it yourself. Two, delegate it. Three, have it done for you; or four, don't do it. Too many attorneys today choose the fourth option of don't do it and they put it off and put it off, until something catastrophic happens, like they get threatened to have their equity taken away or they don't make partner for the second time in a row, because nobody told them that they had to be a rainmaker in order to be considered to be an equity partner or they go out on their own and two, three, four, five years later they're still banging their head against the wall struggling to break a quarter of a million dollars a year in gross revenue. Right?

So, you can't afford to stick your head in the sand and ignore it. You can't not do anything because it will always cost you more every single year that you wait. It will cost you more to get a new client this year than it did last year and it will cost you more to get a new client next year than it did this year, why? Because of the increase in cost of competition. The number of attorneys are not getting fewer, they are getting more in our society and there will always be an attorney or a law firm out there who is willing to do it for less than you can afford to do it.

So, you have the other three options, either number one, do it yourself, number two, delegate it to one of your staff members, or number three, have it done for you by outsourcing some or part of it to an outsource marketing company. There are certain things that you can't delegate and you can't outsource. You can't outsource building personal relationships with your potential referral sources. You have to do that yourself.

There are some things you don't have to do yourself. You shouldn't go about trying to learn how to build your own website. You shouldn't go about blogging because it takes up more time that you could be doing something else. You shouldn't go about trying to spend time on creating your own newsletter when you could delegate it for a few hundred bucks a month or outsource it.

> Business development is a marathon, it's not a sprint. You need to and either you need to do it, or you need to hire someone to do it, or put systems, people, processes in place to help you do that you need to outsource it and have it done for you.
>
> —*Stephen Fairley*

So, you need to decide what are you going to do? I work with a lot of very successful law firms and every single successful one that I've seen spends either time or money and the most of them actually spend both, but you have to do one or the other, either you have to spend your time and invest your time and do it yourself, or you have to spend your money and delegate it or have it done for you on an outsource basis.

Time: How Do I Find the Time for Business Development?

(David King Keller)

Making the 'impossible" possible. See section titled, "*Making The Impossible Possible, Finding Time For Business Development,*" an interview with Scott Kessler in my best-seller ABA book titled, *The Associate as Rainmaker, Building Your Business Br*ain.

Top Two Conversational Tools Every Lawyer Needs

(Tasneem Goodman)

Every lawyer needs to have a *business development* conversation that starts with the response to these two questions: "What do you do?" and "What's new?"

[Also read *Elevator Pitch: One of the Two Most Important Conversational Skills.*]

Touch-Points: How Many Times Does It Take to Get Business?

(Gerry Goldsholle)

When you ask me, based on my 40-plus years of experience as an attorney, "How many touch-points do you need, or how many times do you have to get into that top-of-mind position, with the potential client before you actually get work from that client?," I can't give you an answer to that. It seems to me, there has to be a match between the value you bring and the need the potential client has. But it's not only how much business the client would be able to give you now.

Let me use an example. If you're an insurance lawyer, and the client does not have an insurance problem now, you should keep on dealing with the friend or a colleague or buddy, keep on dealing with that person because he or his company may not have an insurance problem now, but undoubtedly, he is also networking with others and they may talk about an insurance problem they're having; and now because the lawyer kept in touch with his contact he or she knows you're doing that kind of work, and it becomes natural for that person to suggest you and now you're in the hunt. And so, it's not only direct business the people you know will give you, but it's the indirect business and introductions that they can provide that is really valuable in generating meaningful long-term business.

Training and Coaching and Business Development Support Resources

See *Business Development Training.*

Training: the Word "Training"

(David King Keller)

Be sensitive when using the Word "training."

You should know that some lawyers do not like the word "training" in the context of being "trained" in something. Some even find the concept of "being trained" repugnant. You may wish to avoid saying "Business Development Training" and merely choose to say, Business Development, Business Development Coaching, Business Development Best Practices, Business Development Tips, Business Development Strategies, Business Development Techniques, Business Development Workshop/Seminar/Meeting, Strategies That Grow Practice Revenue, or some other phrase suitable for your intended audience. Lawyers are wordsmiths and their opinions on how they parse a word should be respected.

Training: The Word "Training": An Action-Oriented Word

(Bill Flannery)

Anything that requires some physical action, doing something as opposed to just listening, is training. For example, Dallas Cowboy's training camp versus education camp. We train golfers. We train trainers. We train musicians and actors. The Army has basic training. The doing versus just getting knowledge is the clear way to explain why it should be training. Corporations call it sales training not sales education. Ask partners do they educate their associates or do they train them?

[Author's note: Bill Flannery is famous for his workshops where lawyers actually go through the actions of a presentation to a real General Counsel (active or retired). Then the lawyer benefits from the GC's feedback which she/he can take forward into the actual presentations they will conduct in the future to generate new business for the firm. When it comes to using a particular word, e.g., training, it only matters what you and your lawyer(s) feel and believe and simply respond to that reality.]

Trust Building

(David King Keller)

See discussion of a few techniques to rapidly build trust and rapport in my ABA book titled, *The Associate as Rainmaker, Building Your Business Br*ain. URL: http://bit.ly/1dAxob6.

Twitter: Tracking Client Info

(Jill Weber)

Do you want to see the Twitter posts about a client you are tracking?

That's the way Manzama works. It aggregates these news articles. I benchmarked it against Google Alerts, and Google Alerts are useful, but (A) you have to have a separate alert for every company, and (B) it doesn't always catch the breadth of what I find through Manzama, and so they are aggregating it from all kinds of publications. It's a subscription service. They cater to the legal industry, and then you can also pick specific industries if you want . . . In addition, Manzama tracks Twitter posts about companies, so if you have a key client you want to monitor—granted, you can do that separately on Twitter, but most attorneys don't have a Twitter account—with Manzama you can have the news stories and the Twitter feeds all in one place.

Value Proposition

(Scott Kessler)

The best way to state your value proposition is to start with the two words "I help," then follow that with "people" or "companies." Example: I help people injured on the job secure fair treatment for the damages they suffer.

Example: I help companies through the complex dangers and opportunities in a merger or acquisition.

Vendors: Managing

(Allen Chichester)

One expertise that I think is often overlooked in law firms is the ability to manage vendors. Having been a vendor most of my life in an ad agency, I know what it's like to work with someone who gets how to motivate me and get the best out of me, someone that makes me feel good about doing a good job. Honestly, it takes some experience to do it well, and often the law firm management of PR firms and ad agencies and graphic firms devolve down to the lowest level, to entry level people in the law firm and you get a terrible result.

Too often, vendors don't get enough information, or they don't understand what you're really trying to accomplish, or they're not brought in as part of the solution and they only see things at the last minute, or they don't get proper lead times, or you don't listen to them when they tell you what things are going to cost. When you manage vendors from a more senior perspective, guess what? You not only get better selections in terms of who you decide to use, but the results are almost always better because you're managing them better and they feel like they're empowered, like they're partners, so they lend you their perspective and expertise instead of giving you the minimum.

Visibility Roadmap

(Shanda Zavalsky)

We use a Visibility Roadmap. We'll put down the initiative, what the purpose is, who the targets are, and what the action is for each initiative. On the second page we have the Visibility Scorecard. This allows the attorney and our BD team to track everything that is done.

Vision: Does Your Firm's Vision Inspire Business Development

(Dave Bruns)

A vision needs to be realistic. Otherwise, it's just an empty platitude. It becomes a platitude when it doesn't mirror your brand or if it's so unachievable that it's not something that really makes sense. It needs to be a stretch, but it's got to be potentially achievable to effectively motivate.

Warning to Solos, Small Firms, and Small Practice Groups

(Gerry Goldsholle)

People are reluctant in corporate America, to recommend a one-person band. They want to know that you have support. For instance, if you're on vacation, if you're in court, if you're dealing in another client meeting, their needs will be addressed. They need to know it's not only you, you're not the Lone Ranger, you have Tonto besides you, and you all have a whole team of Tonto's in the wings ready to go. That's really important for the solos and small firms out there (and for the associate thinking of going on his or her own). They better have some breadth and depth, and relationships that they work with, on an ongoing recurring basis, so that the client knows she'll be covered.

If you're the best specialist in the world and you get laid up with an illness, you're on vacation, you have a family graduation to attend, the client's needs have to come first, and if the client doesn't think they will, you're not going to be their lawyer, and they are not going to be your client. Be sure to have backup, have relationships—have other lawyers. Make sure your client knows you've have these relationships, so they're never without representation. You need to be able to assure the client that they're always going to be covered, they're always going to be comfortable, and they're going to come first. You give them your cell phone number.

You're going to carry two cell phones. I carry a second cell phone. In case one is busy, or this one is AT&T, this is T-Mobile, so when I'm in Europe, I can get calls on T-Mobile because I can get back immediately. I get good coverage with T-Mobile in Europe, and I don't get good coverage there with Verizon or AT&T. It's a small investment to protect your client. Don't nickel-and-dime the clients. It's a big mistake. This is a long-haul relationship. If a client calls with a question that takes 20 seconds and your "Yes or No" answer takes 10 seconds, and you jot down one-tenth of an hour, you're going to get a client who is really ticked.

Website: Home Page as Magnet

(Karen Bell)

Turn the home page into a client magnet by offering an essential ingredient every client's legal team needs: CLEs. CLEs that provide critical and timely information in-house counsel need to perform their job properly, and their needs to fulfill standard CLE requirements. Offer the full complement using internal and external resources, just as long as they get their CLEs through you.

Put this "Client Magnet" on your website's home page: Offer free CLEs to all In-House Counsel, their Legal Team and the C-Suite executives: Put the "Seminars/CLEs" Tab on Website Home Page. [See *Client Professional Development: A Value Add That Sets Us Apart* by Karen Bell.]

[Author's note: I would suggest that mid to large firms consider labeling one of the website Home Page tabs "Seminars/CLEs," and if Home Page real estate is too precious let "CLEs" light up when the mouse is hovered over "Seminars." Why? Because client legal teams need CLEs but don't always need "seminars" per se.]

Website: How many Times a Week Do You Need to Refresh It?

(Larry Bodine)

Google made a big change in what appears in the first 10 search results and which websites they rank highly. Google wants original material and Google wants the website updated frequently, which makes sense. If you're doing a search, you want to see something that's original and you want to favor websites that are active.

Google likes a website that is refreshed two or three times a week. So, what I do now for two websites that I work with, I update their sites once a day. Here's another key fact. The more you blog, the more business you'll get. There's a direct correlation. Two or three times would be good, but every day is better.

Websites: Why Potential Clients Go There, Primarily

(Erin Meszaros)

Based on a recent client survey we conducted, clients come to our website to learn something specific about the skillset of an attorney, to look up his/her direct phone number, to confirm a referral from a friend which is all information found on the attorney bio pages. In addition, when we review our monthly analytics, the individual attorney pages are the highest percentage of pages visited.

I believe a law firm's website serves as confirmation. I don't think people do Google searches and then pick you because of what they read on your website.

You can, however, use your analytics to help identify a "viable" target which allows you in turn to feel confident pitching your services. One of our lawyers was recently asking about a particular company to target. We have a program that will allow us to pull up the companies who peruse our attorneys' bios and we noted this particular company had been looking at his individual page on the website and accessing certain sections of his bio page for a few weeks. This "confirmed" for him that the company was indeed a viable target as they were accessing his bio page and reading substantive content he was supplying.

Websites: Your Home Page

(David King Keller)

Your website's Home Page should have the four key elements of a verbal business card: Name, Value Proposition, Memorable mind-bite, and a Free Valuable Offer that helps to advance and solidify the connection.

Everyone who comes to your website should be offered an array of goodies that make them say "Yes" I would like that. [FREE Industry Reports; News You Can Use; Avoid These Costly Mistakes; Five Legal Elements for Every Shareholder Report; Report Available: Study Shows 30 Seconds Can Increase Bottom Line; or use the Karen Bell approach of a client development program that is supported by a "Seminars" tab on the McCarthy Tétrault LLP Home Page.]

Zest: A Trick to Add Zest

(David King Keller)

A simple little trick can add more zest and more enjoyment to a lot of your activities. Using a scale of 1 to 10 with 10 being ecstatic joy, simply ask yourself, "What would make this experience more of a 10?" Pause a moment and really explore the question, "What could I do to make this more fun?"

For example, maybe some mood enhancing but non-distracting instrumental music in the background. Maybe you add a favorite food, cookie, or your favorite latte to the experience. Possibly you set up a reward for yourself that will act as a real treat when you are done and that treat serves as a point in the future that literally helps to pull you through the present, like it has a rope around your waist drawing you to that soon-to-be pleasant experience.

Having something pleasurable to look forward to is a powerful motivator. Whether it be a movie, a great meal, a two-hour massage, or romantic date or your favorite sports activity? Maybe it's that email you'll be able to send to your client or partner that the project is done. Maybe you set up a golf game, tennis game, or a card game with friends. Maybe it's an after-hour drink with someone you haven't seen in a while but really enjoy talking to. Set up a date to go to a live stand-up comedy show.

Maybe you take six deep breaths to move your autonomic nervous system from the sympathetic fight-or-flight mode into the parasympathetic higher productivity mode. Maybe you enjoy a brief one-minute mindfulness practice and take advantage of the recent Max Planck Institute research that shows holding some loving and compassionate thoughts for a brief period of time can boost your biochemistry and enhance your mood. In all cases be sure to "toast" yourself with a real or imaginary glass of champagne for a job well done.

This question, "What would make this experience more of a 10," is a great one to ask participants before an event, a training, a coaching session, a retreat, or a client interview. It's a great question to ask your date or family members. Have more fun. What a concept!

Chapter 2's Index of Topic Titles

Chapter 3

Avoid These Disasters

Did you hear the true story about two different practice groups from the same firm who, unbeknownst to each other, approached the same company, and gave the client two different messages on how to approach the client's legal issues? Disaster!

Obviously, to the client, the firm and the practice groups looked like horses' asses. The practice groups proved the firm couldn't even organize itself, so why deliver a complex client matter to them? How closely aligned are your practice groups? How well organized and user-friendly is your Avoid These Disasters CRM software? Does the left hand know what the right hand is doing?

Is it possible that an attorney or new lateral in an office of your firm in a different city and state to have already done work for a company that is on your potential client target list and you not know? Are you set up to avoid this revenue drain and potential embarrassment?

In the previous chapter you learned to master a number of strategies and skills to become a better rainmaker but you can undo all of these positive steps in the right direction—quickly and dramatically—by making some disastrous mistakes. The following comments point out some of the more critical mistakes that need to be avoided in order to be successful in business development.

I recommend that you take a minute right now and go to the **Chapter 3 Index of Topic Titles** at the end of this Chapter on page 320 for a complete listing of disasters to avoid.

Review the egregious errors below to make sure you're not putting your success or your career on the line. Any comment without attribution to a specific contributor are those of this author.

Assuming The Potential Client Knows You Want Their Business.

(David King Keller)

My friend's wife is a writing editor whom I have hired on past writing projects. But it had been over ten months and quite frankly, she had dropped off my radar as I had been using some other freelance editors to review some matters for me. In a conference call we both were on the phone and before signing off he casually reminded me that his wife was still available and had time for more editing work and I sent her two assignments within the next three weeks. So, when lawyers tell me, "Well, you know, people know me. They know I'm a lawyer, so, if they have business, I'm sure they'll give it to me." Human nature doesn't work that way today. People need to be told regularly that you would like their business or the business from someone they can refer you to because you have the capacity and want to fill up the unused hours of yourself or the other members of your firm. Let them know you always have room for more business.

Bad Timing When Introducing a Legal Service

(Mark Usellis)

Some people approach a potential client with the idea, "I'll tell them everything I can do and maybe they'll hear something that will trigger a purchase." That's just wrong and ineffective. Or some might approach the conversation as, absent any knowledge of need or interest, "Hey, I'd really like to introduce you to our real estate lawyers." But that's an imposition on the client, right? You're asking them to give up time and then it's going to be awkward if they don't want to use your real estate lawyers or don't have any need for real estate attorneys. Again, put yourself in the other person's shoes and think about what would be effective.

> Let's say you talk to them about their company's priorities and challenges and they respond with,
>
> "Oh, we've got these real estate problems."
>
> "Oh, really? Well, how do you handle those?"
>
> "We have this firm that's been doing it."
>
> "Well, do you like those guys?"
>
> "Well, yeah, I like them, but the problem is, they don't have enough depth."
>
> "Oh, well if you have overflow work . . . Let me introduce you to someone and we don't need to displace this firm that you like, but if they have depth issues, we could be a second source."

You could say something like this second example, which is a whole different conversation from the first example. [See full discussion in Chapter 2, *Rainmaker Traits: Build Trust Instead of Annoyance*]

Being De-Equitized

A number of attorneys made equity partner, only to be de-equitized later because they failed to achieve any new revenue through business development. So, I recommend CMOs, BDDs, and managing partners have a talk with future and current equity partners and make the distinction between de-equitization and equitization. Lawyers, like the rest of us, like to avoid unpleasant things, and moving away from something can be as big a strategy and motivator as moving toward something. Moving away from being a de-equitized partner is a great motivator.

Being Late With a Matter Can Cost You Business

(David King Keller)

It is worth repeating: the client is always, always, always watching your every move and deciding whether they trust you more or less. If you're a "little bit late", then they're going to think you do not have the bandwidth to take on more, so they're not going to give you more work. Every time a client thinks "where's that matter I assigned to XYZ?" you're losing points. If those points add up you can lose extra business from them, and worse, you could lose them to a law firm that always comes in on time or early. What do you want your reputation to be? Nail biting up to the wire, or sleep-peacefully-at-night-because-[fill in your name]–is-handling-it.

Billing Practices That Lose Clients

(Gerry Goldsholle)

When you make a mistake, admit it. Not too long ago a major law firm was doing some work for us. The firm made a mistake and to correct it required over 30 hours of senior lawyer time. Rather than say, "Hey, we're not going to charge you for those 30 hours we had to spend to correct it," the firm billed us for the time. Needless to say, shortly thereafter we switched counsel.

There's a lawyer that I deal with in San Francisco I'll call "Denny." He is one of the most outstanding corporate lawyers in America, and he charges over $1,000 an hour. I don't mind paying $1,000 an hour, because when he puts in an hour or two of his time, I receive tremendous value, and it's not the hourly rate itself that is significant but the hourly rate of each lawyer multiplied by the number of hours the firm's partners and associates spend. So while a few hours of Denny's time is well worth it, were Denny to bring in a junior partner and an associate who spend lots of time on my matter, even though their rates may be far lower, it would increase my costs several times and I'd likely feel ripped off. From what I've seen, too many firms are overstaffing matters and spend an excessive amount of time on the matter that don't justify the excess work. Yet that's how too many law firms behave.

If you are the attorney who brought in the new client, and want to have that client become a source of recurring business, make sure that your colleagues are not trying to maximize how good they look to the firm by putting in lots of essentially unnecessary hours on your client's matter. Monitor the help that you're getting from your colleagues because otherwise your colleagues can destroy your relationship with the client. They may not fully appreciate how much the client can afford, or is willing to pay. What's important to you is not today's billings but the real value of a long-term relationship with that client. That's me speaking as a client and as a former billing attorney.

Don't nickel-and-dime the clients. It's a big mistake. This is a long-haul relationship. If a client calls with a question that takes 20 seconds and your "Yes or No" answer takes 10 seconds, and you jot down one-tenth of an hour, you're going to get a client who is really ticked.

[For more see Chapter 2, *Advice To An Associates: Going From Skilled Lawyer to Skilled Rainmaker: Part 2, Warning to Solos, Small Firms, and Small Practice Groups*]

Billing: Don't Bite the Hand That Feeds You

(David King Keller)

When billing, a proper description of the time spent on their matter is key to getting paid. I was at a seminar with a panel of in-house counsel and one of the things that this associate general counsel said was, "I got a bill that says, 'seven and a half hours of strategizing.' And the associate counsel told me, "I just sent it back. Wouldn't pay it. Just marked it off. And I thought, if they were smart enough to look at their bill and review my comments . . . then we could discuss it." He found that bill to be infuriating and alienating because it was just so non-descriptive.

Cultural Malaise

(Jeff Berardi)

It really is a culture issue. Our lawyers are the ones on the ground engaging in these client development activities directly and we are trying to train them and give them the tools to do it. So, if we can engage them and if they really embrace the brand and the value proposition, that's a pretty powerful force out there. If you don't have that business development consciousness enmeshed in the firm's culture, if people don't really get it and don't really want to engage in any of that, it's going to be hard to make much of a difference. It's really important that our lawyers are doing the business development directly. Doesn't mean that sometimes my team doesn't accompany them on pitches or sometimes make the introductions. At the end of the day, the salespeople are the lawyers. They are the ones selling the talent that we have and the experience that we have.

Depression: Is Depression Sucking Revenue and Life Out of Your Firm?

(David King Keller)

A January 20, 2014 CNN online published report stated, "One by one, state by state, bar associations say the tally is rising: Lawyers are killing themselves. The Centers for Disease Control and Prevention provided CNN with the latest available data on suicide deaths by profession. Lawyers ranked fourth when the proportion of suicides in that profession is compared to suicides in all other occupations in the study population (adjusted for age). They come right behind dentists, pharmacists, and physicians. Lawyers are also prone to depression, which the American Psychological Association, among others, identified as the most likely trigger for suicide. Lawyers are 3.6 times more likely to suffer from depression than non-lawyers." Source: URL: http://www.cnn.com/2014/01/19/us/lawyer-suicides/

Are you losing revenue, talent, or quality work time to stress, anxiety, or depression? If you are a sizable firm, the answer is probably "Yes." The actual question is "How much?" and "What can you do about it?" Founding partner of Brayton Purcell, Gil Purcell, points out that, "Lawyer depression is a big issue."

> "Lawyer depression is a recurring issue."
>
> —*Gilbert Purcell*
> *Partner, Brayton Purcell LLP*

See resources under "Stress" in Chapter 2 and additional information and resources in Exhibit 27, Stress, Anxiety and Depression.

Different People at Firm Presenting to Same Client and Not Know It

David Bruns, Director of Client Services, at Farella Braun + Martel LLP, points out, "When multiple attorneys are trying to go after a particular client. Why not put them all together and have them act as a team? Firms with multiple offices, increases this problem. Because how embarrassing is it when you're competing against yourself? That's where a firmwide standard business plan template can be a lifesaver."

Frequent Mistake When Conducting Business Development Training/Coaching

(David King Keller)

Many business development coaches and trainers make the mistake of teaching to the program as opposed to teaching to the individual attorney. A training program is only good if it is implemented effectively and with enthusiasm. So, the first order of business in any coaching or business development training program is to ignite the passion and motivation within the individual attorney. The way you do that is to invite the attorney to remind him- or herself of what motivated him or her to get into the practice in the first place and what additional motivations have been discovered and added since then. To optimize the learning experience that is being provided with coaching and training is to optimize the mind that you are seeking to engage; to do that is to create an enthusiastic mental attitude on the part of your coachee/trainee and the way to do that is to support the attorney in getting into a mental state and frame of mind to passionately embrace what you are about to confer. The following 10 questions can help achieve that goal. The first six can be used in a group training session. The last five questions are best done in a 1:1 coaching session.

A trainer in a group training should break the group into dyads to facilitate quick and personal ways to answer the first six questions. If time does not allow the dyads, ask the lawyers to place the answers in their training journal.

(1) What motivated you to go into law?
(2) What is exciting about the legal work you are currently practicing?
(3) Who benefits from your practice as a lawyer?
(4) Are there people who benefit from your law practice that are not clients and, if so, who are they and how are they benefited?
(5) Are there people who benefit from your income as a lawyer other than yourself and, if so, who are they and how?

(6) Describe three of your favorite law practice experiences. (Best done 1:1 or in a dyad breakout).
(7) How would you change your practice to make it even more exciting and more enjoyable?
(8) On a scale of 1 to 10, with 10 being sheer ecstasy, what number would you give your average workday and how could you tweak your current workday to make it more of a 10?
(9) What, if anything, is missing from your work-life balance?
(10) If you could change your practice in any way to make it more enjoyable to you, how would you change it?
(11) If you could pick any client at all, describe three of those ideal clients.

How to Lose a Client Fast: Bill Them for the Origination Bonus

(David King Keller)

This mistake can get your firm fired by in-house counsel no matter how well you are doing.

You can instantly alienate GCs and in-house counsel by making this mistake. A director of legal operations for a global tech firm based in Silicon Valley, Palo Alto, California, told me that it infuriates her when she gets wind of the fact that their company is paying for the firm's finder/originator bonus system or that there is a billing attorney at a meeting who is simply a "finder" and not working on any of the client's matters being discussed.

Yes, you want to reward originators of firm business, but don't let the client get wind that even one dollar of their bill is going to finance some internal finder's fee bonus program. This Silicon Valley in-house counsel indicated a fury at a level that would seem to look for reasons to quickly terminate that relationship. Keep your origination bonus system strictly confidential. Make sure anyone at a meeting is actively engaged in the matter at hand. Let your relationship manager stay away if she/he isn't directly involved as a billing attorney on the matter being reviewed unless it is abundantly clear that their time is not being billed.

One bonus method that can avoid a direct dollar quid pro quo relationship to client's bill is to use points where those points translate to a share of end-of-year profits, or a share of a percentage of a firm's originators' bonus category within the end-of-year profits. This way, a client can't get wind of a dollar amount associated with someone "finding" them for you because it's all based on points. Though, there is no reason that the "points" cannot relate to the amount of billed revenue or realized income. You *must* reward originators and finders as ethically allowed, but keep that knowledge internal and never accessible by the client. You can have a relationship partner who is friend with the client, but never allow that partner to bill for anything other than obvious and clearly defined work for the client.

The danger is getting into an informal chitchat session with a client over drinks and letting it accidently slip that so-and-so is being financially rewarded for somehow bringing the client to the firm.

Most in-house counsel work for companies that compensate salespeople for originating a sale. So, sales commissions are not alien to their culture by a long shot. But their company never bills their client for that salesperson attending a meeting simply because the salesperson made the original sale to that company at some prior time. Don't pad a bill for any reason, right?

Ignore YouTube at Your Peril

(David King Keller)

According to a Larry Bodine blog post on July 24, 2014 YouTube is the Second Largest Search Engine on the Internet.

More than one billion unique users visit YouTube each month. A compelling reason for lawyers to record video is that YouTube reaches more US adults aged 18–34 than any cable network and it is the second largest search engine, after Google. Research shows that more than two-thirds of adults prefer to consume content through video than through any other media format. Every 1 of 2 users on the Internet is on YouTube. If YouTube were a country it would be the largest in the world after China and India. How are you reaching this vast audience that includes many of your potential clients?

Ignoring Eric Schmidt's Advice on Coaching

(David King Keller)

Eric Schmidt, CEO of Google, was asked in a Fortune TV interview, "What was the best advice you ever received?" To which Schmidt responded, "Well, I've received lots of advice. One that comes to mind is to have a coach. My board member John Doer said to me 'You need a coach.' I said, 'Why would I need a coach? I'm an established CEO. Is something wrong?' He said, 'No. No. You need a coach. Everyone needs a coach.' So, Bill Campbell became my coach, which has served Google very well. Every famous athlete, every famous performer has somebody who's a coach. Somebody who can watch what they're doing and say, 'Is that what you really meant? Did you really do that?' They can give them perspective. But one thing that people are never good at, is seeing themselves as others see them. The coaching really, really helps."

To see Eric Schmidt's live interview answer, go to https://www.youtube.com/watch?v=kngyyeMel5c.

Language: Are You Really Speaking the Same Language as Your Potential Client?

(David King Keller)

Research at Stanford University in 2005 demonstrated that there are non-verbal cues that can create trust.

There is "surface" English, which the majority of people use when communicating. It involves speaking English with minimal attention to all of the cues you are sending and the other person is receiving, and all the cues the other person is sending are on multiple levels (words, tone, inflection, phrases, predicate mode, body posture, breathing, eye movement, beliefs expressed and implied, concerns that are obvious and implied, clothes, jewelry, props, surroundings, and much more); and all of these folks are feeling confident that they're speaking the same language as the other person. Entering into a dialogue without having a finely tuned multi-channel radar, in today's competitive environment, is being haphazard, unprofessional, and very, very risky. Knowing your area of law inside and out is a given.

On a just below the conscious level, your audience is looking for "cues" that you can be trusted, or are part of their self-defined "people I can trust" with my life, my reputations, my job security or whatever "trust" means to their brain, both their amygdala and their prefrontal cortex. To survive, early homo sapiens formed security groups, or tribes. That "tribal" mentality runs deep. Early tribes from part of an area did not speak the same language as those from a different geographic area. Today we call those areas countries, but only an amateur in neuroscience or communication thinks they are speaking the same language as another by conversing in the "surface" version of the other person's language, meaning just addressing gross interpretation of the words being spoken. We understand that northerners and southerners have different accents; but there is a lot of truth in that old movie scene where the actor says "you're not from around these here parts, are you, fella?" In New York, this might mean a matter of a different borough, or even just a few blocks, where people can guess whether you're from the Bronx, Brooklyn, or Queens, and so on, and thus determine which "tribe" you're from. You open your mouth and instantly, the other person's brain is computing "trust/don't trust," and moving their internal reaction within the wide spectrum in between.

You can be a lazy communicator and hope your words, phrases, and accent "land" in that part of the brain (the amygdala) that says "Ok, he's/she's safe . . . for now. So far I haven't gotten any danger signals." Where does that "gut" feeling come from? A good deal of it comes from the reptilian/primate part of the brain that is ultimately in charge of survival, the amygdala, the primal fight or flight part of the brain.

Whether it's a client, potential client, trial judge, or your managing partner, everyone speaking English is actually speaking a sub-dialect of the English you speak. You are not a professional communicator until you've mastered the art and science of speaking the other person's "dialect", and I am not referring to their "accent" (unless you can use it and come off as being authentic and not mimicking). I am referring to how their conscious and subconscious processes every iota of data that you are communicating, both verbally and non-verbally.

However, the matter doesn't end there. Just as someone from their own "tribe" can lose the honored position of being trusted, you can do everything possible to speak the other person's dialect and still run afoul of some missed cue. The masters have a calm center that can empathicly tune in to all the messages that surround the words. Ask the firm to sponsor a number of lunch and learns on the unspoken message, bring someone in to present during a retreat, and secure a few great books, podcasts, webinars, and articles on the topic. Your competition is doing this. And many savvy clients can tell if your radar only receives a very narrow bandwidth.

Lateral Miscalculation

(Silvia Coulter)

Rainmakers who have built enviable books of business sometimes find themselves lateralling over to another firm and some of their clients aren't going with them. Now they've got to build part of their practice all over again. As some firms find out, gee, this person isn't living up to what we thought he or she could do. Part of that is because the lateral may have been managing some old client relationships for a long time and they are not aware of changes in the buyers in today's market. It's no longer necessarily the guys at the golf club or whatever worked when they built their practice. It's new faces, new names, new buyers, educated buyers, and very savvy competitors. All of those factors come into play. Why are they trying to make the square peg from yesterday fit into the round hole of today? Again, it's making sure that we help them understand how to reach potential clients and communicate to these new buyers in their language. Otherwise, those clients whom they think are loyal but in reality are not loyal, will stay with their existing firms.

Law Firms: Look for Law Schools Preparing an Attorney to Be Business Savvy

(David King Keller)

Law schools take note: Avoid the disaster of preparing your graduates to be unemployed, or for some, something worse, a job laden with excessive stress because they do not really understanding how to develop a practice from a business development standpoint. Law students want to learn "the business" of law and real-world strategies to grow a law practice. Law firms must include whether the potential hire has had law practice business development training and related skills when hiring a new associate.

Missing Vendor Expertise Opportunities: Capable Vendors But Incapable Staff

(Allen Chichester)

One expertise that I think is often overlooked in law firms is the ability to manage vendors. Having been a vendor most of my life in an ad agency, I know what it's like to work with someone who gets how to motivate me and get the best out of me, someone that makes me feel good about doing a good job. Honestly, it takes some experience to do it well, and often the law firm management of PR firms and ad agencies and graphic firms devolve down to the lowest level, to entry level people in the law firm and you get a terrible result.

Too often, vendors don't get enough information, or they don't understand what you're really trying to accomplish, or they're not brought in as part of the solution and they only see things at the last minute, or they don't get proper lead times, or you don't listen to them when they tell you what things are going to cost. When you manage vendors from a more senior perspective, guess what? You not only get better selections in terms of who you decide to use, but the results are almost always better because you're managing them better and they feel like they're empowered, like they're partners, so they lend you their perspective and expertise instead of giving you the minimum.

Mixed Business Development Messages to Associates

Associates report getting mixed messages. "I tried to join this specific group to expand my business development capabilities and they never let me go to their lunch-and-learn meetings because they're always keeping me in the office during lunch."

Never Do This

Never answer the question, "What do you do?" with "I'm a lawyer." That's a conversation stopper. [See Chapter 2: Elevator Pitch: Never just say, "I'm a lawyer."]

Never Let a Client See Low Tech IQ

(From In-House Counsel Summit Article by David King Keller and Jeffrey Silber)

In a Palo Alto meeting hosted by the Legal Marketing Association billed as the "In-House Counsel Summit," a panel of three legal leaders from prominent Silicon Valley hi-tech companies moderated by David Bruns, director of client services at Farella Braun + Martel LLP, spoke to an audience of more than 50 attendees about "Rising Above Your Competition—What Today's Tech Industry General Counsel Expect From a Law Firm." One of the relationship-killing traits of a firm that would not be rehired was that of costly low-tech IQ. These Silicon Valley counsel were referring to basic Microsoft Office skills like the Word task of global Find and Replace. Examples were given of an associate billing two hours to search a document for one word that needed to be replaced with a different word, when Word's global Find and Replace is able to do that in less than five seconds. Other examples were given of lawyers not knowing basic Excel and PowerPoint skills. It's gotten so bad that one in-house counsel, Casey Flaherty of KIA, has developed a basic technology awareness test that any lawyer working for his corporation must pass prior to being retained or being placed on a consideration list.

> Never exhibit low Tech-IQ about MSFT Office. An associate billing two hours to search a thick document for one word that needed to be replaced with a different word when MSFT Office WORD's global Find and Replace would do that in less than five seconds. Example related by:
>
> —*Lisa Konie, Director, Legal Operations, Adobe Systems*

Never Tell a Lawyer How to Conduct Business Development Before You Do This

(Sally Schmidt)

Figure out what your lawyers like to do.

Prioritizing business development activities is just helping them figure out what they like to do because they're going to be more inclined toward things they enjoy. So, when people tell me—as one young woman did—she said, "I'd rather teach 100 hours than take someone to lunch" . . . my idea there is that she's not real big on networking and let's find other ways for her to get out there. Because if you can find what people like to do . . . If someone loves to write [for example] . . . I'll say, "Well, let's think about a blog or let's think about a quarterly update or, you know, writing a series of articles. Some things may be more effective than others, but they're all going to be more effective if you're targeting the right people and doing something you enjoy. So, it's a lot about just finding them something that they like, that they're going to commit to. Something that's efficient, and there's lots of different options.

[*Author's note:* Sally is right. Years ago some would ask, "What floats your boat?" Today we might say, "What would be so much fun, that you couldn't wait for the next day to start so you could do it again?" Ok. Passion. Forget about work or the law for a minute, or include legal work, and answer this question. What do you absolutely love to do? What else? Ok. What else? Once you have that list fully flushed out, then review the list for anything that could include business development within it. Virtually *anything* that involves other people may have a business development niche within it. If not, what comes as close as possible to their passion that can include business development? If "10" is ecstatic joy, then on a scale of 1 to 10, how can we make this business development activity more of a 10? If you love going to church, what about the church board or some church-related function that puts you in touch with your target audience or people who can refer you to folks in your target audience?]

Not Seeking Client Feedback on Your Legal Service Has Multiple Risks

(Sally Schmidt)

For the top 10 clients, it might be some sort of a client feedback process where somebody goes out and talks to them and says, "What do you think of the firm? Are there other opportunities? Is there anything the firm could be doing for you that it's not?" From my experience over the years, about 50 percent of those interviews result in new business. So that, to me, would be job one.

Overlooking A Bonus Opportunity

(David King Keller)

What?! You don't bonus for origination by a non-billing attorney?! Gosh, ask yourself what's more likely, actions that are rewarded or actions that take up your time but get you nothing?

Do you just pay a one-time bonus to the attorney finder-originator-introducer of a new client who keeps sending checks in year after year after year and helps you retain very valuable attorneys and staff? What is an extra million a year for 10 years' worth to you? Why not reward the gift that keeps on giving with a gift that keeps on giving? Do you really buy the argument that attorneys will do it "for the greater good"? Do you really believe the argument that "but for the excellent service provided by the working/billing attorney the client would not have come on board or would have left, so, all the credit goes to that billing attorney"? You no doubt have heard the expression, "100 percent of zero is zero."

Most clients take "excellent legal skills" for granted, and certain legal work is now viewed at the commodity level. Competition is fierce. At last glance, law schools were graduating 45,000 law students a year, with openings for only 25,000 a year. Clients know this. They know your firm is not the only fish in the sea. You know that as well. What you cannot afford to take for granted is an opportunity provided to you to deliver your firm's excellent legal skills to this client. Whichever attorney brought you that opportunity, whether by chance conversation or by a lifetime of association, the reward must be fast, clear, emotionally gratifying, in substance relative to the new business, and ongoing as long as that new revenue stream continues to deliver to your bottom line. Yes, ok, maybe over time you decrease the amount of the reward if that attorney does zero to keep the relationship going. But don't look a gift horse in the mouth, or you'll just end up seeing its rearend as it walks away toward greener pastures.

Remember Pavlov: reward behavior you want repeated. Ring that bell! And keep ringing that bell as long as the new gold keeps jingling as it falls into your pocket. Another firm would have paid a lot more than you ever will for that revenue-generating lead that got away to you, their competitor. What message are you sending to every member of the firm? Before you answer that, ask yourself, "What's an extra $500,000 a year, $2 million a year, or $20 million a year worth to you?" And, yes, SalesForce says they have a program that can easily track that for you.

What is the residual long-term value of a new happy client? Might that client provide other matters? Might that client become a raving fan referring you to new business from their friends? What is the revenue multiplier factor of a new client? What is the revenue loss factor had that client gone to a competitor? Should you bonus the attorney "finder" of that new client for referrals by that new client to other new clients? What bonus strategy is going to increase your bottom line the most over time?

Overlooking an Industry-Based Marketing Group Opportunity

(Sally Schmidt)

Another opportunity for firmwide revenue growth that I love is industry marketing. You may review your clients and find 10 that are in the food and beverage industry. So you need to ask, "What are we doing to use them as a platform to get more business in the food and beverage industry?" Or, hospitality. Or, energy. Or, whatever industry grouping may apply. Law firms traditionally haven't been very good at looking at their clients that way; they tend to look at them from a practice group standpoint and try to market tax or try to market real estate as opposed to what the clients need. So, a lot of times, we'll help a firm set up an industry-focused marketing group, for example, create a new sports law group or a new hospitality law group—and it's interdisciplinary. There are usually very good opportunities, because we might have a contractor that we're doing litigation for and it's a family-owned business, but we have never talked to them about succession planning. So, you start to bring lawyers from different practices together around client types. The idea is to get the firm to think "client types" and "industry types." This creates a cross-selling mechanism right within the structure. In fact, you don't even have to talk about cross-selling if you have the right people on the team. Put it together prospectively, thinking about, for example, what any life sciences company needs—from patents to product liability to whatever—and then have all of those people on the team.

Potential Future Scenario That Holds Risks if a Firm Isn't Careful

(Sally Schmidt)

I believe it makes sense to align yourself with other professional service companies that don't do what you do, but do what a lot of your clients need . . . Many companies would appreciate a one-source solution to various common business needs. I think it could be a very smart move.

I can give you an example. We did a focus group for a client of mine who does a lot of a middle-market company work. We had a number of companies in the market participate and they were not necessarily clients. It was interesting because they basically said that they don't care where they buy their legal services. They don't care if they are offered by an accounting firm. They like the idea of simplicity. So, as we see more people dip their toe in the legal market, it could be scary if we aren't thinking ahead of them. [See full discussion in Chapter 2, *Future Trend: New Opportunity: New Risk.*]

Potential Time Waster: Meetings: Who Is Selling Who?

(Sally Schmidt)

Many attorneys might be thinking they're doing a lot of marketing because they're going to a lot of lunches, but it's because they're getting invitations from brokers or insurance agents and different people that want to see them, but not necessarily the people the lawyers need to see in order to grow their practices.

[*Author's note:* If you find yourself in a meeting with someone who is not a potential client convert that person into a referral source. Ask the vendor/contact how she would sell your practice. Also ask the vendor, using the Milton Erickson pre-question set-up for three leads for your business followed by a Pavlovian enhancement. (Read more at Chapter 2, *Rainmaker Traits: Convert the Vendor's Sales Pitch into a Referral Source*). Lunch saved!]

Quickest Way to Lose a Business Opportunity: Outdated Bio

(David King Keller)

I met a founding CEO for a fairly mature and successful startup (with global companies already signing up for their unique product). He was now looking for an attorney to help them with a merger, acquisition, or an IPO. I called one of my IP coaching clients who is a partner working for a well-known law firm that has a substantial presence in Silicon Valley. My client referred me to his capital markets partner, saying that the partner had more than 25 years of experience in that area. The startup CEO and I pulled up that partner's bio on the website and we both had the same reaction when the most recent information in his bio referred to the Palm Pilot: "WTF, this guy is yesterday's news and is not current with what's happening today!" In fact, this attorney may actually be one of the brightest capital markets minds in Silicon Valley, but the startup CEO would never find out because he said he would look to other resources for his legal needs without even making a further inquiry into anything about that specific partner. It's really too bad because at a minimum, that partner's bio could have put that information within a contemporary context, explaining how his past experience assisted his current clients in today's market. But unfortunately, that was not the case, and that partner will never know how close he came to getting a call for a great capital markets opportunity.

Risk of Losing Control of Your Multi-Office Marketing and BD Staff

One of the things that tends to happen in law firms is that marketing people who are working in an office away from HQ tend to identify more with that office than with the marketing group or the firm overall. So you tend to see silos get created, or cultural hot spots.

Saying, "Just Figure It Out!"

One of the things we hear from associates, for example, is "how do you expect me to put one more thing on my plate when I am crunching the kind of hours I'm crunching?" We have to approach that with some sensitivity because they are under a lot of pressure, but at the same time, there are a number of associates that have done it and it's better for them to hear from those associates than people who have never been an associate. They have to hear it from somebody that has credibility and not necessarily a partner who says, well, if you want to make it, you better figure it out. That's not helpful. Don't say, "Just Figure It Out!" Have one of the associate's peers, someone at their exact same level, give them examples on how they've done it.

Sitting on News?

Are you sitting on news that could make you top-of-mind to clients, potential clients, friends, alumni, and referral sources? Blast that news out there in various ways, including using something like **Adrian Dayton's ClearView Social** to create a scalable **social** marketing tool.

Stop Wasting Time on Meetings That Have No Business Development Value

(Sally Schmidt)

I find sometimes that what the attorneys are doing for marketing is being so poorly done that they shouldn't even do it at all. They think they are marketing, for example, by going to a chamber of commerce lunch or something like that, but they get there late, they sit right down at the table, they miss the networking time, they listen to the speaker and, as soon as he is done, they get up and run back to the office. They haven't used any of the opportunities in that situation to network or build relationships. [See full discussion in Chapter 2, Business Development: Finding The Time.]

The Expensive CRM with All the Bells and Whistles That Isn't Being Used

(Sally Schmidt)

The key is that you don't want to buy more than you need. And that's what I find firms do. They'll invest in some six-figure CRM and it's only being used by the marketing department. Many firms are like that. The CRM is just being used to generate lists for materials that go out and for seminars and activities like that. The whole point of CRM is for everybody to manage their relationships. But if that's not happening then I think it's not worth the money.

The Trap of Telling a Client or Prospect that You're Really, Really Busy

Telling a client you're really busy may make you sound important to yourself, and even to them, but it can cost you business.

Be sure to qualify any "busy" statement with "and we still have plenty of time to work on matters I or my firm might be able to help you with." If a client hears you are "really busy" and you're a little late on one of their existing matters, then, they may decide you're too busy to be sent more work.

If a client is asked, "Would you recommend them to others?" They might say, "Well, you know, I like them enough to do that, but I'd hate to do it if it means it's going to pull them away from my matters because they're already really busy."

Don't ask for a referral unless you have clear feedback that the client is assured it won't distract from their work. Getting their work in early (versus just on time or late) will send the message that you, indeed, have extra bandwidth to take on more work.

Think like a client: This lawyer did a good job but was late. How does that make me look to my boss? What if I give them another matter that has a do or die deadline, a critical business deadline, does this lawyer have the time to get it done on time? I may need to be testing out a back-up lawyer to cover my reputation and protect my job and my business. The message must always be, "Thank you, and I'm ready for more."

Websites: Don't Get Caught With a Low "Sticky Factor"

(David King Keller)

How many gifts are you offering just for visiting your website? If "none," you're losing business and valuable mind-time. Gifts your website can include might be articles, webinars, CLEs, e-books, "Third Friday" Lunch and Learns for In-House Counsel, etc.

Websites: Home Page Should Have the Four Key Elements of a Verbal Business Card

(David King Keller)

Every law firm should consider the following for their home page: name, value proposition, memorable mind-bite, and a value offer that advances the connection. Plus an obvious "Contact" tab on the opening screen. I cannot tell you how many websites make you search or scroll around to find that "Contact" button.

Everyone who comes to your website should be offered an array of goodies that make them say "Yes, I would like that." [FREE Industry Reports; News You Can Use; Avoid These Five Costly Mistakes; How to Look Good to Your Boss/Shareholders; 30 Seconds That Can Increase ROI and Bottom Line, etc.]

Many value propositions start with "We help . . ."

Chapter 3's Index of Topic Titles

Chapter 4

Summary and Conclusion

My goal in writing this book was to provide you with the definitive guide to business development for lawyers. From the contributors to the editors, everyone involved in *Building Rainmakers* hopes that this book becomes a valuable resource that you can refer to throughout your professional legal services career, and then serve as a gift you can pass on to others who are facing the classic issues addressed in these pages.

There are 400+ business development strategies presented in this book. Here are just a few:

- **Make client-centered face time a priority.** The single most productive rainmaker activity with the greatest ROI is face time with individual client decision makers. This is where client-centered, not firm-centered, conversations should take place. To achieve this, the client or potential client should be doing most of the talking because you should be asking the right questions to draw out the client's known and unknown legal needs. Sounds simple enough, yet how much time, energy, and money is spent on other activities?
- **Take a full-service, full-firm approach to every client.** Two big mistakes a law firm can make are: one, not knowing what percentage of the client's total legal billing you currently enjoy, and two, not taking a full-service, full-firm approach to every client. There are some partners who don't want to share their client with the firm's other practice groups. Another big mistake. Those overly-protective partners are endangering the relationship with their client because other law firms are taking a full-service, full-firm approach to that same client, which may get your firm bumped from the client's roster.
- **Think like in-house counsel and be a strategic "functional" business partner to your clients.** Don't be known as *just* a legal services provider to your clients, *be a valued strategic business*

partner—think like in-house counsel and bring as wide a range of your firm's resources as possible to meet as many of the client's legal and business needs as you can. You should continually, 24/7, look for ways to introduce your client to contacts who can increase the client's business. A client receiving that level of partnership support from you is not going anywhere.

- **Make your clients look good.** Rainmakers treat their client contacts like best friends. You have their back and they know it. You make every effort to make the people who hired you look good to the people they report to because that's what friends do. If you treat every dollar of the client's money like it is your own money, they'll notice and reward you with increased loyalty.
- **Write a business development plan and find someone to hold you accountable.** First, obviously, put your business development plan in writing under the guidance of a trained business development professional such as your Chief Marketing Officer, Business Development Director, or certified business development coach. Have regularly scheduled accountability follow-up sessions on business development plan implementation.
- **Seek professional guidance.** Every elite performer has a coach or mentor. So, use your in-house business development team or a skilled outside coach to help you continue to hone the necessary skills to grow your book of business. These include: a well-rehearsed verbal business card, 4 questions for everyone you meet, understanding what the sales world has learned about "advancing" a prospect and knowing more than one way to ask for the business. Smart firm leadership knows that simulated "live" presentations are a fast way to polish pitching skills, and that external coaches are essential because many attorneys—often out of fear of damaging their carefully cultivated internal image—will not disclose all of their professional and personal challenges to anyone on the "inside."
- **Continue to fine tune your Business Development IQ.** A good exercise is to periodically test your knowledge against the 300+ business development questions in the back of this book, Exhibit 29.
- **Get started now.** Pick a course of action from the vast menu of actions provided in this manual. Measure the results. Adjust the rudder on your business development ship until you are sailing smoothly and have achieved your desired results. Inertia is your worst enemy. Take that first step, knowing that it may not be the perfect step, but you won't know until you take it, and you can always improve on it when you take the second step.

I've only given you a taste of the sumptuous banquet of information that precedes these remarks. If you avail yourself of the wisdom and experience provided in this book, you will have great success in building rainmakers.

In conclusion, **if you are passionate about your work, it will show**. If you treat everyone with respect and as a potential client or a potential referral source, your business will grow. The golden rule of business development still applies: people do business with people they like, respect, and trust.

Rainmakers work smart and hard, yes, but they play smart and hard, too. Rainmakers know you have to be healthy, physically and mentally, to play at the rainmaker level. There's a difference between workload stress and anxiety-based stress. Know the difference and manage both.

Arianna Huffington, who built a business worth over a billion dollars, keenly remembers the time her mother told her that **failure is not the opposite of success—it's a step toward success**. Rainmakers know this. Louise Muldoon paid a lot of dues to achieve her level of leadership, knowledge, and success. Matt Taylor didn't acquire an eight-digit book of business without overcoming many obstacles. Jill Weber had to go through a number of iterations before her *Fast Forward* rainmaker training program became refined and desired by other law firms. Karen Bell had to "work-out" like any great athlete to become a national leader at her firm and an in-demand speaker at legal marketing conferences.

All of our contributors to this guide have experienced trying times—Adam, Allen, Barbara, Bill, Casey, Clare, Dan, Dave, David, Despina, Don, Erin, Gerry, Gil, Hans, Jan, Jeanne, Jeff, Jeffrey, Jill, Jon, Jonathan, Karen, Karie, Larry, Lisa, Louise, Marian, Marilyn, Mark, Matt, Melanie, Michael, Michele, Mike, Nancy, Peter, Roger, Sally, Scott, Shanda, Silvia, Stephen, Steve, Tasneem, Tom, and Wayne—and they all found a way to be resilient, which added to their leadership abilities. All of their experiences, from overcoming daunting challenges to savoring the high-five wins, have helped to give them the skills to build rainmakers, and the kindness and wisdom to share those skills with us.

To all of our contributors, we say thank you.

—David

Exhibits 1-4: Questions For Strangers/Potential Clients/ Clients

Exhibit 1

Five Good Questions Upon Meeting Someone

By Larry Bodine

You might consider yourself a little introverted, but you can create a potential business relationship if you're able to go up to somebody and ask them these five good questions:

(1) What's going on with them?
(2) What's happening in their business?
(3) What challenges are they facing?
(4) What are they going to do about it?
(5) What would happen if they didn't do anything?

These questions very quickly lead to people discussing their business and telling you their problems. Most lawyers view rainmaking as pitching. They believe you have to have a good pitch or a good 30-second commercial and I would say worry less about your pitch and worry more about the questions you're going to ask. Anybody can ask a question. You don't need to be brilliant or handsome or loquacious.

Exhibit 2

Twenty Questions you Should Ask Current and Prospective Clients

By William J. Flannery, Jr., JD

You've done your research about the client or prospect, thought about communication strategies, and completed your pre-interview plan, but you may still be wondering: *What do I say? Where do I start?* Here's where rainmaking often turns into drought. Lawyers inexperienced in business development often make the crucial mistake of assuming that they're the ones who are supposed to do all the talking. For lack of anything better to do, they start their sales pitch. Or they try to convince clients or prospective clients that the firm has a number of good lawyers who can help them. Or more likely, they start with small talk as their way of trying to build rapport. For the first 45 minutes, they focus on sports, the weather, or subject matter that borders on the trivial, and is, often, inappropriately personal.

But clients and prospective clients don't want a poorly thought out sales pitch, and they don't need to be told about your lawyering skills. They probably assume you're good at what you do, or you wouldn't have gotten this far. And they certainly don't want personal, small talk. They're as busy as you are. What they want is to feel comfortable with you as a professional and to see where you and your firm might fit in with their business objectives. To make them comfortable, you must get them to talk about themselves and their business objectives.

Your efforts should focus on listening to their responses. The more they talk, the more you'll learn. And the more you learn, the more natural the process becomes. In business development, information is always power—because it means knowing what they need.

Knowing what to ask and how to ask is an art and a science. The 20 essential questions proposed here are broad enough to apply to most types of clients—both current and prospective—yet specific enough to elicit the concrete information essential for effective business development. While many of these questions appear to target new clients, it is surprising how much lawyers don't know about the clients they've been serving for years. When those lawyers take the time to learn they often find that there is substantial business going elsewhere which, with a little effort, could be kept in the family.

First, here are a few basic rules:

- **Show respect for your client's time.** Demonstrate your ability to perform due diligence before a meeting, by asking questions that show you have mastered basic background information on the person you're meeting with, his or her company and industry, and the company's overall legal matters. Much of this is easily obtained from publicly available resources or in pre-meeting conversations with support personnel.
- **Don't neglect the long-term perspective.** When they hear you asking about their plans three to five years hence, they begin to think of you as a 30-year ally.
- **Don't worry about asking new clients direct questions.** This is information they tell their brokers, their PR staffs, the stockholders, the press, and others in the business world. Further, they expect a high degree of confidentiality when talking to a lawyer, and they certainly want to talk candidly about their business because they want to trust their lawyers.
- **Ask current clients direct questions, too.** They will appreciate your interest and may even realize that such expert listening is the crux of delivering quality legal services.
- **You cannot and should not try to "sell" legal services to unwilling buyers.** Don't
- try to close the business at the first available lull in the conversation. Avoid the "sales pitch," as they may not be in the "catching" mode.
- **Never put them on the defensive.** Don't use the style of questioning you would use in a deposition or while cross-examining a hostile witness. The interview should be a win-win. The better they feel about talking now, the better they'll feel about hiring you later. Let them be the ones to bring up sensitive or painful matters.
- **Try to avoid the "why" questions.** Such questions are often received as judgmental, even when you intend no such thing. It's empathy and rapport that you're after.
- **Make all your questions as open ended as possible.** A "yes" or "no" answer will seldom do you any good. Phrase questions in such

a way as to give them the opportunity to supply as much information as possible.

- **Don't feel you need to respond to everything they tell you.** Much of what they say should be filed away for future use at a more appropriate moment. Silence can help build informational savings accounts.

The needs-analysis process during an interview follows its own course and cannot be rigidly structured into a pre-determined sequence of the essential 20 questions or any other questions. In general, however, you may plan to start by asking general questions about their business: what products or services they offer and to whom. There's nothing they'd rather talk about. Then explore how they've structured their organizations. Finally, focus on their legal needs: how they've met those needs in the past and intend to do so in the future.

In the course of that discussion, these are the 20 essential questions you will want answered:

(1) **What do you want your organization to look like in one year, two years, or five years?**

This question is a good opener, because it allows buyers to begin talking about any aspect of their business they choose. But you also have your own tactical reason for asking it, which is to determine if they've formulated a strategic plan and, if so, what that plan involves.

You should know the plan before you visit, by looking at their website and industry trends. You are simply validating the known plans. What you really need to know is what they see as the unknowns.

Asking about strategic planning also tells you what kind of self-knowledge they have. Do they have a specific vision of what they want for themselves, or are they playing the field, reacting to events and market developments as they happen? Getting a feel for them in this way may tell you volumes about how they deal with every other aspect of their business, including hiring lawyers.

(2) **When and where do you plan to open new offices or plants?**

This seemingly innocuous question is more than just a further refinement of the strategic planning issue. It will help you focus on a whole range of possible legal services, from real estate and lease negotiations to benefits planning for new staffs. In addition, it's information that will give you a real sense of just how aggressive and confident they are. It's one thing to talk about a strategic plan. It's another thing to state boldly, "We intend to open 10 new branches in the next two years." This is a global market and you will need to know how they see it.

(3) **What new products, services, or major changes are you anticipating?**

What if a retailer has decided that it wants to offer a discount brokerage service? You may have had no idea that the client or prospect intended to do this, and they may have had no idea that your firm has a securities practice. Here, the opportunity speaks for itself—thunderously.

(4) **What kind of research and development do you see as necessary for you to meet your strategic objectives?**

Legal counsel is itself a form of R&D for clients, particularly where they will be breaking new ground. As they talk more about their plans—how much they plan to invest, and the kind of research they'll be doing—you may get a glimpse of your own future: the practice areas you'll need to develop to be at the cutting edge five or 10 years down the road.

(5) **What is the profile of your typical customers and how do you market to them?**

Getting a clearer sense of who their customers are may help you determine how they themselves behave as customers. Are their buyers highly sophisticated and demanding, and to what extent? If so, they may want to see some evidence that you also treat your clients as peers. Understanding how they market their products or services will naturally give you some clues as to how you should be approaching them. If they de-emphasize the direct pitch, maybe you should, too. But there's another reason to explore their marketing approach. How they structure their sales force, whether it's decentralized or pyramidal, and the quota pressures under which those salespeople operate, will give you crucial insights into their culture. What the company expects from its district managers it may also expect from you. Refine this question as much as possible, to show you have already learned what you can about the company's business. If possible, this question will sound more sophisticated to the client if you can start it like this: "Given that your customer profile is X and marketing to that demographic is changing in Y ways, what changes do you see in the next five years in marketing?"

(6) **What are your employee relations concerns?**

How they manage their sales force leads to a broader issue: how they manage their entire work force. This line of inquiry will strengthen your sense of their culture and its impact on their legal needs. Is it a paternalistic milieu or a demanding and confrontational one?

Querying their concerns here also will help accomplish two other basic objectives. First, it will indicate current or future labor/employee problems: collective bargaining, wrongful discharge, benefits planning, etc. Second, it will increase their comfort level with you. Whether they are a closely held business or a Fortune 500 giant, there's nothing they fret about more—and nothing they'd rather talk over with a lawyer.

(7) **How do you see your competitive landscape changing?**

Here's another opportunity to get a sense of the business climate in which they are operating. Where there's an ongoing survival struggle with competitors, there are myriad legal issues, like commercial litigation, that the decision maker may not yet be pondering but ought to be. Conversely, less intense competitive environments may direct the client dialogue elsewhere.

(8) **What strategic changes in the business do you see in light of the financial climate you operate in, and which changes in the global economy concern you most?**

Use care here. This is information you need to have, but the question must be presented in as non-threatening a way as possible. You don't want to put anyone on the defensive. And you certainly don't want them thinking you're worried about who's going to pay the bill. You're really trying to accomplish something very different. If they are in distress, they may want to think about spinning off a division, or even tapping your or your firm's bankruptcy expertise. Or perhaps you will eventually want to suggest custom-designed billing methods. You may even want to mention that you have helped other companies under the gun. Once you have a sense of where they are in the marketplace, shift the focus somewhat. Find out what makes them tick.

They have something on their minds; otherwise they wouldn't be talking to a lawyer. Some of them may want to jump right in and tell you about a serious problem that's been keeping them awake at night. Others will prefer to talk about bewildering regulatory, political, or market changes. But even generalities will highlight what they need from you today, as well as how you might be solving their other problems tomorrow and the day after tomorrow.

Depending on the answer, you may be on the verge of making an absolutely crucial determination: does this person want proactive counseling or crisis management? You're not going to use the same tone with a client who wants you to co-pilot long-range business strategy that you'd use for someone who needs you as a safety net. To know which tone will make them most comfortable, listen carefully to the tone they use with you.

(9) **Before we talk about how decisions really get made, can you walk me through the critical parts of your organization chart and talk about the legal and purchasing decision-making process?**

You're really trying to gauge the organization's level of complexity. Is it a flat organization or hierarchical? Are there dozens of subsidiaries, or is it a one-cell organism? You don't necessarily need the whole organization chart, just enough information to know with whom you're dealing. You may uncover reporting relationships between their divisions or subsidiaries that you never suspected. The names of the key executives are also important at this juncture. You may never actually meet, say, the CFO, but you certainly don't want to sound ignorant later if that person's name comes up.

(10) **Now, in practical terms, how are decisions made and who makes them?**

Here, you're fleshing out the political underpinnings of the organizational setup. How bureaucratic is it? How autocratic? How many meetings will be needed before decisions, including retention decisions, are made? For lawyers in particular, it's vital to know who specifically makes the decisions. You need a firm grasp of all levels of the organization and key decision makers and must be prepared, with or without the presence of a general counsel, to work with a variety of non-legal executives who influence or outright control the buying decision. This also is your chance to learn more about the leadership style and personalities of those people before you meet them. You may learn that the leadership style emphasizes consensus-building. That's a cue to suggest setting up other meetings with as many of those important team players as possible. Even brief introductions are useful. The more decision makers you meet, the more opportunities open up.

(11) **In light of all that, how is the legal department organized and how does its role change depending on involvement in decisions from elsewhere in the company?**

Obviously, you need to know how this legal department really functions and how much influence and independence it has internally. But be careful here. The general counsel may be out of the decision-making loop altogether. Let the client or prospect describe the role of their legal department and then you can draw your own conclusions. But ask to meet the members of the legal department in any event. There's no point in alienating your in-house counterparts.

(12) **What do you see outside counsel accomplishing for you or your organization?**

Again, the question is broad enough so that the client supplies the essential information. Let them tell you what they want to buy, not just react to what you assume they need. They state their needs. You decide if you can fill them.

(13) **What has been your experience with value billing methods and who gets involved in determining ROI?**

The new buyers of legal services are far more focused on the financial aspects of buying legal services. By offering some that can be compared using rates per hour has made the job of comparative performance about lawyers and law firms easy targets for discounts. The concept of pricing based on the value provided has proved to be challenging for all parties. Many firms have hired pricing analysts. The problem for these analysts is that their calculations are based on the law firm's costs rather than the value to the business. All legal services can be easily measured: the services either help the client grow assets or protect assets.

Licensing of IP by companies is a clear example of opportunities to grow and protect assets at the same time. Helping clients with real property tax audits that reduce the tax bills are another.

(14) **How big an upside does the company expect to see from a new business opportunity before committing to a legal and business strategy?**

Ultimately, your greatest potential lies in breaking free from tight budgets drawn with existing legal needs in mind. Before you propose that the client invest in your services to execute a plan it hadn't budgeted for, you need a clear sense of the client's risk tolerance and how large a bottom-line benefit must be before it gets the client's attention. If, in this part of the conversation, you hear the client agree that some amount of ROI would make approval of a new initiative likely, you may find it useful later on in this process to repeat that back to the client.

(15) **What sort of legal services are you currently using, and do you expect any changes?**

Perhaps they've been relying on outside counsel for, say, garden variety tax work or ERISA. If so, ask yourself why they're talking to you now. Maybe some new and critical situation is in the offing, and they feel the need to shop around. Or perhaps they're just dissatisfied with their current counsel and are looking to turn everything over to another firm.

This line of inquiry is also helpful because you'll be able to compare their current legal needs with the services they're now buying. Something may well be missing on the service end. With new or first-time buyers, there may be particularly glaring omissions. With long-term clients, watch for certain recurring patterns. Some of them may be turning to Firm X for, say, tax work, and to Firm Y for litigation. Do they even know that many firms offer the best of both? One-stop-shopping is a powerful lure for most clients and prospective clients. Consolidating to fewer and fewer outside firms has been the most compelling "one-stop-shopping" trend in recent history.

For less sophisticated buyers, modify the questions. Ask them to imagine the best-case lawyer/client scenarios, as well as the worst.

(16) **What do you like about what other firms do, and what do you wish they would do differently?**

Learn from your competitors' mistakes without attacking them directly. In fact, never make negative comments about your competitors. It reflects on the judgment of the buyer! Identify where competitors have fallen short in order to determine where you'll need to do better. It's helpful to find out who those other firms are, because they're likely to continue to compete with you for future work. The buyer may mention their names without your having to ask. This could turn out to be the most important question about your opportunity to replace the competition.

(17) **How much detail do you like to get from your lawyers?**

Here is where you can get a real picture of their legal environment, and how much knowledge of the law they're bringing to the table. That knowledge will have a direct impact on your business development efforts. They may not be interested in hearing about all the details of your most recent case and aren't likely to appreciate your trying to dazzle them with displays of esoteric legalese.

By the same token, if they demand chapter and verse on every deal, they may well expect to be talking shop before they hire anyone. Incidentally, if they take pride in their legal knowledge, they probably have invested power in their general counsel, at least in determining which firms get what business.

(18) **How do you perceive our firm in particular?**

You should be listening here to two things. First, what is it that has interested them enough to consider hiring you? Is it a particular practice area or your firm's overall reputation? Define that strength and, whatever it is, reinforce it in your discussions. But note also what even the most admiring clients fail to perceive about your firm. Remember, you're trying to build a long-term relationship. That means going beyond the one or two areas of expertise that they have seen fit to mention.

(19) **What criteria do you use in selecting lawyers? What makes a good lawyer?**

A good lawyer may be variously defined as someone who wins cases, returns phone calls, respects in-house counsel, or keeps costs down. Sometimes they have no particular impression of you or your firm. They may just be spreading their nets, talking to as many lawyers as possible. So don't guess what they're looking for. Ask them.

(20) **How does your budgeting for legal services compare to what you spend on other resources?**

Get a sense of the cost pressures beleaguering them. Sophisticated buyers aren't looking for bargain-basement rates, but they are attracted to lawyers who are sensitive to their need to stay within reasonable limits. Again, the main issue is their comfort level. They're going to want to know that you're someone they can deal with. You will need to assist in the budgeting process. Helping clients establish budgets, manage matters and use attractive fee arrangements (AFAs) have grown increasingly commonplace in the "New Normal." Many firms will have to develop desktop and laptop technology programs to communicate with clients' systems.

The last question you may want to ask is the one that will lead to a commitment. Building relationships is a process, and one in which clients and prospective clients themselves participate. So ask your client or prospective client for help in determining what the next step might be rather than begging for the business using antique "closing" techniques.

Exhibit 3

Rainmaking Advantage® Key Talking Points/Scripts

(This form has been generously provided by the LawVision Group.)

Tips

- Be confident and clear with your message. Know your goal for the call or meeting ahead of time. Focus on building or strengthening the relationship.
- Make sure there is a follow up step and it's in your court. Add it to your calendar so you'll remember to call/schedule meeting or whatever else was decided is a good next step.
- Remember that staying connected will lead to business in the future and that people like to hear from you—it shows you are thinking of them and the message is that they matter.

Below are some helpful scripts when calling or meeting with people:

(1) ***For clients with whom you have completed some work but no long-term, ongoing relationship yet.***

I've enjoyed working with you/getting to know you [whichever is most appropriate] and would welcome your thoughts and advice on how to continue to build a relationship with COMPANY for potential opportunities to work together. [Then let him/her answer and go from there]

(2) ***For referral sources/potential referral sources who have existing counsel relationships.***

We know COMPANY has good options when it comes to referring work to counsel. I'm very interested in hearing from you, what you think our next step should be to continue to strengthen our relationship with COMPANY. [Listen to how he/she responds and think of a next question that leads him/her closer to suggesting a next step for you to take for building the relationship which could include meeting more of the team from COMPANY at their location or at the firm.]

(3) ***For inactive clients/contacts with whom you have not spoken in a few or more years. (The objective is to rebuild the relationship and not discuss BD right away)***

It's been a while since we connected and I wanted to touch base to say hello and hear how things are going. [Pause and let them answer or leave this as a message for them to return call]. I would welcome the opportunity to schedule a time to talk with you to hear what's going on with you, your business, etc. OR I would welcome the opportunity to schedule a time to meet—I'd be happy to come over to your office. Let's look at calendars and figure out a good time. Remember, you are back at the beginning stages of the sales cycle—Assess Needs!

(4) ***For connecting with your existing contacts who will introduce you to someone else in their organization.***

Two parts to this one: Who else in the company do you recommend I meet to continue to build our relationship with XYZ Company. How should I go about meeting him/her?

To follow up on that: NAME, you've been great to offer to introduce me to XXX. I'm calling to follow up on your recommendation about next steps.

Tip: When you leave a meeting or call, try to make sure you have an action step. If your contact says they will call you to follow up, be sure to respond by letting them know if you don't hear from them by a specific date (e.g., if I don't hear from you by XXX, I'll give you a call)

(5) ***For turning friends/neighbors into potential business opportunities.***

At a social outing or neighborhood meeting, you might say: "Cynthia, I'm going to give you a call at your office next week to find out more about your business and to discuss ways in which we might have opportunities to work together."

You may say once you do have a meeting: "Our friendship is of utmost importance to me and I don't want to jeopardize that. At the same time, it seems that we could pursue opportunities for working together." Do you agree?

(6) ***For following up with individuals who say they will send you a deal/piece of work in the future.***

It was good to see you/speak with you. Thank you for offering to send me an upcoming deal/piece of litigation/project. I will give you a call in the next few weeks to follow up on what my next steps should be. I look forward to the opportunity to work with you and your team.

Exhibit 4

Five Tips for Turning Introductions into Opportunities

By Deborah Shames & Jonathan R. Fitzgarrald

It is 7:45 a.m. Cup of coffee in hand, you find a seat and wait for the networking meeting to begin—you are visiting for the first time. The meeting facilitator welcomes everyone and says, "With so many new faces today, I thought it would be a good idea to go around the room and have everyone take a few moments to introduce themselves and what they do."

"Oh great, here comes a glorified roll call," you think. Short of watching paint dry, nothing is as mind numbing as listening to a group of professionals introduce themselves through clichés, generalities, and generic value statements.

Elevator speeches, 15-second pitches, brief introductions—whatever you call them—are attempts to connect and stir the interest of a prospect or referral source in a short amount of time. With forethought and preparation, introductions can be an effective way of building your book of business and even of starting a process that may lead to a strategic alliance.

FIRST, consider your intention. Intention is the driving force behind every successful presentation (and yes, an introduction should be considered a presentation). It is the singular message or impression you want to leave with your audience. Pick one intention and make it active. Want more of a particular type of work? Align your message accordingly.

All too often, lawyers think their intention is to educate or inform their audience as to the litany of services they provide. David Booth, co-author of *Own the Room: Business Presentations that Persuade, Engage and Get Results*, says, "If you educate people, you get them to think, but if you persuade them, you get them to act."

Sometimes lawyers fear that by delivering only one message or focusing on one service, their audience will not grasp the full extent of their capabilities. In fact, listeners will absorb the one thing you focus on, which helps gain trust and further understanding. Once trust is established, listeners can (and will) approach you to learn more about the full range of your services.

SECOND, demonstrate your intention through storytelling. Avoid reciting a menu of services or the history and reputation of your firm. Instead, think of your intro as an opportunity to tell a story—engage your audience, differentiate yourself and your message, and be memorable.

THIRD, catch your audience's attention through a dynamic opening. Rather than beginning with "Thank you for having me," "Good morning," or "I'd like to tell you a story," dive off a cliff and deliver an attention grabber.

You might reference a current news item, tell a personal story, reveal a lesson learned, share your perspective on a controversial topic, ask a thought-provoking question, or relate a matter/case you recently handled. Use specifics and paint a picture. If your audience can visualize what you describe, they are engaged.

Avoid the common mistake of beginning with such a colorful opening that it becomes the focus of your introduction, rather than the story that demonstrates how you assist clients. If you were to map out the structure of an introduction, it would look like: Open (to grab attention), Transition (to relate the opening to the intention), Body of Content (your services and/or methodology), Close (name and firm).

FOURTH, construct your story. Identify the obstacle. What is at stake? Is there a tight deadline? What is it that requires your expertise and experience to overcome? The obstacle is typically the client's problem or issue for which they hired you in the first place.

Next, reveal the solution you implemented by stating three specific processes that you used to solve the client's problem. Communicate the steps you took to solve a client's issue will demonstrate your capabilities as a business professional and is far more effective than merely telling someone what you're capable of.

Close with your name and firm. Speakers have a honeymoon period of 30 seconds or less to capture an audience's attention. Since there is nothing novel or surprising about your name or the name of your firm, why start at a disadvantage? By putting your name and firm at the end of your introduction, you encourage the audience to place the most important of details into long-term memory.

FIFTH, practice. Once you have an overall structure for your introduction, rehearse it. "Winging it" is a recipe for disaster. Initially, you will probably include too much information, or new thoughts will come to you as you say your speech aloud. It is all part of the creative process.

Rehearsals are where you decide what to include and what to eliminate, and how to keep everything within the allotted time. During a scene in the movie This Is It, Michael Jackson rehearses dance moves with his band. When the music conductor apologizes for getting the timing wrong, Michael says, "It's OK, that is why we practice!" Despite his unbelievable talent and years of experience, Michael understood the need to practice.

Delivery of your introduction should be similar to having a conversation across a dining room table. Many of us were taught that to be taken seriously in business we had to be formal, rigid, and official in our posture and language. The reverse is true. When lawyers show an easygoing, relaxed demeanor, they exhibit true confidence and approachability. When you make eye contact around the room, the audience feels included.

You never get a second chance to make a dynamic first impression. Ninety-nine percent of all lawyers cannot extemporaneously deliver an introduction that is succinct, colorful and serves as a business magnet. To achieve mastery requires commitment, training, rehearsal and experience.

The more authentic you are, the more people will be drawn to you. To thrive in this fiercely competitive marketplace, speaking is among the best ways to be seen as the go-to person in your field. Would you prefer to captivate your audience or watch them mentally walk out the door? If it's captivate you want, deliver a well-crafted introduction.

****

Deborah Shames is the co-founder of Éloqui—training lawyers to achieve a competitive advantage through enhanced communications and presentation skills.

Jonathan R. Fitzgarrald, is Managing Partner of Equinox Strategy Partners. Drawing upon more than 15 years of sales and marketing experience, Jonathan provides strategic counsel to professional services firms to drive revenue, market visibility, and client satisfaction.

Exhibits 5-10: How to Identify and Create Ideal Target Client List

Exhibit 5

Answer Five Questions to Identify and Find New Clients

By Merrilyn Astin Tarlton
Partner/Catalyst at Attorney at Work blog, founding member of the Legal Marketing Association

When you finish up a big case or put the final signatures on a long-time-closing contract, things can get slow around your office. You might begin feeling a little panicky. It's dangerously easy at that point to slip into thinking you'd take any old legal work you could lay your hands on—just to keep the cash flowing. And sure enough, that's what you do—jump on your horse and gallop off in all directions looking for work. And, sure enough, you bring in "any old legal work."

Now let's back up: What if instead of panicking, you spent your quieter times bringing in work that you'd **love** doing? And, since you are expending all that business development effort anyway, what if you made your marketing tasks pay off over the long-term as well as this month? Yeah, that's what we thought, too. So this article is dedicated to the proposition that you actually can draw a bead on exactly the kind of work you want to do.

There Are Just Five Simple Questions to Answer

Sit down with pencil and pad, and let's quickly figure out the equation to get you started off right. Take the following questions in order, and answer them thoughtfully. In some instances, you may need to pause and do a bit of research.

(1) **What kind of work would you really like to do?** Perhaps you took a wrong turn a little ways back, taking case after case outside your initial area of focus. Or maybe, over time, you've learned that certain matters are like sandpaper on your skin, while others feel just right. Better yet, perhaps you have a driving passion to make *something* happen in the world and want to find paying legal work that furthers that goal. Well, now's a good time

to get back on track. Just for the sake of illustration, let's say the work you really want to do can best be described as "business start-ups."

(2) **Who hires lawyers to do that kind of work?** Right away, this question allows you to carve away a certain percentage of the market you might otherwise waste your time on. Your potential clients are certainly not in-house counsel with established companies. Nor are they injured individuals looking to sue. Grossly stated, the people who might hire you to do this type of work are people who are moving in the direction of starting a new business. (I know, duh.) But you can get a bit more specific: inventors, highly specialized professionals who want to bail out of corporate life, B-school grads with a hot idea. For our purposes, let's choose those people who are tired of what they have to put up with to get a paycheck and want to head out on their own.

(3) **Where do they get their information?** Assuming Mr. Darcy, VP of Human Resources with x-Zooper Corp., wants to make his exit in a sophisticated and professional manner, he isn't going to randomly ask around for the names of lawyers who can help him. That could lead to an exit before he's quite ready, right? No, he's going to conduct his search for a lawyer in a very confidential fashion. So ask yourself (or ask Google) what do corporate HR directors read? What organizations do they belong to? What are their daily blog reads?

(4) **Who do they listen to?** At the same time, you'll want to think about who might recommend you to Mr. Darcy. Whose opinion would he value on this question? Now, this is challenging because of concerns about confidentiality, but there will be some people whose advice he will seek out … or whose recommendation he will value if he can receive it without tipping his own hand about his plans. The list starts with people who have, themselves, left the corporate world and successfully launched a business.

(5) **How can you get in front of those parades?** Here's the payoff for all that research—and where your to-do list begins to develop. Understanding what we do now about *who* might hire you to do simple business start-ups, you can focus on *what* to do. For example:

- Join and participate in a couple of LinkedIn groups: LinkedIn Human Resources Group and On Startups—The Community for Entrepreneurs. Don't lurk. Actively post and participate in online discussions about topics related to the law and business entity creation. Remember, you want to be seen. And you want to be impressive on *your topic*. If you're not experienced with LinkedIn groups, you'll learn quickly enough.

- Identify a local publication likely read by HR professionals or entrepreneurs (smart people read about where they want to go) and pursue opportunities to write creatively on your topic. (If you live in Colorado, as I do, you'd be looking at the Denver Business Journal.) Find out if there's a chance to develop a series of articles for publication or even a regular column. Be easy to deal with. Write well. Please the editors. They'll want you to write more.
- Volunteer and get involved with a local organization focused on training entrepreneurs and new business owners. Again, in Colorado, you might look at the University of Colorado's Deming Center for Entrepreneurship or Colorado State University's Center for Entrepreneurship. Or, you may live near one of these top 25 colleges for entrepreneurs. Talk, teach and write about legal issues related to start-up businesses. Do it right and the young people you work with will come to see you as *the* business startup lawyer—and call you when they start up their businesses.
- Write a book. Better yet, write a pamphlet—a downloadable one—and make it available to anyone interested in starting a business. Maybe it's a "how to" or "pitfalls to avoid" guide, or a "new business start-up checklist." Promote it via social media and offer it through your website or blog. While you're at it, offer a list of other free publications that are useful to new business owners.
- Pull together a list of people you have already helped to launch their businesses and schedule lunches and coffee dates. Find out how their business is going. Build relationships. Network. Introduce these people to others who might help them in their business. And, yes, remind them of your capabilities and ask them to share your name with anyone who may be looking for legal help for their own startup.

There's more—a lot more—you can do. Start. Once you've focused in on the best activities, you'll be surprised at how simple it is to build a reputation and a network to support getting exactly the kind of work you want. And it's so much easier (and cheaper) than galloping off in all directions!

Merrilyn Astin Tarlton has been helping lawyers and law firms think differently about the business of practicing law since 1984. She is the Partner/Catalyst at Attorney at Work. A founding member of the Legal Marketing Association, she is a past President of the College of Law Practice Management and an LMA Hall of Fame inductee. Follow her on Twitter @ astintarlton.

Exhibit 6

Developing a Target Market Prospect List

(This form has been generously provided by the LawVision Group.)

Getting Organized/Identifying Targets

This step of the sales process can take some time but once it's completed, it's only necessary to update the information on a regular basis (annually). When developing a target list of specific identified prospects for building/strengthening your and the firm's brand, here is a useful guideline to follow. Start by creating a spreadsheet that has the following columns:

Name of company, address, web site URL and phone number

Name of decision-maker(s); CFO and GC if applicable

A column for each quarter of the year

One last column for Next Steps

(1) Understand Demonstrable Experience—where are our individual/collective strengths
  (a) For litigators, is there specific opposing counsel that attorneys/firm has success against—if so, set up alerts on those attorneys/firms, and pursue the companies they are initiating legal action against
  (b) What are we known for that our perceived (market-centric) experience can sell for us?
  (c) What strengths/experience do we have that the market may not know us for? For these areas, we'll need to rely more on our experience, pricing, and the market opportunity.

(2) Identify the potential market—common characteristics may include the following (and can also be a combination of some of the following):
- Number of employees
- Industry segment (e.g., Oil & Gas; Pharma; Pet Products)
- Geographic jurisdiction (e.g., Top 100 companies in XXX Region/State/Country)
- Common ranking (e.g., Inc. 100; Forbes 100; Global 100)
- Common characteristics (individuals with incomes of more than XXX; companies with revenues of XXX; companies with significant patent portfolios)
- Look for historical combinations of legal activity trends & company revenue trends—i.e. companies that are increasing specific areas of litigation by a certain % while revenues are increasing or decreasing by a certain %

(3) Identify the companies (clients and contacts) you or the firm already has in these markets
- Review the firm's database
- Review your Outlook files
- Review firm billing records (it's useful to go back up to 7 years or even more) to identify current and past client companies in these industries or market segments
- Ask Finance, Marketing and IT (or those individuals in the firm who oversee these responsibilities) to assist
- Add clients and contacts' names to the list and identify the relationship lawyer (if it is not you) next to the name of the individual
- Note: you may want to do Step 2 in each geographic jurisdiction of the firm

(4) Cross-check the company and individual names with your social media contacts.
- Check against LinkedIn, Facebook and other social media databases to identify potential connections you have to the targeted individuals and companies. Go to the site and log in, then one at a time (this is a good step to delegate as well) enter in the company name and see if anyone you are connected to is connected to someone at the company.
- Add any names (connections/links) to the spreadsheet—these will be individuals who know you and who know someone at the target company.

(5) Research the competition.

- Once a market/industry segment has been identified, it's wise to know which other firms are targeting and working with this market. In many cases, the best way to determine this information is to ask the Library/Information Resource team at the firm to help. If the firm is small and does not have many resources in this research area, ask Marketing or one of your suppliers (Lexis/Nexis, Thomson/West and others) to help.
- The Internet can be useful for this type of data but unlikely will give the results in the kind of detail that is most helpful. An industry association can help here too. Researching key words may pull up articles or presentations by competitors.
- Look at which firms are representing the client in all areas (to the extent that can be determined, such as litigation, M & A/Securities, and IP transactions)
    - Consider all representation—Does the client retain single firms for multiple areas of representation? What size firms do they hire for various types of representation? Do they retain firms from lower cost markets for more commoditized types of work? Are firms with significant experience in your primary area(s) of expertise handling work in other areas for the client currently?
    - Much of the pricing data is now available—what is the average collected rate and demand level trends by timekeeper, by market, by practice area?
        - For example, a large retail coffee company typically uses a national GP firm to handle labor & employment work, but most of the attorneys handling the representation in high cost jurisdictions are based in low cost markets

(6) Identify the industry/target market association(s) related to this market.

- This is most easily accomplished by conducting an Internet search using key words. For larger firms, a librarian may be of significant help with identifying related organizations/associations.
- Review the information about the association and select one or two to explore further.
- Attend an industry association event to determine if in fact this is the right association for you to develop additional contacts, to learn about the industry and at which to be visible.

- Meet and build a relationship with the Association's Administrative Director and join a committee—get involved where possible. Getting involved will help you to raise your profile.

(7) Build strong referral relationships.
- Identify which other types of businesses also sell to the target industry. Consider accounting firms, insurance companies, other service providers and competitors (for conflicts).
- List up to ten companies for each potential referral market (e.g., 10 accounting firms; 10 consulting firms, etc.)
- Go to each company's website and type in the key industry segment and information about which individual at the company focuses on this industry will come up in the search. Note the individuals' name(s) on the spreadsheet. These are people with whom you will want to connect directly to discuss the target market, obtain information and build relationships.

Now that the referral sources and target companies and individuals have been identified, develop a strong annual plan for reaching out to these individuals that includes in person relationship-building with referral sources and connecting with prospects by using effective "Approach" strategies. For more information about the rest of the sales process, please visit our website at www.lawvisiongroup.com and contact one of our business development consultants.

###

Exhibit 7

The Best Way to Catch New Clients: Find Their Associations and Get Actively Involved

By John Remsen, Jr., President

The Remsen Group, http://www.theremsengroup.com

Generally speaking, I find that many (maybe even most) younger attorneys I meet—say those born after 1960—are willing and, in many cases, eager to "market." They realize that marketing and business development are part and parcel of being a successful lawyer and essential to operating a successful law firm.

In most law firms, existing client relationships tend to be controlled by more senior lawyers. That means that junior lawyers must go outside the firm to find clients and build their books of business. And we all know, it's just not that easy.

Studies tell us that it takes 8-11 "impressions" to convert a prospect to a client. On top of that, it takes 5-7 times more time, effort and energy to generate a new matter from a new client than from an existing one. Needless to say, finding new clients takes time (non-billable), commitment and perseverance.

So what should a young lawyer who wants to build a book of business do in order to create these 8-11 impressions? Where is the best place to invest that precious time, effort and energy?

To use a fishing analogy, you've got to first figure out what kind of fish you want to catch and then hang out where they do. The "fish," of course, are the prospective clients. The place they hang out—the "reef," if you will—is their association. It's where they go to be with others like them. It's where they learn and keep abreast of industry trends. And you need to be there . . . one of the fish, part of the school, actively involved and, one day, leading the way.

When it comes to organizational involvement, most lawyers join and seldom go. Or they pick the wrong organization for marketing and business development purposes. Our October "Marketing Tip of the Month" counts down our top ten recommendations to maximize your ROI from involvement in associations.

#10) Stay Out of The Bars

Your parents always said that hanging out in bars can only lead to trouble. And, from a marketing and business development perspective, spending lots of time in bar associations is probably not the best place to meet and build relationships with prospective clients. Alas, many lawyers find comfort here among other lawyers and they call it "marketing." But I'm going to suggest that you find somewhere else to go.

#9) Figure Out What You Want to Catch

Here we are back to that fishing analogy. But it proves my point. The more clearly and narrowly you define your target audience—the kinds of clients you want—the more effective your marketing and business development efforts will be. Let me repeat that. The more clearly and narrowly you define your target audience, the more effective your marketing and business development efforts will be.

This is half the battle for most lawyers and law firms. They tend to want to be all things to all people and they try to market every tiny little thing they do. But if you spread your marketing time and dollars too thin, you wind up catching nothing.

Another important consideration: Market what you *want*, not what you *do*.

#8) Think Industry, Not Area of Law

Most lawyers and law firms like to market their areas of law, such as corporate, tax, environmental or litigation. Clients, on the other hand, look for lawyers and law firms with knowledge and experience in their industries, such as construction, entertainment, transportation and health care. There is a growing body of research that supports this most important distinction.

The moral of the story: Market to an industry, not your area of law. That suggests that you should get involved in an industry trade association. Many law firms, following the lead of banks and CPA firms, have taken the next logical step and created Industry Practice Groups.

#7) Do Your Research and Develop a Short List

There are associations for just about everything. And if you live in a large metropolitan area or state capital, chances are you can find a number of organizations to consider. For example, if you are a banking lawyer, check out your State Bankers Association. If you are a female real estate lawyer, take a look at an organization called Commercial Real Estate Women (CREW).

Do some online research. Talk to clients and prospective clients about the organizations to which they belong. Check out these organizations' websites. Take a look at the Board of Directors. What about the rank and file members? Are they decision makers? Can they hire or influence the decision to hire lawyers? Talk to a Board member about upcoming meetings and opportunities for you and your firm to get involved. Find out what other lawyers or law firms are involved. You are looking for a target rich environment where you will have the opportunity to get involved. Do your homework and develop a short list of organizations to consider.

#6) Pick One and Go Deep

Next, go to a meeting or two of each group you have identified. Ask one of your clients if you can go to an upcoming meeting as a guest. This is the time to conduct some due diligence, because once you find the right organization, you must become active and invest lots of time there to make it pay off.

Although there is nothing wrong with the Chamber of Commerce or the United Way, these groups cross industry lines. They are too diverse and their memberships are typically too fragmented. I submit that you'll find a more target rich environment if you stick with an industry trade association.

My advice is to find the right group—just one—and go deep. That will be far more effective than peripheral involvement in three or four organizations.

Finally, if the organization you seek isn't out there, start it. That's what we've done with the Managing Partner Forum and we've worked with many law firms to create similar opportunities.

#5) Jump in With Both Feet

Once you've found the right organization, you've got to get actively involved. And, frankly, this is where most lawyers and law firms fall down. They join and then never go. Too busy. Kid's softball game. Conflicts. Whatever.

Well, guess what? Getting meaningful results through organizational involvement is like joining the gym. If you want results, you have to go and you have to exercise. You've got to make it a top priority.

You get involved by going to monthly meetings. And you go religiously. You start to meet people. You develop friendships. Remember those 8-11 impressions? Here's where they start to happen fast and, in time, it will start to pay off.

It's an investment in you. Make it part of your routine. A little bit every week.

#4) Join a Committee and Perform

Early on, you should join a Committee and I often suggest the Program or Membership Committee. Both tend to be active and visible within the organization and will afford you the opportunity to meet lots of people. Once you've selected your Committee, volunteer to lead a highly visible project and perform like crazy. Do what you say. Meet deadlines. Exceed expectations. Do a great job and people will notice.

Remember those 8-11 impressions? Here's where they start to happen really, really fast . . . and it all happens very naturally.

#3) Throw Some Money At Them

Ask the firm to sponsor a meeting or two, or run an ad in the membership directory. Make an impact with your dollars and resist the temptation to spread them too thin. For example, it is far more effective to pick one high profile annual event and own it as the primary sponsor, rather than being one of three dozen bronze sponsors for a multitude of events throughout the year.

#2) Befriend Future Leaders

Make it a point to befriend key leaders (both current and future) of the organization. Seek them out at meetings. Set up a breakfast or lunch meeting twice a month with selected Board members and Committee Chairs. Do some research ahead of time and ask questions about their company, its plans for the future and their role in the organization. Get to know them on a personal level. Be sincere and, by all means, don't ask for business too soon. You've got to build trust and that takes time. . . . it takes 8-11 impressions.

#1) Achieve a Leadership Position

In time, you should seek to Chair a Committee. In most organizations, this can be realistically achieved within two years. A year or so later, you are likely to find yourself in a position to run for a seat on the Board of Directors. I guarantee that you can become President of almost any organization you want within five years if you set your sights on the prize and go for it. It's not hard. It just takes time, commitment and perseverance,

As you climb within the organization, seek opportunities for you (or your colleagues at the firm) to participate in programs and contribute articles to the newsletter or website on a regular basis. Talk to the Program Chair and the Newsletter Editor about your interest in helping them put on good programs and provide timely and relevant articles for the members. Chances are you will be pleased by the responses you get. Find out what they need and help them get it.

Conclusion

If you find the right organization and do the things we've set forth in this article, it won't be too long before you and your firm are recognized as can-do people who know and understand the concerns and issues facing the industry. Along the way, you will have developed relationships with persons in a position to hire or refer you. It doesn't get much better than that.

But it takes time, commitment and perseverance. Get out there. Get active. Start today.

Exhibit 8

How to Identify Your Ideal Client Target List

By Allen Fuqua, CMO, Winstead PC, Dallas, TX

Targeting is the life blood of any productive business development effort or plan. However what qualifies as a real target and how to identify the target continues to be a challenge for many attorneys.

First and foremost understand what a target is: A target is a named person; not a title/position, not a company, not an industry, not a legal practice or need ('I'm targeting companies that need litigation'). Either you have a name or you are still in the process of identifying the target.

Without this clarity, many attorneys continue to wonder why their efforts do not deliver new business for themselves or their firms.

Here's what I counsel attorneys to aspire to on targets:

(1) You need 4—6 Tier 1 targets which you have decided are your top priorities. You decide how you will increase the relationship and deliver value to the target (review Chapter 2 in this book for ways to increase the relationship). You plan the 4—6 touches for the year.

(2) You identify 10—15 Tier 2 relationships which could result in new business for you or your firm. You think in terms of 2—3 touches in the year.

(3) You identify about 200 targets with whom you find a way to develop visibility and value. Over time many of these will become Tier 2 and then Tier 1 targets as others fall off those lists. For most attorneys, this is a large number, but it should push you to get yourself out there meeting the right people.

Once you are clear on the kinds of matters and clients you are after, you need to identify your process for choosing your targets.

Actually this can vary with the level of experience of the attorney.

Starting From Scratch - You Have No Targets At All

Let's assume you have nothing, nada, zippo. Ask yourself these questions and begin to add targets from the answers:

- What clients do you have or recently had that have other work that you or your firm is relevant to?
- What people do you know from your schools, kids' friends' parents, church, other social activities that you sincerely enjoy, who are in a relevant business career and you would enjoy learning more about and developing a relationship with. Add those to your list and begin the process.

You Have a Practice But It is Leveled Out or Is Moribund and Possibly Languishing

- Be sober about your current clients: has your work with them become so price sensitive that you can see a day when you will be priced out of serving them? If so, these are not good targets. Please be sober about this. I've seen too many wonderful attorneys work themselves into a dead end alley where their practice with their clients can no longer support their career. And they haven't invested in any other targets.
- Look at your current clients and identify where their company business (not legal work; the client's own business) is going. Discuss with your colleagues how your services might make a difference for that company or those targets within the company.
- Ask your current clients what organizations they belong to, join those organizations and see if you can find new targets that broaden your opportunities. Take at least 6 months, 4 meetings to get a good feel for the organization before you evaluate its potential value. Then begin to add targets from that organization.
- Use the ideas from the group above.

You Have a Successful Practice But Would Like to Take It to the Next Level

- Do a review of your portfolio of work. What part of it is price sensitive versus price insensitive? What clients are you doing less work for than in the past? Don't ignore the trends there. Which of your clients are experiencing the most change? We make money based on the absolute value of client change. Focus on the targets where change is highest (good or bad), where you get a better rate and where the trend is positive.

- For the clients whose work is decreasing, have an open discussion about their business (once again not your legal business, their business), where it is going and what its goals are. Then ask them how they would like to manage their legal needs? You'll know whether they are a good target to invest in for the future.
- Take a step back from yourself and your career. Ask yourself what industries, business issues or types of work you are really interested in. Choose one area and then project what people would that bring you into contact with. Then find out where those people go, meet, etc. Put yourself there, ask them questions about their business and work and see where it goes. Once again, give it at least four meetings before evaluating anything. And see if you have targets that you are pleased with.
- As you probably understand, you'll take your practice to the next level not by luck, but by focusing on the better targets and the hard work of developing a better relationship with those targets than your competitors.

Keep reminding yourself that you have a track record of success. And all you need is to be meeting and developing business relationships with the right people. Review your targets every six months to ensure you are putting time into the right people.

People make the world go around and certainly for attorneys they determine the quantity and quality of their practice.

Exhibit 9

Save Client Targeting Time & Money—80/20 Approach

By Carol Schiro Greenwald, PhD
MarketingPartners: Building Professional Practices (An Excerpt)

It's a big world out there. Random networking can be frustrating—so much time, so few live leads. To maximize the effectiveness of your rainmaking consider focusing on the most perfect kind of client for you, your firm, your practice group, your specific practice area, industry/business group(s), and industry/business sub-group(s). Create a persona to guide you toward that goal. To create a persona, follow these steps.

Understand where you are right now

(1) Start from where you are now. Do an analysis of your "80/20"—the handful of clients that provide 80% of your revenue. Chart five years back if you can:
  (a) Identify the name of the client, their location, product/service, revenue each of the five years they were with you, and client relationship attorney.
  (b) If you work primarily with individuals, not businesses, the product/service becomes their demographic cohort, and all the rest stays the same.

(2) Once you have this client overview, think about what parts of working with them you like best because it is easier to sell something you really want to do, e.g., do you like the people, the problems, the legal strategy?

Select one of the "80/20" clients to be the basis for your ideal client persona.

(1) Prospects: use your knowledge about them as an indicator of how you would be able to work with them. By choosing a client/client

type that you know well you can build on your knowledge about them and begin your prospect search one step ahead of other.

(2) Construct the persona as a stand-in for your perfect client.

(3) Personal characteristics:

   (a) Business or individual
   (b) Business' location on their growth trajectory (early, pre-IPO, still growing, mature, declining) or individual's age/demographic cohort.
   (c) Location(s), geographic reach
   (d) Business' product or service lines and revenue range; individual's financial picture and sources of revenue
   (e) Chemistry factors—culture similarities. Do you get along personally? Do you have the same work ethic? Do you share the same views of collaboration or confrontation?
   (f) Problems/opportunities they bring to you
      (i) Potential to cross-sell other services
      (ii) Frequency—i.e., a one-time divorce or multiple contracts
   (g) Kind of results they want
   (h) How they work with you—i.e., very involved, very hands-off, in-between
   (i) How they get information they value and accept:
      (i) Groups they belong to
      (ii) What they read
      (iii) Internet usage patterns

Exhibit 10

Defining the Ideal Client: Using PRIZM

By Veronica J. Williams, Director of Marketing & Client Development, Downs Rachlin Martin

In determining the ideal client for our general practice firm here's the process I went through:

I interviewed nearly half of our attorneys to identify the buyer type they are trying to target (I couldn't do it by industry/employees/revenue because we are a general practice firm). I then collated that information and discovered that typically it broke down into 4 major categories: CEO/Owner, In-house counsel, Media, and Potential lateral hires.

Then, I researched our best contacts in those categories to identify the "ideal" and then utilized PRIZM data from www.claritas.com to create a "representative" (not actual because the attorneys get very caught up in the exact details) persona. I currently use stock images of people to represent the category, but would eventually prefer avatars that are reflective of our brand. I keep these personas posted on my walls—it helps inform all the marketing decisions I need to make to support the attorneys' business development efforts. While I also list some major demographics and psychographics on these client posters, the image itself speaks volumes. I have 4 posters, one for each target, including a photo and then the demographics/psychographic below.

According to the Claritas website, "The PRIZM program defines every U.S. household in terms of 66 demographically and behaviorally distinct types, or "segments," to help marketers discern those consumers' likes, dislikes, lifestyles and purchase behaviors. Used by thousands of marketers within Fortune 500 companies, PRIZM provides the "common language" for marketing in an increasingly diverse and complex American marketplace. PRIZM enables marketers to create a complete portrait of their customers by answering these important questions: Who are my best customers? What are my best customers like? Where can I find my best customers?

How can I reach my best customers? With PRIZM segmentation marketers can better understand their customers and prospects, and reach them with tailored messages and products designed just for them. Captured by catchy nicknames, images and behavioral snapshots that bring the segment to life for marketers, PRIZM segments are memorable and summarize complex consumer profiles in a way that is intuitive and easy to communicate."

Exhibits 11-16: Business Development Plan Templates

Exhibit 11

Individual Marketing/Business Development Action Plan ("IMAP"sm)

(This form has been generously provided by the LawVision Group.)

(Form has been reduced in length, rows for notes deleted, and spacing compacted to accommodate this book.)

Marketing/Business Development Action Plan for:
Direct Phone: **Email:**
Next Meeting/Phone Update:

This Individual Marketing/Business Development Action Plan ("IMAP sm") was created to help you achieve your goals and stay focused on the clients, prospects and activities that offer the best opportunity for securing new business.

My Primary Goals & Objectives for the Next Twelve to Eighteen Months
1.
2.
3.

***Target Markets** describes the target companies/individuals you would like to have as clients. Examples: pharmaceutical companies; real estate developers; healthcare institutions; energy companies; wealthy individuals. By targeting your efforts, you will begin to build your "brand" in the industry/*

among the client group, and you will be better able to understand the key issues relative to those companies/individuals.

Target Markets:
1.
2.
3.

Target Referral Markets *describes the target companies/individuals who may send you business. They are individuals who may also be involved in the target industry on which you are focusing or strong contacts who are your peers. Examples include: accountants; lawyers; industry consultants; existing clients, etc. Target referrals are individuals with whom you will proactively develop relationships.*

Target Referral Markets:
1.
2.
3.

Key Groups and Organizations *describes your participation in networking and relationship development activities for the current year. Examples include conferences you will attend, referral networks, trade associations, leadership positions with industry groups, alumni networks, civic or charitable organizations, clubs, boards.*

Key Groups and Organizations for the Upcoming Year
1.
2.
3.

Please describe one or more value propositions (hot issues) which will enable you to proactively open doors with current or prospective clients. Examples include briefings on new legislation, regulatory compliance audits, sourcing contract reviews, newsworthy occurrences in the marketplace with legal ramifications; CLE programs, IP portfolio reviews, international trademark updates, investigation compliance reviews, etc.

Value Propositions
1.
2.
3.

List your top clients. Include key contacts for relationship development in the current year. This initial list will broaden into your Contact Activity Tracker list as you continue on in the process.

	Top 5 Clients	**Key Contacts**
1.		
2.		
3.		
4.		
5.		

List your top potential clients. Include key contacts for relationship development in the current year. Potential clients are target decision-makers from companies in key industries or areas of focus described in your "Target Markets" above. This initial list will broaden into your Contact Activity Tracker.

	Top 5 Prospective Clients	**Key Contacts**
1.		
2.		
3.		
4.		
5.		

List your top competitors. MVPs are names of individual lawyers who are superstars at the competitor.

	Top 5 Competitors	MVPs
1.		
2.		
3.		
4.		
5.		

From month to month it will be important to have attainable action steps. By creating a manageable few each month, you will stay on track and keep the ball rolling.

	Action Steps	Date for Completion
1.		
2.		
3.		
4.		
5.		
6.		
7.		
8.		

Exhibit 12

Business Development Contact Activity Tracker

(This form has been generously provided by the LawVision Group.)

Name: **Date:**

Contact Name	Client ✔	Company	Telephone Email	Email/Phone				In Person		Next Step
				Q1	Q2	Q3	Q4	1st Half	2nd Half	

Exhibit 13

Business Development Tracking Form: By Category

(Word doc. Insert rows as needed. Row height expands to hold data.)
Courtesy of Peter Johnson/www.LawPracticeConsultants.com

Name: **Date:**

Client Name	Contact (Name & title)	Goal	Activities	Deadline	Results	Next Steps/ Deadline
1. EXISTING CLIENTS: Getting additional work/building and strengthening relationships						
2. NEW CLIENTS: Developing relationships with potential clients						
3: REFERRAL SOURCES: Developing/strengthening relationships						
4. GENERAL NETWORKING						
5. REPUTATION BUILDING/CREDENTIALING (writing, speaking)						
6. Cross Selling						
7. Professional Development (developing legal expertise/improving your skills)						

Exhibit 14

Business Development Tracking Form: Activities

(Four page form reduced to fit this book. Insert rows as needed.)
Courtesy of Peter Johnson/www.LawPracticeConsultants.com

Name:
Weeks of:

For each of the categories below, briefly describe the nature of the business development activity, and note any particular highlight. (Include the following; Name, Contact Information, Date, Next Steps, Follow up Date.)

(1) **Strengthening relationships with existing clients and referral sources.**

Activities/Notes:

Future Activities Scheduled:

---

(2) **Developing relationships with new clients/new referral sources.**

Activities/Notes:

---

(3) **General networking activities.**

Activities/Notes:

Future Activities Scheduled:

---

(4) **Getting known internally/internal networking.**

Activities/Notes:

Future Activities Scheduled:

(5) **Cross Selling Activities.**

Activities/Notes:

Future Activities Scheduled:

(6) **Developing reputation/name recognition externally.**

Activities/Notes:

Future Activities Scheduled:

(7) **Professional development/developing expertise/improving skills.**

Activities/Notes:

Future Activities Scheduled:

Notes:

Exhibit 15

Business Development Tracking Form: By Name

Business Development Tracking Form

Reduced in size; columns narrowed; row ht increased; words hyphenated; changed from landscape to portait to fit this book page.
(Excel doc. Insert rows as needed. Row height expands to hold data. Color keyed words changed to black for book.)
Courtesy of Peter Johnson/www.LawPracticeConsultants.com

Name of Person	Company	Relationship	Goal	Form of Contact	Date of Contact	Result of Contact	How Will You Follow-up?	Date of Next Contact
		(C)lient (P)rospect (R)eferral (O)ther	(Be Specific)	(M)eeting (P)hone call (S)eminar (O)ther				
CURRENT/ FORMER CLIENTS								
CLIENT PROSPECTS								
Smith, Mary	ABC	Prospect	Handle ABC Co's abitrations re issues X, Y and Z	Lunch	2/1/2012	Learned more about the arbitrations. Learned that Mary's colleague Joe picks outside litigation counsel. Mary agreed to introduce us by email.	Email to remind her on 2/14. Set up lunch with Mary and Joe.	Goal: Lunch by 3/1.
Schmo, Joe	ABC	Prospect	Handle ABC Co's abitrations re issues Q and R	Lunch	15-Mar	Discussed arbitrations and ABC criteria for choosing counsel. Joe said he'd keep me in mind.	Invite Joe to CLE on 4/1, find something relevant to send by 4/15, another in-person by 5/1.	
				Meeting	1-Apr	Saw Joe at CLE. Talked about getting together with a few other colleagues.	Identify right internal team, schedule lunch for late April	
REFERRAL SOURCES								
FIRM COLLEAGUES (Internal Marketing)								

Exhibit 16

Sample Associate Professional Development Plan

by Morrison Duane, Esquire

Professional Development Plan
January 1, 20__ through December 31, 20__

Professional Goals

- Become a member of the American Bar Association Business Law Section and its Blue Sky subcommittee.
  - **WILL COMPLETE BY:** End of First Quarter
- Prepare subcommittee seminar materials for spring meeting and attend meeting with senior members of the Corporate Department.
  - **WILL COMPLETE BY:** End of First Quarter
- Complete one article on recent developments in the area of securities law and attempt publication locally and nationally.
  - **WILL COMPLETE BY:** End of Third Quarter

Client Development Goals

- Meet a law school or college classmate for lunch at least once a quarter.
- Attend at least two client lunches with partners in the practice group.
  - **WILL COMPLETE BY:** End of Fourth Quarter
- Use securities law article as the basis for a one-hour internal CLE.
  - **WILL COMPLETE BY:** End of Second Quarter

Pro Bono/Community Involvement Goals

- Accept one transactional matter from local pro bono legal services group.
  - **WILL COMPLETE BY:** End of First Quarter

- Participate in local law school alumni events and offer to participate in the organization of one event for 2015.
  - **WILL COMPLETE BY:** End of Fourth Quarter
- Join and participate in local literacy project.
  - **WILL COMPLETE BY:** End of Third Quarter

Firm Involvement Goals

- Participate in a community involvement program sponsored by the firm.
- Assist with other in-house CLE programs given by the practice group.
  - **WILL COMPLETE BY:** End of Fourth Quarter

Strategy for Effective Use of Continuing Legal Education Requirements

- Attend two-day seminar addressing "Developments in Securities Law" in New York in October 2015 to build knowledge in this area.
  - **WILL COMPLETE BY:** End of Fourth Quarter
- Complete three hour online course addressing advanced issues in Mergers & Acquisitions by July 2015 to strengthen knowledge and practice skills in this area.
  - **WILL COMPLETE BY:** End of Third Quarter
- Attend bar-sponsored ½ day seminar on "Effective Negotiating Strategies" (scheduled for May 2015 to improve negotiating skills (noted in my evaluations as area for improvement).
  - **WILL COMPLETE BY:** End of Second Quarter

Exhibits 17-20: Understanding the Sales Process

Exhibit 17

A Brief Summary of The Sales Process

By David King Keller, PhD © 2015

In sales you must answer 3 essential questions.

(1) What's my product?
(2) Who's my buyer?
(3) How am I actively connecting my product to my buyer?

The answer to the third question is the "sales process."

It's very similar to persuading a jury that your client's story (the product) is the one the jury (the buyer) should agree to believe (buy).

Key elements of the **Sales Process** are:

Product/Service is clearly defined.

Identify Target Audience: Clearly define potential client pool of product/service buyers.

Market: Create awareness of your product/service within the target audience. Ask "discovery" questions (open/closed) of potential client to unearth their needs, pain points, and opportunities.

Lead generation**:** Develop some interest in product/service on the part of someone, now called a "lead."

Qualify the lead: verify the lead has a need for your product/service and has the ability to pay.

Prospect creation**:** You "advance" the lead to the "prospect" stage by motivating the lead to engage with you, e.g., a free consultation, a meeting, a proposal, concerns/ objections addressed, value demonstrated.

Sale/Client created: Ask for the business. Prospect becomes Client/ Buyer via engagement letter, payment; called the "close"/"closing the sale." A "sale" has occurred. Product bought /Service engaged.

Client Service/Referrals Requested: An essential part of a sale is the service that follows. This is the stage where a client can become a raving fan and a key referral source for new clients, or not.

Many will represent the sales process steps as a "sales pipeline" where you start at one end of a pipe and advance the party to the other end; or represent the sales process stages as a "sales funnel" where you place a large number in the wide open top of the funnel, and filter out the non-clients as you advance parties down through and to the funnel's narrow bottom with only clients coming out. People will ask you where are you along the sales pipeline with XYZ party, or what stage are they within the sales funnel?

Example of need satisfaction selling: As a Sales Executive with XEROX, I uncovered a need of one prospect and invented an accessory to a $250,000 machine to satisfy that need. My invention opened up a whole class of heretofore unavailable clients that increased XEROX sales by $98 million a year.

If you love your product then selling it is sharing your passion with those that can benefit. A win-win.

Exhibit 18

Comparing Legal Skills To Sales Skills During Client/Buyer Acquisition Steps

By David King Keller, PhD © 2015

The Client/Buyer Acquisition Steps	
Comparison of Legal Skills to Sales Skills	
(Partial List)	
Legal Skills	**Sales Skills**
Must clearly define service/product	Must clearly define service/product
Must clearly define potential client/buyer	Must clearly define potential client/buyer
Knows multiple ways to connect client/buyer with service/product	Knows multiple ways to connect client/buyer with service/product
Can effectively describe and communicate value of service/product	Can effectively describe and communicate value of service/product
Resourceful: Knows how, who, where to get help	Resourceful: Knows how, who, where to get help
Proactive listening skills; empathic listeners excel	Proactive listening skills; empathic listeners excel
Discovery: Need for service/product discovery skills via open/closed questioning	Discovery: Need for service/product discovery skills via open/closed questioning
Lead /Prospect location and identification process	Lead /Prospect location and identification process
Client/Buyer identification process	Client/Buyer identification process

(*Continued*)

Legal Skills	Sales Skills
Concerns elicitation/Objection handling skills	Concerns elicitation/Objection handling skills
Pace and lead conversation skills; body language interpreter; rapport and trust building skills.	Pace and lead conversation skills body language interpreter; rapport and trust building skills.
Message: "I truly want to help, not just sell."	Message: "I truly want to help, not just sell."
Negotiation skills	Negotiation skills
Good closer: Knows multiple ways to ask for the business/order.	Good closer: Knows multiple ways to ask for the business/order.
Engagement/Retainer/Invoice/Sales Process	Engagement/Retainer/Invoice/Sales Process
Effective payment/billing/collection methods	Effective payment/billing/collection methods
Client Service following engagement/sale	Client Service following engagement/sale
Ability to retain and re-sell existing clients	Ability to retain and re-sell existing clients
Referral source creation skills	Referral source creation skills

Exhibit 19

The Business Development Cycle

Courtesy of Silvia Coulter and LawVision
Copyright LawVision, Inc. 2010

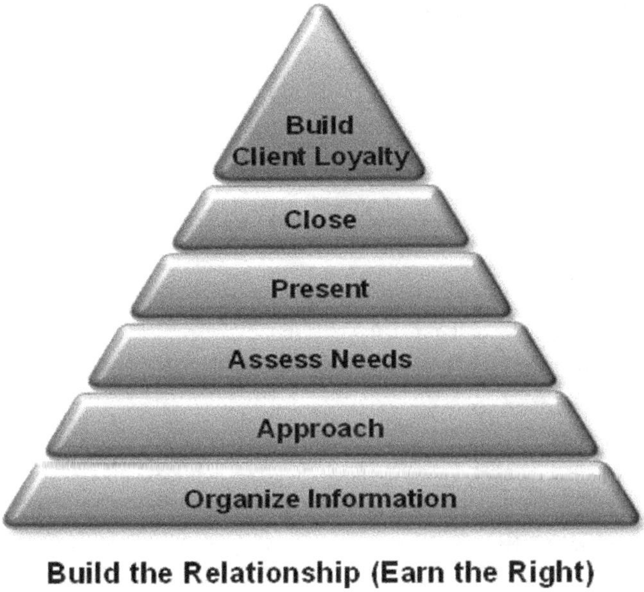

(1) Organize information—Develop a list of at least 50 contacts with whom you will be in touch quarterly.

(2) Approach—Phone or visit clients, prospective clients and good referral sources regularly. Send information to them to stay top of mind.

(3) Assess Needs—Ask lots of questions. Talk 20% Listen 80% of the time. Find out about their goals, strategies, needs and organization.

(4) Present—Based on Needs Assessment, discuss how you/your firm can address their needs. Bridge whatever you say to something that is important to them. Otherwise, it's nice to know versus need to know information.
(5) Close—Ask for the business. You will not get business unless you ask for it; even from friends.
(6) Build loyalty—Conduct regular annual "audits" to check in and see how things are going. Clients very much appreciate this.

Exhibit 20

10 Ways To Ask For The Order

By David King Keller, PhD © 2015

There are many types of closing 'techniques.' Here are 10 plus.

Four of the most well- known closing techniques are:

#1: **Trial Close**

Used to check if they are ready to engage your services.

"If you give us the green light *now* we could get started on this first thing tomorrow."

#2: **Confident Close/Assume-The-Sale Close**

"When would you like us to have that draft M&A agreement to you?"

#3. **Alternative Choice Close**

"Would you prefer to have us do the estate planning for just the C- Suite executives or all senior level managers?"

#4. **Fear of Loss/Consequences Close**

"The statute of limitations is about to run out should we get started on this today?"

#5: **The Easy Conversational Close:** The soft gentle test close:

"So...what do *you* see as the next step?"[1]

[1]The more sophisticated attorney will have been listening for "predicate mode" cues given by the client/potential client; and if a dominant predicate mode is detected, be it visual, auditory or kinesthetic, then use their language, their dialect, their predicate mode when asking the question. "See" is a visual predicate mode. "What 'feels' like the next best step" is using kinesthetic predicate mode. "Please 'tell' me what you think is the next best step" would be using the auditory predicate mode.

#6.—#10.+ Ask the top 2 rainmakers from each practice group to record the different ways they ask for the business. Make those available during business development instruction and on your firm's private intranet. If you're a solo, ask the President and Section Chair of your County and State Bar and/or Section or Forum Chair of the American Bar Association for assistance with examples that have worked for them and other members.
Select three "closes" and practice them until they are second nature.

Exhibits 21-25: Marketing Firm/Self

Exhibit 21

Role of Marketing and Business Development During Client's Hiring Process

(Courtesy of Bill Flannery and WJF Institute)

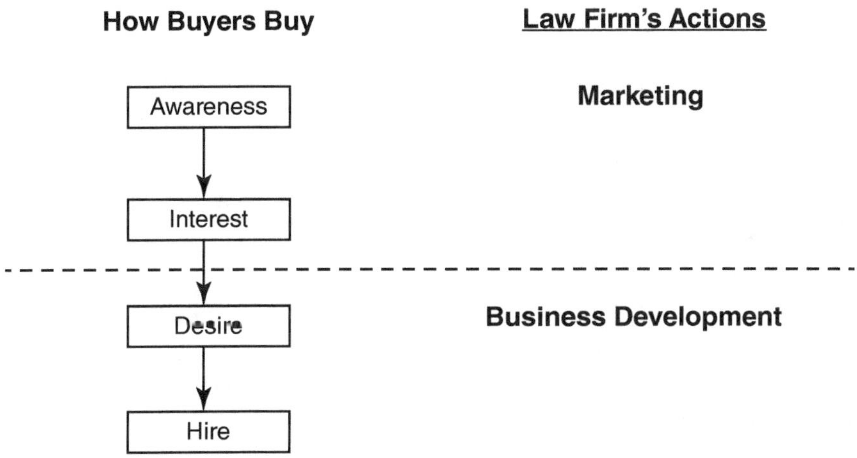

Rule : Your Mission In Marketing and Business Development Is To Change The Buyer's Behavior.

The above graphic helps to identify the role of law firm marketing and business development as it aligns with the client hiring process

Exhibit 22

The Ten Most Effective Law Firm Marketing Techniques

By Larry Bodine

Many lawyers don't get new clients and files because they don't do enough business development activities, or they waste time on the wrong activities, or they don't get face-to-face with potential clients.

What you'll read next are the most effective marketing techniques. These tips are based on scientific research that I have conducted where we asked 377 marketing partners and marketing professionals in the professional services fields what they did that worked. I'm going to cover 10 particular points.

Number one: You have to spend at least 2.5 percent of your gross revenues on marketing. Otherwise, you're just pretending to market. That 2.5 percent does not include the salaries of any of the people that you may have hired to perform the work. This is money that is spent on generating new business, on taking clients out to lunch, on visiting clients - it's all direct marketing activities. You have to put your money where your mouth is. If you're not spending 2.5 percent, you're not being serious about marketing, and you're not going to get any results.

The second technique is to put video on your website. The reason that I bring this up is you may have noticed that YouTube is sponsoring presidential debates. It's the number four most popular website online on the internet. That's because roughly 30 percent of the population has grown up with the internet always present in their lives. Just as I grew up with fax machines, touch-tone phones, and microwave ovens - they were something I always accepted as being there. All of these people - the 30 percent of the population that has always had the internet - are looking for video. That's what they expect. It's very easy to record a video and put it online. If you don't have any video on your site, you're really missing a good trick. It's a great opportunity to present how you look, how you talk, what you're like, and make yourself more attractive to clients. It's a great business-getting technique.

The third point: Don't waste any money on marketing that is not measurable. If you can't measure it, don't do it. For instance, advertising and public relations are widely used, but after you've spent $20,000 on it, do you have any way that you can check to see if it actually generated any results? I don't think so. What I would suggest you do is pursue the techniques that you can measure. That would include blogs. You can publish up a blog and see how many people visited. On a blog, you can also see how many people commented. If you really have to advertise, take out a banner ad. A banner will tell you how many people took a look at your banner and how many people clicked on it. The same thing is true with email newsletters. It's possible to send out an email newsletter and get a report on how many people actually opened it, and if there are links inside it, how many of the links were clicked on and who clicked on them. Those are all measurable activities.

Number four: When it comes to business development, start with the low-hanging fruit, and that is your own clients. These are people who love you, they trust you, they send you work, they are sending you checks. It's incumbent upon you to get to know them better to see if you can generate additional files from them. It's much easier to open a new file from a current client than it is to originate a brand new client. Again, this is something that you can measure. You can measure the number of times the attorneys in your firm have actually visited the client, how many times they had lunch with a client or a referral source. Or, if you have an event at your firm, you can count the number of attendees, keep track of all their contact information, and then trace in the new matter reports how many of them turned into new files. The bottom line is you should start at the *beginning* of any sort of marketing initiative by figuring out how are you going to measure it. If you don't do that, you have no way of knowing whether it succeeded or not.

The next thing is to cultivate referral sources. A lot of lawyers get most of their business from referrals, and that's a wonderful thing, but the point is that it doesn't just happen all by itself. The people who get these referrals are lawyers who cultivated them.

- Where I would start is with clients. Again, these are people that you're doing work for, but *unless you tell them that they're supposed to send you new work* and that you would welcome this new work, they won't know that they're supposed to do so. You actually have to tell them.
- Step two is you tell them what kind of work you're seeking. If you're doing a lot of commercial real estate transactions and they're

sending you matrimonial cases, you haven't explained the kind of work that you're looking for.

- There are lots of other referral sources besides clients. There are people that you will know in other professions such as investment brokers, accountants, and bankers. These are all people that can send you business so long as you tell them that you would like them to and what kind of work to send.
- The same thing is true with law school classmates. These are people who know you. If you're a litigator, obviously you don't want to approach the litigators because they're in competition with you. Approach all the people who have a transaction practice. Chances are they're going to have some sort of a transaction that went south, and they're going to need your help.

Number six: Get active in a trade association, and get on the board of directors. You'll notice that I said, trade association, and not bar association. You should join an association of clients. You want to get in front of a room full of clients, people who can potentially hire you. You find out about these trade associations by asking your current clients what meetings they go to. Then it's a simple matter of saying, "I'd like to join you at the meeting. Would you introduce me to your friends?" These friends, of course, are all potential clients for you. It's no good just going to the meeting; you have to be *visible.* Your goal when you join a trade association is not to be just a face in the crowd. Your goal is to get on the board of directors. The way you do that is you seek out the president and you volunteer. You volunteer to help put together programs; you volunteer to help with the newsletter; you volunteer to help in any sort of activity that is going to lead to a board position.

Number seven: Only after you've done all of these things, then pursue target clients. What I mean by "target" is a business executive whom you already know. You don't have to make any cold calls. Whom you're contacting could be a neighbor. It could be another dad or mom at a little league game. I originated a Fortune 500 company by just talking to another dad at a little league game and asking him what line of work he was in and what kind of business problems he faced. You can meet targets in the religious organizations that you go to and the clubs that you belong to and the charities that you're active in - these are all people who have businesses - that's what you looking for - and they all have careers. Ask them questions about it.

Number eight: If you do have a business plan, write it down. It's not real until you write it down. What you want to be writing down is whom you're going to call, when you're going to meet them, and some sort of an outcome that you're expecting to have. The idea of writing it down is now you've moved it on to your calendar. Once it's on your to-do list, you're going to do it.

Number nine: A question I get a lot is "How much time should I devote to business development?" Point number nine is I would recommend 200 hours a year. That may sound like a lot, but when you break it down by week, it's really only four hours a week. You can meet somebody for coffee at Starbucks in the morning. You can meet a client. You can meet a referral source for lunch. You can go to a trade association meeting in the evening. All of this you can weave into your ordinary to-do list, and before you know it, you've devoted 400 hours. I guarantee you are going to get way more back in new business and new clients than the value of the effort that you devoted.

My closing point, number ten, is to track your results. If you are undertaking a marketing initiative such as, "joining the local business owners club, make a point of writing down the people that you want to meet before you go. After you've met your targets, asked them about their business challenges, later you can to go back and ask yourself, "Did this work? Did I get a new file?" I recall working with a lawyer who was spending money on radio ads, and he was reaching a huge number of people, but he examined his new clients and none of them came from the radio. He wasn't getting any new business out of it at all, so he discontinued it. That's the approach you have to make, but you only will be able to do that if you track your results.

So count to ten, pick the ideas you will pursue, and just do it. The more activities you choose, the more clients and revenue you'll bring in.

Exhibit 23

This One Statistic Will Define Your Entire Client Strategy

By Michael B. Rynowecer
President and Founder of The BTI Consulting Group

One statistic stands out as most compelling: The typical large company uses 47 law firms.

The typical middle market company commonly uses about 8 law firms. Each of these law firms wants to grow between 5% and 7%. This means most law firms will not be able to get their increased share of business without taking this business from another law firm. This will only happen by developing business with each client in a manner which is better than the other law firms. It also means the law firm with the best client service is best positioned to get the business.

Exhibit 24

Turn Every Vendor Into a Potential Referral Source

By David King Keller, PhD © 2015

If a vendor comes into your law firm selling you something, never let them leave without asking them for referrals.

More than likely the person that you're speaking with has been in the business for some time and they know a great number of people many of whom are potential clients of yours. There are many ways to ask that person for a referral. Here is one way:

Mike, I know we're talking about our firm using your service and I know you've been in this business for a while and you've spoken to a lot of different firms and companies many of them could actually become clients of this firm. And I know you did not come in here with a list of 12 other companies or firms that could hire us but if you were to think of two or three *right now* who would you mention? (Then be absolutely silent while their brain processes the question particularly in the form in which you just presented it.)

Yes, the above technique employs a little bit of what would be called an Ericksonian auto-suggestion strategy. Compare the above example to: "Hey Mike, know anybody that could hire our firm?" It might get the same result, but the odds are that the first approach sets them up for a more considered answer.

And don't forget Pavlov!

Associate your request with something that brings them pleasure. Following their response to your referral request give them a Starbucks card or a small box of chocolate or a discount coupon to a local restaurant or validate their parking. You should have a drawer full of very low cost goodies that you can present to people to reward behavior that you would like to see repeated. Use your imagination when it comes to this small, very low cost, reward.

Exhibit 25

Developing an Effective Elevator Pitch

(Courtesy of Melanie Green and Faegre Baker Daniels)

An elevator pitch is a quick and concise way to communicate who you are, what you do, and why you can do it better than the competition. You should have an elevator pitch prepared for when you run into an acquaintance, when you meet someone new, or when someone asks what you do. Your pitch should be descriptive and catchy so you can keep the conversation going, convey your essential messages succinctly, and showcase your practice in a way that gets people excited and thinking.

Why is an elevator pitch important?

When you don't have an elevator pitch ready and you give short, non-descriptive answers to introductory questions, the conversation dies and developing the relationship becomes difficult. For example:

Q: What do you do?

A1: "I'm a lawyer."

A2: "I'm an employment lawyer who helps advertising agencies comply with state and federal wage and hour regulations to avoid costly penalties and litigation. I've counseled several international agencies on proper employee classification and kept them out of court at a time when many agencies were facing expensive lawsuits."

Q: How is work going?

A1: "Busy" or "fine."

A2: Right now I'm focused on guiding a medical device company during a product recall. Fortunately, I assisted this client with due diligence before the product launched, so we are prepared with the proper documentation, recall plan and employee training to help our client weather this setback while minimizing financial and reputational harm to the business.

Tips for your elevator pitch:

(1) **Make it memorable:** Describe your core service from a client's perspective and tell why you and the firm are unique.
(2) **Solve a problem:** Explain what needs you meet.
(3) **Turn adversity into opportunity:** Lay out your prescription for the problems you solve. Boil down the unique elements of your approach into one or two sentences.
(4) **Lay out the benefits:** You're not pitching a great idea, team or product. You're pitching what your idea, team and product will do for clients and businesses.
(5) **Conclude with a call to action:** Different audiences prompt different requests. Ask clients and contacts if they know anyone experiencing the problem you solve, working on something similar or working in the industry you counsel. Ask if they will make an introduction or tell them you will follow up next week.
(6) **Make it tangible:** Talk in tangibles, not abstractions. Kill J.D., MBA and tech-speak. Keep it short and at a level people can understand. Include client names as appropriate.

Show your passion: Let your passion be evident as you describe solving clients' problems. Get them excited about your work.

Questions to consider when developing your elevator pitch:

What problem(s) do I solve?
For whom do I solve those problems?
How am I different or how is my work compelling?
What is a good-fit situation for my work?
Why should this person care?
What do clients say about me?

For assistance developing your elevator pitch, contact your group's business development and marketing liaison.

Exhibits 26-28: Key Business Development Topics

Exhibit 26

How to Hire a First-Year Associate Who has Rainmaker Awareness

By David King Keller, PhD © 2015

Can you spot a future rainmaker in a first-year associate hire?

One researcher mentioned that any sales experience at all, even a lemonade stand as a child was an indicator of potential rainmaker capabilities.

After determining excellent legal skills and training commiserate with his/her experience level, how do you interview for first-year associates who have better-than-average likelihood of being rainmakers based on some awareness of sales, finance and how businesses function. Law firms need to add business awareness skills to their interview process. Following is a partial list:

(1) Have they participated in a "hands on" lawyer experience training program like that offered by Florida State University Law School (endowed by book contributor Wayne Hogan), or the Colorado Law business awareness training program (designed by book contributor Bill Mooz)?
(2) Ever worked in a business?
(3) Ever have a boss?
(4) Any newspaper routes?
(5) Lemonade stands?
(6) Any part-time or full-time jobs?
(7) Ever been a wait person? Bar tender. Barista?
(8) Ever raised money for a charity?
(9) Ever work with a budget?
(10) Any sales experience?
(11) Familiar with business org chart?
(12) Ever sell to another business?

(13) Ever sell to consumers?
(14) Ever made anything that you then sold?
(15) Project management awareness?
(16) Does the General Counsel of a Corporation have a boss?
(17) Own stocks? Invest in stocks?
(18) Owner or shareholder in a company?
(19) Ever done legal work for anyone? A business?
(20) Ever worked for in-house counsel?
(21) Ever done legal work for anyone? A business?
(22) Ever had a legal discussion with in-house counsel?
(23) Ever set up a business?
(24) Ever sold a business?
(25) Ever valuated a business?
(26) Ever priced a product? Examining costs and margins? Cost analysis?
(27) Ever produce a financial report?
(28) Besides moot court, have you ever been in the role of persuading someone?
(29) Play chess? Poker? Golf? Tennis? Row? Sail? Team sports?
(30) C-Suite Experience?
(31) Ever worked with P&L Statements?
(32) Ever invented anything?
(33) Ever been in a business that required very happy clients to stay in business?
(34) Ever been on a board of directors?
(35) Ever worked on a fund raising campaign?
(36) Ever been involved with the media, newspaper, magazine, press, radio, TV, YouTube channel?
(37) On LinkedIn? Facebook? Other social media?
(38) Done public speaking?
(39) Been on stage? Acting? Improv?
(40) How many LinkedIn connections do you have?
(41) Do you blog?
(42) Have you written any published articles?
(43) Leadership roles? In business, sports, non-profit, or other setting?
(44) Boy Scouts? Girl Scouts? Clubs?
(45) Marketed or sold anything live or online?
(46) Worked with financial or accounting software?
(47) Do you have family or friends who could potentially hire a law firm like ours?

This is not an exhaustive list nor in any way conclusive. You could hire a first-year who has zero work and sales experience but has family and friend connections that can bring in business, or has demonstrated other skill sets that cause you to believe this person has rainmaker abilities.

This list is designed to elicit a certain level of applicant's comfort with the business of creating satisfied clients out of strangers and understanding the P&L issues every in-house counsel is facing and would like to know that outside counsel is in a position to understand and appreciate.

Happy hiring.

Exhibit 27

Stress, Anxiety and Depression

By David King Keller, PhD © 2015

This Is Not Medical Advice.

Depression can be like a punch in the stomach and take the wind out of any skilled attorney's ability to perform his or her legal duties, and, obviously, to an even greater extent their ability to perform business development functions.

Everyone at every level of management at a law firm can benefit from having some awareness about depression and its signs, and need to have developed a protocol when and if they come face-to-face with someone who says they are depressed. Your initial response is to say that they should immediately meet with their healthcare professional, and then verify that this was done. A secondary response, of course, is to say, how can the firm, if at all possible, help reduce your level of stress, anxiety, and/or depression?

For those of us who want to do some personal research for our own benefit and curiosity, then the following book by Peter Symons might be of interest, *Brain-Fuel Depletion: Making Sense of Anxiety and Depression.* Symons points out that the cause of anxiety and depression for many may be lack of the "brain fuels" that support neurotransmitter activity, specifically the proper messaging between axons and dendrites. Therapeutic levels of sleep, exercise, proper nutrition, vitamin D and a high quality omega supplement have all been shown in Symons research to support the brain's neurotransmitter functions. Another resource for research and potential relief is attorney Jeena Cho's website, TheAnxiousLawyer.com, and Don Goewey's book, *The End of Stress.* My doctoral dissertation was on *Micro-Mindfulness*, a practice that takes 30 seconds and is supported by published studies that shows it can reduce heart rate, enhance mood, switch the body from the sympathetic autonomic nervous system (geared for producing the stress response hormone cortisol and fight or flight) to the calmer, less-stressed parasympathetic autonomic nervous system. The first step is six deep breaths. That is enough in some cases to reduce heart rate and slow or stop cortisol production. Research at Ohio State and elsewhere showed that a break lasting only 30 seconds every two hours can significantly reduce errors and increase productivity.

I always recommend to my attorney coaching clients to set their smart phone to vibrate every 2 hours. I use 9am, 11am, 1pm, and 3pm. Associates should add 5pm and 7pm. Stop. Take six deep breaths, move your body a little or a lot, then dictate a voice-to-text email exactly what you're doing for a client in detail in the active voice and send it to yourself or accounting for review later when structuring your client invoice. Just knowing that you're on top of your billing is stress reducing, and as we know from comments in this book, *Building Rainmakers,* that clients really appreciate more, not less, detail when it comes to billing. According to a 2001 Cornell/Lockheed Martin study a thirty second break every two hours reduces errors and increases productivity. Reduce stress, increase productivity, and improve billing. Very good use of a 30 to 60 second break.

More information on stress reduction if you send a request to david@kbdag.com.

Exhibit 28

Draft Law School Curricula On Law Practice Business Development

Using Building Rainmakers Book As Supporting Text

By David King Keller, PhD

Partial List of Lecture/Discussion Topics

Defining Law Practice and Law Practice Development
Practice Area Options: Public, Private, Commercial, Consumer
Professional Development vs Business Development
The Economics of a Comm'l Law Practice: Solo vs Associate/Partner Firms
Defining Your Law Practice, and Defining Your Desired Client Base
How To Connect Your Law Practice With Your Desired Client Base
Defining Your Value Proposition
Define Success and Who Succeeds In Today's Legal Market
The Role of Branding, Marketing, Networking and Selling in a Comm'l Legal Practice
Defining Client Service That Creates Referrals
The Business Development Plan
Eight Ways to Measure Law Firm Business Development Activity
Attorney Work-life Balance, Stress, Resilience
The Art and Science of Being a Law Practice Rainmaker

Nota Bene: See Exhibit 29 which has over 300 law practice business development questions answered by this book, Building Rainmakers,

The Definitive Guide To Business Development For Lawyers. These questions can form the basis for classroom discussions, homework assignments, quizzes, tests, and exams. Becoming an adjunct professor and bringing law practice business development awareness and skills to law school students is a career goal of this author.

Exhibit 29: 300 Questions to Test Your BD IQ/Answers in The Book

Exhibit 29

Over 300 Business Development Questions

Answered by Building Rainmakers Book

In most cases at least one location for the answer is referenced within parentheses following the question.

(1) What is a typical reaction when a potential client is asked for their business? (Taylor)

(2) Can you name one sure fire way to turn a client into a raving fan? (Karen Bell)

(3) Who are the best attorneys to invest your limited business development coaching dollars? (Coulter)

(4) What is SPIN and how does it add new clients and new client matters? (Flannery)

(5) Can you name 8 categories of business development activities to measure? (Fitzgarrald)

(6) What is one way to automatically ensure that cross-selling takes place? (Schmidt, Various)

(7) Your verbal business card should be able to answer what four questions? (Schmidt)

(8) What are the three most important traits of a Rainmaker in securing new business? (Keller, Various)

(9) Can you name 5 ways to motivate an attorney to pursue new business? (Ackert)

(10) What are three different methods to teach an associate business development? (Goldsholle, Severson, Taylor, Usellis, Berardi, Hammerstrom, Muldoon, Chichester, Weber, K. Bell, Lee, Green, S. Bell, Kostakos, Febeo, Haglund, Zavalsky, Meszaros, Bruns, Various)

(11) What is one bit of advice you can give an introvert to feel more comfortable at a networking event, or at a meeting with a potential client? (Bodine, Keller)
(12) Can you name 3 ways a client's bill can cost you their business? (Goldsholle, Keller, Schmidt, Various)
(13) How can white space/green space analysis increase business development? (Zavalsky, Green)
(14) What's the first activity an associate should take to learn about the firm's people and resources? (Taylor)
(15) What is the sales process? (Coulter, Keller, Exhibit 20, 22, Various)
(16) According to research at Stanford what is one non-verbal way to build rapport with someone in a face to face meeting? (Keller, Various)
(17) Can you name two non-law school indicators of potential rainmaker success when hiring a new associate? (Keller, Various)
(18) What does a "tactical" approach to business development mean? (Haglund)
(19) What is a pipeline meeting? (Hammerstrom)
(20) How often can a client feedback survey result in new business? (Schmidt)
(21) What is a client professional development program? (K Bell)
(22) What is content marketing, and how do you use it to increase SEO? (Bodine)
(23) What would be an example of a free value-add a lawyer can offer his client to introduce a lawyer from another practice area? (Freeman, K. Bell, Keller)
(24) When you meet a potential client for the first time it's the quality of your *what* that demonstrates your expert in your field? (Fairley)
(25) Can you name the United States Supreme Court Justice, who said, "Everything I ever did I was afraid to do"? (Keller)
(26) What is one technique that some people have successfully used to overcome shyness and introversion? (Keller)
(27) How do lawyer skills compare to sales skills when addressing a potential client? (O'Horo, Keller, Various, Exhibit 21)
(28) Beyond excellent legal skills, what are some of the qualities that in-house counsel are looking for when hiring new outside counsel? (Keller, Silber)
(29) As outside counsel what can you offer to do for free for in-house counsel that will make their day? (Flaherty)
(30) What one factor causes many to believe an external coach is essential? (Keller, Silber)

(31) What key question can elicit an attorney's desire to excel in business development? (Keller)

(32) Can you name three billing mistakes that can cost you a client? (Schmidt, Goldsholle)

(33) Can you name one way to quickly handle stress? (Keller, Goewey)

(34) Does it help your business to tell a client "business is booming I'm really busy"? (Schmidt, C4)

(35) Never tell a lawyer how to conduct business development before you do what? (Schmidt, C4)

(36) What is the best way to hold an attorney accountable for their business development activity? (Haglund, Johnson, Fitzgarrald, Kostakos, Fairley, Keller, Meszaros, Various)

(37) What are 4 business development activities to discuss with your associates? (Severson)

(38) What is the *Fast Forward* business development program? (Weber)

(39) What's a network map? (Kostakos, Febeo) When should business development training begin? (Meszaros)

(40) What is the Legal Mocktail? (Hammerstrom)

(41) How often should business development activity be conducted? (Bruns)

(42) How can a firmwide business development standard template become a firm lifesaver? (Bruns)

(43) Is there a difference between a sales pipeline, sales funnel, sales cycle and the sales process? (Various)

(44) What are the three broad categories of challenges to business development facing an attorney? (Johnson)

(45) What is the minimum number of words in a new article on your website to attract attention by Google? (Bodine)

(46) What is the optimum rate at which you should update new content on your firm's website? (Bodine)

(47) What is another two word term for "cross-selling" that conveys the intended purpose behind the activity? (Severson)

(48) What role can your admin staff play in business development? (Keller)

(49) What are five good questions to ask anyone you meet particularly a potential client? (Exhibit 1, Exhibit 2)

(50) Can you name two famous people who had overcome shyness in order to be successful? (Keller)

(51) What role does the anterior cingulate cortex play in your career?(Keller)

(52) What is the second largest search engine on the Internet? (Keller, C4)
(53) What, on average, is one essential criteria to receive business from a potential client? (Coulter, Muldoon, Flannery, Various)
(54) What is the best way to prepare an associate for the associate to partner transition? (Taylor, Johnson, Lee, Haglund, Flannery, Various)
(55) What's the typical reaction of most associates when they become a new partner? (Weber, Various)
(56) When associates are asked to contact their former classmates, how do you handle the objection when they state, "Yeah, but my friends will think I'm marketing to them." (Coulter, Various)
(57) According to patent litigator Jon Waldrop, is business development relational or transactional? (Waldrop)
(58) Why does Jill Weber call the associate-to-partner transition "the sweet spot?" (Weber)
(59) According to Allen Chichester what's the best way for the business development staff to treat the firm's attorneys? (Chichester)
(60) Should you give an origination bonus to an associate? (Goodman, Coulter, Various)
(61) Is the bill sent to a client just an invoice, nothing else? (Goldsholle, Schmidt, Green, Keller, Schmidt, Various)
(62) Can you name 2 ways a client's bill can improve your chances of increasing client loyalty? (Green, Goldsholle, Schmidt)
(63) How important is an attorney's website bio? (Zavalsky, Salazar, Kartson, Various)
(64) When someone visits your firm's website, how often is it to look at an attorney's bio? (Keller)
(65) Can blogging generate new business? (Salazar, Flaherty, Bodine, Various)
(66) Should an attorney consider blogging? (Bodine, Flaherty)
(67) According to Larry Bodine what activity increases business as you increase that activity? (Bodine)
(68) According to Silvia Coulter what's more important blogging or face-to-face meetings? (Coulter)
(69) According to Tasneem Goodman what's the best way to encourage attorney BD behavior? (Goodman)
(70) Who said rewarding BD activity failure can be a good idea? (Flannery)
(71) What is a proven formula for business development success? (Silvia Coulter)
(72) Is there a distinction between coaching, training and consulting? (Johnson)

(73) Should your firm have a business development committee separate from the board of directors? (Weber)
(74) Should the business development plan be simple or complex? (Kartson)
(75) Should you have a business development/marketing checklist for associates by year? (Hammerstrom)
(76) Do you need a business development resource library? (Keller)
(77) Does brand development take precedent over business development?
(78) What is a good ratio of business development/marketing staff to total firm attorneys?
(79) Can you name one extremely effective way your attorney can meet a high level targeted potential client executive?
(80) What do you say to an attorney who hates to socialize but needs to increase his/her book of business?
(81) Do you have a 24/7 video access business development instruction library?
(82) What is a SWOT? (see Index)
(83) What is DIRP? (see Index)
(84) What is the "sales pipeline?" (Coulter, Keller, Exhibit, Various)
(85) What is the "sales funnel?" (Coulter, Keller, Exhibit, Various)
(86) Can you name two ways to build rapport with someone on a phone call? (Keller, Various)
(87) What is your firm's referral source compensation strategy? (Self)
(88) Should you conduct business development education with partners and associates at the same time? (Johnson, Coulter, Various)
(89) Who are your best internal rainmaker instructors for associates? (Coulter, Muldoon, Various)
(90) What single activity practiced at Barnes & Thornburg achieved fast business development awareness results? (Chichester)
(91) What are the core business development competencies you need to develop as an associate? (Lee)
(92) Does personality research/profiling help when working with attorneys on business development? (Various, see Index)
(93) Do you train associates/partners in addressing a client upset over a bill? (Various)
(94) Do you have a resiliency- awareness program?
(95) Do you have an organized approach to stress awareness and reduction?
(96) Is business development in your firm's DNA? (Taylor)
(97) How valuable is a time management education program? Do you have one? (Various)

(98) What is one key skill an aspiring rainmaker should have in order to take a holistic approach to a client relationship, and what is one way to develop and enhance that essential skill? (Muldoon)
(99) Is it important for your talent management team to work in close consultation with the business development team? (Muldoon)
(100) What's the best time during the week to train lawyers with a short program? (Kartson, Berardi)
(101) How organized and detailed should your firmwide business development be? (Chichester)
(102) Should everyone at the firm receive the same business development training? (Usellis)
(103) If you're the firm's first CMO, what do you do? (Lauterbach)
(104) What is the "tiered" approach to business development training? (Fitzgarrald)
(105) What is the best strategy when a launching a half-day group training with new instructors and firm attendees from other offices who may not know each other? (Johnson)
(106) How effective is a PowerPoint when teaching business development skills? (Kostakos, Febeo, Flannery)
(107) Is there a one-size-fits-all BD model that can work for all firm offices? (Berardi)
(108) Can you, should you develop a catalog of BD learning modules? (Berardi)
(109) Can you standardize a BD plan template? (Meszaros)
(110) Can anyone be a rainmaker? (Bodine)
(111) Your best BD instructors are fellow attorneys or outside BD consultants? (Berardi , Various)
(112) What's better, role-playing a client presentation or one-on-one coaching? (Bell, Flannery, Various)
(113) Do some people introduce Summers to business development?
(114) Who uses a mock pitch in their business development education program?
(115) What role, if any, does senior management play in the business development program? (Schmidt)
(116) What is a "Visibility Road Map"? (Zavalsky)
(117) What is a "client team?" (Severson)
(118) What does one-size-fit-one approach mean and where is it applied? (Severson)
(119) Is poor marketing better than no marketing? (Schmidt)
(120) How do you find time for business development? (Lauterbach, Various)

(121) What are two designs for a business development plan template? (Taylor, Meszaros, Johnson, Various)

(122) What is the difference between an internal coach and external coach and when should each be used?

(123) What is the next step after meeting someone in a networking event? (Hammerstrom)

(124) Besides asking a trusted colleague what is another good way to locate an outside consultant trainer or coach? (Keller)

(125) What is the "attorney marketing action plan"? (Fairley)

(126) Can you name one way to prioritize business development time? (Schmidt)

(127) Can you define the role of the chief marketing officer versus the business development manager versus the marketing coordinator versus the marketing assistant? (Fitzgarrald)

(128) What is the "Ready, Aim, Fire: Your Personal Brand" approach to business development? (Zavalsky)

(129) What is the practice group "one pager process"? (Zavalsky)

(130) What are two roles the rainmaker can play to help educate other attorneys on their rainmaking process? (Zavalsky)

(131) How does the pay-it-forward concept work within a mentoring program? (Zavalsky)

(132) What is the associate marketing checklist and where can I get one? (Zavalsky, Index, Various)

(133) What is meant by the power of checklists? (Keller)

(134) What is a CCO? (Bell)

(135) What is one famous instance of former trial adversaries coming together and changing the course of legal history because they practice civility when they were on opposite sides of another very famous case? (Keller)

(136) What is the 70/30 rule? (Haglund)

(137) How can the Australia legal market help us with business development in the US legal marketplace? (Muldoon)

(138) What is the role of education with a client? (Bell)

(139) How often should you conduct a client satisfaction survey at an institutional level? (Muldoon)

(140) Can lowering your billing rate increase revenue? (Meszaros)

(141) Can you name one client magnet being effectively used by a national firm? (Bell)

(142) What is the ideal ratio between law firm attorneys and in-house attorneys at that initial meeting? (Keller)

(143) How often should you have an off the clock meeting with your client? (Kartson)
(144) What is the "fishing hole concept" to locating new clients? (S Bell)
(145) What is meant by conducting a client "needs assessment"? (S Bell)
(146) When the Chief Sales & Marketing Officer for Womble Carlyle says, "Everything, everything, everything comes back to this." What does he mean? (S Bell)
(147) What is meant by a "client team"? (K Bell, Various)
(148) From a best practice standpoint is the client perceived as an entity or as an individual? (S Bell)
(149) How important is it that your law firm attorneys can speak C-Suite? (Various)
(150) What is a "key client program"? (Kartson)
(151) How essential is an external coach? (Silber, Green, Kartson, Trujillo, Keller, Various))
(152) What does the Google CEO say about having a coach? (Keller)
(153) What is one possibility as to why "the coaching just didn't work?" (Coulter)
(154) What is the Markowitz program and how did it double origination after two or three years in the program? (Trujillo)
(155) What are the three pillars of the 12 month rainmaker Coaching the Coaches program at Bryan Cave? (Trujillo)
(156) After 14 years of coaching the Law Practice Consultants group has increased or decreased the ratio of workshops to one-on-one coaching has increased or decreased? (Johnson)
(157) What is a good first step prior to starting a business development training and coaching program at a law firm? (Johnson)
(158) Is there more than one way to bring accountability to an attorney's business development program? (Johnson)
(159) What is meant by "the ask"? (Johnson)
(160) What is one good way to measure the success of an attorney one-on-one coaching program? (Johnson)
(161) What is the benefit to "code your clients"? (Schmidt)
(162) Would it help to survey the firm's attorneys with this question, "does the firm's compensation program fully incentivize you to conduct business development"? (Mooz)
(163) Is it true that, generally, people do what's measured and rewarded? (Johnson)
(164) Does your firm's compensation program support the firm's expectations of its attorneys? (Johnson)
(165) Is it a good idea to share the origination credit? (Coulter)

(166) What are four commonly accepted approaches to become successful as an attorney consumer advocate? (Boies, Hogan, Purcell)
(167) According to recent research are people finding attorneys more by asking a friend or colleague, or by going online? (Bodine)
(168) When considering search engine optimization does Google have a preference to new content from third-party sources or from original content written by you? (Bodine)
(169) Is there more than one way to define "rainmaking"? (Epstein)
(170) How often should you refresh your business development plan? (Epstein, Various)
(171) If you have to criticize someone can you name one technique that could minimize the negative impact of that criticism? (Stock)
(172) Can you name three CRM programs used by thought leaders in the legal field? (Hammerstrom, Fairley, Zavalsky, Various)
(173) Can you name one program that will provide you with business intelligence before walking into a client or potential client meeting? (Zavalsky, Various)
(174) Does a client team increase or decrease cross selling? (Usellis)
(175) Is there a difference between cross-marketing and cross-selling? (Berardi)
(176) When was your last whitespace/green space analysis to uncover BD opportunities? (Zavalsky, Green)
(177) How does white space analysis support cross-selling? (Zavalsky)
(178) Should you credit an attorney in one practice for introducing her client to another attorney in another practice in which a new matter is generated? (Keller)
(179) Does your law firm's compensation program and origination credit policy fully support the cross-selling activity? (Kessler)
(180) Does cross-selling help prevent a client from being poached by another firm? (Coulter)
(181) Does cross-selling improve comradery within a law firm? (Muldoon)
(182) What is a client collaboration group? (Green)
(183) What value is a firm's industry marketing group in support of cross-selling?
(184) To what degree does a firm's culture impact business development? (Bruns, Various)
(185) What law firm set up a formal institution within the firm for business development and professional development training? (Chichester)
(186) Who said "I think the true salespeople need to be the lawyers"? (JB)

(187) What is the purpose of this national firm's Dialogue Project Management® system, which is based on the general principles of the Project Management Institute? (K Bell)
(188) Does an MBA held a CMO? (Bruns)
(189) What does a director of business development need to do to stay on top of the marketplace? (Bruns)
(190) What role can the firm's rainmakers play in creating a firm's verbal business card AKA elevator pitch? (Kostakos)
(191) What are 4 qualities of a well- designed verbal business card /elevator itch? (Keller)
(192) What are the two best words to start an elevator pitch? (Kessler)
(193) Have you considered creating a brief comment that describes the firm and is circulated throughout the firm such as the one created by this AmLaw 5 law firm? (Muldoon)
(194) What are two common questions people ask you to which you need to have a simple direct answer? (Goodman)
(195) Can you name three ways to use an email as an online marketing tool? (Salazar, Various)
(196) What is the technique of partnering people with two different skill sets and backgrounds at an event? (Bruns)
(197) How should your attorneys think about Facebook and Twitter? (Salazar)
(198) What is one way to educate your attorneys on discussing pricing and alternative fee agreements with potential clients? (K. Bell)
(199) Can you name one element of a business development mindset culture to cultivate within a law firm? (Kartson)
(200) How essential is it that firm leadership conspicuously support a business development program? (Haglund)
(201) Does it work to pair a baby boomer as a business development mentor to a millennial? (Flannery, Various)
(202) Should you be sensitive when using the word "training"? (Flannery, Keller)
(203) Do you need to be cautious about using the word "sales"? (Various)
(204) What is one surefire way to separate yourself from the legal crowd when meeting with a potential client? (Flannery, K. Bell, Various)
(205) What is one of the most revenue generating activities that you can track that is a predictor of who will be a successful rainmaker or not? (Flannery)
(206) What is meant by rewarding failure in order to encourage business development activity? (Flannery)

(207) What does the client need to do in order to hire your firm for the first time? (Flannery)
(208) According to the Flannery training method what is the best way to educate an attorney on how to be a rainmaker? (Flannery)
(209) What is one precaution you need to take before speaking with someone at your potential client in terms of their decision-making authority? (Flannery)
(210) What is one way you can make the in-house attorney you are working for look good? (Flannery)
(211) What, according to Sylvia Coulter, is a proven formula for business development success? (Coulter)
(212) What is one business affiliation that major law firms should consider in order to further secure their work with certain clients? (Schmidt)
(213) How do you hire a new CMO? (Bruns)
(214) What is one firm action they can assure that cross-selling will occur? (Schmidt)
(215) Can you name three information aggregators? (Weber, S. Bell, Haglund, Hammerstrom, Various)
(216) When it comes to in-house counsel is the trend toward more billable hours or alternative fee agreements? (Keller, Silber)
(217) What is a "10% collar around a fixed fee"? (Keller, Silber)
(218) What is the role of diversity when being hired by in-house counsel? (Keller, Silber)
(219) Who does the GC have to answer to? (Keller, Silber)
(220) When quoting a group of GC panelists, what is the missing word in this sentence, "Building _____ was everything."? (Keller, Silber)
(221) According to one group of GC panelists are marketing leave-behinds reviewed? (Keller, Silber)
(222) What does in-house counsel Flaherty mean when he says when you are working on a case think in terms of "systems"? (Flaherty)
(223) How should an attorney treat the client's money? (Flaherty)
(224) What is one way outside counsel can introduce and ingratiate themselves to the legal department of a targeted client? (Keller)
(225) According to one GC, what is the missing word in this sentence, "We don't buy legal services; we buy _________" ? (Flaherty)
(226) How does a GC feel when outside counsel interacts with their internal clients? (Flaherty)
(227) What is your legal tech audit IQ? (Flaherty)
(228) As long as your end product is excellent, does in-house counsel care about your Microsoft Word and Excel skills? (Flaherty)

(229) Can you name two ways to help a lateral acquire new clients? (Coulter, Keller, Various)
(230) Can you name three ways to acquire new clients using LinkedIn? (Berardi, Salazar, Keller, Various)
(231) According to Erin Meszaros what are the three tiers that litigation cases now fall into? (Meszaros)
(232) According to one consultant in what year did the legal profession shift to a buyer's market after 25 years of being a seller's market? (O'Horo)
(233) What is a marketing audit? (Schmidt)
(234) What is a good ratio between marketing and business development support staff to the number of attorneys? (Chichester, Various)
(235) Can a formal mentoring program work? (Berardi, Various)
(236) Is mentoring essential for success? (Kloke, Various)
(237) What are 3 must-haves on your website homepage?
(238) When do you begin associate business development training?
(239) How can LTA –IQ help or hurt your chances with a GC. (See Flaherty)
(240) Can you name one networking trick to help mix at a networking event?
(241) What are the best first two words to use when introducing yourself?
(242) Should we have a formal mentoring program?
(243) When it comes to metrics, what are the best business development activities to measure?
(244) How do I educate associates in business development?
(245) Who makes more money, the generalist or the specialist?
(246) What is the best response to, "I don't have time for business development"?
(247) Should you pay an origination bonus to an associate?
(248) Does personality type awareness help in business development?
(249) Who said, "Pipelines eat business plans for lunch"?
(250) Can you name one pitch training program that makes a difference?
(251) What's one fast way to find a connection who knows someone at your targeted client?
(252) Can you name one way to achieve free PR?
(253) What is a sure fire way to assure cross-selling?
(254) How can you increase an attorney's resilience?
(255) What is one way to reduce shyness, introversion and fear of connecting?
(256) Is there a just-in-time technique available to help me prep for a pitch tomorrow?

(257) What is a tactical approach to a business development plan?
(258) What's one way to help a lawyer set aside time for business development that's in their total control?
(259) How can you help your lawyers speak C-Suite?
(260) Can you name four rainmaker traits?
(261) How would you rate your attorneys' EQ?
(262) Can you name 3 ways to compensate a non-attorney referral source?
(263) What is your non-firm attorney referral compensation program?
(264) What's the Golden Rule of business development?
(265) What's the Platinum Rule of business development?
(266) How do legal skills compare to sales skills?
(267) What's the worst answer when you ask a client for their business?
(268) How many marketing and business development support staff do you need for every 25 attorneys?
(269) Can you name two broad categories of stress?
(270) When should business development training begin?
(271) What's a good indicator that a newly hired associate attorney has an experience that is a rainmaker indicator?
(272) What are the 3 dominant communication modes you need to know about when your client is speaking?
(273) Do you have a vendor referral development program?
(274) How often do you need to refresh your website? (Bodine)
(275) Are your lawyers aware of the multiple dimensions of communication? (Keller, Chapter 4 = C4)
(276) Is proper English and correct legal references the only communication concerns of your lawyer in a client meeting? (Keller, Chapter 4 = C4)
(277) Are your lawyers aware of their dominant communication predicate mode and how uncomfortable it is, consciously or unconsciously, to a client who operates in an entirely different predicate mode? (Keller, Chapter 4 = C4)
(278) Do your attorneys know not to sit on news? (C4)
(279) Are your associates aware of what "de-equitized" means and how to avoid it? (C4)
(280) Are you in danger of cultural malaise? (Berardi, C4)
(281) How can you avoid different people from a multi-office firm presenting to the same client and not be aware of it? (Bruns, C1, C4)
(282) Did you purchase an expensive CRM only to have it ignored by the attorneys? (Schmidt, C4)
(283) Have you lost control of some of your multi-office BD staff due to local office politics? (Chichester, C4)

(284) Is there a wrong way to tell a client about other legal services your firm offers? (Usellis, C4)
(285) Are you aware of the buyer's motivations inside the book that you believe is coming over with a new lateral? (Coulter, C4)
(286) Do you know 10 questions you should ask your lawyers before sending them into a business development training session? (Keller, C4)
(287) Do your lawyers know how to turn a meeting with a vendor selling them a product into a business development opportunity for the firm? (Schmidt, Keller, C4)
(288) How dangerous is it to new business from an existing client if one of their matters is just a little bit late on delivery? (Keller, C4)
(289) How dangerous is it to a relationship if one of your attorneys takes a quick 30 second call from a client and bills the client for one-tenth of an hour? (Goldsholle, C4)
(290) How important is the description of time spent on a matter within the bill from the client's perspective? (Keller, C2, C4)
(291) What is the example in the book where an associate counsel marked off 7 ½ hours in a firm's bill because it said "7 ½ hours of strategizing" and why? (Keller C4)
(292) If an attorney at the firm makes a mistake on a client's matter and it requires 30 hours to fix that mistake how much of that time should be billed to the client? (Goldsholle, C4)
(293) Can lawyer depression reduce firm revenue? (Keller, C4)
(294) If a friend knows you are a lawyer, do you really need to tell him or her that you would like their business or would like them to refer some business to you? (Keller, C4)
(295) What did Eric Schmidt, CEO of Google, say about coaching? (Keller, C4)
(296) Is it important for a non-billing attorney to receive a bonus for origination? (Keller, C4)
(297) Is there any business opportunity for the firm to have an industry-based marketing group? (Schmidt, C4)
(298) Is it effective when an associate has a legal question to be told "just figure it out"? (Chichester, C4)
(299) Is it okay to bill a client for the origination bonus? (Keller, C4)
(300) Approximately what percentage of users on the Internet are on YouTube? (Keller, C4)
(301) How important should YouTube be in your business development plans? (Keller, C4)

(302) When hiring an associate how high on your radar is the question, "did you take a business of law course or a law firm business development course"? (Keller, C4)

(303) Are you getting the maximum business development potential in marketing potential out of your business development and marketing vendors? (Chichester, C4)

(304) What is a lawyer's worst answer to the question, "what do you do"? (Keller's, C4)

(305) Are clients sensitive to technology awareness issues by your billing attorneys? (Keller, Silber, C4)

(306) How important is it that your lawyers are tested for fundamental Microsoft Word and Microsoft Excel features and how to use them? (Keller, Silber, C4)

(307) Are all of your attorneys aware of the Microsoft Word global find and replace feature which can make the difference between a two hour task and a five second task as highlighted by the director of legal operations for Adobe? (Keller, Silber, C4)

(308) How often should you conduct a client service feedback survey of your top 10 clients? (Schmidt, C4)

(309) Is it enough for the lawyer to say s/he went to a Chamber of Commerce meeting? (Schmidt, C4)

(310) What are website "sticky factors" and are they a part of your website? (Keller, C4)

(311) What are four essential elements for the home page of your website? (Keller, C4)

(312) Name one tab you can put on your website home page to make it "sticky" and more attractive to in-house counsel? (K. Bell)

(313) Is it important to know what percentage of a client's legal business you have? (Flannery, Various)

(314) If you could only pick one rainmaker activity, what would it be? (Flannery, Keller, Chapter 5)

(315) What is a competitive analysis in the form of a legal services "gap analysis"? (Severson)

Exhibits Index of Topic Titles

Appendix A

Biographies of Contributors

David Ackert, MA, is President and Founder of The Ackert Advisory business development firm, a company that helps lawyers, accountants, and advisors grow their books of business through coaching, training, and e-learning. Business Development Mentor to service professionals and executives since 1997. Founder of Practice Boomers, a business development e-learning program for law firms and winner of two LMA Your Honor Awards. (See www.PracticeBoomers.com for testimonials and results.) Founder of Practice Pipeline, an online platform for client prospecting. Founder of The Business Development Symposium, an online forum that brings together lawyers with thought-leaders in legal marketing and client development. Former Chief Marketing Officer for Libertas Law. Written for and contributed to dozens of articles in publications including the *LA Times, The National Review, The Daily Journal, Voice America, Attorney at Work, the Los Angeles Business Journal,* and quoted in several trade publications and business books. Participated on numerous panels and lectured in seminars on business development, effective communication, and time management techniques. Public speaker (visit http://bit.ly/e8H7m9 for upcoming engagements). Guest lecturer at UCLA School of Law, USC's Marshall School of Business and Carnegie Mellon University. Former instructor at UCLA Extension on strategic planning and business development for professional services.

Karen KH Bell, LLB, is the national Senior Director, Professional & Client Education at McCarthy Tétrault LLP. Karen is responsible for developing and delivering a broadly based Capabilities Curriculum under the platform McCarthy Tétrault *Advance*™. This includes education programming for clients. A lawyer for over 30 years, Karen has worked with law firms and legal departments to drive productivity and growth by focusing on efficiency and client service, building resilience to risk and developing business strategically. She practiced as a business litigator for 20 years and then assumed a variety of practice advisory roles: as external Risk Management Counsel to LAWPRO where she created practicePRO®, a risk and change management program; as a partner at a large national firm leading the development and implementation of a multi-faceted knowledge strategy; and as a consultant advising law firms and legal departments on practice efficiency, resilience to risk and business development. Karen has been active in the legal community throughout her career – pioneering new approaches to practice, educating about professional responsibility and risk management; presenting to legal organizations across the country and internationally; and writing for legal publications including LAWPRO Magazine, The Lawyers' Weekly and Canadian Lawyer.

Steven Bell, BA, is the Chief Sales & Marketing Officer for Womble Carlyle Sandridge & Rice LLP's global sales and marketing operations working out of their of Washington DC office. Womble Carlyle is a global firm with over 550 lawyers in 14 offices, US and Worldwide. Steve currently serves as Regional Vice Chair of Marketing – Americas for Lex Mundi, the world's leading association of independent law firms. Steve's publications, presentations and co-presentations include: *Big Data for Legal Marketers – Doing the Right Things and Doing Things Right for Bigger ROI, 8 No-Fuss No-Muss Steps to Sales Nirvana, From Sherpa to Guide—Driving Revenue through Sales Coaching, A Small Law Department's Guide to Working Effectively with Your Outside Counsel, A Day in the Life of a Law Firm Salesman, Use of 'Sales' Pipelines and 'Sales' Models in Law Firms - What Works, What Doesn't, How Leading Law Firm Marketers Are Positioning Their Firms and People to Succeed, FirmReady to Co-Brand, Social Media and Lex Mundi Lawyers: Why and How this New Communications Medium Affects Your Practice, Crystal Balls and Hockey Pucks, Increasing Your Social Media Intelligence,* and *Point/Counterpoint—Client Teams Suck/ Client Teams Rock!* Follow Steven Bell on Twitter at @SteveMBell and at his New Legal Normal blog.

Jeff Berardi, MBA, is the Chief Marketing Officer (CMO) for the global law firm K&L Gates. As CMO, Jeff leads marketing and business development efforts for the firm's nearly 50 offices located across five continents. Within this role, he maintains primary responsibility for the various function areas in the department, including strategic planning, regional and practice-based business development, PR/media relations, creative direction, and digital communications. K&L Gates has been recognized among the top law firm brands in the world by several leading market research surveys, including Acritas and BTI Consulting Group. In 2014, BTI noted K&L Gates in its prestigious "BTI Brand Elite" ranking, naming the firm as one of just a few "Best Brand Builder" firms that exhibited "an outstanding upward trajectory" in their brands. The firm was also ranked in 2014 for a third consecutive year in the elite "BTI Client Service 30" ranking. Jeff currently serves as a Seven Generations Board Member for the international nonprofit organization City Year, a Governing Body member of the CMO Collective (NY Chapter), and he is a past member of the Global Editorial Advisory board for Managing Partner Magazine.

Larry Bodine, JD, is the Editor-in-Chief of Lawyers.com, a service of LexisNexis that publishes legal news for consumers, directing editorial operations across the site. Bodine worked previously as a law firm marketing consultant, Attorney at law, and columnist. Prior to his work at Lawyers.com, Bodine spent 11 years as a business development advisor who advised more than 250 law firms and other businesses on attracting new customers and generating revenue. He has advised businesses from a 3,000-lawyer global law firm to a one-person website startup. A former litigator, Bodine also served as an expert witness in litigation involving Internet marketing disputes and launched several online ventures that share information about law firm marketing. Bodine began his career in journalism as a news reporter for the New York Daily News, The Star-Ledger, and Paterson News from 1972 to 1978 and then worked as an assistant editor at the National Law Journal from 1978 to 1981. Bodine also served as editor and publisher of the American Bar Association Journal from 1982 to 1989 and then Lawyers USA from 1989 to 1991. In 2003 Bodine received the "Edge Award" for his writing in the American Bar Association's Law Practice Management magazine. Bodine was called "the best known marketing and website consultant to the legal profession" by Immigration Daily.

David Boies, JD, is Chairman of Boies, Schiller & Flexner LLP, a law firm with offices in New York, Washington D.C., California, Florida, Nevada, and New Hampshire. Mr. Boies has been selected as one of the 100 Most Influential People in the World by *Time Magazine* (2010). He has been named Global International Litigator of the Year by Who's Who Legal an unprecedented seven times, including 2013. Mr. Boies is the recipient of Honorary Doctor of Laws from New York Law School (2007), University of New Hampshire School of Law (2013), and New York University (2013). Mr. Boies served as Chief Counsel and Staff Director of the United States Senate Antitrust Subcommittee in 1978 and Chief Counsel and Staff Director of the United States Senate Judiciary Committee in 1979. In 1991–1993, Mr. Boies was counsel to the Federal Deposit Insurance Corporation, recovering $1.2 billion from companies who sold junk bonds to failed savings and loan associations. Mr. Boies also served as the lead counsel for former Vice-President Al Gore in connection with litigation relating to the 2000 election Florida vote count. As co-lead counsel for the plaintiffs in Perry v. Brown, he won judgments establishing the constitutional right to marry for gay and lesbian citizens in California.

Dave Bruns, MS, is the Director of Client Services at Farella Braun + Martel. Dave creates and implements the business development and marketing programs for the firm, its practice groups and individual attorneys. Dave recently developed a firm-wide business development training program with two goals: action and culture change. To accomplish the goals, the program used intensive group training, one-on-one consulting, firm-wide programming and training/messaging within the political constituencies of the firm. He is the lynch pin in most of Farella's business development efforts. From strategic cross selling to new client development, Dave leverages proven tactics from inside and outside of the legal industry into action-based activities that blend traditional and electronic client touch points. His approach is founded in solid metrics and requires a deep understanding of law firm economics, practice-based value propositions, corporate marketing tactics and the voice of the client obtained through the client interview process.

Allen Chichester, MBA, is the chief marketing officer at Barnes & Thornburg LLP. Reporting to the executive director, Mr. Chichester is responsible for marketing, communications and business development. He joined the firm in 2009. Prior to joining Barnes & Thornburg, Mr. Chichester held various leadership positions in advertising, marketing and business development for the past 25 years. These include chairman and chief executive officer of North Asia for Leo Burnett International, chief marketing officer for DLA Piper US LLP, and owner and principal of Chichester Consulting LLC. Mr. Chichester is past chairman of the Association of Accredited Advertising Agencies in Hong Kong, a member of the Legal Marketing Association, and has been appointed as a Commissioner for the Architectural Review Committee for the town of Bannockburn, IL. He is currently on the board of the Midwest LMA. Mr. Chichester received a B.A. in multi-disciplinary social science as well as an M.B.A. from Michigan State University in 1982.

Silvia Coulter, MS, is a founding Partner of LawVision Group and leads the firm's Client Development and Strategic Growth Practice. Law firms rely on Silvia's substantial experience in collaborating with them on their business development and key client retention and growth strategies, client service strategies and process improvement initiatives. Prior to cofounding LawVision Group, Silvia chaired the Client Development Practice at Hildebrandt. She is a recognized leader in law firm business development strategy and is a frequent speaker at legal industry conferences, and law firm retreats. Silvia has spent twenty years as a consultant to the industry and has served as chief marketing and business development officer at two Global 50 firms. She is an adjunct faculty member of the Law Firm Management Master's Degree Program at the George Washington University College of Professional Studies.

Roger Epstein, JD, is chair of the Tax Department of Cades Schutte and has extensive experience in all areas of tax law handled by the Tax Department. His areas of practice include corporate tax law, partnership tax law, real estate tax law, international tax law, tax planning, Hawaii state taxation, and tax controversies. Mr. Epstein has substantial expertise in international tax transactions and international estate planning. Prior to joining Cades Schutte in 1972, Mr. Epstein was a Tax Law Specialist with the National Office of the Internal Revenue Service in Washington, D.C. and prior to that, he was an Internal Revenue Agent in Washington D.C. Mr. Epstein is a frequent lecturer at tax presentations in Hawaii on the U.S. mainland and internationally. Mr. Epstein is A.V. rated by Martindale Hubbell and is listed in both Who's Who in American Law and Best Lawyers in America (every edition since the publication began). A graduate with honors in 1972 from Georgetown University Law Center. His admissions include Hawaii State Bar (1973), United States District Court for the District of Hawaii, United States Tax Court, United States Court of Federal Claims, and United States Court of Appeals for the Ninth Circuit.

Stephen Fairley, PsyD, is a two-time international best-selling author, Stephen Fairley is the Founder and CEO of The Rainmaker Institute, the nation's largest law firm marketing company specializing in lead generation, lead conversion, and client retention for small to mid-sized law firms. Over 10,000 attorneys nationwide have benefited from learning and implementing the proven Rainmaker Marketing System. Stephen was academically trained as a clinical psychologist and ran 2 successful small businesses prior to focusing on the legal marketplace. Over the last 14 years, he has become a nationally recognized legal marketing expert and been named, "America's Top Marketing Coach." He has spoken numerous times for over 35 of the nation's largest state and local bar associations and has built an international following among attorneys with over 200,000 followers on Facebook, Twitter and LinkedIn. Stephen is a nationally syndicated columnist for Attorney at Law magazines. He has been featured and cited in dozens of websites and magazines including: Inc magazine, the *Chicago Tribune, TheStreet.com*, and *Entrepreneur magazines.* Stephen has authored 12 books, taken 15 cruises, and traveled to 42 countries. He resides in Phoenix with his wife of 19 years.

Karen Febeo, JD, joined Goodwin Procter in 2005 and is the firm's Managing Director of Professional Development & Training. In this role, she leads all aspects of professional development and training for attorneys and professional staff. She aligns a training strategy with the firm's development frameworks and the evolving marketplace to ensure that Goodwin Procter's attorneys are leaders in client service. Her programs primarily focus on leadership, business development and project management. In 2012, in collaboration with the firm's Marketing team, she created a revenue generation coaching program to help the firm's attorneys systematize their approach to business development and sales techniques. Ms. Febeo also leads engagement, retention, feedback, diversity and inclusion, and integration initiatives at Goodwin Procter. Prior to joining the firm, Ms. Febeo served as Director of Human Relations at Testa, Hurwitz & Thibeault, where she focused on associate life and served as a counseling resource for associates. Ms. Febeo is also an attorney, and practiced intellectual property law at Testa, Hurwitz & Thibeault from 1996 to 2004. Ms. Febeo received her A.B. (cum laude) from Dartmouth College and her J.D. (with honors) from the University of Connecticut.

Jonathan Fitzgarrald, BA, is Managing Partner of Equinox Strategy Partners. Drawing upon more than 15 years of sales and marketing experience, Jonathan provides strategic counsel to professional services firms to drive revenue, market visibility, and client satisfaction. Prior to Equinox, Jonathan directed the business development, marketing, and public relations functions at three separate law firms. Prior to his focus in legal marketing, Jonathan held senior-level communications positions at various public and private companies within the high-tech, telecommunications, electronics, health care, and consumer products industries. A clear, dynamic, and diplomatic communicator, Jonathan regularly speaks and presents to professional audiences on various marketing and business development topics. He has been quoted in such publications as The Wall Street Journal, Los Angeles Times, the National Law Journal, The Recorder, ABA Journal, Strategies: The Journal of Legal Marketing, City News Service and on The CBS Evening News with Katie Couric, KNBC.com and Law.com. For five years, Jonathan was a broadcast journalist and news anchor for a television network in San

Francisco. He is an accomplished equestrian, fluent in Spanish, and also known as Jonathan "I get sh*t done!" Fitzgarrald.

D. Casey Flaherty, JD, is corporate counsel at KIA Motors America, Inc. where he oversees dealer-related legal matters and electronic discovery. Before moving in-house, Casey served time in BigLaw where his practice focused on complex commercial litigation and electronic discovery. Based on what he witnessed in BigLaw, Casey developed a Legal Technology Audit (LTA) that he administers to his outside counsel. In conjunction with Suffolk University Law School's Institute on Law Practice Technology & Innovation and a group of advisers from across the legal spectrum, Casey's audit has been automated. LTA registrations are open (http://www.legaltechaudit.com/). The LTA is not associated with KIA Motors America. Casey regularly writes and speaks about his audit, legal technology, legal operations, electronic discovery, budgeting, and other topics. Casey's Tech Toolbox is the first monthly technology column to be featured in the ACC Docket. Casey is on the Board of and a regular contributor to *Law Technology News*. His work has been featured in the *ABA Journal, The American Lawyer, Corporate Counsel*, etc. Casey has been recognized as an ABA Legal Rebel, one of the Fastcase 50, an Innovator, and a Rising Star. The opinions Casey expresses are his own and not those of KIA Motors America.

William J. Flannery, Jr., JD, ("Bill") is the President of The WJF Institute, located in Austin, Texas. The Institute's primary focus is client development and client relationship management, law firm marketing and marketing support programs. The WJF Institute trains lawyers and provides related consulting services in law firm management and leadership. Over the past twenty-three years, The WJF Institute has conducted intensive, small group training sessions for over 16,000 attendees. Bill started his career in 1966 at the Department of Justice as an instructor. While at IBM, he obtained his Juris Doctorate in 1973 from the University of Baltimore Law School. He attended the IBM/Harvard Advanced Business Executive Education Institute Program. His IBM career included assignments in marketing training, corporate marketing planning, large system management, corporate strategic planning, finance, litigation management, and computer technology for the legal profession where his responsibilities included IBM's relationships with key law firm computer customers, corporate law departments' in-house legal systems managers and IBM's outside counsel. He left IBM in 1988 and founded The WJF Institute. Bill has been a special advisor to the ABA and the Association of Legal Administrators (ALA) on technology and marketing. He has served as a member of the ALA's Long Range

Planning Committee. The WJF Institute's Client Development and Relationship Management workshop was recognized by *Inc.* magazine's Marketing Masters Awards in 1997. He has published numerous articles on marketing and law firm management. Bill is a frequent speaker at various legal conferences and meetings.

David H. Freeman, JD, CEO of David Freeman Consulting Group and founder of Law Firm CultureShift®, is a best-selling author and an award-winning consultant. For the third consecutive year, he was voted the "Top Law Firm Business Development Coach and Consultant" in nation-wide National Law Journal surveys. For over two decades, he has shown thousands of law firm leaders and lawyers how to generate more revenue, profitability and growth. He has worked with hundreds of firms world-wide, including over 1/3 of the AmLaw 200, and he is a highly regarded keynote speaker at law firms, industry conferences, bar associations and law schools. David specializes in providing consulting, training and coaching services in the areas of leadership, business development, cross-selling, client service, retreats and strategic planning, and he is also the author of three books: *The Law Firm Leader's Reference Guide for Creating a Business Development Culture, Secrets of the Masters: The Business Development Guide for Lawyers,* and *Weekly Reminders for Revenue-Focused Leaders.* David can be reached at David@LawFirmCultureShift.com and 949-715-0819.

Don Joseph Goewey, BA, is managing partner of ProAttitude, a human performance firm with the mission of ending work stress, and the author of *The End of Stress ~ Four Steps to Rewiring Your Brain.* Don also managed Stanford's Department of Psychiatry, directed one of the first regional emergency medical services systems, and headed ICAH, an internationally recognized institute that pioneered a psycho-social approach to overcoming catastrophic life events. ICAH worked in some of the most stressful places on the planet, with people facing terminal illness, in grief groups with parents who'd lost children, with prisoners serving life sentences, and inside refugee camps during the genocidal war in Bosnia. In the six years that led to his founding ProAttitude, Don directed a research team that developed a solution to stress based on breakthroughs in neuroscience. The model facilitates the specific shift in mindset that literally changes brain structure to quiet stress reactions and stimulate higher brain function, expanding the fluid, emotional, and social intelligence that predicts both success and a higher quality of life. Don's clients have included Fenwick and West LLP, Cades Schutte LLP, Wells Fargo Bank, Cisco Systems, LA Sheriff's Department, and San Mateo County, to name a few.

Gerry H. Goldsholle, JD, has been an attorney for over 50 years, and became an Internet pioneer in 1995 when he founded the first major consumer legal website, FreeAdvice.com, which generates over 20 million consumer visits each year. An honors graduate of the College of William & Mary and Columbia Law School, who also did graduate work in business at Stanford, Gerry began his legal career as a litigator at the New York regional office of the Securities & Exchange Commission, where he headed its special enforcement unit. He later practiced as a litigation and corporate associate in Manhattan, and served for many years as Assistant General Counsel of Metropolitan Life Insurance Company. He retired from MetLife as its Chief Brokerage Executive and the President and CEO of MetLife Marketing Corporation. Now senior partner in a San Francisco area based law firm representing consumers nationwide, Gerry has chaired numerous committees of the American Bar Association, including service as a section officer and Council member, the California State Bar, and the New York City Bar Association.

Tasneem Goodman, JD, is a Partner at Akina Corp. Tasneem has spent over ten years in the legal industry working with lawyers to grow their practices and helping firms make the most of their relationships with their clients, attorneys and recruits. Prior to joining Akina, Tasneem was a partner and the Director of Marketing at Katten Muchin Rosenman, where she led the firm's marketing and business development team. Tasneem previously practiced law in the corporate department of Latham & Watkins, where she represented publicly-traded and privately-held companies in mergers, acquisitions and securities offerings, and in the restructuring group of Kirkland & Ellis, where she represented corporate debtors in bankruptcy planning, negotiation and litigation. Before her career in law, Tasneem was an event planner in the University of Chicago's student life office. Tasneem serves on the board of directors of Lawyers Lend-A-Hand to Youth, a nonprofit organization that channels the legal community's resources to promote mentoring programs in disadvantaged communities, and the Alumni Board of Governors of the University of Chicago, which cultivates engagement of the worldwide University of Chicago alumni community through volunteerism, philanthropy and participation. She graduated from the University of Chicago Law School and earned her Bachelor's degree, with honors, from the University of Chicago.

Melanie S. Green, BJ, is the Chief Client Development Officer at Faegre Baker Daniels responsible for developing and managing strategic marketing and business development, including the client feedback program. She works closely with firm management on identifying and implementing strategic initiatives and goals. Melanie also supervises the firm's media relations, corporate identity and advertising programs, business development training, website and external communications, client entertainment and appreciation efforts, contributions and sponsorships, alumni program, and market research, and is on the firm's Diversity & Inclusion Advisory Group, and Women's Forum for Achievement — Leadership Council. Prior to joining Faegre Baker Daniels, Melanie Green was director of marketing for Lewis Roca Rothberger LLP and the membership services coordinator for the Maricopa County Bar Association in Phoenix. Professional associations include: the Legal Marketing Association, Lex Mundi — Marketing and Business Development Committee, and Legal PR Chicago. Civic activities include (have included) Indiana Sports Corporation, Indianapolis 2012 Super Bowl, Big Ten 2011 Football Championship, NCAA Basketball Men's and Women's Final Fours, Fiesta Bowl, Maricopa County Sports Commission. Presentations include: *Quick Fixes: Innovative Solutions in Law Firm Business Development, Law Firm CMOs: Right Now, Tomorrow and a View Ahead, Business Development Thought Leadership & Best Practices,* and *Creating and Implementing a Sales and Business Development Culture in Your Firm.*

Hans T. Haglund, BS, is the Chief Business Development and Marketing Officer at Blank Rome LLP, bringing more than 20 years of experience to the Firm. Hans directs strategic business development and marketing across all the Firm's practices and geographies by leveraging his significant experience in practice and market development, customer relationship management, and sales training and management development. Prior to joining Blank Rome, Hans was the Chief Business Development and Marketing Officer for an Am Law 100 firm in Washington, D.C. and a former director of global business development for one of the twenty largest law firms in the world, where he directed a strategic account management initiative for clients from the global financial services sector. He also cofounded two software companies (both providing solutions to the legal profession) and a renewable chemical company earlier in his professional career. He is a member of several M&A and venture capital professional organizations, and a board member of two emerging growth companies. Hans received his Bachelor of Science degree in Business from the University of the Redlands.

Jeanne Hammerstrom, BS, is Chief Marketing Officer for Benesch, a business law firm with offices in Cleveland, Columbus, Hackensack, Indianapolis, Philadelphia, Shanghai and Wilmington. Ms Hammerstrom brings 25 years of legal marketing experience to her post, and has firm wide responsibility for marketing, communications and practice development. She oversees a staff of business development, client service, public relations, advertising, event planning and other professionals. She also participates in the firm's Executive Committee, Strategic Growth Committee and Client Service Committee. Active in the legal industry, Ms. Hammerstrom was recently named a Fellow of the College of Law Practice Management. She is a former President of the International Legal Marketing Association (LMA), Chair of LMA's 2009 Annual Conference and a past-President of LMA's Pittsburgh Chapter. She is a frequent presenter at industry conferences and has authored many articles in the professional service industry. Under Ms. Hammerstrom's leadership, Benesch was ranked the highest of any non-AmLaw 200 firm in the country by Marketing the Law Firm's 2012 national ranking list. Active in the legal industry, Ms. Hammerstrom was recently named a Fellow of the College of Law Practice Management. She is a former President of the International Legal Marketing Association (LMA), Chair of LMA's 2009 Annual Conference and a past-President of LMA's Pittsburgh Chapter.

Michael R. Haven, JD, is the Senior Counsel for Legal Operations and Litigation at NetApp, Inc. (NASDAQ: NTAP), a Fortune 500 storage and data management provider. He joined NetApp from K&L Gates LLP, where he was a partner in the firm's Palo Alto office. As an outside litigator and trial lawyer for more than 12 years, Mike represented corporate clients in complex intellectual property, employment, and commercial disputes, handling all phases of challenging cases from inception through trial and appeal. In February 2013, he brought his vast experience in-house to NetApp, where he now oversees litigation generally across the global enterprise and also is responsible for the business function of the legal organization. In this multi-faceted role, Mike has been on the cutting edge of litigation and partner management initiatives. Along with his award-winning team, Mike has created, implemented and developed some of the world's most innovative policies, procedures, and tools for efficient operation of the NetApp legal department and its business partners.

Tom C. Helm, BA, is senior marketing and business development manager with Bryan Cave LLP, a 1,000-lawyer firm with a diversified practice across the U.S., U.K., Continental Europe and Asia. Tom has over 13 years of legal services marketing and business development experience, which includes management of business development programs, attorney coaching initiatives, and marketing, public relations and branding campaigns. At Bryan Cave, he works with his firm's Atlanta and Charlotte offices, as well as firm-wide corporate practice teams. Tom's early career includes resource development and client education programs for a national nonprofit health agency. He is a past president and active member of the Legal Marketing Association's Southeastern Chapter.

Wayne Hogan, JD, is a past-president of the Florida Justice Association, a Florida and National Board Certified Civil Trial Lawyer and was educated at the Florida State University (B.A. 1969; J.D., with High Honors, 1972). He has chaired the Florida Bar Civil Procedure Rules Committee, twice has served on the Code and Rules of Evidence Committee, and has held leadership positions in American Association for Justice, Public Justice, and the American Board of Trial Advocates. He chairs the Federal Judicial Nominating Conference for the Middle District of Florida. Hogan is president of the Terrell Hogan Yegelwel personal injury and wrongful death law firm, founded in 1974, and served on the team of trial lawyers who represented the State of Florida against the cigarette industry. He has been president of the Florida State University College of Law Alumni Association and he and his wife, Pat, have supported the Summer for Undergraduates Program which has been honored by the American Bar Association for its Diversity Pipeline contributions to legal education.

Peter A. Johnson, M.Ed, JD, is the founder of Law Practice Consultants, LLC. Peter offers a valuable combination of skill and experience in law firm management, sales, marketing and counseling. He evaluates and assists law firms and lawyers in business development, client retention and management related issues. He consults with firms in the areas of succession planning, practice group management, compensation system reviews, and assessing and improving law firm profitability. Peter performs client interviews to evaluate satisfaction and assess existing and future needs. This information is used by the firms to design and implement client-based strategic planning and business development coaching programs for partners and associates. Marketing the Law Firm, ranked Peter's 2002 article on client interviews one of the top ten best of that year. Over the last ten years Peter has designed coaching and business development training programs for lawyers of all levels of experience, in firms of all sizes, and has "coached" over 400 attorneys on a one-on-one basis. He speaks frequently on a variety of law firm management topics for organizations such as the Legal Marketing Association, Association of Legal Administrators and many bar associations. Previously, Peter practiced law for seventeen years, concentrating on business litigation at a mid-size Boston firm where he served as chair of the firm's compensation committee and managing partner.

Despina C. Kartson, BS, is the chief business development and marketing officer for Morgan Lewis. In this capacity, Ms. Kartson is responsible for leading Morgan Lewis's global business development and marketing strategies across 26 offices in the U.S., Europe, Asia, and the Middle East. Ms. Kartson oversees a global business development, marketing, and communications department, which includes strategic planning, marketing, practice development, client development, public relations, creative services, internal, external, and online communications. Prior to joining Morgan Lewis in 2013, Ms. Kartson held the position of chief marketing officer for a global law firm. She also held leadership positions in business development, strategy, and technology for service providers to the legal and financial services industries as well as other global law firms. Ms. Kartson earned her B.S. in journalism from Bowling Green State University.

Jan Kang, JD, is vice president and general counsel for AOptix Technologies, Inc. where she oversees the company's legal function. Prior to joining AOptix, **Jan** provided strategic and tactical legal support for companies of varying sizes from Fortune 1000 to startups. During this time, **Jan** gained tremendous experience in various industries such as semiconductor capital equipment, software, ecommerce, engineering and construction and open source. Her broad expertise includes corporate governance, contracts, litigation, financing, labor and employment law, mergers and acquisitions, and intellectual property. **Jan** was General Counsel for Cupertino Electric, Inc., Asera, Inc., Myteam, Inc., and Prism Solutions, Inc., and was associate general counsel at Lam Research Corporation. She holds a degree in Philosophy, Logic of Formal Systems, from Stanford University and a J.D. from the University Of Michigan School Of Law. She is a member of the Silicon Valley Association of General Counsel and the Bay Area Association of Asian American General Counsel and a founder of WGCN (Women's General Counsel Network).

Mark C. Karkazis, BA, is Director of Marketing at Ungaretti & Harris. Mark has been helping professional service firms generate business, increase profits and enhance their brands since the early 1990s. With a background in sales and direct marketing, he utilizes high-impact methods to achieve tangible results for law, accounting and consulting firms. He has also advised attorneys regarding lateral recruitment and integration, origination credit systems, individual performance assessment, pricing and alternative fee arrangements, succession planning and other strategic issues. Mark has served as Marketing Director for a prominent mid-sized law firm in Chicago and helped execute a cutting-edge key client initiative for a global law firm. Before working in-house at law firms, Mark focused his career on marketing and selling consulting and accounting services to CEOs, division presidents, business owners and other executives.

Scott Kessler, JD, helps lawyers and other professionals achieve their professional and personal goals. When asked to define his work, Scott likens it to being a *passion* coach - he believes that uncovering and feeding your passions is the easiest way to achieve whatever goals you set. "Whatever my job title, my real job is to help people uncover their passions, to empower them to keep that passion alive throughout each day, and to, ultimately, live fuller, richer lives." In addition to his coaching work, Scott has helped lawyers to develop and execute personalized business development and marketing plans. "Finding ways to grow a legal practice is not a 'one-size-fits-all' proposition - it requires individualized planning, consistent effort, and regular tweaking. My ultimate goal is to fuel a passion for business development within each attorney with whom I work." Since 2001, Scott has held positions with Shearman & Sterling, Seyfarth, Deloitte, Brobeck, and The Wall Street Journal. Scott was also a search consultant with Major, Lindsey & Africa, where he advised large and mid-sized law firms in their efforts to fill senior and mid-level management positions. Having worked inside law firms as both an attorney and as a business development manager, Scott's clients considered him to be uniquely qualified to provide the advice and guidance needed to make the best hires. "I believe I was much more than a 'head-hunter," Scott received his JD from Hofstra University School of Law and practiced law in New York before finding his true passion.

Marilyn Klinger, JD, the Chair Emeritus of Sedgwick's Construction Practices Group, is located in the Los Angeles office, and is involved in all aspects of construction law on a state and national level. She represents the full spectrum of the construction industry, from owners, contractors, subcontractors, and sureties. Her practice includes time-related claims and litigation (e.g., delay/impact), legal advice and counsel regarding the contracting process (e.g., bidding and contract disputes/performance bond claims), payment enforcement/defense (e.g. payment bonds/mechanic's liens/stop payment notices), administrative and scope claims and litigation (e.g., differing site conditions, change and extra work orders/inadequate plans and specifications, and subcontractor substitutions), and counseling and transactional services to the construction industry (e.g., general advice and counsel, including contract preparation, evaluation, and negotiation). In addition, Ms. Klinger has extensive experience in dispute resolution including litigation, trial, appeals, arbitration, and mediation. Ms. Klinger regularly presents and writes articles on issues impacting the construction industry. She has served as an annual guest lecturer at Stanford University's Graduate School of Engineering, Construction Management since 1993 and has also spoken on numerous panels for the ABA Forum on the Construction Industry since 1985. A very long, yet partial, list of attorney Klinger's numerous affiliations, civic activities, accomplishments and speaking engagements may be found on the Sedgewick website.

Daniel Kloke, JD, specializes in intellectual property law with an emphasis on patent prosecution, strategic patent counseling, patent litigation, drafting and negotiating intellectual property licensing agreements, and counseling on open source as well as standards-setting issues. Mr. Kloke has also participated in numerous post grant review proceedings including ex parte and inter partes reexaminations and reissue proceedings. In addition to his patent practice, Mr. Kloke has extensive experience as a litigating attorney in complex commercial litigation matters. Over his career, Mr. Kloke works closely with clients to create market power and promote valuation through implementation of sound legal strategies to leverage intellectual property assets and investments. In addition to intellectual property portfolio development, Daniel has assisted businesses and counsel to analyze patents and other intellectual property to prepare for and support litigation.

Lisa Konie, JD, is Director, Associate General Counsel at Adobe Systems and also the Efficiency and Process Change Agent - Legal Services. Responsible for operations of the international Legal Department: strategy planning and operations planning, outside counsel management, acquisition integration activities, legal tools and technology, contract management, knowledge management, departmental training and communications. Prior responsibilities included: Adobe Systems Legal Operations Manager, Adobe Systems Sr. Legal Counsel, responsible for ISV/OEM teams, Supported Strategic Alliances and partners, Drove efficiency project for legal sales team, Implemented process improvements around negotiation positions and fallbacks, Adobe Systems Corporate Counsel, Supported East and Government sales transactions, Lead strategic alliances team - supporting all key strategic partners, Supported key product teams - knowledge worker and mobile users, Hitachi Data Systems Corporate Counsel, and Wilson Sonsini Goodrich and Rosati Associate in technology transactions group.

Nancy Kostakos, AB, serves as Goodwin Procter's Managing Director of Marketing and is responsible for the development of marketing plans, collateral and technologies that help the firm and its practices to be widely recognized in the marketplace. Prior to joining Goodwin Procter, Ms. Kostakos served in the same capacity for nearly 13 years at another large national law firm. Prior to that she held marketing and business development positions in architecture firms in both Boston and Atlanta. Ms. Kostakos began her marketing career as a merchandise marketing manager at Liz Claiborne, Inc. in New York. She earned her A.B. degree in Fine Arts from Harvard College.

Barbara Lauterbach, BA, MBA (2015), is Director of Business Development for Daniel Coker Horton & Bell, P.A., a Mississippi-based firm that focuses primarily in commercial and business litigation. Barbara moved to Daniel Coker from McKenna Long & Aldridge in Atlanta, Georgia. She is a graduate of Marquette University in Milwaukee, Wisconsin and is currently pursuing an Executive Masters in Business Administration. Barbara began her legal marketing career shortly after the Supreme Court permitted legal advertising, and worked closely with the founders of Law Line, the nation's first free legal information and referral network. She moved into "big law" in the 1990's training under David Milberg and Marceline Johnson at Schiff Hardin in Chicago.

Marian Lee, JD, is the Director of Legal Talent at Brownstein Hyatt Farber Schreck. Marian is in charge of promoting the professional growth of the firm's attorneys which is a high priority at Brownstein Hyatt Farber Schreck. Marian, an attorney with over sixteen years of practice experience and former professional development consultant, is the firm's Director of Legal Talent. Based in Denver, Marian directs the firm's professional development programs for attorneys in all offices, including orientation, in-house training, outside CLE opportunities, evaluation systems, and other programs that support the professional growth of the firm's associates and shareholders. Marian serves as a member of both the firm's Pro Bono Committee and the Inclusiveness & Diversity Committee. Marian has created and presented training programs on Success as a New Associate, Effective Legal Writing, Generational Differences in Recruiting and Retaining Lawyers, How to be a Mentor, and Outstanding Client Service, among others. She is the author of published articles in local and national publications on how firms can motivate associates, upward evaluations, effective management of support staff, and encouraging the professional growth of attorneys.

Erin Corbin Meszaros, BS, is the Chief Marketing and Business Development Officer for Sutherland Asbill & Brennan LLP. With more than two decades of hands-on marketing experience, and more than half of those years in law firms, Erin Corbin Meszaros helps Sutherland attorneys turn business strategies into business successes. Guiding firm initiatives from marketing to public relations, Erin focuses on developing innovative solutions and programs to enhance client satisfaction and increase brand awareness. Erin works one-on-one with attorneys on their professional and business development to help integrate and align their individual initiatives with the firm's overall business development plan. She also guides and supports practice groups and sections to ensure the firm's strategic goals are met. Erin's career includes numerous successful marketing initiatives, such as implementing and executing a firm's business development program, initiating and completing a re-branding campaign, conducting an in-depth client relations coaching program for firm partners and creating a unique customer relationship management (CRM) database course, which effectively increased firm-wide usage. Awards and Rankings: National Law Journal's Top 50 Business of Law Trailblazers (2013), Fulton County Daily Report's Top Atlanta Legal Marketers (2012), and named Most Respected Business Person by the Indiana University Kelley School of Business, Business Class X104 (2009). Professional Activities include: Co-Chair, Legal Marketing Association National Conference - Quick Start Program (2013). Presentations include: CMO Best Practices.

Bill Mooz, JD, serves as a Scholar in Residence at the University of Colorado Law School where he runs the highly acclaimed Tech Lawyer Accelerator program. Bill has over 25 years' experience helping law firms, law departments, and the companies they represent develop and implement strategies for driving revenue growth and improving profitability. Bill began his career as a lawyer at Holland & Hart, LLP, an AmLaw 200 firm, where, as a partner, he cofounded and managed the firm's Boulder, CO office, helping grow it into one of the firm's most profitable branches. Bill left private practice in 1996 and served as Deputy General Counsel at Sun Microsystems, Inc. where he led efforts to streamline large parts of the company's contracting infrastructure and to build and implement a scalable model for using joint ventures to expand market share and improve profitability in emerging markets. At Sun, Bill also spent several years working in a business role, first running business development and strategy for the company's multi-billion dollar support services business and later founding and running the company's utility computing services business. Bill moved to VMware, Inc. where he led a number of initiatives to improve business agility, shorten transaction cycle times and reduce legal costs by re-architecting portions of the company's M&A diligence and integration process, streamlining contract templates, automating large portions of the contracting process, and outsourcing a wide variety of legal activities to India. Bill is a JD from the University of Colorado.

Louise J. Muldoon is the North American Director of Business Development, Marketing and Communications at Baker & McKenzie. Louise is qualified as a lawyer in the UK, France and Australia and practiced as a litigator with Lovell White Durrant (now Hogan Lovells) in London and Paris, before moving to Australia to join Baker & McKenzie in Sydney in 1998. After handling litigation and advisory work for a range of global and Australian clients, she moved into a business development role with the Firm to direct and further develop the Firm's business development, marketing and communications capabilities in Australia. Based in Chicago, Louise has been Baker & McKenzie's North American Director of Business Development, Marketing and Communications for the last four years. During this time, she has led a complete restructure of its operations across these areas in the US and Canada, in tandem with implementing new client programs and initiatives. Baker & McKenzie is ranked as the world's strongest law firm brand by Acritas and has 5,600 fee earners and 5,300 professional staff in 77 offices in 47 countries.

Mike O'Horo, BA, is known throughout the law business for the past 20 years simply as "The Coach." Mike is best described as a "serial innovator." Mike's most recent breakthrough is RainmakerVT, the first just-in-time interactive virtual rainmaking training that not only teaches lawyers how to earn high-value clients, but also enables them to gain practical experience in the virtual world far in excess of anything available to them in the real world. In this virtual world, lawyers manage an avatar through a series of decisions as they progress through simulated networking events, sales calls, beauty contests and other typical market activities. Through context-sensitive video coaching at each decision point, they learn, make mistakes, and practice in the safety of a private virtual world where no one sees their mistakes. He also conceived and developed *TeamPath*, the opt-in, role-specific client team process that, in addition to growing the client strategically and economically, teaches lawyers how to develop business relationships based on knowledge of the client's business. In early 2009, Mike created *Decisive Advantage*, a success-based contingency sales coaching service for lawyers.

Clare Ota, BA, is the Marketing Manager at Murphy Pearson Bradley & Feeney, a 50 attorney litigation firm with offices in San Francisco, Sacramento and Los Angeles, California. Ms. Ota manages business development initiatives, including the Firm's business development coaching program, Association of Professional Women, as well as traditional marketing communication initiatives, such as building and maintaining media relations, purchasing advertising, and creating collateral materials. Ms. Ota has worked in law firms more than 15 years, formerly as a paralegal and currently in business development and marketing. Ms. Ota serves on the board of the Bay Area Chapter of the Legal Marketing Association and is a member of International Legal Technology Association and the Bar Association of San Francisco.

Gilbert L. Purcell, JD, is founding partner of Brayton Purcell, LLP, which, at 55 lawyers, is the largest plaintiff law firm in California, with offices in Washington, Oregon, and Utah. Nationally regarded as the leading plaintiff attorney in asbestos cases with his juries regularly returning seven and eight figure verdicts. In addition to his extensive trials Purcell has successfully argued appeals in federal circuit courts and state supreme courts including California where the justices, in a unanimous opinion on certified questions from the Ninth Circuit, established a separate statute of limitations trigger for latent cancers, without which significant numbers of Californians would have no remedy. Purcell was named the Recorder's 2011 Attorney of the Year award and ATLA's Trial Lawyers Care Hero Award for pro bono representation of victims of 9/11. Serving on the board of the Consumer Attorneys of California since 1998 he has been board-certified by the National Board of Trial Advocates since 2002 and is the youngest to ever achieve **American Board of Trial Advocates's** highest rank of diplomat. He serves on the American Bar Association trial advocacy panels and California Judicial Council Trial Committee. Purcell is a Pepperdine University School of Law graduate and gave Pepperdine's 2013 commencement address. Purcell lives in Sausalito where he and his life companion, Roxanne, regularly host charitable events at their historic home.

Lisa Salazar, JD, is the interactive marketing senior manager for Norton Rose Fulbright in the US market. With over ten years of experience in digital, she is responsible for all US digital assets as well as all global social media efforts. A thought leader in the legal industry for internet marketing, she has revolutionized and reinvigorated marketing processes by integrating digital strategies to bring "big law" brands and practice areas into all digital realms through the use of social media, search engine optimization and content management. A licensed attorney, she works with Norton Rose Fulbright's leadership, lawyers, marketing groups, public relations and IT, deal with high-level, deadline-driven, time-sensitive projects to grow the business's legal practice.

Sally J. Schmidt, MBA, is President of Schmidt Marketing, Inc. in Edina, Minnesota, offering marketing services to law firms. The company's clients have included over 450 law firms throughout the world, ranging in size from two to more than 3,000 attorneys. Ms. Schmidt received her MBA and B.S. from the University of Minnesota, and was formerly the Director of Client Relations and Marketing for a law firm in Minneapolis, Minnesota. She was a founder and the first President of the Legal Marketing Association (LMA). In 1994, Ms. Schmidt was inducted as a Fellow into the inaugural class of the College of Law Practice Management. In 2007, she was inducted into the inaugural class of the Legal Marketing Association's Hall of Fame. A frequent industry presenter, Ms. Schmidt has spoken at more than 200 national and international seminars and conferences for the legal profession. Her 250+ articles have appeared in every major legal trade publication, and she has a monthly post on marketing the "Attorney at Work" website. Ms. Schmidt is author of two books: *Marketing the Law Firm: Business Development Techniques* (Law Journal Press, updated semi-annually) and *Business Development for Lawyers: Strategies for Getting and Keeping Clients* (ALM Publishing, 2006).

Adam Severson is the chief marketing and business development officer at Baker Donelson in Nashville, Tennessee. He is responsible for the strategic direction and execution of the Firm's business development and marketing initiatives, and collaborates with the Firm's lawyers and professional staff to maintain a client focus, increase marketplace awareness and facilitate cross-office and cross-practice collaboration. Mr. Severson is very active in the International Legal Marketing Association and is the 2015 president for the LMA. He also served three years on the LMA International Board of Directors. He has received several industry awards including recognition as the #1 Business Development & Marketing team by Marketing the Law Firm and "Best of Industry" for outstanding achievement in web development. He is a nationally-recognized presenter and leader in the legal marketing and business development community. Prior to joining Baker Donelson, he held similar roles as director of business development and marketing at Faegre & Benson LLP and director of business development at Dorsey & Whitney.

Jeffrey F. Silber, CPA, MBA, is a partner of Silber, Vasquez & Associates a San Francisco-based International Executive Coaching firm specializing in legal marketing at the individual lawyer level. Jeffrey began his career on Wall St. with Arthur Andersen & Co. focusing on stock brokerage, venture capital, commodities trading and other financial companies; he was the Executive Vice President of a real estate investment and financial services company in Los Angeles; Jeffrey then studied at the Covey Leadership Center with Stephen R. Covey and returned to New York teaching the Seven Habits of Highly Effective People primarily in law firm; for seventeen he was based in Mexico City as the Director of Latin American Operations for Martindale-Hubbell; and in parallel he pursued an advanced degree in Business and Life and Coaching. Today, together with his partner, they have an extensive practice in the United States, Mexico and Brazil. In 2014, their clients were named Mexican National Law Firm of the Year, Most Innovative North American Law Firm and were listed among the Most Admired Law Firms in Brazil. He is a CPA in New York and California, holds an MBA in Finances and is a Certified Master Life, Legal and Business Coach. Jeffrey is fluent in Spanish and Portuguese.

Michele Silva, BA, was a "collaborative marketer" for 25 years for high tech companies such as IBM, Acer, Sybase and Access Commerce (France). For the last 12 years, she has facilitated collaboration among members of the San Francisco Chapters of the Association of Corporate Counsel (ACC) and the Association of Business Trial Lawyers (ABTL) as their Executive Director. Ms. Silva designs program formats that encourage networking between members to benefit from referrals and leads from fellow members for business they cannot pursue due to conflicts of interest or because they are outside their practice areas. The programs for in-house counsel allowed attorneys of all levels to feel comfortable brainstorming with fellow attendees to resolve issues they had not encountered before, which is frequent in the Silicon Valley/San Francisco legal community that continuously is setting precedents and pioneering previously unexplored areas of the law. The collaboration also fosters civility when members are opponents in the courtroom. The collaborative atmosphere of these continuing legal education programs brings high ratings from attendants (attorneys and judges alike) and provides a collegial and relaxed venue in which to learn and network. Ms. Silva can be emailed at abtl-ncal@comcast.net.

Adam L. Stock, BS, is the Chief Marketing and Client Services Officer at Allen Matkins. Adam leads marketing and client development initiatives for firm members as well as practice areas and industry groups. He oversees the firm's branding, external communications and client relationship support. Prior to joining Allen Matkins, Adam was the Chief Sales and Marketing Officer at Dorsey and Whitney LLP. Adam brings his passion of marketing and technology to helping law firms doing a better job providing value to their clients. Before joining the legal profession, Adam hired outside law firms as a high technology executive for Adobe Systems, Auctiva Corporation, Electronics for Imaging, Inc., and several startup companies. He is frequent speaker on law firm sales, technology and video. Adam has been the Chair of and instrumental in growing the Legal Marketing Technology

Conference/West into the premier technology conference for legal marketing. He serves on the board of Legal Marketing Association. He is a Board Member of the Legal Sales and Service Organization (LSSO). Included among his many achievements: 2014 LMA Bay Area Chapter Presidents' Chair, Chairman of LMA Bay Area's Legal Marketing Technology Conference, founded a successful online auction management services company, key contributor at six startup companies, closed partnership deals with Fortune-500 companies including AOL, Cablevision, Comcast, HP & IBM, and presented at over 100 professional conferences.

Dr. Peter Symons, a veterinarian and member of the Sydney 2000 International Olympic Committee Medical Commission, teamed with Clyde Jumeaux MD - a medical doctor - to develop a new, logical and intuitive physiological explanation of depression called "Brain-Fuel Depletion" or BFD. Their research is explained in their book - *Brain-Fuel Depletion: Making Sense of Anxiety and Depression.* Symons, an avid sportsman who has completed a duo swim of the English Channel, met Dr Jumeaux after months of suffering horrific insomnia and anxiety leading to suicidal feelings. Dr Jumeaux, an Associate Professor at University of Western Australia Rural Clinical School, regularly saw patients who did not fit the usual 'depression' or 'anxiety' pigeon-holes but had similar symptoms. Together they developed their BFD model which shows how the depletion of our neurotransmitters ('brain-fuels') plus an associated increase in adrenaline explains how 'anxiety' and 'depression' can develop; and why this results in a myriad of confusing symptoms. They have reinterpreted current neuroscientific evidence to take the mystery out of 'depression' and 'anxiety'. By replacing these two ambiguous names and descriptions they have changed, for many, a 'mental disorder' into a medical problem. These are problems that, for some, can be addressed with physical and lifestyle adjustments; not unlike someone who addresses low blood sugar with diet and lifestyle changes. BFD can remove the stigma of 'depression'; making dealing with this condition similar to addressing a physical complaint. At the same time, they recognize that some people might need additional support including psychological help, medication (such as selective serotonin reuptake inhibitors), and physiological support.

Matthew A. Taylor, JD, is Chairman of Duane Morris' Trial Practice Group, which consists of approximately 350 attorneys in 18 offices. Mr. Taylor also serves on the firm's Executive Committee and his home office is in Philadelphia. Mr. Taylor practices in the area of commercial litigation, handling matters in state and federal courts across the United States. Mr. Taylor also represents corporate boards and individual corporate officers and directors in internal and government investigations and related proceedings. He is an active trial lawyer dealing with matters in banking and securities law, RICO, corporate governance, commercial real estate, computer software and hardware, product liability (with a concentration in medical devices), and corporate directors and officers liability and indemnification. Mr. Taylor handles a wide range of employment matters involving noncompete, trade secrets and business related torts. Mr. Taylor represents medical device manufacturers nationally in product liability matters and in connection with commercial disputes between the manufacturer and its distributors. Admitted to practice in Pennsylvania and New York, Mr. Taylor is a Fellow of the American College of Trial Lawyers, is a member of the Pennsylvania and Philadelphia bar associations, the International Association of Defense Counsel and the Drug and Medical Device Committee of the Defense Research Institute. He is listed in *Chambers USA: America's Leading Lawyers for Business* in general commercial litigation. Mr. Taylor is a 1989 graduate of the Georgetown University Law Center and a graduate of Boston College.

Karie Trujillo, BA, is the Director of Marketing at the business litigation boutique law firm Markowitz Herbold PC in Portland, Oregon. She handles all aspects of the firm's marketing efforts including business development, advertising, media relations, social media, online strategy and the firm's very successful attorney coaching program. Prior to joining Markowitz Herbold, Karie was a Business Development Manager at a large national law firm. Karie is the Sponsorships Chair of the Pacific Northwest Chapter of the Legal Marketing Association, serves on the Public Outreach Committee of the Multnomah Bar Foundation, is a member of the Portland Business Alliance's President's Council, and chairs the Portland Farmers Market board of directors.

Mark Usellis, MPA, is Chief Strategy Officer at Davis Wright Tremaine LLP where he was also the firm's Chief Marketing Officer in the years 2007 to 2012. Mark served on the Board of the international Legal Marketing Association (LMA) in 2013–2014. He also served as Co-Chair of the LMA Annual Conference Committee (2011–2012) and Co-Editor of "Strategies," the LMA magazine. He was Principal of End2End Strategies a management consulting firm focused primarily on helping professional services firms with strategy, business development, client service and profitability. He has also been Director, Business Development at Perkins Coie LLP, Vice President - Public Affairs at APCO Worldwide, Director - Public Affairs at U.S. WEST, Legislative Director for U.S. Rep. Ron Wyden, Legislative

Assistant for U.S. Rep. Fortney H. Pete Stark, and a Financial Analyst at Provident National Bank. He was a Henry R. Luce Scholar in 1989–1990, during which time he worked in Kuala Lumpur, Malaysia.

Jonathan K. Waldrop, JD, is a Partner at Kasowitz, Benson, Torres & Friedman LLP. Jon represents industry leading companies in patent and trademark litigation involving interactive web technologies, video-on-demand telecommunications, cable technology, computer-assisted sales processes, medical devices, cooking ovens, gaming systems and complex financial transactions. He is also experienced in handling commercial and anti-trust litigation matters. Jon's clients include Google, YouTube and Adobe, world-leading global technology companies, and Cox Communications, the third largest cable television provider in the United States. He has acted as lead trial counsel in many cases for his clients and has a history of achieving favorable jury verdicts. In a recent example, Jon acted as trial counsel representing Google and YouTube in a case with such broad potential implications that Wired.com declared, "Texas Jury Strikes Down Patent Troll's Claim to Own the Interactive Web." In a separate patent litigation, Jon achieved a verdict touted as the largest verdict of the year in the district in which it was handed down. Jon is recognized in the 2015 edition of "The Best Lawyers in America" and listed as a "Rising Star" in the 2014 edition of *Georgia Super Lawyers*. He is registered to practice before the U.S. Patent and Trademark Office.

Jill Weber, BA, is Chief Marketing and Business Development Officer for Stinson Leonard Street, where she is responsible for creating and executing marketing and business development strategies, including Fast Forward®, a nationally recognized integrated business development initiative. Jill was named to the National Law Journal's inaugural list of 50 Business of Law Trailblazers & Pioneers; was recognized as a 2009 "Unsung Legal Hero" by Minnesota Lawyer; was the recipient of the 2007 EXCEL Minnesota Award, sponsored by the Minnesota Chapter of the International Association of Business Communicators; and has received three national and 15 local Legal Marketing Association (LMA) "Your Honor" awards. She serves on the LMA Board of Directors, and was co-chair of the 2012 LMA Annual Conference. Jill offers more than 20 years of experience creating marketing and business development strategies for professional service firms, including law firms, accounting firms and financial institutions. Her experience includes strategic and tactical planning, business development training and coaching, lateral integration, client service, client interviews, branding, media relations, social media and advertising. She oversees a staff of

16 business development, marketing, communications, event planning and marketing technology professionals. Jill is a regular speaker on marketing and business development, and is the author of numerous articles on professional services marketing.

Shanda Zavalsky, BA, is the Director of Marketing and Business Development at Brownstein Hyatt Farber Schreck. For more than 20 years, Shanda has worked for leading professional service organizations including Arthur Andersen, Brownstein Hyatt Farber Schreck, Dorsey & Whitney and Ernst & Young. Shanda guides both individuals and teams through the development and implementation of successful marketing and business development initiatives designed to engage targets with innovative, strategic tactics and tools. She develops customized marketing strategies based on an attorney's skills and comfort, industry niche, objectives and audience to generate measurable and timely results. She regularly coaches attorneys on techniques and best practices to enhance their business development efforts.

Appendix B

Author's Request

Please email me your comments, testimonials, recommendations, typos found, and suggestions of any type.

All compliments will be gratefully received and forwarded to our 50+ Contributors.

Your additional ideas, different topic suggestions, disagreements, complaints, and/or expanded comments on a given subject category are requested for consideration for future editions of *Building Rainmakers, The Definitive Guide To Business Development For Lawyers.* You will receive full credit for any new material from you used in a future edition.

Likewise, please send me a reference or link to your favorite rainmaker websites, blogs, newsletters, articles, books, consultants, coaches, trainers, vendors and other business development resources that have proven valuable to you.

Possible email subject lines: "ABA book"; or "Building Rainmakers"; or "Hey, Dave . . ."

Please let me know your opinion of Best Tips, Not-So-Great Tips.

Please tell me how you are using *Building Rainmakers.*

I would really appreciate hearing of your success stories.

Thank you!
–David

David King Keller, PhD, MBA
Author, Speaker, Instructor, Consultant, Coach
www.buildingrainmakers.com
www.kbdag.com

Email: David@kbdag.com

Acknowledgments and Dedications

This book is dedicated to the officers and membership of the American Bar Association and all those helping to sustain the health, fairness, and sustainability of the rule of law.

To all of the book's contributors. It was both humbling and exciting to be able to spend time with these incredibly busy professionals and to be given the privilege to serve as their messenger to convey to the readers many of the successful strategies that they originated, developed and refined over years and decades of experience. I say thank you to each of our contributors for your friendship and allowing me to share your valuable insights in this book.

To the chief marketing officer, business development director, managing partner, practice group leader, firm executive, professional development director, client services director, sales director, associate, partner, management team member, librarian, consultant, and coach, you are helping to maintain the health and livelihood of the firm through your business development efforts. You are making a tremendous contribution. You are helping people enjoy the fruits of their skills. You are helping people have the life that they want to have, and you are helping people enjoy their work while accomplishing their professional goals.

To the wonderful people at the American Bar Association book publishing division who worked so hard with their amazing skills to produce this book, and especially to our guiding editors who coordinated all of us in its final, most important phase, Jason Stauter, Kevin Commins, and John Palmer.

To my Dad (deceased), and my forever young Mom whose heartfelt intelligence and love of people permeates the lives of all with whom she comes into contact. To my parents in Florida. To my brothers Andrew, Michael, Paul, Mark, John, Thomas, and Rick. To my sisters Ann Marie, Susan, Mary, and Teresa. To my relatives, friends, and colleagues who inspire me. To David Adams who provided timely insight into the book's subtitle. To Andy Gordon who provided an extensive review of the manuscript. To Gerry Goldsholle, Karen Bell, Barbara Lauterbach, Shanda Zavalsky and

David Adams for their enthusiastic support and editorial comments on the book's opening and closing remarks. To two people I am privileged to know and who have contributed to my life, Melba Patillo Beals and Howard LaGardé.

To my clients who inspire me with their enthusiasm, high standards, and desire to excel.

And most especially to my partner in life, **my wife, Carmen**, without whose support this book would not exist.

About the Author

I help law firms increase revenue by providing their lawyers with strategies to acquire new clients and new client matters. Whenever I can, I will actually connect the lawyer to a desired client, like the time I introduced a litigator to Wal-Mart's General Counsel in charge of litigation. One of my passions is helping others achieve their professional and personal goals.

—David King Keller, PhD
Author, Speaker, Instructor, Consultant, Coach

David King Keller, MBA, Ph.D., is the author of the best-selling ABA book, *The Associate As Rainmaker, Building Your Business Brain*, and the award-winning book, *100 Ways To Grow A Thriving Law Practice.* David addresses national and state-wide legal conferences, appears on radio and TV, and delivers "glued-to-their seats" lunch and learns. Dozens of his articles on marketing, technology, and law firm business development have appeared in legal publications, Attorney Journal magazines, and the popular Attorney At Work blog.

Clients hire David as a business development consultant, coach, trainer, keynote speaker, retreat presenter, and as an ethics, bias, and substance abuse CLE instructor. One popular ethics CLE for annual conferences and retreats is titled *Ethical Business Development Strategies That Can Grow Revenue and Add New Clients* with one sub-section on *The Neuroscience of Going from Stranger to Trusted Advisor* that includes recent brain and relationship research out of Stanford University. In the past two years The Recorder, a highly regarded daily legal publication, declared David King Keller as the *#1 Law Firm Business Development Coach.*

David is Founder/CEO of the Keller Business Development Advisory Group. He holds three international executive coaching and life-coaching certifications, is a member of the Bar Association of San Francisco Legal Ethics Committee, has lectured at UC Hastings School of Law, and was on the Board of the international Legal Marketing Association –Bay Area Chapter.

David invented four products in four different business categories including the SDT for XEROX Corporation which increased sales by $98 million a year when he was a Senior Sales Executive with XEROX. The other three industries with new products from David include the food industry, the financial services industry and the field of stress reduction. David has an MBA from Pepperdine University and a PhD in East-West Psychology from the California Institute of Integral Studies. David's doctoral dissertation is on a thirty second process he created that can increase resilience, and is supported by published research showing that his MicroMindfulness technique can reduce heart rate, improve mood and increase productivity.

David has served on numerous non-profit Boards including Meals on Wheels, The Center For Attitudinal Healing, an Advisory Board to the San Francisco Unified School District, and as Trustee of the California Institute of Integral Studies graduate school. He resides with his wife in Sausalito, California and enjoys bicycling and scuba diving. You are invited to connect with David on LinkedIn and contact David through his website www.kbdag.com, or david@kbdag.com.

Index

A

C

F

G

H

N

X

Y

Z